PRESIDENTIAL ELECTIONS

Strategies and Structures of American Politics

Fifteenth Edition

NELSON W. POLSBY
University of California, Berkeley

AARON WILDAVSKY
University of California, Berkeley

STEVEN E. SCHIER
Carleton College

DAVID A. HOPKINS
Boston College

ROWMAN & LITTLEFIELD
Lanham • Boulder • New York • London

Executive Editor: Traci Crowell
Editorial Assistant: Deni Remsberg
Executive Marketing Manager: Amy Whitaker
Cover Designer: Amanda Wilson

Credits and acknowledgments for material borrowed from other sources, and reproduced with permission, appear on the appropriate pages within the text.

Published by Rowman & Littlefield
An imprint of The Rowman & Littlefield Publishing Group, Inc.
4501 Forbes Boulevard, Suite 200, Lanham, Maryland 20706
www.rowman.com

6 Tinworth Street, London SE11 5AL, United Kingdom

British Library Cataloguing in Publication Information Available

Library of Congress Cataloging-in-Publication Data
Names: Polsby, Nelson W., author.
Title: Presidential elections : strategies and structures of American politics / Nelson W. Polsby, University of California, Berkeley, Aaron Wildavsky, University of California, Berkeley, Steven E. Schier, Carleton College, David A. Hopkins, Boston College.
Description: Fifteenth Edition. | Lanham : Rowman & Littlefield, [2019] | "Fourteenth edition 2016"—T.p. verso. | Includes bibliographical references and index.
Identifiers: LCCN 2019016335 (print) | LCCN 2019018099 (ebook) | ISBN 9781538125120 (ebook) | ISBN 9781538125106 | ISBN 9781538125106 (cloth : alk. paper) | ISBN 9781538125113 (paperback : alk. paper)
Subjects: LCSH: Presidents—United States—Election.
Classification: LCC JK528 (ebook) | LCC JK528 .P63 2019 (print) | DDC 324.973—dc23
LC record available at https://lccn.loc.gov/2019016335

By Nelson A. Polsby and Aaron Wildavsky—
To our grandchildren
Benjamin Polsby Stern
Eva Miriam Wildavsky
Aaron Alexander Wildavsky
Edward Polsby Stern
Saul Abraham Wildavsky

By Steven E. Schier—
To my family
Mary, Anna, and Teresa Schier

By David A. Hopkins—
To my family and friends

Contents

Figures, Tables, and Boxes

FIGURE

TABLES

BOXES

Preface

■ ■ ■

THE ELECTION OF A PRESIDENT is a long and complicated process. A large and diverse population of interested actors works to influence the nation's choice of a chief executive, beginning years before the first votes are cast. These engaged Americans include candidates and other politicians, consultants and advisers, interest group leaders, party officials, convention delegates, journalists and commentators, issue activists, and ordinary citizens—all situated at different locations and playing distinct roles within the political arena. The impact and behavior of these individuals, in turn, can only be understood by recognizing the larger set of political structures within which they operate and that shape their strategic calculations in vital ways. These institutional constraints include the operation of party organizations: the Electoral College and other constitutional provisions; legal rules, such as campaign finance regulations and voter registration requirements; the norms and incentives of the news media; campaign milestones like national conventions and televised debates; and the highly complex, ever-evolving mechanism of presidential nominations.

But the story of a presidential election does not end once the votes have all been counted and the winning candidate inaugurated. The means by which we choose presidents fundamentally determines what kind of leaders will govern us, and whose demands they will heed while in office. The procedures that determine how presidents are elected have effects that endure long after the election itself is over. In particular, changes over time in the nature and functioning of the two major political parties—the institutions responsible for providing Americans a choice of candidates for the presidency every four years—have exerted a powerful impact on the character of the political system as a whole—and thus on the nation itself.

These critical observations motivated Nelson W. Polsby and Aaron Wildavsky to publish *Presidential Elections* for the first time in 1964, and they remain at the heart of this newly revised fifteenth edition. But even as the fundamental insights originally developed by Polsby and Wildavsky stay as relevant as ever, much about American politics has changed over the intervening decades. Today, a candidate's resources not only must include money and endorsements, but also the ability to construct and maintain an attractive social media presence. The customs of campaign decorum have eroded as attacks and responses between candidates have become more harsh and pointed. A profusion of candidates and information outlets have made presidential nomination debates crowded and unpredictable events. The opportunities provided by digital platforms have provided once-improbable candidates with new means of furthering their causes. Campaign finance regulations have evolved as the scale of fund-raising has mushroomed. The presidential nomination calendar remains in flux from one election to the next, requiring that campaign strategies accommodate ever-changing rules. Candidates scramble to catch up with new electoral realities, particularly the evolving traits and priorities of the electorate itself.

The historic 2016 election produced even more than the usual number of new issues, questions, and milestones. This new edition of *Presidential Elections* reflects a series of remarkable recent developments in American politics, including the unusual popularity of outsider candidates like Donald Trump and Bernie Sanders; the explosion of small-donor fund-raising conducted over the Internet; the increasingly central role of social media platforms in mobilizing voters and spreading information (or misinformation); and the growing political salience of divisions in American society that fall along the lines of race, gender, and national identity. The events of 2016 also provoked energetic, and sometimes divisive, national debates over the proper role of party leaders in the presidential nomination process, the power of news media coverage to influence the electoral preferences of voters, and the increasingly visible consequences of ideological polarization among national officeholders—all subjects that receive extensive attention and discussion in the pages that follow.

This fifteenth edition of *Presidential Elections* is the third to be produced via collaboration between Steven E. Schier and David A. Hopkins. Dave—one of Nelson W. Polsby's last doctoral students in the Department of Political Science at the University of California, Berkeley—also assisted in the creation of two previous editions. We hope that the vitality, imagination, wit, and commitment to fair and accurate political science that marked the distinguished careers of the two founding authors are as apparent to new generations of readers as they are to us as we carry the book forward into a second half century. We are indebted to Linda O. Polsby and Mary Wildavsky, and to Lisa, Emily, and Dan Polsby, for their continued faith. Thanks also to Jon Sisk and Traci Crowell at Rowman & Littlefield for their encouragement, support, and enthusiasm. We express our gratitude to William Higgins and Marissa Marandola for research assistance, to Jonathan Bernstein for his invaluable contributions to previous editions, and to Kathleen Donovan and Wendy L. Johnston for their comments and suggestions for improving the edition you hold in your hands. We also benefit from much constructive kibitzing by the colleagues and students who have sustained our morale every day at Carleton College and Boston College.

Steven E. Schier
Northfield, Minnesota

David A. Hopkins
Chestnut Hill, Massachusetts

PART I

The Strategic Environment

The strategies of all the participants in presidential elections are to a certain extent constrained, and to a certain extent driven, by the ways in which actors are situated within a set of political conditions over which they have limited control. Here are some examples: the rules governing how votes are counted, the sequence in which primary elections occur, the accepted practices of campaign journalism, whether candidates are incumbents or challengers, and the habits of voters. All these conditions need to be taken account of by participants and need to be understood by observers.

1

Voters

■ ■ ■

MORE THAN 137 MILLION AMERICANS voted in the 2016 presidential election. Millions more who were old enough to vote—about 108 million in 2016—did not. Parties and candidates depend on their supporters to turn out in large numbers. And so it is important for them to know why some people show up at the polls and why others do not. In two respects, Americans are different from citizens of other democratic nations. A smaller proportion of Americans will usually vote in any given election than the citizens of most other democracies, but Americans collectively vote much more often, and on more matters, than anyone else.[1] Who votes? Who doesn't vote? Who votes for which candidate and why? Each of these questions is the subject of extensive study.

WHY PEOPLE DON'T VOTE

A lot of elections, not just presidential contests but also congressional, state, and local elections, take place in the United States. Americans are noted for their lukewarm levels of participation as compared with voters in most world democracies, especially those of Western Europe. Table 1.1 compares the voter turnout rate of Americans in the most recent election for president, when participation is highest in the United States, to the most recent turnout figures in the national elections of other democratic countries. Why don't Americans vote more, or at least more like Europeans? In some respects, to be sure, the elections being compared are not exactly the same. Parliamentary elections in many places, for example the United Kingdom, require voters to do only one thing—place a single X on a ballot to fill an office more or less like that of a US representative in Congress. Who ends up running the government in these countries depends on how many parliamentarians of each political party are elected (from more than 600 constituencies in the UK), and so most voters cast party-line votes and do not much care about the identity of individuals on the ballot.[2] Ballots in US presidential elections are longer and more complex: they require voting for president and vice president, members of the House of Representatives, senators (two-thirds of the time), various state and local offices, ballot propositions, and so on. American ballots therefore demand quite a lot of knowledge from voters. In general, Americans do not invest their time and energy in becoming knowledgeable about all the choices they are required to make.[3]

Table 1.1 Voter Turnout in Selected World Democracies

Country	Turnout of Voting Age Population (%)	Compulsory Voting	Eligible Required to Register
Belgium	87.2	Yes	Automatic
Sweden	82.6	No	Automatic
Denmark	80.3	No	Automatic
Australia	79.0	Yes	Automatic
South Korea	77.9	No	Automatic
Netherlands	77.3	No	Automatic
Israel	76.1	No	Automatic
New Zealand	75.7	No	Automatic
Finland	73.1	No	Automatic
Norway	70.6	No	Automatic
Germany	69.1	No	Automatic
France	67.9	No	Automatic
Mexico	66.0	Yes	Yes
United Kingdom	63.3	No	Automatic
Canada	62.1	No	Automatic
Spain	61.1	No	Automatic
Ireland	58.0	No	Automatic
United States	*55.7*	*No*	*Yes*
Poland	53.8	No	Automatic
Switzerland	38.6	No	Automatic

Source: Drew DeSilver, "U.S. Trails Most Developed Countries in Voter Turnout," Pew Research Center, May 21, 2018, http://www.pewresearch.org/fact-tank/2018/05/21/u-s-voter-turnout-trails-most-developed-countries.

Note: The percentage listed for each country is the proportion of the voting-age population casting ballots in the most recent national election as of 2018.

But American voters do turn out for presidential elections more conscientiously than for midterm congressional elections, so the complexity of presidential elections is clearly not a deterrent to voting (see table 1.2). To the contrary, the added publicity of a presidential campaign obviously helps turnout, as do the greater sums of money spent by candidates and the increased level of campaign activity in presidential elections by political activists and interest groups.[4]

An often-heard explanation of low turnout in the United States (low by the standards of other Western democracies) is that Americans are unusually disaffected from politics and that abstention from voting is their method of showing their disapproval of, or alienation from, the political system. Scholars have been deeply interested in the subject of political alienation, but they have shown that this explanation of low turnout is at best incomplete.

There are several elements to their demonstration. First, scholars note that the constellation of sentiments associated with alienation—disaffection, loss of trust in government, and so on—are equally or even more prevalent in many other countries where turnout is relatively high. Compared to the citizens of other nations, Americans also rank high in other forms of political participation:

Table 1.2 Turnout of Eligible Voting-Age Population in Presidential and Midterm Elections, 1960–2018

Year	Presidential Elections (%)	Year	Midterm Elections (%)
1960	63.8	1962	47.7
1964	62.8	1966	48.7
1968	62.5	1970	47.3
1972	56.2	1974	39.1
1976	54.8	1978	39.0
1980	54.2	1982	42.0
1984	55.2	1986	38.1
1988	52.8	1990	38.4
1992	58.1	1994	41.1
1996	51.7	1998	38.1
2000	54.2	2002	39.5
2004	60.1	2006	40.4
2008	61.6	2010	41.0
2012	58.6	2014	36.7
2016	60.1	2018	50.3

Source: Michael P. McDonald, United States Elections Project, http://www.electproject.org.

expressing interest in politics, discussing politics with others, trying to persuade others during elections, and working for candidates or parties of their choice.[5] Within the United States, people who don't like or don't trust government vote about as frequently as people who do.[6] And although Americans increasingly voice negative feelings about government, turnout rates in recent elections were not much lower than they were in the 1950s and 1960s, when collective trust was much higher.[7]

A better explanation for what really distinguishes Americans from their more participatory counterparts elsewhere is the existence of stringent voter registration requirements in the United States. While most other democratic nations either consider all of their citizens to be automatically registered to vote, requiring no special initiative on the part of the prospective voter, or combine voter registration with enrollment for universal benefits such as health insurance or pension programs, nearly all American states require citizens to apply to their city, town, or county government specifically in order to participate in elections, including presidential elections. In many states, registration must be completed at least 30 days before the election, when political interest among the public has yet to peak.

Moreover, American citizens must register all over again each time they change their address, even when they move within the same state or city. Because the United States is an unusually mobile nation—in any given two-year period, roughly one-third of the American public will have moved at least once—a lot of re-registering is required in order to maintain voting rights.[8] Most states also have laws permitting or requiring regular purges of the voting rolls to remove citizens who have not voted for a certain number of years or who are believed—sometimes incorrectly—to have moved, died, or become ineligible to vote due to a criminal conviction; if they are indeed still among the eligible living, these individuals must register again in order to resume electoral participation.[9] Unsurprisingly, the costs imposed by this system of voter registration depress American participation rates relative to those in Europe. The turnout of *registered* voters in the United States is, in fact, comparable to that of other democratic nations; 87 percent of registered voters participated in the 2016 presidential election.[10]

Voting itself takes place not on a national holiday, as in some countries, or over a weekend, but on a regular weekday—for presidential elections, the first Tuesday after the first Monday in November.[11] Presidential primaries (electoral events that play a major role in nominating presidential candidates) take place, state by state, on a series of dates, usually but not always on Tuesdays, stretching from January or February to June of a presidential election year. These primary dates can be, and often are, changed every four years and may or may not be combined with a state's primary elections for other offices. History, geography, and custom thus play a significant part in determining contemporary patterns of turnout.

While the United States now lags behind the performance of most Western democracies in overall levels of voter participation, there was once a time—in an era when the impact of the federal government was remote, mass communication absent, and electronic voting equipment unheard of—when more than 70 percent of potential (not just registered) voters reliably participated in presidential elections: the late nineteenth century, or "Gilded Age," when partisan mobilization in the United States reached extremely high levels. In the election of 1876, for example, 82 percent of the eligible electorate (which at the time consisted only of men) turned out in the nation as a whole. Soon thereafter, however, nearly every state introduced registration requirements cloaked in rhetoric about reducing fraud and corruption but also aimed at keeping down the vote of "undesirable elements" (code words for immigrants and racial minorities). As Stanley Kelley and his collaborators observed, turnout "may have declined and then risen again, not because of changes in the interest of voters in elections, but because of changes in the interest demanded of them. . . . [Not only are] electorates . . . much more the product of political forces than many have appreciated. But also . . . to a considerable extent, they can be political artifacts. Within limits, they can be constructed to a size and composition deemed desirable by those in power."[12]

Declining national turnout rates between the 1960s and the 1990s (see table 1.2) prompted a series of public initiatives intended to reduce the burdens of registration and participation on prospective voters. In 1993, Congress enacted the National Voter Registration Act, commonly known as the "motor voter law." This legislation required voter registration forms to be available at the Department of Motor Vehicles and other government offices in every state, allowed registration by mail-in form, and compelled states to allow citizens to register up to 30 days before an election.

Since the 1990s, many states have taken additional measures to encourage voter turnout. Nineteen states from Maine to California allow same-day voter registration, under which an unregistered citizen may go to a polling place on

Table 1.3 Turnout in States with Same-Day Voter Registration, 2016

	Turnout of Eligible Voting-Age Population (%)
Minnesota	74.7
Maine	72.9
New Hampshire	72.5
Colorado	71.9
Wisconsin	69.5
Iowa	69.1
North Carolina	64.9
Connecticut	64.9
Vermont	64.8
Montana	64.3
Illinois	63.1
North Dakota	61.7
Idaho	60.9
Wyoming	60.2
California	58.2
Hawaii	43.2
U.S. Total	60.1

Source: Michael P. McDonald, "2016 General Election Turnout Rates," http://www.elect-project.org/2016g.

Note: Maryland, Michigan, and Washington enacted same-day registration laws after 2016 that will be in effect for the 2020 election. North Dakota does not require voter registration.

Election Day, register to vote, and immediately cast a ballot. The turnout rate in most of these states is noticeably higher than the national average (see table 1.3).[13] Fifteen states have adopted automatic voter registration, which automatically adds licensed drivers and enrollees in government benefit programs to the state voting rolls unless they take the initiative to opt out.

Other states loosened eligibility requirements for absentee ballots, which were once reserved for those unable to vote in person due to travel or illness. For example, eight states permit voters to register as a "permanent absentee" and receive a ballot automatically by mail before each election; more than 57 percent of the vote in California, the nation's most populous state, was cast by absentee ballot in 2016.[14] Washington, Oregon, and Colorado have dispensed with the traditional polling place altogether, conducting elections entirely by mail. And 36 more states offer early voting, allowing voters to cast ballots in person at designated places in the weeks before Election Day.

These reforms may have contributed to a rebound in the national turnout rate in the presidential elections after 1996, when it reached a modern nadir of slightly over 50 percent of the eligible adult population (see table 1.2), although a series of closely fought elections and renewed voter mobilization efforts by political parties and interest groups have also likely contributed to the recent rise in mass participation. In any case, voters clearly welcome the opportunity to escape the potential inconvenience and long lines of Election Day polling places in states where alternative voting procedures are available. In the 2016 election, an estimated 47 million citizens, or 34.3 percent of the national electorate, cast their ballots via absentee or early voting (as compared to only 7 percent in 1992); in 16 states, more than half of all votes were cast in advance of the nominal date of the election.[15] Candidates and campaigns must compete in an electoral world in which voting increasingly occurs in stages over a period of several weeks rather than on a single day nationwide.

Still, many potential voters are kept out of the electorate. Non-citizens are not allowed to vote, whether legal or illegal aliens. Most states strip convicted felons of their voting rights while incarcerated or on parole; in 12 states, this disenfranchisement may stand for life even if the sentence is completed.[16] These groups are not insignificant in size. Michael P. McDonald has estimated the number of ineligible voting-age residents as roughly 19.5 million people as of 2016, about one-thirteenth of the adult population of the United States.[17]

There is no convincing evidence that the basic human nature of Americans differs from that of citizens of other democratic lands. But the United States has organized itself differently—state by state rather than as a unitary nation—to do political business. The right to vote is administered in a more decentralized fashion than in most democracies, and its exercise usually requires more initiative on the part of the prospective voter (in the form of registration before the election at each new residential address). This seems better than any other explanation to account for much of the difference in turnout between American presidential elections and parliamentary elections in other comparable nations.

WHY PEOPLE DO VOTE: A THEORY OF SOCIAL CONNECTEDNESS

These findings still leave open why the millions of Americans who vote in presidential elections bother to do so. This question is a matter of some interest to candidates and their advisers. Even though in recent years some congressional elections have turned on a handful of votes, and the outcome of the 2000 presidential election was determined by a disputed 537-vote margin in the state of Florida, it cannot possibly be the case that millions of voters have convinced themselves to turn out in presidential elections because each of them believes that he or she will likely cast the deciding vote. Oddly enough, the more votes being aggregated in an election and the more voters expected at the polls, the larger the proportion of those eligible who actually show up, so that presidential elections regularly inspire higher turnout than midterm elections for Congress. But as the psychologist Paul Meehl once noted, the probability of casting the decisive vote in a national election is smaller than the likelihood of being killed in an accident en route to the polling place.[18]

Scholars studying human motivation have argued that voting must in some way or other make people feel good (or better, at least, than if they did not vote), perhaps because they see the act of voting as a civic duty or as an opportunity for personal political expression. Some political scientists argue that voters conclude that the benefits of turning out—which may be psychological rather than instrumental—exceed the costs.[19] We believe that the act of voting is on the whole probably not rationally calculated in this fashion, but is instead a more or less standing decision or habit that citizens fall into as they adopt other forms of public participation in the course of becoming integrated into the ordinary social life of their communities.[20]

Essentially, voting and other forms of political engagement seem to make sense mostly as an act of social participation or civic involvement. In one major study, Kay Lehman Schlozman, Sidney Verba, and Henry E. Brady asked citizen activists why they devoted their time and energy to politics, concluding that many of their subjects did so for reasons that transcended simple personal gain:

> We might have expected that activists would either characterize their own political involvement in cynically self-interested terms or see themselves as spectators at an exciting, if sometimes foolish or dirty, sport. On the contrary, their retrospective interpretations of their activity are replete with mentions of civic motivations and a desire to influence policy. Of course, many participants also report selective material or social gratifications. Still, it is striking the extent to which references to doing one's share and making the community or nation a better place to live run as a thread through activists' reports of the concerns that animated their involvement and the number of participants who discuss nothing but civic motivations for their activity.[21]

It is hardly a surprise, then, that habitual voters tend to be people connected in various ways to the larger society or to their local community, and non-voters are not. Thus people who are settled in one place vote more than people who move around. Married adults vote more frequently than the unmarried. People who belong to civic organizations, religious institutions, or interest groups vote more than non-joiners. Citizens who follow current events and have strong opinions on policy matters vote more than the politically indifferent. The better-educated vote more than the less well-educated. Voting participation generally increases with age until late in life when social participation of all sorts drops away—frequently as the result of declining health or the loss of a spouse. The young, many of whom are unsettled and unmarried, vote much less than their elders, but as they settle down, they begin to vote more often. And people who identify with one or another political party vote more than those who claim no party affiliation or loyalty. Residence, family ties, education, civic participation in general, and party identification all create ties to the larger world, and these ties evidently create social habits that include turning out to vote.[22]

This reasoning also provides a basis for the view that political life is significantly organized according to the social identities of voters. Foremost among the group affiliations that matter are the political parties, organizations that specialize in political activity. Two such organizations, the Democratic Party and the Republican Party, more or less monopolize the loyalties of American voters. Either the Democratic or the Republican nominee has won every presidential election since 1852, and only twice during this time (1860 and 1912) has the candidate of the other party not finished second in both the popular vote and the Electoral College. Over the long term, the two major parties are evenly matched. In the 23 presidential elections since 1928, the Democrats have won 12 times and the Republicans 11 (see table 1.4).

Table 1.4 Presidential Election Results, 1928–2016

Year	Winning Candidate	Electoral Votes	Popular Vote (%)	Losing Candidate	Electoral Votes	Popular Vote (%)
1928	Herbert Hoover (R)	444	58.2	Al Smith (D)	87	40.8
1932	Franklin D. Roosevelt (D)	472	57.4	Herbert Hoover (R)*	59	39.6
1936	Franklin D. Roosevelt (D)*	523	60.8	Alf Landon (R)	8	36.5
1940	Franklin D. Roosevelt (D)*	449	54.7	Wendell Willkie (R)	82	44.8
1944	Franklin D. Roosevelt (D)*	432	53.4	Thomas E. Dewey (R)	99	45.9
1948	Harry Truman (D)*	303	49.5	Thomas E. Dewey (R)	189	45.1
1952	Dwight D. Eisenhower (R)	442	54.9	Adlai Stevenson (D)	89	44.4
1956	Dwight D. Eisenhower (R)*	457	57.4	Adlai Stevenson (D)	73	42.0
1960	John F. Kennedy (D)	303	49.7	Richard Nixon (R)	219	49.5
1964	Lyndon Johnson (D)*	486	61.1	Barry Goldwater (R)	52	38.5
1968	Richard Nixon (R)	301	43.4	Hubert Humphrey (D)	191	42.7
1972	Richard Nixon (R)*	520	60.7	George McGovern (D)	17	37.5
1976	Jimmy Carter (D)	297	50.1	Gerald Ford (R)*	240	48.0
1980	Ronald Reagan (R)	489	50.7	Jimmy Carter (D)*	49	41.0
1984	Ronald Reagan (R)*	525	58.8	Walter Mondale (D)	13	40.6
1988	George H. W. Bush (R)	426	53.4	Michael Dukakis (D)	111	45.6
1992	Bill Clinton (D)	370	43.0	George H. W. Bush (R)*	168	37.4
1996	Bill Clinton (D)*	379	49.2	Bob Dole (R)	159	40.7
2000	George W. Bush (R)	271	47.9	Al Gore (D)	266	48.4
2004	George W. Bush (R)*	286	50.7	John Kerry (D)	251	48.3
2008	Barack Obama (D)	365	52.9	John McCain (R)	173	45.6
2012	Barack Obama (D)*	332	51.0	Mitt Romney (R)	206	47.1
2016	Donald Trump (R)	304	45.9	Hillary Clinton (D)	227	48.0

* Incumbent

PARTY IDENTIFICATION AS SOCIAL IDENTITY

Most Americans vote according to their habitual party affiliation.[23] In other words, because they consider themselves Democrats or Republicans, many people will have made up their minds how to vote in an election before the candidates are even chosen.[24] These party identifiers are likely to be more interested and active in politics and have more political knowledge than people who call themselves political "independents."[25] Party regulars rarely change their minds. They tend to listen mostly to their own side of political arguments and to agree with the policies espoused by their party. They even go so far as to ignore or reject information that they perceive to be unfavorable to the party of their choice.[26]

Thus party identification is important in giving a structure to voters' pictures of reality and in helping them choose their preferred presidential candidate. But where do people get their party affiliations? There seems to be no simple answer. Every individual is born into a social context and consequently inherits a set of beliefs and identities that may contain a political component. People are Democrats or Republicans, in part, because their parents and the other people with whom they interact are Democrats or Republicans.[27] Most individuals come into close contact predominantly with members of only one party.[28] And just as people tend to share social characteristics with their friends and families, such as income and educational level, ethnic identification, religious affiliation, and area of residence, they also tend to share common party preferences.[29] They view their own party as standing for "people like us" and the opposite party as representing an indifferent or even hostile "them."[30]

In recent years, social conflict in the United States has produced a phenomenon known as "negative partisanship" in which "party voters . . . have developed increasingly negative feelings about the opposing party and candidates."[31] Two notable consequences have resulted from this development. First, Americans increasingly vote on the basis of national issues, leaders, and events, as cable television and the Internet have disseminated a single set of partisan images and messages more evenly throughout the citizenry. Secondly, this growing antipathy toward partisan opponents has produced a more vitriolic tone to the country's politics, exemplified by the harsh rhetoric and divisiveness that has become a familiar characteristic of the contemporary era.

PARTIES AS AGGREGATES OF LOYAL VOTERS

Each of the major political parties maintains a reservoir of voting strength among social groups in the public that it can count on from one election to the next (see table 1.5). For example, white Christians—especially evangelical Protestants—mostly identify as Republicans and reliably vote accordingly, as do business owners and managers, military veterans, and the residents of small towns and rural areas (especially in the South). The Democratic Party's most loyal supporters can be found among racial and religious minorities—African Americans, Latinos, Asian Americans, Jews, and the non-observant. Public employees, creative-class professionals such as artists and educators, feminists, gays and lesbians, and city dwellers also contribute disproportionately to the Democratic vote.[32]

But why did these particular social groups come to have these particular loyalties? We must turn to history to find answers to this question. Enough is known about a few groups to make it possible to speculate about what kinds of historical events tend to align groups with a political party.

Here are a few examples. From the end of Reconstruction in 1877 until the rise of the civil rights movement nearly a century later, the historically "Solid South" perennially supported Democratic candidates for president as an expression of lingering sectional bitterness at the outcome of the Civil War and at Northern Republicans' postwar rule over the former Confederate states; only in a

Table 1.5 Party Identification by Social Group, 2016 (in percentages)

	Democrat	Independent	Republican
Nationwide	36	32	28
Men	31	35	30
Women	40	30	26
18–34 years	35	37	24
35–44 years	39	34	20
45–54 years	33	32	32
55–64 years	37	27	32
65 years and older	37	27	33
White	28	33	35
Black	71	19	6
Hispanic/Latino	49	31	15
No college education	36	33	26
Some college	33	33	29
College graduate	32	30	35
Postgraduate degree	45	29	22
Income under $20,000	40	37	17
Income $20,000–$39,999	39	34	22
Income $40,000–$69,999	36	30	30
Income $70,000–$99,000	29	33	35
Income $100,000 and over	34	29	33
Northeast	41	36	19
Midwest	33	30	33
South	33	32	31
West	31	35	30

Source: All adult respondents, National Election Study, 2016.

Note: Party "leaners" are treated as independents.

few mountainous pockets that had remained loyal to the Union did the Southern Republican Party exhibit any mass appeal for generations after the war's conclusion. But as the Democratic Party became more identified with civil rights activism in the 1950s and 1960s—and as Republican leaders became aligned with socially conservative causes such as the pro-life movement in the 1980s and 1990s—white Southerners began to collectively change their partisan minds. By the first decade of the twenty-first century, they had become at least as important a base of support for the Republican Party as they had previously been for the Democrats.[33]

The voting habits of African American citizens, when and where they have historically been permitted to vote, have also been shaped by several large events. The Civil War freed them from slavery and prompted the vast majority to join the Republican Party of Abraham Lincoln and Ulysses S. Grant. But the Southern reaction to Reconstruction disenfranchised them once again, because most blacks at the time lived in the rural South well within the reach of Jim Crow laws preventing them from voting.[34] The growth of American industry brought many African Americans north in the first half of the twentieth century, taking them away from the most severe legal impediments to political participation but not always lifting their burden of economic destitution or racial discrimination.[35] The effects of the Great Depression of the 1930s on African American voters in the North unmoored them from their traditional Republican loyalties and brought them into Democrat Franklin D. Roosevelt's New Deal coalition; Northern blacks have remained overwhelmingly Democratic ever since.[36] In the South, especially after the Voting Rights Act of 1965 was enacted by bipartisan congressional majorities during the Democratic presidency of Lyndon Johnson, newly enfranchised African Americans also voted Democratic. As these voters have observed Democratic politicians (in increasing numbers themselves black) espousing causes in which they believe, they have maintained their high levels of support.

If the historical events of the Civil War in the 1860s and the Great Depression of the 1930s shaped the political heritage of some people, for others the critical forces seem less dramatic and more diffuse. It is possible to see why the poor became Democrats (for the Democratic Party since the 1930s has been in favor of social welfare programs), but why did the rich historically lean toward the Republicans? Undoubtedly, in part, rich voters reacted negatively to the redistributive aspirations of some New Deal initiatives and the inclination of Democratic presidents to expand the role of government in the national economy. But they have also been attracted to the Republican Party by its long-standing record—dating back to the nineteenth century—in favor of measures benefitting business interests.[37] Recent Republican presidents and congressional leaders have upheld the party's traditional advocacy of policies that disproportionately appeal to affluent voters, such as income tax cuts for high earners, reduction or repeal of the federal estate tax, and the relaxation of government regulations of private corporations.

Sometimes party affiliation coincides with ethnic identification because of the political and social circumstances surrounding the entry of particular groups into the country. A dramatic example is the rapid influx of Cuban refugees—many of them well-to-do and solidly middle class or above—into Greater Miami, Florida, after Fidel Castro came to power in 1959. Opposition to Castro's communist regime was an extremely salient personal cause for these Cuban émigrés, and most favored the Republican Party as a result. But the American-born children and grandchildren of these refugees are less concerned with the issue, and are thus more likely to be Democrats.[38] Immigrants from Mexico and Central America who settled in California, Arizona, and Texas, as well as Puerto Ricans who migrated to New York, New Jersey, and other Northeastern states, were especially attracted to a Democratic Party that they viewed as friendly to their culture and economic interests alike. Mindful that Latinos and Hispanics comprise a growing share of the American electorate, Republican leaders attempted to court this voting bloc themselves during the presidency of George W. Bush; these efforts, however, were made more difficult in recent years by Donald Trump's advocacy of restrictions on immigration.

In the decades following the Civil War, politics in most major Northern cities was dominated by the Republican Party and by "Yankees" (Protestants of British ancestry) of substance and high status. During this time, thousands of Irish people—many of them fleeing the potato famine of the mid-nineteenth century and rule in Ireland by the English and Scots-Irish cousins of Yankee Americans—streamed into Boston, New York, and other large population centers in the eastern United States. The Democratic Party welcomed them; the Republicans did not. In due course, the Democratic percentage of the two-party vote began to increase, and Irish politicians, who uniquely among newer immigrants already knew the English language, took over the Democratic Party nearly everywhere they settled.[39] Later generations of those with Irish backgrounds gained in affluence, moved to the suburbs, and became swing voters between the parties. In the Midwest, events such as American involvement in two world wars against Germany under Democratic auspices in many cases shaped the political preferences of Americans of German descent toward the more isolationist Republicans, retaining that orientation is subsequent generations.[40] These are a few examples of the ways in which group membership and historical circumstances have given voters affinity for one party or the other.

Party identification may also be shaped by the identity of the politicians in power when citizens come of political age. The generation of Americans who reached adulthood during the 1930s, for example, became socialized into national politics during the administration of a popular Democratic president, Franklin D. Roosevelt. As a result, most of these voters became lifelong Democrats themselves; 60 years later, members of the now-elderly "New Deal generation" were still more likely to belong to the Democratic Party than voters who first became introduced to politics during the 1950s, when Republican Dwight D. Eisenhower was president. Similarly, the cohort of voters who entered the electorate during Ronald Reagan's presidency in the 1980s remains, even today, significantly more Republican than their slightly younger counterparts who reached adulthood in the 1990s during the Democratic administration of Bill Clinton.[41] The personal popularity of Barack Obama—and unpopularity of Donald Trump—among the millennial and post-millennial generations led younger Americans to exhibit a strong preference for Democratic candidates beginning with the election of 2008; if historical trends are any guide, these generations of voters will likely retain their own partisan distinctiveness for decades in the future.[42]

Once citizens form psychological ties to a political party, a great deal follows. Merely to list the functions that party identification performs for voters—helping them make sense of the day's events, telling them which side to take in a policy debate, providing them with a path to personal engagement with political life—is to suggest the profound significance of parties for voting behavior. The political arena is a complicated place, filled with what seems like an overwhelming number of issues, personalities, and developments. Voters who adopt a partisan identity can simplify their choices and reduce to manageable proportions the time and effort they spend on public affairs simply by supporting the candidates and absorbing the positions of their party. Rather than puzzling over each and every political question, they can defer to the pronouncements of politicians, interest group leaders, media figures, and other partisan authorities. Of course, citizens with greater curiosity about public affairs may investigate matters for themselves. Even so, their party identification provides them with important guidance in learning about the issues that interest them, as well as the many matters on which they cannot possibly be well informed. All of us, including full-time participants in politics, such as the president and other leading politicians, require reliable signals to tell us what to think about topics on which we lack true expertise.[43] For most of the millions who vote, identification with one of the two major political parties performs that indispensable function most of the time.

IDEOLOGIES, ISSUES, AND NATIONAL CONDITIONS IN THE MINDS OF VOTERS

Another method of reducing the costs of information may be for voters to have or acquire a more or less comprehensive set of internally consistent beliefs, sometimes known as an *ideology*. How do ideologies structure political attitudes? Voters may be conscious of having an ideology that shapes their views on specific policy questions; they can use ideological labels as a shortcut in making decisions, or at least they can think of one issue as related to another. Most citizens do not demonstrate ideologically consistent views across a wide range of policy issues, though the smaller segment of the public that is especially knowledgeable about, and active in, partisan politics is more likely to adhere to a coherent philosophy of the left or the right.[44] The ideologically sophisticated stratum of the electorate has grown in size over the past few decades, perhaps due to rising education levels, but remains a minority of the mass public as a whole.[45] Yet many Americans consider themselves liberals or conservatives—and behave accordingly in the voting booth—even if they fail to fully understand the connection between these labels and their associated policy positions.

At the same time, the increasing correlation between ideology and partisanship since the 1980s has reduced the likelihood that voters will desert their favored party due to a cross-cutting ideological proclivity. There were once a large number of conservative Democrats in the American electorate, as well as a smaller but not insignificant share of liberal Republicans. These ideological misfits were occasionally open to widespread electoral defection, such as the Southern conservative Democrats who crossed party lines in sizable numbers to support Republican presidents like Richard Nixon and Ronald Reagan. Today, the number of partisans who identify with the prevailing ideology of the opposite party is much lower than it once was, and thus the capacity for ideological preferences to exert influence on voters' candidate choices independent of their existing partisan alignments is correspondingly small.

Can views on a specific issue prompt voters to abandon their normal partisan habits? In order for this to happen, the issue must reach a high degree of salience for the voter. Voters must know about the issue, they must care about it at least a little, and they must be able to distinguish the positions of the parties and their candidates on the issue. Data from public opinion polls tell us that most people are not well informed about the details of issues most of the time.[46] All but major public issues are unlikely to influence them to desert their usual partisan preferences. And even these major issues may enter the consciousness of most people in only the most rudimentary way.

Once voters have some grasp of the content of a public policy and learn to prefer one outcome over another, they must also find a public leader to espouse their point of view. Discerning differences on policy issues between parties is not always easy. Leaders may deliberately obfuscate an issue for fear of alienating interested actors. They may try to hold divergent factions in the electorate together by glossing over disagreements on many specific issues, or even by misleading elements of the public about their true positions. Even when real party differences on policy exist, many voters may not be aware of them. The subject may be highly technical, or the time required to master the subject may be more than most people are willing to spend. By the time we get down to those who know and care about and can discriminate between party positions on issues, we are usually restricted to a small proportion of the electorate.[47]

What can we say about these people? Their most obvious characteristic is interest in and concern about issues and party positions. These are precisely the same people who are most likely to be strong partisans. Party loyalty thus works against the possibility that voters will shift allegiance just because of a disagreement on one or two issues.[48] Voters who pay only a moderate amount of attention to politics are most likely to be affected by new information on issues. This is because the most attentive are generally committed to a party and that party's position, whereas the least attentive are unavailable to persuasion: since they don't take in political information, they cannot be influenced by it. This leaves the middle group as most open to persuasion. Not being intensely partisan, they are not previously committed, but they learn enough so that it is possible for them to be swayed by new information about issues and by campaigns.[49] The number of issue-oriented "independents"—voters who care a lot about public policy but have no consistent party preference—is very small. Knowledgeable citizens are more likely to have strong opinions about politics, and therefore almost always consider themselves either Democrats or Republicans. Most people who call themselves independents actually lean toward one or another of the two major parties.[50] So purely issue-oriented voters may be distributed on both sides of major policy questions in such a way that gains and losses balance out and the total number of votes gained or lost by the impact of any specific issue is minute.

Even these changes may not amount to much if other issues are also highly salient to voters and work the other way. For if voters were willing to change their votes on one particular issue, why should they not switch their support back because of another? There usually are many issues in a campaign; only if all or most of the issues pointed voters in the same direction would they be likely to switch their votes. What is the likelihood that candidates will arrange their policies along a broad ideological front, forcing large numbers of weak party identifiers or "independent" voters from or into the fold? It is low, but not nonexistent. In 1964 the Republicans, led by extreme conservative Barry Goldwater, did so. And in 1972 the Democratic candidate, George McGovern, "was perceived as so far left on the issues that his Republican opponent, Richard Nixon, was generally closer to the electorate's average issue position on 11 out of 14 separate issues."[51] Supporters of the Goldwater and McGovern campaigns argued that enthusiasm for their candidates' more extreme issue positions would inspire a massive increase in turnout among disaffected citizens who previously declined to participate in politics (a claim known as the "hidden vote theory"). Instead, Goldwater and McGovern merely alienated large numbers of Americans who already voted regularly, including many members of their own party, resulting in landslide victories for the opposition.

Issues that arouse deep feelings can alter longer-term voting patterns, but this usually occurs when one party changes its position on, or fails to adapt to, a matter of special concern to a specific group within the American public—or if a new crisis emerges that disrupts old party loyalties. As we have seen, the Great Depression, the civil rights movement, and the political mobilization of evangelical Christians all worked to alter the group coalitions and the issue agendas of the Democrats and Republicans. Most of the time, however, the two major parties' policy platforms and popular bases of support remain relatively consistent from one election to the next, and the issue positions of voters work more to reinforce than to limit the influence of partisan identity on their electoral choices.

The rise of negative partisanship also reduces the capacity of issues to sway voters—even if they differ with their own party on one subject or another, fewer Americans are tempted to cross over to the distrusted opposition. The 2016 general election contest between Donald Trump and Hillary Clinton featured a high proportion of negative television ads—only 20 percent were positive.[52] TV ad spending in 2016 was the lowest for presidential candidates since 2000, however, as campaigning migrated further to the Internet and social media, where much of the content remained sharply critical in tone. Both Clinton and Trump emerged from the campaign with low levels of personal popularity, but party loyalty remained high—partisans who disagreed with their own side's nominee mostly supported him or her anyway, because their views of the opposing candidate's policies were even less favorable.

The successful or unsuccessful performance of an incumbent presidential administration will seldom shake strong partisans from their existing loyalties, but it can still sway enough swing voters to influence the outcome of an election. Figure 1.1 illustrates how closely the vote for the president's party tracks

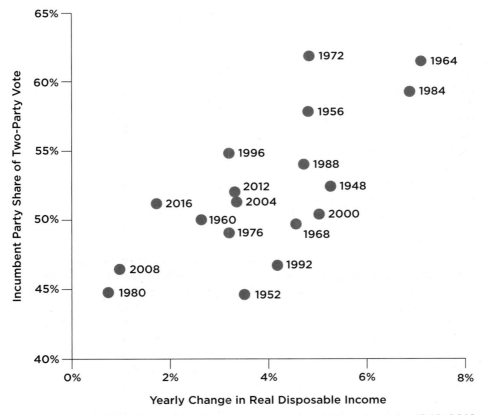

Figure 1.1 The Effect of Income Growth on Incumbent Party Success, 1948–2016

Source: Compiled by authors from Federal Reserve Economic Data, https://fred.stlouisfed.org/series/DPIC96.

the contemporary performance of the economy, as measured by the growth of Americans' real disposable income in the year of the election.[53] Stung by "stagflation," a politically deadly combination of high inflation and high unemployment, and dismayed over what they perceived to be President Jimmy Carter's lack of leadership, voters in 1980 chose Republican nominee Ronald Reagan despite uneasiness about Reagan's conservative issue positions. They may have thought that under then-current conditions of uncertainty about the economy, a new administration would do better. A strong economic recovery brought Reagan renewed support and a resounding victory in 1984.

News of an economic turnaround came too late to save George H. W. Bush in 1992. He lost his bid for reelection despite his tremendous popularity two years earlier at the time of the Persian Gulf War, when he orchestrated the international defense of Kuwait against Iraqi aggression. By the fall of 1992, however, Americans were more concerned with the state of the economy than with the nation's military successes. The president fell victim to negative retrospective evaluations of his performance on domestic matters and to popular feelings that he demonstrated insufficient concern about a recession that had occurred on his watch, even though the economy had entered a period of recovery by the time of the election itself. Bush ultimately received only 38 percent of the popular vote in a three-way race.[54]

His son George W. Bush's unpopular economic stewardship in 2008 created serious political problems for Republican nominee John McCain, who was running to succeed the younger Bush as president. An unprecedented financial crisis, threatening the survival of several prominent private investment banks and insurance companies, erupted just weeks before the November election in the midst of an existing recession. This development made the management of the national economy the dominant issue of the fall campaign. McCain's career-long focus on national security concerns did not position him well to address this matter, allowing his Democratic opponent Barack Obama to charge that McCain would simply continue Bush's policies if elected. Obama's solid victory, by a popular margin of 53 percent to 46 percent, reflected voters' historical tendency to hold the incumbent party responsible for poor economic conditions. Even so, Republican voters remained loyal to their party, casting 90 percent of their votes for McCain.

Obama's reelection campaign in 2012 also faced the problem of a middling economy that had recovered from the depths of the prior recession but still suffered from historically high rates of unemployment and low economic growth. His opponent, former Massachusetts governor Mitt Romney, failed to capitalize on this issue. The Obama campaign successfully portrayed Romney as a wealthy "out of touch" multimillionaire, an image reinforced by Romney's maladroit comments during the fall campaign. This candidate "framing," combined with a relatively quiet international scene and the successful assassination of terrorist mastermind Osama bin Laden during Obama's first term, allowed the incumbent to win re-election by a margin of 51 percent to 47 percent.

Sluggish job growth and a static unemployment rate hindered the campaign of the "status quo" candidate Hillary Clinton in 2016. Donald Trump's surprising victories in the industrial states of Wisconsin, Pennsylvania, Michigan, and Ohio that had lagged during the slow economic recovery helped propel him into the White House, despite losing the national popular vote by 2 percentage points. As figure 1.1 suggests, economic conditions predicted a very close 2016 presidential election, as it proved to be.

So while ideology, issues, and performance in office are all capable of affecting who wins, party matters almost all the time for most individual voters. Candidates know that activating the loyalties of their own party faithful is a necessary step on the path to electoral victory, and that the vast majority of the opposition will remain resistant to their appeals, no matter how hard they try to reach out across the party divide.

CHANGES IN PARTY IDENTIFICATION: SOCIAL HABIT VERSUS CONTEMPORARY EVALUATION

Thus far we have considered factors that might cause voters to deviate in voting from their underlying party allegiance. Under what conditions do they actually change their party identification?

The prevailing model of party identification holds that it is a strong social habit. It begins early in life; is remarkably stable; resists short-run political forces; and changes only through reaction to long-lasting and powerful political events, such as the Great Depression of the 1930s. This view was authoritatively propounded in 1960 by the authors of *The American Voter*. At its core is the idea that party identification constitutes a strong emotional bond and is therefore "firm but not immovable."[55] This leaves at least a little room for candidate and issue-related changes and for a more active evaluative role on the part of voters. One classic study shows that those who change party from one election to the next generally are sympathetic to some key policies of their new party. "Standpatters," in contrast, tend to agree with major policies of their existing party.[56]

It is often difficult to determine whether citizens choose a party in accordance with their pre-existing political beliefs or instead adopt a party's positions after affiliating with it for other reasons, such as ethnic, religious, or class identity or affinity for a particular political leader. Almost certainly, both processes are having an impact on the electorate. One synthesis that combines long-term habit with more contemporaneous evaluations concludes that "there is substantial continuity in partisanship from one point in time to the next" and that party identification "can be interpreted as the individual's accumulated evaluation of the parties."[57]

In addition to extremely rare tidal waves that change the party preferences of large groups of voters, there are also more common squalls that affect the life experiences of smaller numbers of individuals and from time to time lead a relatively few voters to alter their party identifications. Since these eddies in the larger flow of events lack a common origin, they usually cancel one another out in their net effects. Thus the big picture of relatively stable aggregate partisanship in the overall electorate can be reconciled with a more complicated picture of occasional individual change.[58] Both the thinking and feeling individuals who change parties once in a while and the large masses of people who are caught up in infrequent movements away from or toward certain parties are galvanized by their reactions to shared experiences.[59]

Thus people whose partisanship was not firmly fixed early in life, perhaps because politics was seldom discussed in the home, may develop party identifications in their twenties or thirties. They adjust their party loyalties to their policy preferences or to the views of the groups with which they associate. But they do not make these adjustments often. As Charles Franklin tells us, "[C]itizens remain open to change throughout life, though as experience with the parties accumulates, it is accorded greater weight."[60]

Is party identification a durable standing decision to vote a certain way, as the authors of *The American Voter* put it, or, as Morris Fiorina argues, a "running tally of retrospective evaluations of party promises and performance" subject to significant change based on unfolding political events?[61] Scholars find that citizen assessment of party performance on major dimensions of public policy—war and peace, employment, inflation, race relations—does matter.[62] Nevertheless, most changes of party identification involve switching in and out of the independent category rather than between the two major parties.[63] This seemed to happen in 2008, for example, as Republican identifiers temporarily decreased in number while the number of independents grew. Donald Kinder sums up:

> So party identification is *not* immovable; it is influenced by the performance of government, by policy disagreements, and by the emergence of new candidates. The loyalty citizens feel for party is at least partially a function of what governments and parties do, and what they fail to do. . . . I do not mean to press this too hard, however. Although party identification does respond to political events, it does so sluggishly. It is one thing for Republicans to feel less enthusiastic toward their party after a period of sustained national difficulty presided over by a Republican administration; it is quite another to embrace the opposition. The latter seldom happens.[64]

Has there been an overall decline in party identification in the United States? From 1964 onward, an increasing share of Americans identified themselves as independents. By the late 1990s, more Americans classified themselves as independents than identified with each of the two major parties. In 2016, Democrats had slightly more adherents (33 percent) than did Republicans (29 percent) alongside a large group of independents (34 percent), according to a survey by the Pew Research Center for the People and the Press.[65] These trends have prompted some observers to claim that parties do not affect the behavior of voters nearly as much as they once did.[66]

However, more than two-thirds of nominal independents report that they "lean" toward either the Democratic or Republican Party.[67] These partisan independents are far more knowledgeable and participate much more actively in politics than "pure," non-leaning independents; they also show a far greater tendency to vote, and they nearly always vote for the party toward which they lean. In short, independents who lean toward a party behave much more like avowed partisans than like truly independent voters. By separating party identification into seven categories rather than three, table 1.6 shows that the number of pure independents is closer to 10 or 15 percent than to the 35 percent often cited.[68] Many voters claim independent status because they perceive it as more socially or psychologically desirable than openly admitting a partisan identity, or as a means of symbolically declaring their frustration with today's polarized political debates.

Table 1.6 Party Identification, 1952–2016 (in percentages)

Year	Democrats			Pure Independent	Republicans		
	Strong	Weak	Independent	Independent	Independent	Weak	Strong
1952	22	25	10	6	7	14	14
1962	23	23	7	8	6	16	12
1972	15	26	11	13	10	13	10
1982	20	24	11	11	8	14	10
1992	18	18	14	12	12	14	11
2002	16	17	15	8	13	16	14
2008	19	15	17	11	11	13	13
2012	20	15	12	14	12	12	15
2016	21	13	12	14	12	12	17

Source: Harold W. Stanley and Richard G. Niemi, *Vital Statistics on American Politics, 2013–2014* (Washington, DC: CQ Press, 2014), based on data from the National Election Studies; 2016 National Election Study.

But they are still unlikely to be truly indifferent between the two partisan choices that they face in the voting booth.[69]

Americans are a lot more stable in their party identifications than in the policy preferences that are sometimes held to underlie party allegiances.[70] But lifelong identification with a party does not ensure that a voter will always support that party's nominees for public office; in the past, there have often been significant defections of partisan identifiers to the other party's candidate in presidential elections. From 1952 to 1968, Democrats defected, on average, about twice as often as Republicans (19 percent to 10 percent). After 1972, Republican defection rates stayed about the same, but Democratic defections increased, averaging 25 percent from 1976 to 1988.

Recent elections, however, have been different. Bill Clinton, after losing about a quarter of Democratic voters in 1992 to Republican George H. W. Bush and independent candidate Ross Perot, received 85 percent of the Democratic vote in 1996. For the first time in many years, Republicans were slightly less loyal than Democrats, with defections totaling 27 percent in 1992 and 20 percent in 1996. Both major candidates received overwhelming support—ranging from 89 to 93 percent—from their parties' identifiers in the closely fought 2000, 2004, 2008, and 2012 elections, reflecting the highly polarized nature of contemporary electoral politics.[71] Party loyalty was only slightly lower in 2016, with Hillary Clinton receiving support from 89 percent of Democrats and Donald Trump 88 percent of Republicans (box 1.1).[72]

So party as an orientation point is still very important. Most people, especially most voters (since those without any party preference are much less likely to vote), identify with or lean toward one party or the other. There are always defections, however, and the parties cannot automatically count on all their identifiers to give them unqualified support in every election. Even if crossing party lines is much less common than it used to be, the consistently close margins of national elections in the twenty-first century suggest that even a small difference in the relative loyalty of Democrats and Republicans could turn out to decide the winner.

Box 1.1 ■ In the Arena: 2016 Trump and Clinton Voters Speak on Issues, Ideology, and Candidates

Issues

"I would vote for Trump. He is the only candidate I have seen be taken seriously after calling for the reassertion of U.S. sovereignty and withdrawing from the numerous terrible international trade treaties the country has signed off on."

"Hillary all the way as she LOVES all people of ALL colors and religions and lifestyles NOT just the white Christian heterosexuals. She will NOT raise taxes on the poor and middle class but on the wealthy who should be doing their share anyway!"

Ideology

"Hillary is going to destroy our Constitution and take away many of our rights given to us by that document. She will do this by Supreme Court appointees. If you want to lose your gun rights and religious freedom, vote for her."

"As a social liberal . . . who also just happens to believe that we need to rein in spending (other people's money) on many fronts, it's readily apparent that Hillary's the best choice vis a vis foreign relations and American interests in that arena. And she's liberal enough on social issues, too."

Candidates

"I am voting for Hillary Rodham Clinton, because I think she has a more positive image than Donald Trump, is more qualified to do the actual work as head of state than any candidate, and is experienced enough to fight dirty when bullied."

"I will be voting for Donald TRUMP! He can't be bought by donors. He will end corrupt government and give the country back to us Americans and enforce the immigration laws of our country."

Source: Posted comments to the question: "Who will you be voting for this election and why?" Located at https://answers.yahoo.com/question/index?qid=20160801181704AAAm CRc&page=11.

A CENTRAL STRATEGIC PROBLEM: THE ATTENTIVENESS OF VOTERS

A remarkably consistent picture emerges from the study of American voters over the past several decades:

1. Most voters (about 70 percent, or up to 90 percent if independent "leaners" are included) have a party allegiance, which determines their vote most of the time. The strategic implication for presidential candidates is that there is such a thing as a party base. Major-party candidates must mobilize this base so that the party faithful turn out at high rates, and they must strive to minimize defections; the overwhelming evidence is that efforts in this direction will be rewarded.

2. In any election, the number of voters making a judgment to desert their customary party of preference will ordinarily be small. If there is a tide of such evaluations in a single direction, this can be decisive for the outcome.

Mostly, these tides are expressed as decisions to move from partisan loyalty to weaker loyalty, or from weak loyalty to a weakened resolution to vote at all.

3. Most citizens do not pay much notice to politics or keep well informed about the substantive details of current events. The world inhabited by politicians, full of public policy and of contention over complex issues, is only dimly perceived by ordinary voters. Politicians must expend resources and work very hard to give meaning to the choices that voters ordinarily make according to party habit. For a candidate to become visible as an individual to the electorate is a difficult task. Much of the activity during an election campaign reflects the eternal truth that most voters are not attentive to the specifics of public affairs, ideologically sophisticated in their views, or spontaneously eager to change their habitual orientations to politics. Politicians must therefore strive to capture their attention.

4. Voters participate in politics in accordance with their social loyalties and involvements. They retain and sometimes exercise their capacity to make contemporary judgments on issues. Partisanship and ideological convictions increasingly overlap in the American electorate. In recent years partisanship has turned more negative, adding a harsher tone to our politics. Voters' behavior is critically influenced by the ways in which they are organized into social groups, especially political parties.

In the heat of a fall presidential campaign, voters are not always coolly rational in their choices. That makes presidential candidates and parties all the more eager to find a way to reach and influence them. "Persuadable" voters, those not anchored by partisanship or ideology and less attentive to politics, become a central campaign focus. Larry M. Bartels notes that "recent studies offer abundant evidence that election outcomes can be powerfully affected by factors unrelated to the competence and convictions of the candidates. But if voters are so whimsical, choose the candidate with the most competent-looking face or most recent television ad, how do they manage to sound so sensible? Most people seem able to provide cogent-sounding reasons for voting the way they do. However, careful observation suggests that these "reasons" often are merely rationalizations from readily available campaign rhetoric to justify preferences formed on other grounds."[73]

Discovering the true reasons why citizens vote the way they do—party identification, retrospective performance, issue positions, perceptions of candidates—and attempting to influence these decisions is the central objective of presidential campaigns.

2
Groups

■ ■ ■

THE PRESIDENTIAL VOTE AS AN AGGREGATION
OF INTEREST GROUPS

In each election, members of the various social groups that make up the American voting population turn out to vote, dividing their loyalties in varying ways between the major parties. Turnout varies enormously among different groups in the population, rising with age, education, income, occupational status, and political interest. The active electorate is therefore not a perfect representation of the larger national population from which it is drawn, and this disparity can provide one party or the other with a systematic advantage. For example, citizens with postgraduate degrees are more likely to vote than those with less educational attainment, which in today's political climate tends to help Democrats, while the elderly are more likely to turn out than the young, which now tends to help Republicans.

The two major parties are constituted differently as voting blocs.[1] Democrats appeal especially to voters organized as conscious groups with specific programmatic agendas for governmental action. The Democratic Party is a broad coalition of social minorities, and Democratic candidates win presidential elections by appealing to these groups' distinct identities and interests in order to stimulate enthusiastic turnout by their membership. Even in years when Democrats lose the presidency, they tend to do well with these groups (see table 2.1). No large social group votes as overwhelmingly Republican as African Americans vote Democratic, and several other groups vote nearly as lopsidedly for Democrats.

Republicans win presidential elections by doing slightly better than Democrats and better than usual for Republicans among big aggregates of voters who think of themselves less as discrete social group members than as "regular Americans," such as white voters (71 percent of the electorate in 2016), voters in their middle years or older, married voters, and observant Christians. In years when Republicans do slightly less well among these very large segments of the population, Democrats win (see table 2.2).

Democrats once held a substantial numerical advantage over Republicans in the national electorate that was balanced out by the greater openness of some Democratic voters to crossing party lines to support Republicans for president. Party loyalty among Democrats increased after the 1980s, with defection rates falling to become comparable with those of Republicans. Unfortunately for the Democratic Party, this trend occurred at the same time as an erosion in the

Table 2.1 The Democratic Party Base: Small but Loyal Groups

Groups	Percentage of 2016 Electorate	Percentage of Group Voting Democratic									
		2016	2012	2008	2004	2000	1996	1992	1988	1984	1980
Blacks	12	89	93	95	88	90	84	83	86	90	85
Latinos	11	66	71	67	56	67	72	61	69	62	59
Asian Americans	4	65	73	62	56	55	43	31	—	—	—
Jews	3	71	70	78	74	79	78	80	64	67	45
Nonreligious	26	65	70	75	67	60	59	62	62	59	41
Union Household	18	51	58	59	59	59	59	55	57	53	49
Family Income <$30,000*	17	53	63	63	65	61	55	49	55	46	50
Big City Residents	34	60	69	70	60	71	68	58	62	63	—
Gays, Lesbians, Bisexuals	5	77	76	70	77	71	71	72	—	—	—
All Voters	100	48	51	53	48	48	49	43	45	40	41

Sources: Marjorie Connelly, "How Americans Voted: A Political Portrait," *New York Times*, November 7, 2004, sec. 4, 4; "Exit Polls," MSNBC, available at http://www.msnbc.msn.com/id/5297138; for 2008, "CNN Presidential Exit Poll," http://www.cnn.com/ELECTION/2008/results/polls/#val=USP00p1; for 2012, "CNN Presidential Exit Poll," http://www.cnn.com/election/2012/results/race/president; for 2016, "CNN Presidential Exit Poll," https://www.cnn.com/election/2016/results/president; and Pew Research Center, "For Most Trump Voters, 'Very Warm' Feelings for Him Endured," August 2018, http://assets.pewresearch.org/wp-content/uploads/sites/5/2018/08/09174248/8-9-2018-Validated-voters-release1-3.pdf.

* The income category is $25,000 annually or lower for elections 1988 or earlier.

Table 2.2 The Republican Party Base: Larger, Less-Conscious Groups

Groups	Percentage of 2016 Electorate	Percentage of Group Voting Republican									
		2016	2012	2008	2004	2000	1996	1992	1988	1984	1980
Whites	71	57	59	55	58	54	46	40	59	64	56
White Protestants	35	68	69	65	67	63	53	47	66	72	63
Married	59	52	56	52	57	53	46	41	57	62	62
Suburbanites	49	49	50	48	52	49	42	39	57	61	61
All Voters	100	46	47	46	51	48	41	38	53	59	59

Sources: See table 2.1.

Democratic edge in party identification. Whereas Democratic identifiers outnumbered Republicans among all adult citizens by 47 percent to 28 percent in 1952's National Election Study, by 2018 this gap had declined to just three percentage points (30 percent to 27 percent), according to data from the Gallup poll. The traditional Democratic edge in party identification, however, did reemerge in 2008 and 2012. In both years, Democrats benefited from record high turnout among a reliably partisan group, African Americans mobilized by Barack Obama's candidacy, and a large identification advantage among voters under the age of 30. Turnout among those groups declined in 2016, as Hillary Clinton failed to stimulate the same degree of excitement as Obama. The national exit poll reported that Democrats' share of voters exceeded that of the GOP by 39 to 32 percent in 2008 and 38 to 32 percent in 2012, but shrank to 36 to 33 percent in 2016—less than half of its size eight years earlier.[2]

To determine the contribution that a particular social group makes to the electoral coalitions of the parties, it is necessary to know three things: how big the group is, how many of its members actually vote, and how devoted its members are to one party or another. For example, consider the voting preferences of poor people—defined as those whose household incomes are in the bottom one-sixth of the total population. As table 2.3 shows, the proportion of the total Democratic vote supplied by poor voters has ranged from 12 to 19 percent in presidential elections over the past five decades.[3] Often, more than 90 percent

Table 2.3 The Parties as Coalitions of Social Groups, 1952–2016

Year	Democratic Coalition						Republican Coalition					
	P	NW	U	CJO	F	C	NP	W	NU	Pro	M	SR
1952	15	8	37	40	50	39	86	99	79	76	48	71
1956	12	6	37	38	48	28	88	98	78	75	46	77
1960	12	8	33	46	49	28	87	97	81	90	45	82
1964	17	13	32	36	56	31	88	100	87	79	48	76
1968	13	20	29	41	58	33	89	98	80	80	44	79
1972	19	25	31	41	60	35	87	96	77	72	47	81
1976	13	20	31	39	56	30	93	96	82	73	44	76
1980	19	29	33	35	59	39	90	96	79	68	48	82
1984	15	29	31	46	61	32	94	92	83	66	47	84
1988	15	34	26	42	59	32	91	92	84	70	48	83
1992	15	31	21	46	59	33	92	90	86	69	48	81
1996	15	33	27	46	60	31	94	92	87	66	55	79
2000	12	31	19	48	60	36	94	89	87	59	49	83
2004	13	38	27	48	55	—	90	86	85	59	51	—
2008	13	35	15	49	59	—	92	95	88	68	45	—
2012	17	41	20	51	57	—	96	90	86	64	45	—
2016	19	45	19	58	60	42	93	88	81	63	53	75

Source: National Election Studies, 2012 and 2016 CNN exit polls. Measures adapted in part from Robert Axelrod, "Presidential Election Coalitions in 1984," *American Political Science Review* 80 (March 1986): 281–84.

Notes: Figures represent the percentage of each party's votes supplied by each social group in each presidential election.

P/NP—Poor (household income in lowest sixth of national population)/Nonpoor
NW/W—Nonwhite (Black, Latino, Asian, Native American)/White
U/NU—Union member in household/Nonunion
CJO/Pro—Catholic, Jewish, other, or no religion/Protestant
F/M—Female/Male
C/SR—City/Suburb or rural area

(93 percent in 2016) of the Republican vote comes from the non-poor—voters whose incomes place them in the top five-sixths of the population. Poor voters therefore regularly constitute a higher proportion of the Democratic electoral coalition (about 15–20 percent) than the Republican coalition (10 percent or less; about 7 percent in 2016).

Most people have overlapping characteristics. Thus a single individual can be white, female, Catholic, and a union member all at the same time. It would be useful to try to identify the contribution of each attribute alone. By separating subjective identification with the working class from belonging to a union, scholars have shown that living in a household with at least one union member creates a strong push toward Democratic allegiance. Being female, non-white, or non-Protestant also makes Democratic identification more likely.[4]

Black voters and other racial minorities have established themselves as a substantial component of the Democratic coalition over the past 40 years. During this time, blacks have remained a relatively constant 12 to 13 percent of the total population. African American voters' vastly increased contribution to the Democratic vote since the 1960s has been the result of a near doubling of their turnout throughout the nation (thanks largely to the Voting Rights Act of 1965, which allowed many southern blacks to vote for the first time), of their high loyalty to the Democratic Party (85 to 95 percent of black voters consistently support Democratic candidates), and of fluctuations in Democratic voting by white voters. The growing Hispanic or Latino population, less heavily Democratic than African Americans but still significantly more so than whites, has also contributed an increasing number of votes to the Democratic coalition in recent elections. Voters of Asian descent, while less numerous, also vote Democratic at a higher rate than whites, while the Native American population, small nationwide but electorally important in a few Western states, tends to be heavily Democratic as well. In 2016, a record high 45 percent of the votes for the Democratic presidential candidate came from nonwhite voters, while the Republican coalition remained overwhelmingly white (see table 2.3).

Members of labor unions and their families have also historically been an important source of electoral support for the Democratic Party. But as the proportion of American workers affiliated with a union has declined since the 1950s, the labor vote has become a smaller component of the Democratic electoral coalition. Whereas union households contributed four times as many votes as African Americans and other minorities to the Democratic Party in 1960 (33 percent of the total), by the 1990s Democratic candidates had begun to receive many more total votes from nonwhites than from union members and their families (see table 2.3). In 2016, more than twice as many Democratic votes came from nonwhites as from union households.

Roman Catholic voters represent another traditional source of support for Democratic candidates that has weakened in recent decades. Catholic loyalty to the Democratic Party dated back to the mid-nineteenth century and was cemented by the advent of the New Deal in the 1930s. Even in 1952, when Republican Dwight D. Eisenhower defeated Democrat Adlai Stevenson by 55 to 44 percent nationwide, Stevenson won 56 percent of the Catholic vote. In 1960, when the Democrats nominated Senator John F. Kennedy of Massachusetts, a Catholic, for president, they captured 78 percent of the vote among Catholics.[5]

But as anti-Catholic prejudice in society declined and Catholics became less socioeconomically distinct from other Americans, they began to vote more like the rest of the nation. White Catholics are no longer a mostly Democratic group, and Democratic candidates can no longer count on automatic Catholic support. For the first time since 1960, the Democrats nominated a Catholic politician for president in 2004, but unlike Kennedy, John Kerry did not benefit from strong loyalty among his fellow Catholics. In fact, he lost the Catholic vote to George W. Bush by 52 to 47 percent.[6] At the same time, the smaller populations of Jews, members of other religions, and the non-religious have either maintained or increased their high levels of support for Democratic candidates since the 1970s and 1980s. In 2016, Hillary Clinton received more than half of her votes from non-Protestants, while almost two-thirds of Trump voters were Protestant (see table 2.3).

An even more dramatic change in partisan preferences occurred among Southern whites. In 1952 and 1956, Southerners voted about 10 percentage points more Democratic than the rest of the country. Republicans began to make inroads among this group in the 1960s and 1970s, though Southern voters moved back to the Democrats in 1976 and 1980, when former governor Jimmy Carter of Georgia headed the Democratic ticket. Since 1984, the Republicans have consistently received very strong support from Southern whites; according to the National Election Studies, Donald Trump outpolled Hillary Clinton by a roughly two-to-one margin among these voters in 2016.

What about the voting habits of young people, those under 30 years of age? Until 1972, they were not consistently a significant component of either party's coalition and their comparatively low turnout reduced any impact that their 18 percent share of the voting-age population might have given them. After the voting age was lowered in 1971 from 21 (in most states) to 18 nationwide, and because of the baby boom after World War II, the proportion of the voting-age population under the age of 30 increased to 28 percent, and in the 1970s there was much talk of young people as a separate, presumably more liberal, voting bloc. As the baby boomers aged, young people decreased as a proportion of all voters, representing 19 percent of the electorate in 2016. Are they now making a big difference?

The belief that the youth vote is usually pro-Democratic dates to the 1960s and 1970s, but it has only been consistently true since 2008 (see table 2.4). Obama won 66 percent of the under-30 vote that year (to 32 percent for his opponent

Table 2.4 Vote for Democratic Presidential Candidate by Age Group, 1968–2016

Age	2016	2012	2008	2004	2000	1996	1992	1988	1984	1980	1976	1972	1968
18–29	55	60	66	54	48	53	43	47	40	44	51	47	38
30–44	52	52	52	46	48	48	41	45	42	36	49	34	47
45–59	44	51	49	48	48	48	41	42	40	39	47	31	37
60+	45	56	47	56	51	48	50	49	39	41	47	29	40

Source: For 1964–1972, National Election Studies; for 1976–2004, Marjorie Connelly, "How Americans Voted: A Political Portrait," *New York Times*, November 7, 2004, sec. 4, p. 4; for 2008, "CNN Presidential Exit Poll," http://www.cnn.com/ELECTION/2008/results/polls/#val=USP00p; for 2012, "CNN Presidential Exit Poll," http://www.cnn.com/election/2012/results/race/president; for 2016, "CNN Presidential Exit Poll," https://www.cnn.com/election/2016/results/president.

John McCain), the largest pro-Democratic margin in this age group since the Johnson landslide of 1964. Hillary Clinton received 55 percent of younger votes in 2016 compared to Donald Trump's 36 percent, with the remaining 9 percent captured by third-party candidates.

What is the Republican electoral coalition? White people, who constitute about three-quarters of all voters, usually vote more Republican than the total electorate, by a margin of 12 percent in 2008 and 2012 and 11 percent in 2016. Historically, the overwhelming majority of Republican votes came from whites: 98 percent, on average, between 1952 and 1980. After the 1980s, nonwhites became a slightly larger component of the Republican vote, but whites still constituted 88 percent of Donald Trump's electoral coalition in 2016. If one can conceive of nonunion families and Protestants as "social groups" in the usual sense, they made up about 81 percent and 63 percent of the 2016 GOP presidential coalition, respectively, and consistently vote 5 to 10 percent more Republican than the nation as a whole.

The Republican Party gets its vote, then, predominantly from white people, middle- and upper-income earners, non-union members, and Protestants—especially evangelical Protestants—outside large cities. Republicans received majorities of 60 percent or better from all these groups in their landslide victories of 1972 and 1984. In 1992 and 1996, defections to Democrat Bill Clinton and independent candidate Ross Perot held Republicans to under 50 percent of the vote in most of these groups, making victory impossible. George W. Bush improved his party's standing among these voters in 2000 and 2004, winning 54 and 58 percent of the white vote, respectively, including about two out of every three votes among Southern whites and white Protestants.[7] John McCain in 2008 and Mitt Romney in 2012 also won a majority of the white vote but were unable to offset Obama's much larger electoral margin among nonwhites. A decline in minority turnout in 2016, coupled with a more favorable distribution of Republican votes within battleground states, allowed Trump's 20-point advantage over Clinton (57 percent to 37 percent) to deliver an Electoral College majority despite his second-place finish in the national popular vote.

The 2016 election, however, did reveal demographic trends among three groups that augur well for Democrats in the future. The Latino proportion of the electorate has grown from 6 percent in 2004 to 11 percent in 2016, and the Democratic advantage among Latino voters rose to 66 to 28 percent in 2016 from 56 to 44 percent in 2004.[8] Also increasing was the percentage of Americans claiming no religious affiliation, which grew from 9 percent in 2000 to 15 percent in 2016. Secular Americans awarded Democrats 65 percent of their 2016 votes, up from 60 percent in 2000. Voters with postgraduate degrees, a growing share of the electorate in the last three presidential elections, have also regularly given most of their support to Democrats: 58 percent in 2016 and 2008, 55 percent in 2004 and 2012, and 52 percent in 2000. All three groups bring distinct advantages to Democrats in presidential elections. Latinos promise to continue to grow as a percentage of the electorate, and secular Americans may well increase as well in accord with recent trends. Secular Americans in recent years have demonstrated increased activism by forming national interest groups.[9] An increasing Democratic margin among those with postgraduate degrees also pays dividends because such people are disproportionately likely to contribute to candidates and serve as campaign volunteers.

To sum up, while there has been no case of abrupt partisan realignment in the years since 1932, the coalitions of both parties have evolved substantially since the New Deal era. Roman Catholics, union members, and Southern whites have become much less important components of the Democrats' electoral base over time, while the party is increasingly dependent on votes from nonwhites, non-Christians, younger voters, and well-educated professionals. The Republican Party has maintained its long-term advantage among the business class, adding substantial support over the past several decades from religiously observant white Protestants—especially in the South—and Catholics. Since the 1990s, these partisan coalitions of social groups have translated into relatively stable geographic bases in presidential elections for both parties, with the Democrats holding an advantage within the Northeast, urban Midwest, and Pacific Coast, while Republicans predominate across most of the South, Great Plains, and Rocky Mountains.[10]

VARIATIONS AMONG INTEREST GROUPS

Interest groups are collections of people who are similarly situated with respect to one or more policies of government and who organize to do something about it. The interest groups most significant for elections in our society are those having one or more of the following characteristics:

1. They have a mass base—that is, they are composed of many members.
2. They are concentrated geographically, rather than dispersed thinly over the entire map.
3. They represent major resource investments of members—such as sugar cane growers, whose entire livelihoods may be tied up in the industry involved, as compared to the consumers of sugar, for whom government policy on the issue is not anywhere near as important.
4. They involve characteristics that give people status in society, such as race or ethnicity.
5. They evoke feelings about a single issue that are so intense as to eclipse the concerns of their members about other issues.
6. They are composed of people who are able to participate actively in politics—that is, people who have time or money to spare.

Interest groups having these characteristics matter most in national elections because these characteristics are most likely to claim the loyalties of large numbers of voters and form the basis for the mobilization of their preferences and their votes. Moreover, they reflect the fact that America is organized into geographic entities—states and congressional districts—as the basis of political representation. Interest groups may be more or less organized and more or less vigilant and alert on policy matters that concern, or ought to concern, them. They are not necessarily organized in ways that make them politically effective; very often, the paid lobbyists of interest groups spend more time trying to alert their own members to the implications of government policies than they spend lobbying politicians.[11]

In American politics, interest group activity is lively and can be found nearly everywhere, even when it is not particularly effective or meaningful for policy outcomes. Three characteristics of interest groups are especially important for presidential elections. First, membership in these groups may give voters a sense of affiliation and political location. In this respect, interest groups act much the way parties do, filling in the voter's map of the world with preferences, priorities, and facts. Interest groups act as agents of intermediation that help voters identify their political preferences quickly by actively soliciting their members' interest on behalf of specific candidates and parties and, more important, by providing still another anchor to voters' identities. This helps voters fix their own position quickly and economically in what otherwise would be a confusing and contradictory political environment. Second, interest groups frequently undertake partisan political activities; they may actively recruit supporters for candidates and aid materially in campaigns.

Third, interest groups may influence party policy by making demands of candidates with respect to issues in return for their own mobilized support. The extent to which interest groups can "deliver" members' votes, however, is always a problem; to a great degree, interest group leaders are the prisoners of past alliances their group has made. This means that they may not be able to prevent their followers from voting for their traditional allies, even when group leaders fall out with politicians. In 1993, labor union leaders vowed revenge on Democratic members of Congress who voted for the North American Free Trade Agreement (NAFTA),[12] but in the 1994 election, 63 percent of union families still voted Democratic in elections for the House of Representatives, as they had in 1980, 1986, and 1988. This was only one point worse than in 1984 when Walter Mondale, a conspicuous friend of labor, headed the Democratic presidential ticket.[13]

Various ethnic and religious votes, the farm vote, the labor vote, the youth vote, the consumer vote, and many other "votes" are sometimes discussed as though they were political commodities that interest group leaders could manipulate easily in behalf of one or another candidate. This is not as easy as it sounds. Seventy years ago or more, when the analysis of election statistics and opinion polls was an esoteric discipline, most politicians could only evaluate intuitively claims to guarantee group support or threats to withdraw it, and no one could tell with any certainty whether interest group leaders maintained sufficient influence among their constituents to deliver on their promises. The development of the craft of public opinion analysis now makes it easier to assess these political claims (box 2.1).

The usual argument is that if one or another candidate captures the allegiance of a particular bloc, that bloc's pivotal position or large population in a key state will enable the fortunate candidate to capture all of the state's electoral votes and thus win the election. Many states with large numbers of electoral votes contain significant populations of traditional Democratic voting blocs: racial minorities, union members, post-graduate degree-holders, and secular voters. During the hard-fought 2008 Democratic primary campaign between Barack Obama and Hillary Clinton, the candidates and their advisers regularly traded competing claims of superior interest-group mobilization capacity. Obama argued that his selection as the Democratic standard-bearer would inspire high rates of participation and support in the general election among racial minorities, young voters, and political independents, while Clinton countered that her nomination would

Box 2.1 ■ In the Arena: 2016 Group Endorsements for Trump and Clinton

For Trump

American Energy Alliance: "The contrast between the two candidates' energy platforms could not be greater. Donald Trump's message is one of optimism, prosperity, and abundance where the needs of consumers and workers are put first. Hillary Clinton's message is one of political favors and cronyism that puts the agenda of her favored special interests above all else. . . . Where Donald Trump promises prosperity and growth, Hillary Clinton promises a third term of President Obama's regressive climate agenda."

National Rifle Association: "In all of history, there's always been a time and a place when patriots stand up and rise up against the decree of the elites and shout, 'No more! Get your hands off my freedom!' That time and place is now. We stand together. We stand and we fight like hell for freedom. The revolution to take America back starts here. It starts on this day, and by God, we will elect our next president, we will save our freedom and America truly will be great again."

For Clinton

Sierra Club: "We firmly believe Secretary Clinton will be the strong environmental champion that we need to lead our country, which is why the Sierra Club is proud to endorse her and her vision for America. Secretary Clinton has a long record on the environment and is the leader we need to build on this progress made by President Obama and the climate movement. She has listened to the grassroots and crafted detailed plans to safeguard our climate, air, water, and public lands, to protect the most vulnerable from environmental injustice, and to continue the rapid expansion of our clean energy economy."

AFL-CIO: "Hillary Clinton is a proven leader who shares our values. Throughout the campaign, she has demonstrated a strong commitment to the issues that matter to working people, and our members have taken notice. The activism of working people has already been a major force in this election and is now poised to elect Hillary Clinton and move America forward. . . . Beginning immediately, the AFL-CIO will put in motion its ground campaign to elect Hillary Clinton and union-endorsed candidates across the country."

Sources: https://www.americanenergyalliance.org/2016/07/12/aea-endorses-donald-trump-for-president; https://www.politico.com/story/2016/05/nra-trump-endorsement-223422; https://content.sierraclub.org/press-releases/2016/06/sierra-club-endorses-hillary-clinton-president; https://aflcio.org/2016/6/15/working-people-afl-cio-endorse-hillary-clinton-president.

generate particular enthusiasm for the party among women and working-class voters. Of course, no single combination of states totaling more than a majority of electoral votes is more critical, valuable, or pivotal than any other such combination. In a fairly close election, the shifting of any number of combinations of voting blocs or states to one side or the other could spell the difference between victory and defeat.

There is little doubt that under certain conditions and at particular times some social characteristics of voters and candidates may have relevance to the election results. Finding the actual conditions under which specified social characteristics become relevant to voter choice is difficult. We know that in a competitive political system various participants (parties, political leaders) back candidates with the hope of capturing the allegiance of various social groups. It is rarely wise to appeal to one group alone; in a very large electorate, the support of only one group will not be enough to win. Many different groups exist, with all sorts of policy preferences, and each individual voter has many social characteristics that are potentially relevant to his or her voting decision. While some people may be so single-minded that they have only one interest that is important in determining their vote—their race, religion, ethnic background, income, feelings about gun control or abortion or the State of Israel—most of us have multiple interests. Sometimes these interests conflict. Environmental organizations, for example, may have less success in mobilizing voters in areas where environmental regula- tion is believed to reduce employment opportunities than in areas where the two do not compete. The worse the economic conditions, the sharper the perceived conflict. Concern about increasing unemployment may influence how some vot- ers feel about governmental support of the unemployed. Much depends on the tides of events, which may bring one or another issue to the forefront of the voters' consciousness and incline them toward the candidate they believe best represents their preferences on that particular matter.[14]

One of the largest social groups of all, women, provides an example of a group membership whose political importance has changed significantly since the 1980s. At one time, gender could not be shown to have a strong effect on parti- sanship or voting habits; what weak tendency existed at the time of *The American Voter* (1960) showed women to be slightly more Republican than men.[15] In 1980, however, women were substantially less supportive of Ronald Reagan's candidacy than were men and thus made up a much larger part of the Democratic than of the Republican coalition (see tables 2.3 and 2.5), marking the first appearance of the modern "gender gap."[16] By the 2000 election, the gender gap had reached a then-record size: Al Gore carried the women's vote by 11 percentage points, but lost among men to George W. Bush by the same margin. In 2004 and 2008, how- ever, the difference between the sexes appeared to narrow a bit, with exit polls showing only a seven-point gap in the presidential vote between men and women. By 2012, the gap was back up to 10 points. In 2016, it climbed further to 13 points, reflecting the Democrats' nomination of Hillary Clinton to be the nation's first female president and the controversies surrounding Republican nominee Donald Trump's remarks toward women.[17]

But the case of the "women's vote" should also alert us to some of the complexities of group interest. Generalizations about social groups, especially groups—like women—that encompass a majority of the electorate, may obscure important internal differences among their members. For example, less-educated women tend to identify as Republicans and better-educated women as Democrats, just like men. Group memberships do not necessarily organize voters along a single dimension; the "interests" of a given group may be of greatest interest to only a subset of members. While organized interest groups claiming to represent women's preferences concentrate much of their lobbying activity on pressuring policy makers to maintain or expand legal access to abortion in order to protect "a woman's right to choose," Karen M. Kaufmann notes that public opinion sur- veys find "few, if any, significant differences between women and men on abor- tion attitudes and issues of female equality" within the American electorate.[18] Hillary Clinton's status as the first female major-party presidential nominee in

Table 2.5 The Gender Gap: Votes in Presidential Elections by Sex, 1960–2016

Year	Men			Women		
	Democrat	Republican	Independent	Democrat	Republican	Independent
1960	52	48		49	51	
1964	60	40		62	38	
1968	41	43	16	45	43	12
1972	37	63		38	62	
1976	50	48		50	48	
1980	36	55	7	45	47	7
1984	37	62		44	56	
1988	41	57		49	50	
1992	41	38	21	45	37	17
1996	43	44	10	54	38	7
2000	42	53	3	54	43	2
2004	44	55		51	48	
2008	49	48		56	43	
2012	45	52		55	44	
2016	41	52		54	41	

Source: For 1960–1972, Harold W. Stanley and Richard G. Niemi, *Vital Statistics on American Politics, 2005–2006* (Washington, DC: CQ Press, 2005), 122; for 1976–2004, Marjorie Connelly, "How Americans Voted: A Political Portrait," *New York Times*, November 7, 2004, sec. 4, 4; for 2008, "CNN Presidential Exit Poll," http://www.cnn.com/ELECTION/2008/results/polls/#val=USP00p1; for 2012, "CNN Presidential Exit Poll," http://www.cnn.com/election/2012/results/race/president; for 2016, "CNN Presidential Exit Poll," https://www.cnn.com/election/2016/results/race/president.

Note: Independent candidates were George Wallace in 1968, John Anderson in 1980, Ross Perot in 1992 and 1996, and Ralph Nader in 2000.

2016 energized many Democratic feminists behind her candidacy, but she had little success in attracting support from Republican women, despite their shared gender identity.

Instead, recent research indicates a growing political divide between older, married, traditionalist, religiously observant women and younger, single, secular, professional women, with the first group becoming more ideologically conservative and pro-Republican over time and the latter more liberal and Democratic.[19] As Barbara Norrander and Clyde Wilcox point out, the gender gap "is as much one of divisions among women as differences between the sexes."[20] In addition, though the rise of the gender gap over the past several decades is usually portrayed in news media accounts as the result of a movement among women toward the political left and the Democratic Party, evidence also exists of increasing conservatism (and Republicanism) among men during the same period.[21] The especially large gender gap in attitudes toward Donald Trump, evident in the 2016 election results as well as subsequent public opinion polling during his presidency, marks a continuation of these trends.

Democratic candidates have a problem attracting white men and Republicans have a problem attracting women in general. There is no doubt about the numbers, only about the explanation. It is possible that the egalitarian bent of the Democratic Party has appealed to women and repelled men. The argument for this view would be that Democrats include women among the deprived minorities for whom beneficial policies are in order, leaving white males above the poverty line as the residual category who must help all the rest. The Republican Party's emphasis on opportunity rather than on more equal outcomes, by contrast, leaves the existing status or privileges of white and more affluent men untouched. In a corresponding manner, white women of low income may see the Democratic Party as providing them with concrete benefits, while middle- and upper-middle-income women, many of them influenced by the feminist movement, may see Republicans as opposed to their views on cultural matters.[22] Women are also more concerned with egalitarian or "compassion" issues—fairness to the poor, unemployment—and tend to be less likely than men to support increased defense spending and the use of military force.[23] Thus women differ from men on specific issue positions as well as on party identification and candidate choice, though not necessarily on the stereotypical "women's issues" commonly assumed to account for the contemporary gender gap.

"SPECIAL" INTERESTS, CAMPAIGN SPENDING, AND PUBLIC INTEREST GROUPS

Is there any difference between interest groups, as we have described them here, and the "special" interests that attract so much criticism from politicians and the news media? Not as far as we can tell. Americans have always organized themselves into interest groups. Groups may have interests that are broad or narrow, but it is hard to see why interests that are narrow, and therefore presumably more "special," are any less legitimate than broad interests, which presumably require more common resources to satisfy. The language of political competition in American elections frequently requires political actors to disparage the claims of others by labeling them "special" interests and therefore somehow not worthy of consideration. "We" are presumably "the people" and "they" are "special interests." But of course the "people" have interests too. In a democracy, leaders are supposed to inform themselves about and sympathize with the policies that people want. Paying attention to these concerns of the people looks to us very much like attending to the needs of special interests.

The rise of rhetoric stigmatizing interests as "special" interests is in part the result of the rise of vocal and deeply concerned groups claiming to represent the "public" interest rather than the private or pecuniary interests of their members. Although interest groups in the past have differed over policy, they have not (at least since the acceptance of industrial unions in the 1930s and African American organizations in the 1960s) denied the rights of opponents to advocate their policy preferences. But, in one significant respect, that is no longer true. "Public interest" lobbies have attacked the legitimacy of "private interest" groups. Political parties, labor unions, trade associations, and religious groups are examples of such private interest groups, intermediary organizations that link citizens and their government. Many are indeed "special interest" groups—groups, that is, with special interests in public policy. Part of the program of public interest groups such as Common Cause or Ralph Nader's various organizations is to reduce the power of private, special interests and substitute their own services as intermediary organizations. Typically, public interest groups have fewer—sometimes vastly fewer—members than private interest groups.[24] They rely on journalists, newsletters, and the Internet to carry their messages to the population at large, and their success is an indication of the extent to which American voters now rely on mass media rather than group membership to obtain their political orientations and opinions.

A remarkable example of the ways in which the mass media have to a certain extent transformed the interest-group environment of elections is the proliferation of specialized media sources as instruments for the crystallization of political opinions. Radio talk show hosts with compelling personalities—exemplified by conservative mainstay Rush Limbaugh—can, over a relatively short period of time mobilize strong expressions of opinion by many listeners and callers, in effect creating interest groups out of thin air by giving voice mainly to exasperated anti-government and other negative sentiments. Limbaugh has an estimated 26 million listeners each week. His books have sold millions of copies.[25] The large population of political blogs and websites—such as Daily Kos and Talking Points Memo on the left and Townhall and RedState on the right—on the Internet also remain an important source of campaign information and analysis and influence more mainstream media outlets. In recent years, social media sites such as Facebook, YouTube, and Instagram—each with well over 100 million monthly active users in America—now act as major avenues where political news and views are shared, and where political action can be stimulated almost instantaneously.

Laws have been passed and constitutional amendments proposed by public interest groups that restrict the amounts of money unions and corporations can contribute to political campaigns and use in lobbying. On the whole, however, these laws have been unsuccessful in curbing interest-group activity. What has happened is that interest groups have found new ways within the law to advance their interests. The history of campaign finance since the 1970s is a story of interests finding new ways to legally spend unlimited funds in election campaigns.

A long-standing device for group spending is the political action committee (PAC), an organization devoted to the disbursement of campaign money from interest groups to candidates. From 1976 to 1984, the number of political action committees organized by business and unions almost tripled, increasing from 657 to 1,845; from 1980 to 1988, PACs of all types (including those unconnected to business and unions) rose from 1,997 to 3,308, remaining relatively stable ever since. (See table 2.6.) The bulk of the original increase was accounted for by the rise in corporate PACs from 433 in 1974 to 1,616 in 1988, but the number of these corporate PACs has slightly declined over the last 28 years, reaching a total of 1,460 in 2016.

PACs are created to collect and disburse political contributions. They must contribute to more than one candidate, and the amount they may give to any one candidate is limited. In 1976, amendments to the Federal Election Campaign Act enabled individual companies or labor unions to establish multiple PACs, thus multiplying the amount of money they could funnel to any single candidate. Surprisingly, corporate PACs did not originally favor Republican campaigns as much as might be expected. Corporate PACs usually support incumbents over challengers, and for much of the 1970s and 1980s, Democratic officeholders outnumbered Republicans at both the federal and state levels. Accordingly, they reaped contributions from corporate PACs.[26] After the Republican Party gained

Table 2.6 The Rise of Political Action Committees (PACs), 1976–2016

Year	Corporate	Labor	Professional Groups	Cooperatives	Corporation without Stock	Nonconnected	Total
1976	433	224	489	—	—	—	1,146
1980	1,037	225	463	27	44	201	1,997
1984	1,584	261	598	51	117	576	3,187
1988	1,616	256	633	51	122	630	3,308
1992	1,514	255	633	48	114	534	3,098
1996	1,470	236	650	41	109	529	3,035
2000	1,365	236	662	37	94	670	3,064
2004	1,402	206	722	34	75	819	3,258
2008	1,470	203	794	39	84	1,023	3,613
2012	1,223	137	700	29	55	902	3,046
2016	1,460	180	879	35	63	1,364	3,981

Source: Campaign Finance Institute, "Number of Political Action Committees Making Contributions to Candidates 1976–2016," http://www.cfinst.org/pdf/vital/VitalStats_t9.pdf.

Note: Nonconnected PACs do not have a sponsoring organization.

a majority in both houses of Congress in the 1994 election, corporate PAC contributions favored the GOP, but shifted back to the Democrats when they retook control of the legislative branch from 2006 to 2010.[27]

The Supreme Court decision in *Buckley v. Valeo* (1976) removed any contribution restrictions from PACs. Thanks to this ruling, "a corporate or union political action committee can collect donations and contribute an unlimited sum of money to unspecified numbers of candidates or committees so long as no single contribution exceeds $5,000."[28] In addition, once a PAC "contributes to five or more federal candidates, [it] can make unlimited independent expenditures on behalf of candidates or parties" (e.g., advertising on behalf of a candidate independent of that candidate's campaign in print or electronic media).[29] Not surprisingly, prospective presidential candidates themselves now organize PACs as a way of developing political alliances.

A 2010 decision of the D.C. District Court of Appeals, *SpeechNow.org v. FEC*, allowed the formation of "Super PACs." These PACs can accept previously prohibited amounts and sources of funds, including large individual, corporate, and union contributions, as long as the PAC only makes independent expenditures—those not coordinated with a candidate—and does not contribute to candidates. "527 groups" are named for the federal tax code provision that authorizes them, can accept unlimited contributions, and can spend unlimited funds in elections on explicit behalf of candidates but must disclose their donors and their amounts donated to the Federal Election Commission. "501(c)(4) groups" can also raise unlimited contributions but do not have to disclose their donors. They are primarily supposed to lobby, but can also engage in unlimited independent spending and endorse candidates as long as those campaign activities are not a "substantial" share of the organization's activities—a restriction that in practice has proved hard to enforce. 501(c)(4) organizations do not have to disclose their donors or the amount they have donated.

Yet another venue for deploying election cash is the "Hybrid PAC," also known as the Carey PAC. Rear Admiral James Carey of the National Defense PAC brought suit in 2011 against the Federal Election Commission, seeking permission to operate as a "Super Duper PAC" that would be, as a single entity, both an independent expenditure-only Super PAC and a traditional PAC that makes direct contributions to candidates. The Federal District Court in the District of Columbia approved Carey's request, ruling that FEC restrictions on such activity were too restrictive of First Amendment free speech rights.[30] Carey committees must have a separate bank account for each purpose. The committee can collect unlimited contributions from almost any source for its independent expenditure account, but may not use those funds for its traditional PAC contributions.

Groups and wealthy individuals were further aided in their efforts to deploy campaign money by two recent Supreme Court decisions. In the 2010 decision *Citizens United v. FEC*, a 5–4 majority held, "No sufficient governmental interest justifies limits on the speech of nonprofit and for-profit corporations."[31] This ruling allowed unlimited independent spending in election campaigns by both corporations and unions. In *McCutcheon v. FEC*, a 2013 ruling, the Court by another 5–4 vote voided aggregate personal contribution limits by individuals to candidates (indexed to inflation since 2002 and then $123,200 annually), finding that "the aggregate limits on contributions . . . intrude without justification on a citizen's ability to exercise 'the most fundamental First Amendment activities.'"[32]

This more permissive campaign finance regime led to a large tide of independent group spending in the 2016 presidential contest. Outside groups spent $75 million in independent expenditures on Donald Trump's behalf, primarily by Carey PACs and Super PACs created as 501(c)(4) organizations. Hillary Clinton in 2016 benefited from $231 million of such spending. In comparison, the Trump campaign itself spent $333 million and the Clinton campaign $563 million.[33] Trump's celebrity status, however, earned him an estimated $5.8 billion in free media time in 2016, compared to Clinton's estimated $2.8 billion.[34] Total presidential election spending on behalf of the two major party candidates in 2016 did decline from the record total of over $1 billion spent on behalf of each 2012 major party candidate, Barack Obama and Mitt Romney.[35]

Massive election spending by groups nominally independent of the candidates and parties seems to have become a permanent fixture of American politics. Both candidates and voters confront new campaign problems as a result. Independent spending produces a clutter of campaign messages that reduces the ability of candidates to dominate campaign discourse. The resulting blizzard of campaign messages also produces accountability difficulties for voters. Who is behind which message? Often contributors are not disclosed and organizations adopt vague and reassuring monikers that reveal little about their aims. The two biggest independent spenders in the 2016 presidential election were the 501(c)(4) Super PAC "Priorities USA" and the Carey PAC "Great American PAC." The first spent $192 million to elect Clinton, and the latter funded efforts on Trump's behalf totaling more than $28 million.

Prominent public interest lobbies since the 1970s have opposed the new avenues of presidential campaign spending. The lobbies represent not direct material interests as corporations and unions do, but "issue" interests such as campaign finance reform and tort reform.[36] They have also sought to weaken the power of party leaders and strong party identifiers and to strengthen citizens who are weakly identified with parties and who emerge briefly during a particular election campaign or in response to a current issue. The stress on ease of entry into internal party affairs—more primaries, more conferences, more frequent and more open elections to party bodies—leads to the domination of parties by activists who have time and education and are able to take the trouble to go to meetings, given the fact that party membership occurs in the first place by self-activation.

What kinds of people have these characteristics? Among others, they are the middle- and upper-middle-class professionals who predominate in supporting Common Cause, Nader's Raiders, and other public interest lobbies. Thus, among interest groups, if money matters less as a resource, business matters less; if time and talk and education matter more, ordinary workers matter less. As leaders of labor, business, and the parties lose power, organizers of public interest lobbies gain. These public interest lobbies are not necessarily all on one side of the ideological spectrum. People who defend corporate capitalism as well as those who attack it can organize in the public interest. And they do.

Two advantages have helped public interest groups expand their influence. One is a product of modern technology and the other has been generated by government. The use of computerized mailing lists and communication via the Internet has permitted these groups to tap contributions from large numbers of people who do not otherwise participate directly in group activities but receive mail and social media messages—and thus become privileged spectators to group leaders' battles over public policy. This opportunity for vicarious participation not only generates ready cash but also simplifies somewhat the tasks of leadership. Instead of having to satisfy an active membership that might make diverse or contradictory demands, only the top leadership of public interest groups need be consulted. Leaders of public interest groups are frequently poorly paid, accepting low income as a sacrifice for their cause, but they exercise strong influence on the groups they lead.

The second advantage is that people who contribute to public interest groups are entitled to count these monies as tax-deductible. When the group wishes to undertake activities incompatible with eligibility for deduction, it often establishes a separate educational or litigating arm that can receive non-tax-deductible contributions. Without tax deductibility, the survival of some of these groups would be in doubt. The tradeoff is that they are required to engage in educational activities rather than overt lobbying, even though this may be a distinction without a difference. In addition, some of these groups achieve a status as legally authorized interveners before regulatory commissions, a role that entitles them to payment for their activity. In this sense, public interest groups are sometimes partially subsidized by government.

POLITICAL PARTIES AS ORGANIZATIONS

A third aspect of the social framework, along with voters and interest groups, that will help us account for the strategies of participants in presidential elections is the nature of political parties in the United States. Here we discuss parties as organizations rather than as symbols for voters.

Party organizations are composed of three basic groups. First, employees of the party at the national and state levels staff the party offices and perform tasks on behalf of the party, augmented by a universe of professional operatives situated in outside firms aligned with the party who conduct polling, research, consulting, media relations, and other campaign activities. Second, candidates and elected officials affiliated with the party carry the party label when they run for public office. Third, party activists are involved in party activities such as candidate recruitment, fund-raising, and getting out the vote. Each group plays a different role in party activities, and sometimes their interests conflict.

The primary goal of party professionals is to run an organization that will maintain or increase the power of the party. We define power in this situation as the ability to influence decisions made by government. Parties obtain this power by helping to elect individuals affiliated with their organization and through control of the appointive jobs that officials ordinarily bestow on members of their own party.[37] For party representatives—candidates and elected officials—and party activists, however, increasing the power of the party as an organization is often a secondary goal; other interests may be more important.

Thus party professionals cannot always count on their party's candidates to share the goals of the central organization. What might be the most effective strategy for a candidate to adopt in a given campaign or legislative situation may not fit with the party's overall plan or policy platform. Conflicts are certain to arise. Aware of this, party organizations have developed strategies aimed at keeping candidates and elected officials loyal to their goals.

Most significant is the fund-raising that national party organizations perform in order to spend money on behalf of the party's candidates for the presidency and other federal offices. In the late 1970s, the Republican National Committee (RNC), under Chairman William Brock, began to raise large sums of money from a broad network of individual donors to provide aid to state parties and to help candidates and state parties professionalize their operations.[38] The Democratic National Committee (DNC), more haltingly and less successfully, began to follow suit. This process was accelerated when the Supreme Court ruled in the 1996 case of *Colorado Republican Campaign Committee v. Federal Election Commission* that the First Amendment protected the right of political parties to campaign on behalf of their candidates and policy positions. In 2002, Congress raised the limit on individual contributions to national party committees from $20,000 to $25,000 per year, and indexed it to increases over time in the national cost of living (so that the limit on individual contributions to national parties is $35,500 in 2020). As table 2.7 makes clear, the growth in fund-raising by the national party committees (the DNC, RNC, and House and Senate campaign committees on both sides) has increased over the past few presidential election cycles.

Parties at times experience tensions between two of their primary goals. On the one hand, they must satisfy their activists and interest-group supporters by committing, or appearing to commit, to policies of concern to them. On the other hand, they are trying to lure enough people uncommitted on these policies in order to win the election. In a close election, the ability of a party to increase its support within one critical electoral group from, say, 20 to 30 percent may be crucial, even though that group still votes overwhelmingly for the opposition. The strategic implications of these remarks color all of national campaign politics: when they are trying to win, the parties try to do things that will please the groups consistently allied to them without unduly alienating other voters.

Table 2.7 The Rise of National Party Fund-Raising, 1983–2016 (in millions of dollars)

	Democratic Party Funds Raised	Republican Party Funds Raised	Total
1983–1984	84.4	289.0	373.4
1987–1988	116.1	257.5	373.6
1991–1992	163.3	264.9	428.2
1995–1996	221.6	416.5	638.1
1999–2000	275.2	465.8	741.0
2003–2004	678.8	782.4	1,461.2
2007–2008	763.3	792.9	1,556.2
2011–2012	805.6	806.9	1,612.5
2015–2016	870.2	752.4	1622.6

Source: Harold W. Stanley and Richard G. Niemi, *Vital Statistics on American Politics, 2013–2014* (Washington, DC: CQ Press, 2014), table 2–6; for 2015–16, Federal Election Commission, "Statistical Summary of 24-Month Campaign Activity of the 2015–2016 Election Cycle," https://www.fec.gov/updates/statistical-summary-24-month-campaign-activity-2015–2016-election-cycle.

It is even more difficult to predict how these aggregations of actual and potential interest groups might react to shifts in party policy positions, and still more hazardous to prophesy what different policy commitments might do to the margin of votes required for victory. This pervasive problem of uncertainty makes the calculations of gain from changes in policies both difficult and risky. It suggests that the interests of parties and candidates frequently are best served by ambiguous or contradictory policy statements that will be unlikely to offend anyone. The advantages of vagueness about policy are strengthened by the facts that many persuadable voters are not interested in policy or are narrowly focused on a small number of issues.

Yet, despite all this, political leaders and parties do, at times, make policy commitments that are surprisingly precise, specific, and logically consistent. Thus we must go beyond our consideration of why the parties sometimes blur issues and avoid commitments to ask why they often commit themselves to policies more readily than their interest in acquiring or retaining office would seem to require.

Part of the answer may arise from the fact that the parties depend on their party activists and that many of these activists, especially the purists among them, demand specific policy commitments from the party. The activists are the heart of any party organization; they are the volunteers and donors for campaigns, the people who stimulate participation in their communities, and most likely they are the party's strongest supporters and most dependable voters. Unlike most citizens, who are largely disengaged from politics except in the final weeks of a national campaign, activists are likely to have elaborate political opinions and preferences and to act on them even when an election is not imminent. They often make demands on the party leadership for policy positions that are reasonably clear and forthright, and they are capable of enforcing these demands by participating in primary elections on behalf of candidates who pledge to satisfy them.[39] Pressure of this sort contributes to the ongoing ideological polarization of the two political parties. The national Democratic Party is now more uniformly liberal in its policy positions and the national Republican Party more thoroughly conservative in its stands than they were 30 years ago.[40]

Furthermore, the interest groups most closely allied with each party make policy demands that parties must to some extent meet. Even more than voters, who are generally interested at most in only a few specific policies, interest-group leaders and their full-time bureaucracies are manifestly concerned citizens and often party activists as well. If they feel that the interests they represent are being harmed, they may so inform their members or even attempt to withdraw support from the party at a particular election. Should voters find that groups with which they identify are opposed to the party with which they identify, they may temporarily support the opposition party, or, more likely, they may withdraw from participation and not vote at all. Consequently, the party finds that it risks losing elections by ignoring the demands of interest groups, especially those that are key elements of the party base.

The demands of many of these groups conflict, however. If unions object to party or candidate advocacy of antipollution devices on automobiles because they increase costs and decrease car sales, for example, Democratic leaders will find it impossible to satisfy both labor and environmental groups. If business interests wish immigration levels to be raised to increase the supply of labor while nationalist groups push for greater restrictions, Republican leaders may be unable to choose a side without alienating an important party constituency. Therefore, the parties may attempt to mediate among interest groups, hoping to strike compromises that, though they give no one group everything, give something to as many groups as they can. But ideologically motivated party activists and interest groups devoted to a single policy goal are not always satisfied by such partial victories.

What at the national level used to be a loose federation of state parties is slowly being converted, by changes in party rules and by judicial decisions, into a somewhat more centralized structure. Thus our national parties combine elements of both decentralization and centralization. The most obvious indicator of continuing decentralization is that national parties are organized on a geographical basis with the state units as the constituent elements. The party organizations from different states meet formally by sending delegates to national committee meetings and, most important, by coming together every four years at national conventions to nominate a president.

The strongest indicators of nationalization are the guidelines set out at the national level, which, especially for Democrats, are important in determining who these delegates will be.[41] Still, it is the states which choose their representatives to national party bodies; the national committees and conventions do not choose officers of state parties. Both parties' national organizations now have sizable staffs who recommend effective campaign managers, consultants, pollsters, and accountants, going so far as to buy blocks of services that then can be allocated to close races. In addition, they assist state parties and candidate campaigns with fund-raising contacts, political strategy, and media relations.[42] National party committees may also spend unlimited amounts of money on behalf of candidates for the presidency and other offices, as long as the expenditures are formally uncoordinated with the candidates' own campaigns.

Much of the institutional apparatus of the two major parties now exists outside the national, state, and local party committees. What some scholars call the "extended party networks" tie politicians and activists in both the Democratic and Republican parties to a larger web of allied interest group organizations, campaign professionals, media authorities, and financial donors.[43] These networks serve as conduits for mutual influence between partisan officeholders and other political actors, such as the conservative media personalities who have gained substantial power over Republican politics in the era of Fox News Channel. Contemporary party organizations thus properly encompass a variety of figures and groups situated outside as well as within the formal structures of the parties.

THIRD PARTIES

While candidates nominated by parties other than the Democrats and Republicans appear on the ballot in every presidential election, most are virtually invisible to the press and public and attract little support from voters. Occasionally, a more prominent third-party or independent candidate emerges. Independent candidate Ross Perot ended up with an extraordinary 19 percent of the popular vote in 1992, drawn from disgruntled voters across many segments of the population. Because he took votes about equally from both George H. W. Bush and Bill Clinton, Perot's candidacy did not influence the outcome of the election.[44] His support was not widely interpreted as personal devotion to Perot so much as a conveniently visible place to park the negative feelings that the campaign had generated about both major-party candidates. Perot ran again in 1996 as the standard-bearer of the Reform Party, a party that he had personally founded in the interim, and received only 9 percent of the vote; again, his candidacy did not affect the final result. No third-party candidate has matched Perot's popularity in subsequent years, though the outcomes in 2000 and 2016—two very close elections—were possibly influenced by the presence of minor candidates in the race.

It is frequently asserted, and frequently denied, that voters who vote for third parties are throwing away their vote. What is presumably meant is that voting for a third party means not voting for a potential winner of the election. But third-party voters generally understand that they are not backing a winner but rather withholding their vote from a (potential) winner. They may hope that this sends a message of overall dissatisfaction with the main alternatives on offer, and hence this would not necessarily be regarded by the voter as a wasted vote.

Another way of determining whether an individual's vote is wasted is to ask who the voter's first choice is among the major party candidates, or who is the voter's second choice overall. If a third-party vote contributes to the loss of that voter's second choice, and the victory of his or her third choice, then the vote has been thrown away. Thus in the 2000 election, Florida voters for Green Party nominee Ralph Nader who preferred Republican George W. Bush to Democrat Al Gore did not throw away their vote; Nader voters who preferred Gore to Bush did throw away their vote.

Most evidence suggests that a majority of Nader voters would have preferred Gore to Bush. So a Nader vote in any state carried by Gore would therefore not have been thrown away. But in a state like Florida, carried by Bush by 537 votes out of nearly 6 million cast, and where Nader received 97,488 votes, it is plausible to assume that the Nader vote was instrumental in defeating Gore and electing Bush. Nader's reputation as a "spoiler" in 2000 damaged his popularity in subsequent contests. While he received 2.9 million votes nationwide, or 2.7 percent of the total, as the Green Party nominee in 2000, his subsequent independent candidacies in 2004 and 2008 received only 0.4 percent and 0.5 percent of the popular vote, respectively.

The very close national result in 2016—Donald Trump's unexpected victory resulted from narrow popular margins in Wisconsin, Michigan, and Pennsylvania totaling 77,744 votes—led to speculation that Trump owed his upset victory to the presence of minor parties in the race. Hillary Clinton's campaign manager Robby Mook later argued that "part of why we lost . . . [was] because [young voters] went to third-party candidates. That could be, to some extent, because there was a sense that Hillary was going to win and people didn't necessarily think that their vote was as vital to the outcome as it could have been."[45]

If all of the votes cast for Green Party candidate Jill Stein in the three closest states had gone to Clinton instead in 2016, she indeed would have won a majority in the Electoral College. Yet it is implausible to assume that every Green Party voter would have chosen Clinton had Stein not appeared on the ballot.[46] And Clinton would not necessarily have defeated Trump in a strict two-person race; Trump himself may have lost some potential support to Libertarian Party candidate Gary Johnson, a former Republican governor of New Mexico who attracted more than 3 percent of the national popular vote in 2016.

Third-party candidates have a long record of occasional victories in congressional and gubernatorial elections.[47] In recent years, however, such successes have reflected individual efforts, without long-term consequences for party politics in the United States. Third-party candidacies do play a significant role in presidential elections from time to time. They can act as spoilers if they draw votes disproportionately from one major side or the other. They can focus discontent. They can raise issues.[48] But because candidates must place first in a state to receive electoral votes, and must achieve an overall majority in the Electoral College in order to take office, the American electoral system is stacked strongly against third-party candidates actually winning the presidency.[49]

3

Rules and Resources

■ ■ ■

RULES: THE ELECTORAL COLLEGE

American presidential elections are not decided directly by a national popular vote. Instead, every state but two awards all of its electoral votes for the candidate placing first in the statewide popular vote. (The two exceptions, Maine and Nebraska, allocate two electoral votes to the statewide winner and one vote apiece to the candidate placing first in each congressional district within the state.) This "winner take all, loser take nothing" approach is called a "unit rule."[1] In chapter 6 we consider whether votes ought to be counted in this manner. For the moment, however, we concentrate on how the Electoral College works and why it matters.

Each state casts as many electoral votes as it has senators and representatives in Congress. Thus all states, no matter how small, have at least three electoral votes. This means that sparsely populated states are numerically overrepresented in the Electoral College. In 2016, 255,849 voters in Wyoming influenced the disposition of the state's three electoral votes, a ratio of one electoral vote for every 85,283 voters. In Florida, on the other hand, 9,502,747 voters went to the polls and voted for 29 electors, a ratio of one electoral vote for every 327,681 voters. One might conclude, therefore, that each voter in Wyoming had more than three times as much influence on the outcome of the 2016 election as each voter in Florida. But this is not entirely valid.

Why not? Because of the unit rule, which provides that the candidate receiving the most popular votes in a state receives the entire electoral vote of the state. This means that each Wyoming voter was influencing the disposition of all 3 of Wyoming's electoral votes, and each Florida voter was helping decide the fate of all 29 of Florida's votes. Thus, as long as the outcome in Florida is in doubt, Floridians get more collective attention from the campaigns, even though each individual voter does not matter so much. In fact, the present method of electing the president encourages candidates to devote most of their attention to populous, politically competitive states; the bigger the state, the more electoral votes are at stake.

The varying strength of states in the Electoral College matters a great deal for the strategies of presidential nominees seeking a national majority of 270 electoral votes. Because the unit rule renders the popular margin of victory in a state irrelevant to the allocation of its electors, campaigns direct their resources—such as television advertising, candidate appearances, and voter mobilization efforts—to the subset of states considered winnable by either side, while ignoring states in which the outcome is not in doubt. In the 2016 general election, 94 percent of the personal appearances by Donald Trump, Hillary Clinton, and their running mates were concentrated in just 12 states: Arizona, Colorado, Florida, Iowa, Michigan, Nevada, New Hampshire, North Carolina, Ohio, Pennsylvania, Virginia, and Wisconsin. Within this group, the most populous states, casting the most electoral votes, received the largest share of candidate attention; Florida, the nation's biggest swing state, hosted 71 separate candidate events between the July national conventions and the November election.[2]

In previous elections, other candidates have sometimes identified different states as pivotal. But the reason the campaign battleground is concentrated in the big states that might go either way is the unit rule of the Electoral College.

THINKING ABOUT RESOURCES

In thinking about resources and their importance, it is necessary to distinguish between conditions that exist for the official candidates of the two major parties after they are nominated and the situation of prospective candidates—politicians seeking the nomination of their party—during the pre-nomination period. Individual candidates before the nomination do not have the benefit of party support, and the way they look at resources is quite different from the way successful nominees do.

There are many resources that, at any given time, may be disproportionately available to Democrats and Republicans, or to different candidates. Possession of the presidential office, organizational skills, knowledge of substantive policies, a reputation for integrity, facility in speechmaking, the ability to devise appealing campaign issues, personal wealth and fund-raising ability, sheer physical stamina—all can be drawn on to good advantage in a presidential campaign. More resources are available to parties and candidates than any one book could deal with exhaustively. But some resources obviously are going to be more important than others, and the importance of different resources varies from occasion to occasion. It would be sensible to regard as especially important those resources that one side monopolizes (such as the presidency), and those resources that can easily be converted into other resources or directly into public office—such as money, which can be used to buy competent staff, advertising, and so on.

Although political resources are at times distributed unequally between the parties, inequalities in a competitive two-party system rarely run all in the same direction. Sometimes Republican candidates reap the benefits; sometimes Democrats do. One result of these inequalities in access to various resources is that different strategies are more advantageous to each of the two parties, as we see when we examine the effects on election strategies of three resources commonly held to be extremely important: money, control over information, and the presidential office.

RESOURCES: MONEY

Presidential campaigns are terribly expensive. The production and airing of radio, television, and Internet advertising; travel for the candidate and campaign staff; mailings of campaign material; the salaries of consultants and advisers; office space and equipment; lawn signs and bumper stickers; conducting polls and focus groups; registering and mobilizing voters; and fund-raising itself—all cost a great deal of money.[3] In 2016, Donald Trump's successful campaign cost about $333 million, while his Democratic opponent, Hillary Clinton, spent about $564 million; other candidates who sought the Republican nomination for president spent about $324 million in total, while other Democrats spent $249 million ($232 million of which was spent by Clinton's main Democratic rival Bernie Sanders). Candidates for the Senate and House of Representatives in 2016 collectively spent another $1.6 billion. In addition, the two major parties spent more than $1.5 billion in support of candidates at all levels of government. The total amount of federal campaign spending by candidates and parties exceeded $4.6 billion in 2016 (see table 3.1), not including another $1.6 billion in independent expenditures made by outside groups.[4] How do candidates for the presidency manage to raise such large sums in their quest for office?

In answering this question, we note the difference between the presidential primary and caucus period, when candidates are on their own and when raising money may prove to be a severe problem for some of them, and the general election campaign, when the mobilization of party-loyal donors, expenditures by party organizations and independent groups, and other factors come into the picture, shrinking the problem of the availability of money to a more manageable size once a candidate has received the nomination of a major party.

The Beverly Hills Primary

The most important source of money for a candidate seeking a party's nomination for president is the individual private contributor, who, under federal law, may donate up to $2,000 in 2002 dollars to a candidate's primary campaign ($2,700 in 2016 and $2,800 in 2020). In order to avoid playing favorites, national party organizations do not spend money on behalf of any specific candidate as long as the nomination is still in doubt. In addition, most political action committees (PACs) prefer to avoid pre-nomination campaigns and the high-risk politics associated with them. Some presidential candidates, especially on the Democratic side, also adopt a policy of refusing PAC contributions. The result is that direct donations from PACs to presidential candidates are negligible—about $2.7 million in total in 2016, less than two-tenths of 1 percent of the $1.53 billion spent by presidential candidates that year.[5]

The traditional way to fund campaigns is for candidates to go where the money is, organizing fund-raising events in areas where large numbers of supporters will attend with checkbooks in hand. One especially well-documented path leads Democrats to Southern California, home of the traditionally liberal entertainment industry; a contested Democratic presidential nomination will invariably feature competing slates of celebrity supporters. In 2008, for example, Senator Barack Obama of Illinois enjoyed the backing of such "A-list" stars as Oprah Winfrey, George Clooney, Robert De Niro, Chris Rock, and Scarlett Johansson. Senator Hillary Clinton of New York received endorsements and contributions from Barbra Streisand, Rob Reiner, Maya Angelou, Amber Tamblyn, Ron Howard, Ted Danson, and Magic Johnson. John Mellencamp and Bonnie Raitt backed former senator John Edwards of North Carolina, while Sean Penn supported Representative Dennis Kucinich of Ohio. For Republican candidates, key

Table 3.1 Federal Campaign Spending, 1972–2016 (in millions of dollars)

Election	Spending by Presidential Candidates	Congressional Candidates	Political Parties	Total Federal Election Spending	Adjusted Total Federal Spending (millions of 2016 dollars)
1972	127	77	13	217	1,235
1976	118	115	46	279	1,161
1980	188	239	216	643	1,815
1984	194	374	420	988	2,265
1988	316	458	424	1,198	2,404
1992	323	680	488	1,491	2,534
1996	405	765	894	2,064	3,141
2000	520	1,006	1,190	2,716	3,765
2004	844	1,157	1,408	3,409	4,308
2008	1,677	1,375	1,513	4,565	5,187
2012	1,360	1,847	1,577	4,784	5,014
2016	1,527	1,597	1,556	4,680	4,680

Sources: Herbert E. Alexander, *Financing the 1972 Election* (Lexington, MA: Lexington Books, 1976), 85–90; Herbert E. Alexander, *Financing the 1976 Election* (Washington, DC: CQ Press, 1979), 171–77; Herbert E. Alexander, *Financing the 1980 Election* (Lexington, MA: Lexington Books, 1983), 113–16, 305, 311; Herbert E. Alexander and Brian A. Haggerty, *Financing the 1984 Election* (Lexington, MA: Lexington Books, 1987), 85–87, 331; Herbert E. Alexander and Monica Bauer, *Financing the 1988 Election* (Boulder, CO: Westview Press, 1991), 12, 41; Herbert E. Alexander and Anthony Corrado, *Financing the 1992 Election* (Armonk, NY: M. E. Sharpe, 1995), 20; Herbert E. Alexander, "Spending in the 1996 Elections," in *Financing the 1996 Election*, ed. John C. Green (Armonk, NY: M. E. Sharpe, 1999), 11–36, at 23; Federal Election Commission, "Congressional Candidates Spend $1.16 Billion during 2003–2004," press release, June 9, 2005, http://www.fec.gov/press/press2005/20050609candidate/20050609candidate.html; Federal Election Commission, "2004 Presidential Campaign Finance Activity Summarized," press release, February 3, 2005, http://www.fec.gov/press/press2005/20050203pressum/20050203pressum.html; Federal Election Commission, "2008 Presidential Campaign Finance Activity Summarized," press release, June 8, 2009, http://www.fec.gov/press/press2009/20090608PresStat.shtml; Federal Election Commission, "Congressional Candidates Raised $1.42 Billion in 2007–2008," press release, December 29, 2009, http://www.fec.gov/press/press2009/2009Dec29Cong/2009Dec29Cong.shtml; Federal Election Commission, "FEC Reports Major Increase in Party Activity for 1995–96," press release, March 19, 1997, http://www.fec.gov/press/press1997/ptyye1.htm; Federal Election Commission, "FEC Reports Increase in Party Fundraising for 2000," press release, May 15, 2001, http://www.fec.gov/press/press2001/051501partyfund/051501partyfund.html; Federal Election Commission, "Party Financial Activity Summarized for the 2004 Election Cycle," press release, March 2, 2005, http://www.fec.gov/press/press2005/20050302party/Party2004final.html; Federal Election Commission, "Party Financial Activity Summarized for the 2008 Election Cycle," press release, May 28, 2009, http://www.fec.gov/press/press2009/05282009Party/20090528Party.shtml; Federal Election Commission, "FEC Summarizes Campaign Activity of the 2011–2012 Election Cycle," press release, April 19, 2013, http://www.fec.gov/press/press2013/20130419_2012-24m-Summary.shtml; Federal Election Commission, "Statistical Summary of 24-Month Campaign Activity of the 2015–2016 Election Cycle," press release, March 23, 2017, https://www.fec.gov/updates/statistical-summary-24-month-campaign-activity-2015-2016-election-cycle.

Notes: Figures correspond to the two-year federal election cycle ending in the year displayed above. Totals do not include convention costs or independent expenditures by organizations formally unaffiliated with the candidates and parties. Party spending includes expenditures by the national party and congressional campaign committees and federally regulated spending by state and local parties. It also includes "soft money" for the 1980–2000 period. Adjusted dollars based on Consumer Price Index calculator from Bureau of Labor Statistics, http://data.bls.gov/cgi-bin/cpi-calc.pl.

stops on the fund-raising circuit include New York (home to Wall Street and much of the financial services industry) and Texas (for energy and real estate interests).

Candidates may also enjoy access to valuable home-state constituencies. For example, Arkansas governor Bill Clinton used his connections in that state to raise more than $2.5 million in his 1992 presidential campaign, a remarkable harvest from a state with a population of only 2.3 million. A single event in Little Rock in late 1991 raised almost $1 million. Many local businesses helped organize Clinton fund-raising events, no doubt mindful of the governor's control over the state's bond market, pension funds, and other regulated businesses. The Worthen National Bank of Arkansas established a credit line worth $3.5 million for the Clinton campaign. This helped tide the campaign over when damaging allegations arose about Clinton's marital infidelity and avoidance of military service.[6]

Barack Obama's presidential campaigns benefited from the strong support of Penny Pritzker, a billionaire businesswoman from his hometown of Chicago whose family owns the Hyatt hotel chain and whose backing had previously helped Obama win the Illinois Democratic primary for the U.S. Senate in 2004. As the chair of the Obama campaign's finance committee, Pritzker used her personal and business connections to raise enough money for Obama to compete effectively against Hillary Clinton in the 2008 Democratic primaries. "Without Penny Pritzker," noted the *New York Times*, "it is unlikely Barack Obama ever would have been elected to the United States Senate or the presidency."[7] Obama later appointed Pritzker as U.S. Secretary of Commerce during his second term in office.

The advent of the Internet has changed fund-raising practices for candidates, allowing those who can stimulate strong personal appeal among politically attentive citizens to collect large sums of money via online contributions outside of the traditional mechanism of in-person events. The first presidential candidate to master online fund-raising was former Vermont governor Howard Dean, whose outsider bid for the Democratic nomination in 2004 was financially fueled via his campaign website by an enthusiastic cadre of committed "Deaniacs." Obama later built on Dean's model by extending his Internet outreach to new heights. His site hosted "meet-ups" for like-minded supporters (an innovation borrowed from Dean) and developed "widgets," portable packets of software code, that allowed supporters to set up their own "fundraising pages, goals, progress indicators (i.e., a thermometer), events and lists."[8] Obama, with a background as a community organizer, used the Internet to create a self-sustaining movement behind his candidacy. Former Federal Elections Commission chair Michael Toner explained the new fund-raising techniques:

> [Previously], if someone was impressed with what a candidate said at a debate or a rally and wished to make a contribution, he or she needed to find their checkbook, figure out the payee, determine where to send the check, and get the check in the mail. Today, if someone likes what a candidate says, he or she can make an online contribution on [an] iPhone in a matter of minutes. Moreover, presidential campaign websites today provide donors with the option of making recurring monthly contributions on their credit cards in $25, $15 or even $5 amounts. . . . In this way, the Internet facilitates the making of political contributions separate and apart from public interest in presidential races. Which may partially account for the record-breaking amounts of money that presidential candidates have raised in recent years.[9]

The online fund-raising champion in the 2016 presidential campaign was Senator Bernie Sanders of Vermont. A self-described democratic socialist without strong ties to the organizational Democratic Party, Sanders was not likely to outraise his opponent Hillary Clinton among the traditional networks of high-dollar campaign contributors. But he found much more success in raising money from devoted citizen supporters, who showered his website with repeated donations. Sanders, who was fond of boasting in his public speeches that the average contribution to his campaign was only $27, ultimately raised more than $200 million online, allowing him to mount an unexpectedly persistent challenge to Clinton's nomination.[10] Clinton's inability to inspire the same degree of personal enthusiasm among small-dollar donors as Sanders, or Obama before him, forced her to depend much more heavily on raising large sums from wealthy contributors who expected personal attention from the candidate in return via phone calls and attendance at private events. "Hillary didn't love fundraising, but . . . she knew her contributors, in particular, needed a lot of hand-holding," noted Jonathan Allen and Amie Parnes.[11] But this much more labor-intensive approach deprived her of time that she could have used to hunt for votes among the public, and it also made her vulnerable to criticism from Sanders and her general election opponent Donald Trump that she preferred the company of the rich to that of regular Americans.

The accumulation of money interacts with the events of the nomination process. Successful candidates can expect to reap a windfall of cash within hours of a victory in a key state primary. But as a less fortunate candidate's defeats add up over the course of the election season, visibility and credibility begin to slip, and fund-raising falls even as expenses mount. Tactical considerations become more and more important as dwindling resources limit the number of states that can be contested. For example, by March 3, 1992, the date of several state Democratic primaries, Nebraska senator Bob Kerrey was forced by financial desperation to limit expenditures in Colorado to one 30-second advertisement, to rely on personal appearances in Georgia to generate enough free press coverage to make up for his lack of any paid airtime, to ignore the Maryland primary entirely, and to hope that $6,600 spent on radio ads in Idaho might influence the outcome in the state's low-turnout caucus. Not surprisingly, none of these tactics paid off, and Kerrey abandoned his campaign two days later.[12]

While presidential challengers cope with financial shortages and strategic dilemmas, incumbents, who are always well-funded and frequently unopposed for renomination, can use the primary period to stockpile campaign money until a nominee emerges in the other party. For example, George W. Bush was able to attract to his 2004 reelection campaign some of the most prominent Republican fund-raisers. Supporters who solicited, collected, and delivered large donations to the Bush campaign from a network of personal and business associates, a practice known as "bundling," received a special recognized title from the Bush campaign if the total of their bundled contributions exceeded a certain monetary amount—an innovation designed by Bush campaign aides to encourage aggressive fund-raising. The *New York Times* reported in early 2004 that by late 2003,

> Bush had 350 top-level volunteer fundraisers—Pioneers, who agree to raise at least $100,000 from friends, colleagues, neighbors and anyone else in their phone books, and Rangers, who agree to raise $200,000. That is an increase of more than 100 people over the 2000 Bush campaign. "They've created new networks,

and it's given them better results," said one Pioneer based in Washington. "One thing they don't do is just round up all the usual suspects."

There are now Pioneers and Rangers in 43 states and Washington, D.C., records show. Texas has the most, at 43, followed by Florida at 35, California at 34 and New York at 27, according to Texans for Public Justice, a group that tracks campaign finance. Representing all segments of industry, these fundraisers have gathered at least $48.4 million since Mr. Bush began raising money in May. Mail and phone solicitations brought in $27 million more and the Internet brought in about $3 million, according to the campaign. Fundraisers paint a picture of an organized operation that encourages friendly competition and makes top campaign officials accessible to those raising money out in the field.

"He's been easier to raise money for than many," said former senator Rudy Boschwitz, a Ranger from Minnesota. "He's extremely well organized. He has the same people running the show that he had in 2000, and the group has coalesced." Mr. Bush even started a new class of fundraisers last year, Mavericks, who raise at least $50,000 and are under 40 years old. So far, at least 10 people have raised enough to earn the title and 17 others hold it in addition to Ranger or Pioneer.[13]

An extensive roster of fund-raising bundlers also helped Barack Obama raise a large amount of money in 2011 and 2012 as his Republican opponents fought among themselves for the right to face him in the 2012 general election. The Obama reelection campaign followed the practice of the Bush campaigns in 2000 and 2004 in voluntarily releasing the names of these fund-raisers, though Obama bundlers were not given special campaign titles like the "Pioneer" and "Ranger" designations used by Bush. Well-known figures who raised $500,000 or more for Obama's 2012 campaign included the married couple of actor Will Smith and actress Jada Pinkett-Smith, actress Eva Longoria, Hollywood studio executives Jeffrey Katzenberg and Harvey Weinstein, film director Tyler Perry, *Vogue* editor Anna Wintour, and pop musician Gwen Stefani.[14] Obama raised more than $55 million from bundlers between April and October 2011 alone, helping him gain a significant head start in the money race more than a year before his reelection. Obama's 2012 general election opponent Mitt Romney also benefited from similar fund-raising networks, but the Romney campaign declined to publicly release the names of its own bundlers.[15]

Hillary Clinton's 2016 candidacy benefited from the support of more than 1,100 "Hillblazers"—her campaign's honorific nickname for bundlers who had raised at least $100,000 apiece. This group included celebrities like actor Ben Affleck and former NBA star Magic Johnson, entertainment industry moguls like director-executives Steven Spielberg and George Lucas, business leaders like investor Warren Buffett and Facebook chief operating officer Sheryl Sandberg, and a number of Democratic members of Congress (including her future running mate, Virginia senator Tim Kaine). Like Romney in 2012, Republican nominee Donald Trump chose not to disclose the identities of his own top campaign fund-raisers in 2016.[16]

Campaign Finance in Presidential Primaries

Responding to the campaign finance scandals that came to light in relation to the Watergate affair, in 1974 Congress acted to create a system of partial public financing for candidates seeking their party's presidential nomination. For more than 20 years thereafter, most serious candidates—and all eventual nominees of both parties— participated in the public funding program. Candidates who establish eligibility (by raising at least $5,000 in contributions of $250 or less from individuals in each of 20 states—$100,000 total) can choose to receive public funds matching all individual contributions up to $250 from a pool created by a voluntary check-off on federal income tax returns. This provision thus doubles the value of individuals' contributions up to $250, encouraging candidates who participate in the matching funds program to seek financial support from large numbers of individual contributors.

In exchange for receiving matching funds from the federal government, however, candidates must abide by two key requirements. The first is a restriction on the amount of money a candidate may spend out of his or her own pocket: candidates accepting matching funds cannot contribute more than $50,000 to their campaigns from their own assets or from those of their immediate families. Candidates accepting matching funds must also observe limits on the money spent by their campaigns in the pre-nomination period. Congress established an overall spending limit of $10 million in 1974, which is adjusted every four years for increases in the cost of living. For the 2016 election, the nationwide spending limit required for participation in the matching funds program stood at roughly $48 million, not including various fund-raising and compliance costs not counted against the total. In addition, participating candidates must abide by spending limits in each state based on the size of the state's voting-age population.[17]

Beginning with George W. Bush in 2000, major presidential candidates have opted to decline matching funds and the restrictions that come with them, concluding that they could raise far more money by relying solely on private donations and thus escaping the overall and state-by-state spending caps. Unless Congress acts to provide greater financial incentives for participation, it appears that the system of partial public financing for primary elections is virtually defunct. Some dark horse candidates unable to raise large sums on their own may still be willing to abide by the accompanying restrictions in order to receive matching funds. But those in serious contention for their party's nomination will wish to remain free of spending limits, especially since these limits apply, even after a presumptive nominee has emerged, until the nomination is made official at the party's national convention.

Before the primary contests begin, some politicians considering a bid for the presidency also form pre-candidacy political action committees. Originally, potential candidates founded PACs in order to get around the spending limits in the public financing system. Today, PACs have become just another way to raise money, especially during the early months when prospective candidates have yet to officially enter the race by creating formal presidential campaign organizations. Politicians can test the waters by using their personal PACs to fund visits to Iowa, New Hampshire, and other key primary and caucus states, while also disbursing PAC money to party candidates for other offices— who might be expected to return the favor with endorsements or fund-raising efforts later in the primary season.[18]

During the nomination process, presidential contenders may also benefit from the support of outside groups that are formally unaffiliated with their campaigns but spend money on behalf of their candidacies. A series of federal court decisions—most notably *Citizens United v. Federal Election Commission* (U.S. Supreme Court, 2010) and *SpeechNow.org v. Federal Election Commission*

(U.S. Court of Appeals for the District of Columbia, 2010)—have found that Congress lacks the constitutional authority to restrict contributions to, and expenditures of, certain independent organizations that spend money in order to influence the outcome of elections, as long as these entities do not coordinate their activities with particular candidates or parties. These judicial rulings have allowed for the increasing prevalence of groups that, unlike candidates' own campaign organizations, can accept unlimited donations from individuals and can receive contributions of any size from corporations and labor unions.

One category of outside groups, officially classified as "independent expenditure-only committees" but more commonly known as "Super PACs," has quickly gained influence in presidential nomination politics. During the 2016 presidential primaries, several candidates benefited from the support of nominally independent Super PACs that funded advertising campaigns designed to create positive impressions of their candidacies—or, more commonly, to create negative impressions of their opponents. Priorities USA Action, a Super PAC originally founded to support Barack Obama's 2012 reelection, transferred its loyalties to Hillary Clinton in 2016, ultimately spending more than $130 million on Clinton's behalf during both the Democratic nomination contest and the general election. On the Republican side, the Super PAC Right to Rise USA led the way with more than $87 million spent to promote former Florida governor Jeb Bush, Senator Marco Rubio of Florida benefited from more than $55 million in expenditures by Conservative Solutions PAC, and multiple allied Super PACs collectively spent more than $52 million to boost Senator Ted Cruz of Texas.[19]

Raising and Spending Money in the General Election

The federal public financing system that provided matching funds to candidates running in presidential primaries and caucuses also granted each major-party nominee $20 million in 1974 dollars—$96 million in 2016—to fund a general election campaign, with the stipulation that candidates who accepted public money had to restrict their spending to this amount and refuse additional contributions from individuals or PACs (except to pay the compliance costs incurred in following the law). Just as participation in the matching funds program plummeted after 2000 as candidates increasingly concluded that they could raise greater sums on their own, presidential nominees now routinely refuse public funding in the general election in order to remain free of the corresponding spending limits. Relying instead upon his unique fund-raising prowess, Barack Obama became the first major-party nominee since the creation of the public financing program to privately fund his general election campaign in 2008—allowing him to greatly outspend his Republican rival John McCain, who accepted the public funds and accompanying spending cap. In 2012, both Obama and his opponent Mitt Romney declined public financing, as did both Donald Trump and Hillary Clinton in 2016. As in the presidential nomination phase, individuals may donate up to $2,000 in 2002 dollars ($2,700 in 2016 and $2,800 in 2020) to a candidate's general election campaign; donors who already contributed the maximum legal amount to a candidate during the primaries are allowed to give again in the general election.

Once the nomination races are decided, the money spent by the candidates' own campaign organizations is augmented by additional expenditures made by the national parties. Federal law limits the amount that each party committee is allowed to spend in coordination with the presidential nominees ($23.8 million for each party in 2016); however, the parties may spend unlimited additional funds as long as the activity remains independent of the candidates' own campaigns. The Democratic National Committee spent $347 million in the 2016 election, mostly on behalf of Hillary Clinton's presidential candidacy, while the Republican National Committee spent up to $323 million in support of Donald Trump.[20] Donations to parties are regulated much the same as those to individual candidates. Corporations and labor unions are not allowed to contribute, and donations by an individual citizen to a party committee may not exceed $25,000 in 2002 dollars per calendar year ($33,400 in 2016 and $35,500 in 2020).

But candidates and parties can partially circumvent these limits by creating joint fund-raising committees, or "victory funds," that split the contributions they receive among participating candidates, national parties, and state party committees according to an agreed-upon formula. Candidates and national parties cannot directly accept more funds from any particular donor through a joint fund-raising committee than they could via a traditional contribution, but funds that are ostensibly donated to state parties via a joint fund-raising committee can be, and often are, immediately re-routed back to the national party organization. With the Supreme Court invalidating aggregate federal contributor limits in *McCutcheon v. FEC* (2014), it is legally permissible for a citizen to write a single six-figure check on behalf of a favored presidential nominee. In 2016, each donor could contribute up to $358,800 to the Hillary Victory Fund, or up to $449,400 to Trump Victory, with most of the funds winding up in the bank accounts of the national parties.[21]

Other judicial holdings overturning various congressional regulations contained in the Bipartisan Campaign Reform Act of 2002 hastened the rise of independent groups that raise and spend funds outside the structure of formal candidate campaigns and party organizations. In the wake of the *Citizens United* and *SpeechNow.org* decisions, outside groups such as Super PACs are permitted to accept unlimited donations from individuals, corporations, and unions, and to spend this money on advertising that explicitly advocates the election or defeat of political candidates. Super PACs are still subject to federal laws requiring them to disclose the source and amount of their donations and the size of their expenditures. However, non-profit 501(c)(4) organizations (named after the section of the federal tax code under which they fall) may also fund ads during election campaigns, although the law nominally requires that political activity cannot be the primary purpose of such groups. Unlike Super PACs and other organizations that are regulated by Section 527 of the tax code (and are therefore called "527 committees"), 501(c)(4) groups are not compelled to publicly disclose the sources of their donations—leading reform advocates to dub their spending "dark money."

Independent expenditures by groups formally unconnected with the candidates and parties now represent a significant fraction of campaign spending in the United States. Traditional PACs, Super PACs, 501(c)(4) groups, and other outside entities spent more than $715 million on behalf of presidential candidates in 2016.[22] The vast majority of advertising funded by outside groups is negative in tone. Because these independent groups are not officially tied to the campaigns or parties and may not legally coordinate with them, candidates and party leaders do not bear direct responsibility for these attack ads, even though they are produced for their political benefit. This prohibition on direct coordination between candidates and independent groups prompted Ted Cruz's 2016 presidential campaign to upload 15 hours of unedited video clips of the candidate and his family to YouTube, hoping that pro-Cruz Super PACs would mine them for advertising spots. The footage—publicly available to curious reporters and voters as well as Super PAC ad producers—represented a revealing, and at times awkward, view into the contemporary state of America's campaign finance laws.[23]

Does Money Buy Elections?

The billions of dollars spent on American elections inevitably raise serious questions about the relationship between wealth and decisions in a democracy. Are presidential nominating and electoral contests determined by those who have the most money? Do those who make large contributions exercise substantial or undue influence as a result? Is the victorious candidate under obligation to "pay off " major financial contributors? Do those who pay the piper call the tune?[24]

This was certainly the reasoning that inspired the post-Watergate political reforms of the mid-1970s, which attempted to minimize the influence of money on presidential elections.[25] Before these elaborate limitations were established, however, moneyed interests did not appear to play a decisive role in the outcome of presidential contests. Republicans did spend more than Democrats in most general elections, but the difference was not as overwhelming as some would suppose. The percentage of post-nomination expenditures spent by the Democratic nominee from 1932 to 1980 varied from a low of 33 percent in 1972 to a high of 51 percent in 1960; the average was about 41 percent.[26] Even in the era when the parties were free to spend whatever they could raise and were not subject to the restrictions and regulations established by Congress in 1974, money did not buy election victories. The best-funded candidate and party did not always win; otherwise, Republicans would have won every presidential election but one between 1932 and 2004 (box 3.1).

Democrats have found more fund-raising success in recent elections. In 2008, Barack Obama greatly outspent John McCain—who was subject to the strict spending limits required of participants in the public financing program—in advertising and deployed a much larger network of field offices; at times, in fact, it appeared as if the Obama campaign was raising money faster than it could spend it. With television airwaves in the usual battleground states already saturated with commercials touting Obama, the candidate's advisers expanded their campaign activity into states such as Indiana and North Carolina that were not central to their Electoral College strategy, funded their own dedicated channel ("Obama on Demand") on residential satellite systems that ran continuous programming produced by the campaign, and even purchased advertising in popular video games such as Guitar Hero.[27] But though his overwhelming financial advantage may have added to his ultimate vote margin, Obama almost certainly would have won the election anyway due to the strongly favorable political environment for Democratic candidates in 2008.

Box 3.1 ■ In the Arena: Campaign Finance in the 2016 Campaign

Jeff Weaver, Campaign Manager, Bernie Sanders for President:

"When we started, we understood we were going to be significantly outgunned in terms of establishment support. In terms of money, Secretary Clinton was an excellent fundraiser. She had a Super PAC, multiple Super PACs, a 501(c)(4) that was doing turnout, and our early estimates were that we were going to raise between $30 and $50 million, total. What came as a complete surprise in this campaign that really allowed this campaign to go toe-to-toe was that we ended up raising over $230 million, primarily from small donors online. Like the Trump people, we did not spend a lot of time doing fundraising. It was primarily done by people hitting a button that asked people to send money and, in fact, people did."

Michael Glassner, Deputy Campaign Manager, Donald J. Trump for President:

"New York is a media base and Trump having been embedded in that, in the media in New York, for decades was a tremendous benefit that generated, by some counts, billions of dollars of free media that he didn't have to pay for [resulting in] a very low-budget campaign. . . . Most importantly, with social media and on Twitter, Mr. Trump would say it was like owning the *New York Times* without the overhead or the debt. He could directly communicate his message and it was widely disseminated for zero money."

Corey Lewandowski, Primary Campaign Manager, Donald J. Trump for President:

"[N]ot having to fundraise was a major advantage to us because I could just go to him and ask him to write a check, and that was our fundraising meeting."

Source: Institute of Politics, John F. Kennedy School of Government, Harvard University, *Campaign for President: The Managers Look at 2016* (Lanham, MD: Rowman & Littlefield, 2017), 32, 37.

Note: A 501(c)(4) organization, mentioned above, is a nonprofit organization organized under that provision of the U.S. tax code. It can accept unlimited contributions and may spend up to 50 percent of its funds on politics. It does not have to publicly disclose its donors.

Most likely, the vast sums spent in American presidential elections represent a textbook example of the law of diminishing returns. Candidates, parties, and outside groups on both sides reliably raise more than enough money to hire competent staff, build strong campaign organizations, fund voter registration and mobilization efforts, and blanket the airwaves of battleground states with television advertising for months before the election. By Election Day, the average resident of a key swing state has seen hundreds of campaign ads—one calculation concluded that the typical voter in Cleveland, Ohio, was exposed to 190 different television spots in 2012, aired a total of 1,450 times—and received a constant stream of mailings, telephone calls, and personal visits from representatives of both candidates.[28]

It is difficult to believe that additional expenditures by one side or the other would prove decisive in such a flooded communication environment, and indeed much of the current spending in presidential elections is probably well in excess of the levels at which additional money has a measurable effect on the outcome. David Axelrod, chief strategist for Obama's 2008 and 2012 campaigns, believes that television spending in particular is highly inefficient, even arguing that "there was no ad that ran after the [national] conventions that ever in the modern era won a presidential race; paid media becomes largely irrelevant in the general [election] after the conventions" because voters have become so overloaded with campaign messages.[29] In 2016, the Hillary Clinton campaign, Democratic National Committee, and outside pro-Democratic groups collectively outspent Donald Trump and the Republicans by a margin of $1.16 billion to $720 million, with most of this money devoted to paid advertising. Yet Trump still captured a majority in the Electoral College despite this disadvantage.[30]

Voters are influenced by more than just television ads or campaign mailings. The overall economic health and direction of the nation, the personal qualities and policy positions of the candidates, events of the campaign season such as conventions and debates that receive considerable attention from journalists and pundits, and other considerations enter into the calculation of citizens making up their mind in the voting booth. While advertising can play a role in shaping voters' perceptions, it is not necessarily the dominant means by which they form their evaluations of the candidates, parties, and issues—especially in presidential elections, which provide ample alternative sources of information by inevitably attracting extensive coverage from journalists and stimulating frequent conversations among citizens' personal acquaintances. In 2016, for example, the massive amount of news media attention received by Trump's unorthodox candidacy was, according to one estimate, equivalent to many times the budget of his paid advertising efforts.[31]

Money is a more powerful factor in deciding presidential nomination contests than general elections. Candidates embark on aggressive fund-raising efforts well before the first primaries and caucuses; having enough financial resources to compete effectively in the early states helps raise additional money to sustain candidates throughout the primary season. A well-funded campaign is necessary both to boost a candidate's name recognition among intermittently attentive primary voters and to signal to the press corps that the candidate should be taken seriously as a contender for the nomination. If a candidate's bank account is sufficiently imposing, potential rivals for the nomination might also be dissuaded from jumping into the race.

The dollar amounts necessary for competitiveness have grown greatly over time. In 1952, Dwight D. Eisenhower and Robert Taft each spent about $2.5 million on their campaigns for the Republican presidential nomination.[32] By 2008, expenditures for both major Democratic candidates, Hillary Clinton and Barack Obama, topped $200 million; John Edwards, who dropped out shortly after the first presidential primary in New Hampshire, still managed to spend more than $50 million that year. On the Republican side, Rudy Giuliani, who ended his campaign at the end of January, also spent more than $50 million. Mitt Romney, John McCain's main rival until the beginning of February, expended more than $100 million in funds. McCain himself, though the certain nominee by early March, still spent $190 million during the primary season.[33] By the time that the 2012 Republican nomination contest was effectively decided at the end of March, Romney (running for a second time in four years) had spent $78 million, compared to $35 million by Ron Paul, $21 million by Newt Gingrich, $20 million by Rick Perry, and $19 million by Rick Santorum; of course, these totals were augmented considerably by independent expenditures from Super PACs allied with the candidates.[34] In 2016, Hillary Clinton and Bernie Sanders each spent about $230 million on their Democratic primary campaigns. Ted Cruz topped the Republican field with $86 million in disbursements that year, followed by Donald Trump at $71 million, Ben Carson at $62 million, Marco Rubio at $50 million, Jeb Bush at $35 million, and John Kasich at $19 million.[35]

Money, however, is still only one factor affecting the fortunes of potential nominees. Skill and strategy in using resources matters as much as having them; as Howard Dean discovered in 2004, a large war chest manifestly does not guarantee victory in primaries. Though Dean boasted the biggest bank account of all the Democratic candidates, he did not spend his ample funds wisely. In the weeks before the Iowa caucus, Dean's campaign bused 3,500 young volunteers into the state from elsewhere at great expense to knock on doors in support of his candidacy, renting vans, cell phones, and lodging for them to use during their stay. "I had never seen a campaign spend like this one," Dean's Iowa spokeswoman later remarked. Despite the high cost, this mobilization effort did not persuade most Iowans to vote for Dean. One 19-year-old volunteer who traveled from Vermont to Iowa for the caucus admitted with hindsight that "many voters . . . may have been insulted by out-of-staters rushing in to tell them how to vote." John Kerry's campaign, in contrast, focused more on courting support from veteran Iowa political organizers who cultivated ongoing personal networks within the state; these efforts paid off when Kerry placed first in the Iowa caucus, setting him on a path to the Democratic nomination.[36] Wesley Clark was also a proficient fund-raiser in the weeks before the primary season began, but his decision not to compete in Iowa cost him valuable publicity, and his campaign never recovered despite the money he spent in New Hampshire and subsequent primary states.[37] For Dean, Kerry, and Clark, strategy seemed to weigh more heavily than money in determining their electoral fortunes in 2004.

This was also true for John McCain in the 2008 Republican primaries. McCain benefited from a careful strategic focus on New Hampshire, South Carolina, and Florida, leading to successes in all three state primaries despite limited campaign funds, especially in comparison to his free-spending, partially self-financing rival Mitt Romney. On the Democratic side in 2008, though Hillary Clinton initially outraised Barack Obama, Obama ran a relatively smooth campaign while Clinton's operation was hobbled by strategic errors and organizational disarray that may well have made the difference in the outcome. In addition, the Clinton campaign spent its money far less efficiently than Obama's, requiring Hillary Clinton herself to make $13 million in personal loans to her campaign in order to keep it afloat in the final months of the race—loans that were ultimately never repaid.[38]

Money was hardly irrelevant in the 2016 primaries, but neither was it determinative. A number of candidates who labored to raise funds also struggled to persuade voters. Former Maryland governor Martin O'Malley on the Democratic side and former Pennsylvania senator Rick Santorum, former Arkansas governor Mike Huckabee, and former Virginia governor Jim Gilmore on the Republican side all found trouble raising enough money to build competitive campaigns; all dropped out of the race soon after trailing badly in the first primary events in Iowa and New Hampshire. Some candidates who failed to attract strong financial backing even folded their campaigns before the voting began, such as former Virginia senator Jim Webb and former Rhode Island senator and governor Lincoln Chafee for the Democrats and former Texas governor Rick Perry, Louisiana governor Bobby Jindal, South Carolina senator Lindsey Graham, and former New York governor George Pataki for the Republicans.

But other contenders couldn't blame their defeat at the polls on a lack of available financial resources. One early leader in the race for dollars among Republicans in 2016 was former Florida governor Jeb Bush, who benefited from a strong existing national network of loyal donors as the son and brother of two former presidents; Right to Rise, the well-funded Super PAC aligned with Bush, was initially considered a major asset to his candidacy. Bush's ample bank account and name recognition didn't translate into much popular support, however, and the combined $159 million spent by the Bush campaign and Right to Rise ultimately won him just three pledged delegates to the Republican national convention.[39]

Despite his considerable personal wealth, Donald Trump did not capture the Republican nomination in 2016 by drowning his rivals in money. By the end of March, Trump had become the clear front-runner among voters, yet he still trailed Bush, Ted Cruz, Marco Rubio, and Ben Carson in the money race when both candidate and Super PAC contributions were taken into account. Most of all, Trump owed his electoral success to his unrivaled ability to draw free media attention, as well as a nationalist campaign message that especially resonated with Republican voters. Money did not decide the Democratic contest either in 2016; both Hillary Clinton and Bernie Sanders benefited from equally impressive success in raising funds that allowed each of them to build strong national campaign organizations to publicize their views and mobilize voters.

It is exceedingly difficult to get reliable information on an event that involves a decision not to act, such as a potential candidate's decision not to run because he or she could or would not attract the necessary funds. But undoubtedly there have been some prospective candidates whose inability or unwillingness to raise large sums of money has proved fatal to their chances of being considered for the nomination. Whether their failure represents an inability to satisfy the moneyed classes or to convince enough people that their candidacies were serious and worthy is difficult to say in the abstract. A more important question concerns whether there has been a systematic bias in favor of or against certain candidates that consistently alters the outcomes of presidential nominations. We can immediately dismiss the notion that the richest person automatically comes out on top. If that were the case, Mitt Romney would have bested John McCain for the Republican nomination in 2008, while either Hillary Clinton or John Edwards would have defeated Barack Obama in the Democratic side. Nelson Rockefeller would have triumphed over Barry Goldwater in 1964 and Richard Nixon in 1968, and Robert Taft would have beaten Dwight D. Eisenhower in 1952. In 1976, Ronald Reagan's personal wealth eclipsed Gerald Ford's, as, in 1980, Ted Kennedy's did Jimmy Carter's. Nevertheless, in both these instances, the incumbent president beat the challenger.

Perhaps the best test of the proposition that the richest candidate will win was found in the Republican nomination contest in 1996. Rather than relying on a mixture of small contributions and public matching funds, as every major candidate for the nomination had done since the public financing system was created, multimillionaire publisher Steve Forbes decided to spend his own money in an effort to secure the Republican nomination. His ability and willingness to spend vast sums of money—$37 million, almost as much as eventual nominee Bob Dole and far more than any other candidate for the nomination—convinced the press to treat Forbes as a serious candidate, despite his late entry, lack of organization in Iowa or New Hampshire, and absence of normal qualifications for the presidency. His money was not, however, capable of buying Forbes the nomination. In the critical states of Iowa and New Hampshire, he failed to finish among the top three candidates. While he did win two primaries (one, in Delaware, by default since he was the only candidate to campaign there), he never really threatened to win the nomination.[40] After reinventing himself as a social conservative, Forbes ran again for president in 2000. He spent even more (more than $42 million) the second time around, but fared no better among the voters, withdrawing from the race on February 10 after receiving just 13 percent of the vote in New Hampshire and finishing third in the Delaware primary.[41]

A similar fate befell Mitt Romney in his 2008 campaign for the Republican nomination. Romney "loaned" his campaign $44 million in personal funds, far more than any other major candidate running that year in either party. Yet he was defeated in a series of early primaries by John McCain despite outspending McCain two-to-one on television ads.[42] By the end of February, Romney had spent more than $100 million compared to McCain's $50 million, yet McCain had easily outdistanced Romney among pledged delegates. Romney fared better with the voters when he ran a second time in 2012, ultimately capturing the presidential nomination that had eluded him four years before, but this time he did not contribute financially to his own campaign and relied entirely on donations from others.

Every national campaign needs many millions of dollars to function effectively, and thus either fund-raising ability or personal wealth represents a necessary attribute for any would-be president. But money is just one of many valuable resources in politics, and a candidate cannot expect to win either a nomination or general election simply by outspending his or her opponents. With the rise of social media making it easier for candidates to communicate directly with voters and for voters to make contributions to their favorite candidates, both the practice and the role of political fund-raising continues to evolve—sometimes undergoing dramatic changes from one election to the next.

Campaign Finance Reform

The dissatisfaction of many citizens, especially left-of-center political activists, with the current system of financing political campaigns in the United States has led to an ongoing series of proposals for reform, which Congress has occasionally adopted—most notably in the Federal Election Campaign Act, or FECA (1972, amended in 1974, 1976, and 1979), and the Bipartisan Campaign Reform Act, or BCRA (2002)—and which have then received constitutional scrutiny from the federal judiciary. Four broad issues are raised by the ways in which money is acquired and spent in presidential elections. The first is the issue of public disclosure of campaign financing. The contributions to, and expenditures of, federal candidates, party organizations, PACs, and Super PACs must be reported to the Federal Election Commission, which makes this information available to the public.[43] The federal courts have upheld the constitutionality of disclosure requirements, rejecting claims that public knowledge of citizens' campaign contributions inhibits political expression by chilling support for socially marginal candidates or parties.[44] The growing role of 501(c)(4) organizations in election campaigns has become an area of concern for advocates of reform; these groups are required to disclose their political expenditures but not the source of their contributions.

Under federal law, political communications such as television advertisements and campaign mailings must contain text identifying the sponsoring candidate, party, or organization. The BCRA included a provision, later upheld by the U.S. Supreme Court in *McConnell v. Federal Election Commission* (2003), that requires presidential and congressional candidates to appear in all radio and television advertising produced by their campaigns, stating their names and explicit authorization of the ad, usually with the following format: "I'm [candidate name], and I approve this message." Online advertising, however, is not subject to this requirement.

A second issue raised in presidential campaigns is the question of public funding. The 1974 amendments to FECA created a public financing system for presidential (but not congressional) elections, covering both the pre-and post-nomination stages, in an attempt to promote fairness and reduce the opportunity for corruption. However, the Supreme Court has ruled that such programs must be voluntary, with candidates free to choose whether to take public subsidies (and operate under the corresponding restrictions on donations and spending). Public funding programs also inspire debate over eligibility requirements (such as for minor parties), the generosity of the subsidies, and the desirability of using tax dollars to fund political campaigns.

Although a substantial fraction of the increase in the nominal cost of campaigns since 1972 is due to inflation, the total spending by federal candidates and parties still more than quadrupled in real dollars between 1976 and 2008 (see table 3.1), even before considering the increasing prevalence of independent expenditures by outside groups. The public financing program established in the 1970s did not keep up with the sharply rising costs of campaigns, as well as the easier access to private dollars enjoyed by today's presidential candidates. As a result, it has been abandoned by serious contenders in both the primaries and the general election, and there seems to be little sentiment among elected officials today for reforming the system to make it more attractive to candidates—which would necessarily involve authorizing more than a billion dollars in public subsidies to the presidential campaigns every four years.

A third unresolved question is the advisability of strict regulations on the money spent by national, state, and local party organizations. While the U.S. Supreme Court has mostly upheld congressional regulations of spending by the official party committees, it has taken a much less deferential view towards attempts to enforce similar restrictions on outside groups such as Super PACs. As a result, certain sources of money that may once have been given to parties have not been removed from the political system but are now directed instead toward less visible institutions that lack parties' electoral responsiveness to citizens. "Super PACs and other non-party organizations have many fewer constraints to raise and spend money than parties," notes Raymond J. La Raja. "The result is that money flows increasingly to electioneering groups rather than the formal party organization. Among the many problems this poses . . . is diminished accountability since it is more difficult than ever for voters to apprehend who finances and wages American campaigns."[45]

Finally, the topic of campaign finance reform raises the question of how the regulation of political money should be balanced against the constitutional rights of Americans to engage in political speech. Since the passage of BCRA in 2002, which contained several provisions designed to limit the electoral influence of political actors other than candidates' own campaign organizations, parties, and traditional PACs, federal courts have become increasingly willing to strike down legal and regulatory restrictions on the activity of outside organizations such as corporations and Super PACs. In the *Citizens United* decision of 2010, Justice Anthony Kennedy wrote that "when government seeks to use its full power, including the criminal law, to command where a person may get his or her information or what distrusted source he or she may not hear, it uses censorship to control thought. This is unlawful. The First Amendment confirms the freedom to think for ourselves."[46]

To the minority bloc of liberal justices, this reasoning obscured what they viewed as the very real danger to the political system posed by the excessive influence of special interests over the outcome of elections. In his *Citizens United* dissent, Justice John Paul Stevens argued that the decision "threatens to undermine the integrity of elected institutions across the Nation. . . . While American democracy is imperfect, few outside the majority of this Court would have thought its flaws included a dearth of corporate money in politics." Many Democratic officials and advocates of campaign finance reform echoed this criticism, including Barack Obama, who claimed in his 2010 State of the Union Address that the *Citizens United* case would "open the floodgates for special interests—including foreign corporations—to spend without limit in our elections."

While this debate over the value and constitutionality of campaign finance regulation will no doubt continue, the current state of federal law and judicial precedent has created an increasingly open environment for a variety of politically active groups to engage in voter persuasion efforts during presidential campaigns, and for individuals with the requisite financial means to donate large sums of money to independent organizations involved in producing political communications directed toward the American electorate. What relationships are we observing when we track this money? While some campaign finance reform advocates tend to portray campaign donations, especially those from wealthy individuals, as little more than legalized bribery, it is often difficult to identify examples of politicians changing their policy positions as a result of receiving financial contributions. More commonly, politically engaged citizens donate funds in order to bolster the electoral chances of candidates who already share their views, and the multiplicity of interests within the American public guarantees that political money will be divided among multiple parties and candidates with very different positions on the salient issues of the day.

RESOURCES: CONTROL OVER INFORMATION

Political information is so easy to acquire during a presidential election campaign that it is hard to identify anybody in control of its spread. There are, however, features of the overall system by which information is manufactured and distributed in the United States that materially affect the fortunes of candidates and the ways in which they are perceived by electorates. Campaign professionals generally divide sources of information into free media and paid media. Free media (sometimes called "earned media") consist of publicity that candidates do not have to pay for, as the result of news coverage. Patterns of news coverage matter enormously to candidates, and they spend great effort conforming their campaigns to the professional practices of print, television, and online media.

News organizations customarily assign experienced journalists to campaigns they judge to be "serious," so aspiring candidates must attempt to be taken seriously by media executives; those deemed to have no plausible chance at winning their party's presidential nomination will be largely ignored by the press. As Kathleen Carroll, executive editor of the Associated Press, notes, "You can't cover everybody in depth."[47] To be judged a "serious" candidate usually requires being a well-known public figure and hiring a staff of campaign professionals recognized by journalists as capable. Even receiving free coverage usually requires money, and sometimes quite a lot of money, since journalists often judge the relative standing of presidential candidates during the early stages of the campaign by the size of their campaign war chests. Appearing in pre-nomination debates is one good way for candidates to get publicity while keeping costs down, and being included in debates is another mark of credibility for candidates.

Paid media refers mostly to television, radio, and Internet advertisements, which candidates produce and place on the air or online. Especially during the presidential primary season, when multiple candidates compete for the nomination of each major party, candidates must purchase advertising in order to boost their name recognition and favorability among potential voters. Modern campaigns also hire professional specialists in social media, who attempt to gain attention and support for the candidate by generating a constant stream of posts and video clips designed to be widely shared on Facebook, Twitter, and Instagram.

What constitutes information varies with the various stages of the process, as we discuss in chapter 4. Traditional topics include horse-race information, estimating which candidates are ahead and which are behind, thereby keeping a running tally on the viability and hence the seriousness of different candidacies. The news media also cover what they call "the issues," which may be public policy proposals brought up or emphasized by one or more candidates, social and political questions of the day, or other topics such as the past voting record or personal behavior of a candidate.

Throughout the life of a campaign, the news media generally maintain a rather close consensus about which candidates are serious contenders (and which are not), who is ahead or gaining ground (and who is stalling or slipping behind), and which issues are important to voters. This agreement arises from the sharply competitive conditions under which individual news outlets operate, from the shared perspective that arises because journalists from different organizations hang around together as they cover the travels of campaigning candidates, and because they keep close track of one another's product. Because reporters, editors, and producers read the major newspapers, keep an eye on television coverage, and immerse themselves in social media content, there is a tendency for their stories to converge.

Sometimes this herd mentality leads the news media astray. Most political journalists, for example, viewed Donald Trump as having little chance of winning the Republican nomination when he announced his presidential candidacy in the summer of 2015—or, even after he managed to disprove those assumptions a year later, of then defeating Hillary Clinton in the 2016 general election. Trump's victories came as a shock to professional experts in the news media who had spent long stretches of the campaign portraying him as a hopeless candidate, and who had devoted little attention before the election to discussing how a hypothetical Trump presidency might operate. While the "conventional wisdom" is not dependably accurate, it nonetheless exists as a powerful force shaping campaign coverage, due in large part to the workways of professional reporters and commentators.

Newspapers

Though the onset of the electronic media age has drastically reduced the readership and circulation of most daily newspapers, driving many out of business entirely, print journalism remains a major source of political information for many Americans. Newspaper coverage of current events has maintained its importance even in the Internet era; the websites operated by the *New York Times, Washington Post*, and *USA Today* rank among the most popular online news outlets, while the articles displayed on highly trafficked portal sites are often supplied by newspaper wire services such as Reuters and the Associated Press. Candidates realize the influence of newspaper coverage of their activities, and pay close attention to the treatment they receive from print journalists.

Most studies of political reporters confirm that they are a liberal-leaning group.[48] A 2004 survey of national journalists by the Pew Research Center found that 34 percent described themselves as liberals and just 7 percent as conservatives, with the balance considering themselves ideological moderates.[49] But standards of professional journalistic practice discourage slanted political coverage. While reporters may lean to the left, it is hard, but not impossible, to find this bias in their copy.[50] Overt expressions of partisan bias are regarded as unprofessional in news columns and may even be veiled in articles labeled "analysis." In at least two ways, however, attitudes shared by many journalists influence political coverage in ways that may, in practice, systematically advantage some candidates over others, despite their formal neutrality.

In the first place, it is permissible under standard journalistic norms to entertain a general pro-underdog bias. Journalists pride themselves in their calling to "comfort the afflicted and afflict the comfortable." Comforting any sizable body of afflicted persons may be well beyond the capacities of the news media.[51] It is far easier to afflict the comfortable, since this merely entails maintaining a pro forma skepticism about the presumably self-interested pronouncements of candidates running for office. Politicians escape this presumption only rarely. In the early stages of a foreign crisis, when there is a rally-round-the-flag effect, incumbents are permitted the luxury of being described as speaking on behalf of all the people.

As George H. W. Bush discovered in the early stages of the American invasion of Kuwait in 1991, and his son George W. Bush similarly found after the terrorist attacks of September 11, 2001, this does wonders for their public opinion ratings. Ordinarily, however, Americans are instructed by the media to take their leaders' statements with a grain of salt.[52]

Perhaps for this reason, journalists often submit leading candidates to stricter scrutiny than also-rans. This is particularly true in the presidential primary season, when the candidates are not widely known, making the tone of coverage more influential in shaping voters' opinions—and when reporters have an interest in prolonging the horse race excitement for as long as possible. Thus candidates may emerge from obscurity to pull into contention on the basis of initially positive media coverage, as Howard Dean did in the summer of 2003, only to face an increasingly skeptical press corps once they are anointed as "front-runners." (It didn't help Dean that he had a famously prickly relationship with the correspondents covering his campaign.) In the fall of 2011, a series of Republican presidential candidates each seemed to capture temporary momentum in the nomination contest—Governor Rick Perry of Texas; former House speaker Newt Gingrich; even Georgia businessman Herman Cain, an outsider candidate who had never held elective office—before wilting under the unfamiliar volume of public attention that followed their surge in the polls.

Second, illustrating Bernard Cohen's observation that the news media tell their consumers what to think *about*, there is the issue of "framing." How issues are framed matters over the long run because frames determine the terms within which alternative solutions are debated, and indeed they frequently serve to define the very nature of the problem.[53] Thus whether or not unemployment, inflation, health care reform, education funding, illegal immigration, violent crime, international famine, climate change, or other societal ills are seen as serious problems requiring political solutions at any given time is not entirely dependent on objective measurement of the phenomenon in question.[54] In part, their status as important "issues" of the day is determined by whether people feel that they are important, for whatever reason, and these feelings are in turn partially determined by how, or to what extent, the news media cover them. Thus the very problems our leaders are called on to solve may differ from era to era according to ebbs and flows of public attention.[55] Politicians work hard to seize control of this public agenda and have a considerable impact on its contents.[56] So, too, do the decisions of journalists, who give and withhold credibility to leaders according to their own collective judgments about issues and the seriousness with which politicians are addressing them.

Some candidates become personally popular or unpopular with the reporters who cover them—understandably so during a long election season in which members of the press corps travel across the country with the campaigns for weeks at a stretch. Bias based on such evaluations sometimes seeps into the content sent back home by correspondents on the road. John F. Kennedy's warm relationships with many reporters in 1960 may have given him an advantage over his opponent, Richard Nixon, who repeatedly complained about his own coverage in the newspapers.[57] (At a 1962 press conference announcing his retirement from politics—prematurely, as it turned out—Nixon told the assembled journalists, "You won't have Dick Nixon to kick around anymore.") Nixon, who long had a tense relationship with the press, compensated in his 1972 reelection campaign by largely ignoring national correspondents who might pepper him with hostile questions, benefiting from the norm that anything the incumbent president does constitutes "news."[58]

Ronald Reagan, with his affable personality and long experience in show business, cultivated good relations with the news media during his successful 1980 and 1984 campaigns, while Bill Clinton's charm and communication skills similarly earned him generally if not uniformly positive coverage during the 1992 and 1996 elections.[59] George W. Bush's folksy demeanor appears to have largely won over the traveling press corps during his successful 2000 and 2004 campaigns (especially when compared to his earnest, less outgoing opponents Al Gore and John Kerry); Barack Obama likewise benefited from a relatively friendly press in 2008, though less so in 2012.[60] Most journalists held both Donald Trump and Hillary Clinton in low regard in 2016, and the media's treatment of both candidates was "overwhelmingly negative in tone and extremely light on policy," according to a post-election analysis by Thomas E. Patterson of Harvard University.[61] The candidates differed much more in the relative volume of coverage they received. Many reporters found Trump, a new face in electoral politics who always seemed to have something interesting to say, to be a "better story" than Clinton, a familiar figure whose scripted and emotionally distant manner inspired rather less journalistic fascination.

Just as professional norms in most cases prevent overt bias from coloring campaign coverage, other considerations discourage the slanting of straight news stories. In a time of declining circulation and mounting costs for the newspaper industry, owners can ill afford to offend half their potential readership. Budget constraints have also led to consolidation among newspapers and have forced the reduction of resources devoted to the coverage of current affairs. Today, most newspapers do not maintain their own news bureaus in Washington or generate a great deal of original coverage of national politics. They increasingly rely on stories supplied by wire services or purchase content from the news services maintained by larger newspapers. These news-gathering agencies serve a wide clientele with a broad spectrum of opinion, and therefore endeavor to prepare stories that appear objective and impartial.[62] While every story will not be completely fair to all sides, the final product is much closer to the canons of neutrality than would be the case if each paper prepared stories in accordance with its own editorial positions.

For these reasons, newspaper coverage of campaigns is, on the whole, not consistently slanted in favor of a particular political viewpoint. One meta-analysis of 59 separate studies over 50 years concluded that "across all newspapers and all reporters, there is only negligible, if any, net bias in the coverage of presidential campaigns. To the extent that there are newspapers whose coverage is biased in favor of Democrats, they are offset by newspapers whose coverage is biased in favor of Republicans."[63]

Over the course of a single campaign, journalistic perceptions of electoral momentum have a decided effect on the positive or negative cast with which the press portrays each candidate at any given time. In 2012, for example, Mitt Romney was the target of more negative stories than Barack Obama during the month of September, when he lagged the incumbent narrowly in the race and faced widespread criticism over several verbal gaffes committed on the campaign trail. After Romney bested Obama in the first presidential debate on October 3, however, the tone of news stories immediately reversed, with Obama receiving more negative coverage than his opponent over the subsequent few weeks.[64]

Whatever role the press plays in influencing presidential elections varies enormously with circumstances. In general elections, when the candidates represent opposite parties, take contrasting positions on issues, and have both usually become well-known to the public, the influence of the news media is much lower than it is during the nomination process, when multiple candidates are often still introducing themselves to the electorate and differing party labels cannot help voters choose among them.

Yet the slender margins by which several recent national contests have been decided raises the possibility that even the more muted effects of media coverage on voters' perceptions in general elections have at times been sufficient to influence the outcome. An October 28 letter sent from FBI director James Comey to Congress confirming the reopening of a federal investigation into Clinton's use of a private email server attracted significant press attention in the final days of the 2016 campaign; the candidate and several of her top aides believed in retrospect that this last-minute development was sufficiently damaging to swing the very close election to Donald Trump. "If the election had been held on October 27, I would be your president," Clinton told a reporter the following spring.[65] Elections analyst Nate Silver of FiveThirtyEight agreed with this interpretation, arguing that the Comey letter was "*the* dominant story of the last 10 days of the campaign" and "had a fairly large and measurable impact, probably enough to cost Clinton the election."[66] However, a different study by Aaron C. Weinschenk and Costas Panagopoulos concluded instead that the media furor over Comey's actions "likely exerted minimal effects, at least once the impact of other factors are taken into account," failing to resolve the question of whether press coverage of the FBI director's behavior was indeed responsible for deciding the 2016 election.[67]

Most discussions of the media's capacity to affect the decisions of voters focus on the narrow subject of whether reporters are guilty of producing politically biased content that systematically favors a single party, ideology, or candidate. But citizens' perceptions of the electoral world are shaped by dependable patterns of news coverage that extend far beyond any potential leftward or rightward slant. In the long run, the media's more significant and consistent tendency to prefer the candidate horse race to policy analysis, cynicism to idealism, and novelty to familiarity are likely to be much more consequential (box 3.2).

Television

Television remains the most important and influential news medium in the United States. A 2016 survey by the Pew Research Center found that 78 percent of respondents named television as a primary source for news about political campaigns, compared to 65 percent for the Internet, 44 percent for radio, and 36 for print newspapers.[68] The influence of television on presidential elections extends well beyond the coverage of campaigns by journalists. Expenditures for television advertising dependably constitute the largest single budget item of any serious presidential campaign.

Box 3.2 ■ In the Arena: Newspaper Endorsements in 2016

Evidence of Donald Trump's "outsider" status can be found in his lack of newspaper endorsements in 2016. He received only two endorsements from the hundred largest circulation papers: from the *Las Vegas Journal Review* (owned by GOP contributor Sheldon Adelson) and the *Florida Times-Union* of Jacksonville.[a] Trump only garnered a handful of smaller paper endorsements as well—from places like Waxahachie, Texas; St. Joseph, Missouri; Palmdale and Santa Barbara, California; and Hillsboro, Ohio.[b]

In comparison, Hillary Clinton received 57 endorsements from the top hundred circulation papers. Among the largest circulation papers endorsing Clinton were the *New York Times, Washington Post, Los Angeles Times, Chicago Tribune, Boston Globe, Seattle Times, San Jose Mercury News, Minneapolis Star Tribune, St. Louis Post Dispatch, Houston Chronicle, Denver Post, Dallas Morning News, San Francisco Chronicle, Atlanta Journal-Constitution, Philadelphia Inquirer, Miami Herald, Detroit Free Press,* and *Cleveland Plain Dealer*.

Trump's absence of endorsements was a big departure from previous elections. According to *Editor & Publisher* magazine, in 2012, 212 newspapers endorsed Republican Mitt Romney compared to 191 for Democratic incumbent Barack Obama.[c] In 2008, Obama received 287 endorsements to John McCain's 159, and in 2004, John Kerry received 213 endorsements compared to 205 for George W. Bush.[d]

[a] The American Presidency Project, "2016 General Election Endorsements by Major Newspapers," University of California, Santa Barbara, http://www.presidency.ucsb.edu/data/2016_newspaper_endorsements.php.
[b] Ruriai Arrieta-Kenna, "These Are the Only Six Papers in the Country to Endorse Donald Trump," *Politico*, https://www.politico.com/magazine/story/2016/10/donald-trump-newspaper-endorsements-214390.
[c] Editor and Publisher, "2012 Presidential Endorsements," http://www.editorandpublisher.com/election.
[d] Editor and Publisher, "Tally of Newspaper Endorsements—Obama in a Landslide, at 287 to 159." http://www.editorandpublisher.com/eandp/search/article_display.jsp?vnu_content_id=1003875230.

Many observers consider the "television age" in American politics to have begun in 1960, when presidential candidates John F. Kennedy and Richard Nixon participated in a series of televised debates—inaugurating what has now become a quadrennial tradition. Almost uniformly, accounts of the 1960 campaign treat the debates as decisive events that gave Kennedy a crucial advantage in what turned out to be a very close election. The handsome, poised Kennedy came across very well on television, especially in comparison to Nixon's shifty eyes and five-o'clock shadow. In fact, the belief that Americans who listened to the debates on the radio (and thus judged the candidates purely on the basis of their words, not their looks) considered Nixon the winner, while television viewers favored Kennedy, has become a staple of American campaign lore, although little evidence actually exists to substantiate it.[69]

To candidates, strategists, pundits, and media critics alike, the lesson is clear: television coverage can significantly influence the outcome of elections, and the medium tends to reward superficiality over substance. The truth is probably more complex. Television's moving pictures and sound give it an immediacy that print journalism lacks. The medium is also better suited to covering politics as a battle of personalities than of ideas; in-depth discussions of policy tend to lack the necessary visual images to make compelling television. Yet the same factors that limit the influence of newspapers on the course of electoral campaigns often constrain the effects of electronic media as well. Television coverage of politics is often intentionally bland in order to minimize controversy; many viewers adhere to their previous political beliefs and evaluations even in the face of the contradictory opinions of talking heads; and most Americans won't receive even strong, compelling political messages in the first place. Ratings for current affairs programming routinely pale in comparison to those for prime-time entertainment, talk shows, sporting events, and other staples of the medium; even "news" broadcasts devote considerable attention to human interest stories, celebrity gossip, and other, more popular topics at the expense of political issues or events. More highly flavored cable news programs tend to attract smaller audiences of politically attentive viewers whose existing attitudes are largely reinforced by their favorite television personalities.

As with newspapers, the influence of television appears to peak during the presidential primary season. Contenders for party nominations are usually much less well-known to the national electorate than incumbent presidents or major-party nominees, allowing media coverage to strongly color the public's perceptions of the candidates. Since primary elections are contested by multiple candidates within the same party, substantive differences among them on salient public policy issues tend to be relatively minor, further encouraging television coverage to focus on the contenders' differing personal styles, identities, personalities, and strategies. And the idiosyncrasies of the primary process itself—beginning with the Iowa caucus and New Hampshire primary in January or February of a presidential election year and continuing through months of sequential primary elections and caucuses in every state and U.S. territory—allow for television coverage to exert significant influence on the outcome, as well-publicized news media interpretations of the results in the early states have proven to have an immense effect on the behavior of voters in subsequent primaries (a phenomenon discussed further in chapter 4).

For one thing, candidates do not automatically receive equal attention from reporters. They must be "taken seriously" by the media in order to earn sufficient, respectful coverage. In 2004, for example, former governor Howard Dean of Vermont was initially considered a decided underdog for the Democratic presidential nomination by media consensus in comparison to Senator John Kerry of Massachusetts, Senator John Edwards of North Carolina, Senator Joe Lieberman of Connecticut, and Representative Dick Gephardt of Missouri. Realizing that he needed to attract media coverage in order to gain the attention of voters, Dean began to repeatedly attack his rivals by name for their support of the U.S. invasion of Iraq in early 2003. Since journalists love to cover personal conflict between candidates, Dean's criticisms generated a great deal of valuable publicity. While Dean portrayed himself as motivated by principle, he was not reluctant to comment on the political advantages to be had in adopting such an approach. "It's made me into a candidate who's not a long shot anymore," he told reporters. "It's put me into a position where there are now five significant candidates, not four."[70]

But Dean ultimately suffered as much as he benefited from the ways of modern television journalism. Reporters and pundits obsessed with the state of the horse race anointed Dean not only the front-runner but, in many accounts, the presumptive Democratic nominee by early 2004—even though a single vote had yet to be cast. Media expectations for Dean's performance in the first-in-the-nation Iowa caucus were therefore extraordinarily high. When he placed a distant third on caucus night, well behind Kerry and Edwards, journalists and pundits on the lookout for surprising results that make a good story gleefully piled on.

Dean's energetic concession speech in Iowa included an improvised exhortation to his followers to take their fight to subsequent primaries and caucuses. After naming a number of states, seemingly at random, Dean raised his fist with an enthusiastic shriek. Footage of the "Dean scream" was replayed endlessly on television over the following days, as political analysts who had just weeks before been confidently predicting a certain Dean nomination now eagerly branded him a loser and perhaps something of a nut. For many Americans who had not been following the race closely until the Iowa caucus, their first televised exposure to Dean was therefore decidedly negative. Unsurprisingly, Dean was never able to work his way back into serious contention, withdrawing from the race several weeks later without winning a single state primary.

The large field of contenders seeking the 2012 Republican presidential nomination similarly discovered the potential power of a single moment on live television to reshape the race and profoundly affect the electoral fortunes of candidates. During a Fox News Channel interview on June 12, 2011, former Minnesota governor Tim Pawlenty attacked his absent Republican rival Mitt Romney for enacting universal health care legislation while Romney was governor of Massachusetts, charging that the federal Affordable Care Act signed into law by Barack Obama in 2010 (and which most Republicans strongly opposed) was modeled on Romney's plan. "You don't have to take my word for it," Pawlenty told Fox News host Chris Wallace. "You can take President Obama's word for it. President Obama said that he designed Obamacare after Romneycare and basically made it 'Obamneycare.'"[71] Yet when Pawlenty was invited to repeat his accusations the next day in Romney's presence at a New Hampshire debate attended by both candidates, he declined to confront Romney directly. As *Time* magazine noted, Pawlenty's "wimp out . . . reinforced impressions that the Minnesotan was too mild-mannered for the raucous presidential race," and Pawlenty soon abandoned his campaign after a disappointing performance in an Iowa straw poll.[72]

With Pawlenty out of the running, Governor Rick Perry of Texas loomed as Romney's most formidable potential challenger for the nomination. Perry could boast a more consistently conservative record in office than the ex-Massachusetts governor, hailed from a large state with an extensive network of deep-pocketed Republican donors, and seemingly held the potential to mobilize the electoral support of evangelical Christians in key primary states. Yet Perry, too, was unmade by poor showings in televised debates. In a September 2011 event in Florida, Perry responded to an attack on his immigration policy by suggesting that critics who disagreed with him on the issue didn't "have a heart." This remark produced a sufficiently strong backlash among conservative activists that Perry later felt compelled to issue an apology for his "inappropriate" choice of words. His standing in polls of Republican primary voters began a noticeable slide.[73]

In desperate need of a better performance in subsequent debates, Perry instead suffered another self-inflicted wound. During a November event held in Michigan, Perry, who was running on a platform that called for the elimination of three existing federal cabinet departments, could only recall two of them when discussing the issue (Commerce and Education), frantically searching his mind for the third (Energy) before admitting, "I can't. Sorry. Oops!" The incident was sufficiently awkward that even Perry's rivals, visibly uncomfortable as he fumbled to complete his response, tried to jog his memory by suggesting possible answers; Representative Michele Bachmann of Minnesota told a reporter afterward that "we all felt very bad for him."[74] Perry's unimpressive debate skills fatally damaged his standing in the eyes of the news media, as he became the repeated butt of jokes by political pundits and late-night comedians while video clips of his blunders circulated widely online to general mockery. His campaign never recovered.

The abrupt rise and fall of candidates reveals much about the role of media attention, particularly television coverage, in shaping the outcome of presidential nominations. Television tends to emphasize candidate personalities and the horse race over qualifications or policy prescriptions. It treats politics as entertainment, hoping that keeping the level of excitement high will keep viewers tuning in. So reporters do what they can to hype up the contest, heavily publicizing any apparent shifts in candidate fortunes.[75] Loudly colored "BREAKING NEWS" banners across television screens announce the daily arrival of the latest supposed shake-up in the race (John Sides and Lynn Vavreck counted some 68 media-proclaimed "game changers" during the 2012 election alone), even if the story of the moment is destined to be mostly ignored by voters or forgotten well before Election Day.[76]

Candidate choices continuously interact with media interpretations. Fond of dramaturgical stereotypes (who's the establishment favorite, who's the scrappy insurgent, who's the tragically doomed loser) and perpetually fascinated by the strategic game of politics, journalists may seek to resist acknowledging obvious truths and stable trends in favor of novelty and counterintuitiveness.[77] Since there needs to be "news" to cover all day every day, members of the media are swept along by the tide of events to which they contribute and in which they swim, very much like the rest of us.

For the first 30 years or so of the television age, political coverage was mainly limited to the nightly evening news broadcasts of the three major broadcast networks (NBC, CBS, and ABC), along with various public affairs programs like *Meet the Press*. The rise of all-news cable channels, beginning with CNN in the 1980s, greatly increased the volume of coverage available. CNN, which once stood alone as a news-only network, soon attracted competition from Fox News Channel and MSNBC. Media consultants now speak of a "24-hour news cycle," in which the demand for fresh content for news stories is a round-the-clock constant. Campaigns face a phalanx of journalists and pundits who are perpetually desperate for new things to talk about; as a result, small developments often inspire at least temporary media frenzies. Candidates must be "on" at all times; remarks meant to be private can be picked up by open microphones or intentionally leaked to the press—such as George W. Bush's vulgar description of a *New York Times* reporter in 2000, Barack Obama's 2008 characterization of rural Pennsylvania voters as "bitter" and "cling[ing] to guns or religion or antipathy to people who aren't like them . . . as a way to explain their frustrations," or Hillary Clinton's dismissal of some Trump supporters as a "basket of deplorables" in 2016—and replayed ad infinitum on cable news. These episodes usually pass without major long-term effects, but candidates concerned about their portrayal in the media seek to avoid them whenever possible.

Much of the programming aired on cable news channels does not constitute actual "news" at all. These media outlets often devote less time to original political reporting than to analysis and opinion. Political analysts tend to be primarily interested in describing and elaborating campaign strategy, discussing the results of public opinion polls and other measures of the candidate horse race, and making predictions about the outcome of elections and other major political events (such as the selection of running mates). Commentators often represent a particular ideological or partisan perspective that largely determines their interpretation of the candidates and campaigns. Political junkies may tune in to satisfy their particular interest in the details of the campaign or to receive psychologically pleasing confirmation of their political views, but other Americans tend to be less interested, meaning that the most loyal audience for cable news is the segment of the population that already has its mind made up about which party to support.

The presidential candidacy of Donald Trump in 2016 represents a particularly revealing case study in the television coverage of political campaigns. Trump was already a national television star before he entered politics, having hosted fourteen seasons of the reality series *The Apprentice* on NBC at the apex of a three-decade career as a heavily promoted media personality. He also behaved much differently from other politicians, adopting a uniquely spontaneous and emotionally expressive style while his opponents remained professionally coached and mannered by comparison. Trump's celebrity status and penchant for arousing controversy proved irresistible to television producers, who routinely devoted extensive live coverage to his campaign rallies (a benefit enjoyed by none of his rivals). "I have never seen a candidate get as much . . . free media [attention] as Trump. It isn't even close," observed veteran election analyst Stuart Rothenberg in early 2016, when Trump was still competing for the Republican nomination. "I have been stunned at the amount of [television] time Trump receives. [Networks] do telephone interviews. They cover entire speeches. He seems to be everywhere. It is very unusual."[78] Jeff Roe, campaign manager for Ted Cruz, later recalled that the Cruz campaign office had "three TVs [tuned to] Fox, MSNBC, and CNN. We called it the 'full Trump' when he [appeared on] all three TVs. He had his 27th 'full Trump' in 30 days in August [2015] and we knew [his campaign] was real."[79]

Defenders of this practice maintained that the Trump phenomenon was simply a bigger story than the other campaigns, and that high ratings proved that the media was simply giving its customers what they wanted—the first televised Republican debate in which Trump participated attracted a record 24 million viewers (compared to 3.2 million viewers for the first Republican debate in 2012), which represented the largest audience for a non-sports cable telecast in American history.[80] Katy Tur, who covered the Trump campaign for NBC News, argued that the candidate was inherently newsworthy, in part because of the unusually passionate response he received from voters: "We do it because it is important to show the public who is running for president. It's important to show how they behave. How they think. What they believe. Who they admire and why. Yes, we give Trump a ton of airtime and article space. But that's because he is unlike anything anyone has ever seen. And despite what folks who don't like him might want to argue, he is resonating. And we have an obligation to document it."[81]

But critics suggested that the media's disproportionate focus on Trump distorted the dynamics of the 2016 race, depriving other candidates of valuable exposure (especially during the Republican primaries) and forcing them to respond to his provocations. At a CNN town hall event in March, rival candidate Ted Cruz accused the media of being "engaged in a love fest . . . How many hours of free media do CNN and Fox and every other station [give Trump]? You let him call in [to your network] for a year."[82] After the November election, Hillary Clinton aide Jennifer Palmieri complained to journalists that Trump "gets all the coverage and you guys only covered her when she was talking about him."[83] Though much of the attention paid to Trump by the major television networks and cable channels was openly critical of his behavior, the sheer volume of airtime devoted to a single candidate over an 18-month campaign was thoroughly unprecedented and by far the most distinctive attribute of media coverage in the 2016 election.

Internet Media

A growing number of Americans get most of their news about candidates and campaigns from the Internet via computers, tablets, and cell phones. Young people, in particular, are likely to look online for political information. This trend will only continue to increase over time, making digital content an even more important segment of news media coverage in future elections.

Many of the most widely visited websites for information about current affairs are maintained by established news organizations such as CNN and the *New York Times*, providing a connection between online content and the coverage available in print or on television.[84] But the Internet also offers an unmatched array of unique sources that generate a constant stream of information. Some online enterprises, such as Politico, focus specifically on the political world; others, such as Slate or Buzzfeed, combine political subjects with other forms of news and entertainment content. Many websites cater to audiences with particular ideological or partisan leanings. HuffPost, Salon, ThinkProgress, and Talking Points Memo are popular sites among Democrats, while Republicans prefer the Daily Caller, Breitbart News, Newsmax, and the Blaze. The conservative-leaning Drudge Report has played a highly influential role in the media's coverage of American politics since the 1990s, predictably directing high-volume web traffic to any article linked on its front page. "Drudge basically tells the conservative base, but also the American media, 'Hey, this is what's important. This is newsy. This matters,'" observed media analyst Dylan Byers, while a cable news producer agreed: "Drudge continues to set the agenda for us."[85] With social media platforms such as Facebook and Twitter allowing journalists, campaign professionals, and attentive voters to keep tabs on political events on a minute-by-minute basis over the course of the day (and night), contemporary presidential campaigns occur in a state of permanent media frenzy.

The Internet also provides the opportunity for like-minded citizens to interact with each other and engage in various forms of political activism. A number of websites, most notably Daily Kos (for Democrats) and RedState (for Republicans), allow readers to comment on stories, post their own original content, and engage in political discussions. Users of these sites also coordinate volunteer efforts and hold online fund-raising drives on behalf of favored candidates.

The advent of the Internet age has fundamentally changed the behavior of candidates and campaigns. Its unparalleled capacity for transmitting information—not just text, but audio and video clips as well—around the world means that any political development can be instantly disseminated to the entire nation. Campaigns locked in electoral combat now race to counter any attack from the other side immediately after it emerges; after the rise of social media, Republican campaign strategist Kevin Madden noted, "Rapid response became more rapid. It became almost instantaneous."[86] Tactics have also evolved in response to technological change. Campaign managers now routinely send workers called "trackers" to follow opposing candidates at all public events with a video camera in tow, hoping to capture hard evidence of any misstatement or gaffe that might "go viral" on the Internet—a practice that has been known to ensnare politicians in controversy from time to time.[87]

On September 17, 2012, the website of the liberal opinion magazine *Mother Jones* released excerpts from a surreptitiously filmed video recording of Republican presidential nominee Mitt Romney speaking to a small group of donors at a private fund-raising event in Florida earlier in the year. In the footage, Romney stated that "there are 47 percent of the people who will vote for [Obama] no matter what . . . who are dependent upon government, who believe that they are victims, who believe that government has a responsibility to care for them. . . . These are people who pay no income tax. . . . And so my job is not to worry about these people. I'll never convince them that they should take personal responsibility and care for their lives."[88]

The release of what soon became known as the "47 percent" video immediately roiled the presidential race. At a press conference held a few hours after the first excerpts surfaced, Romney acknowledged that his remarks were "not elegantly stated," but stood behind the substance of his argument.[89] But Romney found it difficult to put the story behind him. After *Mother Jones* uploaded the footage to YouTube, it attracted millions of views in a single week, and the remarks became easy fodder for pundits, talk show hosts, and late-night comedians, as well as the Obama campaign.[90] Several weeks later, after perceiving that he had been damaged politically by the release of the video, Romney reversed course, telling Sean Hannity of Fox News Channel that "I said something that's just completely wrong. . . . My life has shown that I care about 100 percent [of Americans], and that's been demonstrated throughout my life. And this campaign is about the 100 percent."[91]

Presidential campaigns now devote extensive resources to digital media, aiming both to shape the coverage they receive from online journalists and to communicate directly with voters without the intermediating interpretations of news reporters and publishers. Candidate speeches, advertisements, and other forms of content are uploaded regularly to campaign websites, social media accounts, and online video channels like YouTube, attempting to give viewers a sense of membership in the campaign and to stimulate active support and financial contributions. Adviser Stephanie Cutter explained how these tools were used by the Obama reelection campaign in 2012:

> Given our challenges in dealing with the traditional news media, we saw an opportunity to go around that filter and directly to our supporters and those that we needed to persuade, which was a much more valuable communication to them than reading something in a newspaper. We had 33 million people on Facebook following Barack Obama. Those 33 million were friends with 90 percent of Facebook users in the United States. . . . So we could communicate with 90 percent of Facebook users in this country, which in sum total is more than the people that voted for us. So we did that very diligently. It was largely a positive conversation online. Because when you're communicating with people

> on Facebook . . . it's about getting them to share something with their friends. They're more likely to share something if they're proud of it. . . . People trust their information when it's coming from a Facebook friend much more than if it's me on TV saying something.[92]

The interaction between candidate social media use and the journalistic coverage of campaigns reached a new milestone in 2016. Donald Trump's freewheeling Twitter account featured regular unfiltered posts composed personally by the candidate, who often used the platform to launch outraged attacks on his political opponents or the news media. Trump's Tweets routinely received extensive attention on television and in newspapers as well as in the online realm, routinely dominating daily campaign coverage and reaching many citizens who were not themselves active social media users. Trump continued this practice after taking office as president, becoming famous for announcing administration policy and personnel decisions via Twitter—sometimes even before his own staff had been made aware of them.

Pro-Trump accounts also used Facebook and Twitter effectively in 2016 to target potential supporters while directing critical messages about Hillary Clinton to potential voters, like young women and racial minorities, whom they believed might otherwise support Clinton in large numbers. It became increasingly clear over the course of the 2016 campaign that some of this online activity on Trump's behalf was performed by clandestine actors with ties to the government of Russia; in October 2017, Facebook publicly acknowledged that it had identified 80,000 items of campaign content linked to Russian-operated accounts to which at least 126 million users had been exposed.[93] When combined with the illegal theft and strategic release of private email messages and other documents from within the Clinton campaign and the Democratic National Committee during the 2016 campaign, this activity represented an unprecedented intervention by another nation into the American democratic process, and remained the subject of multiple federal investigations more than two years after Trump's narrow victory. The advent of online and social media has revolutionized the behavior of voters, candidates, campaigns, and journalists, but has also opened a new avenue for other figures, both domestic and foreign, to reach potential voters and thus act to influence the outcome of national elections.

INCUMBENCY AS A RESOURCE: THE PRESIDENCY

The presidency is one resource that, in any given election year, must of necessity be monopolized by one party or the other. A president seeking reelection enjoys many special advantages by virtue of incumbency. At the beginning of a campaign, a president is much better known than any challenger can hope to be. Everything the president does is news and is widely reported in the media. The issues to which presidents devote attention are likely to constitute the national agenda because of presidents' unique visibility and capacity to center attention on matters that they deem important. To this extent, presidents are in a position to focus public debate on issues they think are most advantageous. Presidents can act and thereby gain credit. If they cannot act, they can accuse Congress of inaction, as Harry Truman did in 1948 and Gerald Ford did in 1976. Since Truman won and Ford lost, this strategy, like all strategies in an uncertain world, evidently has mixed effects.

Faced with a crisis in foreign affairs, a president can gain politically by handling it well or by calling on the patriotism of the citizenry to support its head of state when the nation is in danger. But if the problem lingers, it soon becomes a nagging liability. A significant example of a foreign crisis took place during the early stages of the 1980 campaign, when Iranian revolutionaries seized the American embassy in Teheran on November 4, 1979, taking American diplomats hostage just as Senator Ted Kennedy of Massachusetts announced that he would run for the Democratic nomination against the incumbent president, Jimmy Carter. Before the hostage crisis began, Kennedy was outdistancing Carter in a poll of potential Democratic primary voters by 54 percent to 31 percent (with 15 percent undecided). When the crisis occurred, voters, including Democrats, rallied around their president, and Carter's support shot up to 48 percent, with 40 percent for Kennedy and 12 percent undecided. Carter announced that he would suspend active campaigning, and he used his presidential responsibilities as a reason to refuse to meet his rival in debates. He continued to campaign from the White House, however, with great success.[94] Unfortunately for the incumbent, the crisis in Iran dragged on too long, and after he had disposed of the Kennedy primary challenge, Carter's popularity suffered a serious decline, reverting to its previous level and causing his defeat in the general election.

As Carter discovered in 1980, sitting presidents benefit from international crises on their watch only as long as the American people have confidence in their ability to handle the problem. A successful resolution of the issue may be rewarded with an impressive surge in popularity, but high approval ratings fade over time as the electorate turns its attention to other issues. George H. W. Bush lost his bid for reelection in 1992 despite reaching a job approval rating of 90 percent after the United States successfully drove the Iraqi Army out of the adjacent nation of Kuwait the year before. By the time of the election, Americans' gratitude for Bush's handling of the Persian Gulf crisis had been superseded by widespread disapproval of the performance of the national economy during his tenure in office.

And if the crisis remains unresolved, impatience sets in. American invasions of Korea in the 1950s, Vietnam in the 1960s, and Iraq in 2003 all initially received broad support from the mass public, but as military operations dragged on for several years without clear evidence of resolution or troop withdrawals, Americans increasingly voiced their disapproval of the wars—and of the presidents who started them. Harry Truman (1952) and Lyndon Johnson (1968) both chose not to seek reelection due to their severely weakened public standing as a result of the events in Korea and Vietnam, respectively, while Democratic victories in the 2006 and 2008 elections reflected voters' growing frustration with the performance of George W. Bush in managing a war in Iraq that unexpectedly continued for years after the initial occupation.

As the symbol of the nation, presidents can travel and make "nonpolitical" speeches to advance their candidacy subtly while attempting to remain above the partisan fray, in contrast to challengers who can be accused of exploiting troubled times for their own political advantage. Presidents can also use the power of their office to pursue specific policies that may appeal to specific electoral groups. In the midst of his reelection campaign in June 2012, Barack Obama signed an executive order loosening the enforcement of immigration laws on individuals who had entered the United States without authorization as children. This policy change was designed to enhance the president's popularity among Latinos, a key voting bloc in the upcoming presidential election. Stuart Stevens of the opposition Romney campaign observed in retrospect that Obama's action "raised the profile of the issue, and that was the sort of thing you can do as president. I felt it was very smartly played. That is an example of the advantage that . . . incumbents have."[95]

A president's life is not necessarily one of undiluted joy, however. If the national economy worsens, if a disaster strikes, or if a battle is lost to hostile forces, the incumbent is likely at least over the long run to be blamed. Whether actually responsible or not, presidents are held accountable for bad times and have to take the consequences.[96] Herbert Hoover felt deeply the sting of this phenomenon when the people punished him as incumbent president for the Great Depression, turning him out of office in a landslide in the election of 1932.[97] The defeat of incumbent presidents Gerald Ford (1976), Jimmy Carter (1980), and George H. W. Bush (1992) were also primarily due to perceptions of weak national economic performance. Incumbents Ronald Reagan, Bill Clinton, and Barack Obama were also blamed for hard economic times in the first two years of their administrations; voters expressed their disapproval with the status quo in the 1982, 1994, and 2010 midterm elections, respectively, by voting out large numbers of the president's partisan allies in Congress. Fortunately for all three presidents, the national economy in each case soon began to recover. By the time each incumbent stood for reelection two years later, voters had become more positive about the direction of the country, and responded by awarding him a second term in the White House.

Incumbents have a record; they have or have not done things, and they may be held accountable for their sins of omission or commission. This is not the case for candidates out of office, who can criticize freely without always presenting realistic alternatives or necessarily taking their own advice once elected. Obama opposed the Iraq war and strongly criticized the George W. Bush administration's handling of the ensuing occupation, but once in office adopted policies quite similar to those in place at the time of his inauguration. The incumbent is naturally cast as the defender of the current administration and the challenger as the attacker who promises better things to come. We cannot expect to hear the person in office say that the opposition could probably perform as well or to hear the challenger declare that he or she really could not do any better than the incumbent, although in a political system that encourages compromise and has enormous built-in inertia, both statements may be close to the truth.

Barring catastrophic events—depression, war, scandal—the political power of modern presidents is strong enough to assure renomination by their own party within the two-term limit imposed by the Twenty-Second Amendment to the Constitution. This is not merely because the presidency is the greatest, most visible office in the land, with claims on the loyalty of many, if not all, potential rivals. The president's party can hardly hope to win by repudiating the president. To refuse the incumbent the nomination would, most politicians feel, be tantamount to confessing political bankruptcy or ineptitude.

This rule was bent but not broken in 1976 by Ronald Reagan's challenge to Gerald Ford in the Republican primaries and in 1980 by Ted Kennedy's opposition to Jimmy Carter for the Democratic nomination. It was not only the fact that Reagan and Kennedy sought to take the nomination away from a sitting president of their own party, but also that they persisted right up through the convention, that hurt the incumbents. Both Ford and Carter were consequently unable to focus on their general election opponents as early as they would have liked. No subsequent president has faced a primary challenger with a serious chance of winning the nomination; Reagan (1984), Bill Clinton (1996), George W. Bush (2004), and Barack Obama (2012) all ran unopposed for renomination, while George H. W. Bush (1992) faced a protest candidate in challenger Pat Buchanan, a former White House aide and conservative columnist who ran an initially energetic campaign but never posed a serious electoral threat.

INCUMBENCY AS A LIABILITY: THE VICE PRESIDENCY

The advantages of incumbency do not necessarily extend to a sitting vice president seeking to succeed a president of the same party, as Richard Nixon discovered in 1960, Hubert Humphrey in 1968, and Al Gore in 2000. A vice president suffers from the disadvantages of having to defend an existing record without necessarily benefiting from it. He or she cannot differ too much with the current administration without alienating the president and causing an internal rift in the party. At the same time, a vice president cannot claim experience in the presidential office. Even voters who approve of the performance of the incumbent administration may not give the vice president any credit for it. This is the most difficult strategic problem of all for candidates.[98]

George H. W. Bush in 1988 was the first sitting vice president to be elected in direct succession to a retiring president since Martin Van Buren succeeded Andrew Jackson in 1836. Why, despite the historical rarity of the event, did Bush win? He obtained the nomination of his party largely, it appears, because primary voters in the Republican Party considered him the logical successor to Ronald Reagan, and Reagan was very popular at the end of his second term. This also explains in part why Bush won the general election. Americans were generally content with the overall direction of the country in 1988, and were therefore more favorably disposed than usual to the promotion of the vice president to the Oval Office.

In the presidential election of 2000, Vice President Al Gore faced the strategic difficulty of claiming credit for the Clinton-Gore administration's popular economic policies while simultaneously distancing himself personally from Bill Clinton in the wake of the Monica Lewinsky affair. Gore was disadvantaged by his proximity to Clinton and the lack of an independent grant of authority by which he could demonstrate that he was his own man. His difficulties ultimately resided in the weak constitutional powers and perceived junior partnership of the vice presidency. Americans often view vice presidents as something of a comic sidekick to the president, which can make it difficult for them to be taken seriously in their own right as strong and capable leaders. Yet the vice president's status as the successor to the presidency on the occasion of the incumbent's death or resignation requires that the position be filled by an experienced and accomplished figure. From this dilemma flow the problems characteristic of the vice presidency.

For much of American history, vice presidents were routinely shut out of the presidential decision-making process. Before Harry Truman assumed the presidency upon the death of Franklin D. Roosevelt in April 1945, for example, he had met with Roosevelt only briefly and infrequently and was largely unaware of the president's declining health. "Boys, if you ever pray, pray for me now," remarked a shaken Truman to a gathering of newspaper reporters the day after becoming president. "I don't know whether you fellows ever had a load of hay fall on you, but when they told me yesterday what had happened, I felt like the moon, the stars, and all the planets had fallen on me." Since the 1970s, however, the vice president has become more likely to serve as a key member of the presidential administration, working closely with the president as a trusted political adviser, liaison to influential interest groups or members of Congress, emissary to foreign leaders, or (in the case of Dick Cheney, vice president under George W. Bush) manager of the federal bureaucracy.

In return for continuous exposure to the entire range of problems confronting the government, vastly improved access to the president, and a closer view of the burdens of the presidency, the modern vice president must also carry some of these burdens. Which burdens are carried, how many, and how far are up to the president. Withholding cooperation would impair the vice president's relationship with the president. This would be bound to affect his or her capacity to fulfill the constitutional obligation of the vice presidency, which is to be genuinely prepared in case of dire need.

Vice presidents can hardly fulfill their constitutional responsibilities by resigning, nor can they be dismissed in the middle of a term. Thus modern vice presidents must discipline themselves to loyalty to the president. This sometimes has painful consequences for vice presidents, especially when they attempt to emerge from the shadow of the president and run for the presidency on their own. The worst modern case was probably Vice President Hubert Humphrey's difficulty in 1968 in persuading opponents of the Vietnam War that he had deeply disagreed with President Johnson's policies, as he had privately done, while publicly defending them. Even after four years out of office, Walter Mondale, vice president under Jimmy Carter, found himself criticized for Carter's perceived failures when he ran for president himself in 1984. In 1988, George H. W. Bush was simultaneously attacked as excessively servile and insufficiently loyal.[99] Al Gore similarly struggled to win credit in 2000 for the peace and prosperity achieved under the presidency of Bill Clinton.

There seems to be no way for vice presidents to avoid the dilemmas built into the office. Unless scrupulously loyal, they cannot get the access to the president that they need to discharge their constitutional function; when loyal to the president, they are saddled, at least in the short run, with whatever characteristics of the president or the administration's program that the president's enemies, or their own, care to fasten on them. A vice president sits there in the limelight, visible, vulnerable, and for the most part, powerless.

From 1836 until 1960, when Richard Nixon was nominated, no incumbent vice president was put forward for the presidency. Since 1960, most vice presidents—Johnson, Humphrey, Ford, Mondale, Bush, Quayle, Gore, and Biden—have run for president in subsequent elections; often succeeding in capturing their party's nomination. Johnson and Ford became presidents before seeking election as their party's presidential nominee, but the others did it on their own. Even defeated vice presidential candidates, from Henry Cabot Lodge to Ed Muskie to Sargent Shriver to Bob Dole to Joe Lieberman to John Edwards, have launched their own presidential campaigns four years later.

As long as vice presidents have some chance to eventually run for the presidency, as they do at present, and are not arbitrarily excluded from further consideration as independent political leaders in their own right, there will be plenty of takers for the vice presidential nomination. This contributes to the strength of political parties. Vice presidential nominees can balance tickets, help unite their party, and campaign effectively before the public (as described further in chapter 4). Thus vice presidential nominees can help elect a president. It is after the campaign is over that the vice president's problems begin.

THE BALANCE OF RESOURCES

Clearly, the social framework within which presidential election strategies must be pursued provides important advantages and disadvantages to candidates and parties on both sides. We have attempted to explain why the unequal distribution of key resources such as money and control over information do not necessarily or automatically lead to election victories for the parties and candidates who possess and use most of these resources. Might there not, however, be a cumulative effect that would greatly assist those who possessed both more money and more control over information?

This effect might develop, but it is not with us at present. The two major parties now seem to maintain a relatively even balance in resources. In 2000, the Republican Party spent more money but the Democrats organized a superior get-out-the-vote effort. In 2004, the spending balance was close to even, with the Republican victory arguably deriving from better strategy, more centralized command of resources, and George W. Bush's status as an incumbent president during wartime. The solid Democratic victory in 2008 came from a clear edge in fund-raising, strategic superiority due to an innovative combination of grassroots tactics supplemented by creative use of new campaign technologies, and, most importantly, a favorable national political environment due to the unpopularity of the sitting Republican president. The narrower Democratic triumph in 2012 reflected a more even financial playing field and Obama's incumbency. In 2016, the Democrats held an edge in the money race while the Republicans benefited from greater media attention and more effective campaign tactics.

It is hard to see a clear pattern of partisan advantage in these recent contests. The fundamental factors shaping presidential outcomes do not strongly and consistently favor either side; whenever one party achieves a strategic breakthrough or innovation, the opposition stands eager to adapt to the new political terrain. We shouldn't be surprised, then, that most presidential elections over the past two decades have been decided by slim margins—and that control of the presidency has regularly passed back and forth between Democrats and Republicans.

PART II
Sequences

The next two chapters follow the chronology of the election year, first describing the procedures governing the nominations of the major candidates, then discussing the course of the campaign leading up to election night. The behavior of candidates, delegates, journalists, and voters can best be understood in the strategic context of the institutional rules structuring the electoral process.

4

The Nomination Process

■ ■ ■

IN ORDER TO BE NOMINATED BY A MAJOR PARTY for president of the United States, a candidate must win support from a simple majority of voting delegates to the party's national convention, held every summer of a presidential election year. Before the 1970s, most delegates were chosen by state party organizations under the control of governors, senators, and other party elites; ambitious politicians seeking a presidential nomination thus spent the years before an election courting the support of these leaders. Now, candidates win nominations by accumulating delegates pledged to their candidacy via a months-long sequence of primary elections and caucuses held in all 50 states, the District of Columbia, and every U.S. territory—a time-consuming, complicated, and costly process.[1]

When the field of potential nominees includes only one major candidate, such as an incumbent president seeking renomination for a second term in office without significant opposition within the party, the rules governing presidential nominations do not matter much. But if two or more serious contenders emerge, the procedural mechanics of the nomination system control the process by which the field of candidates is narrowed to a single party choice. Some rules are unique to the Democrats or the Republicans, while others apply to both sides. Some are consistent and longstanding, while others are the subject of frequent revision. Here are the most important rules in their current form:

1. Both national parties require all pledged delegates (i.e., delegates who are chosen to attend the national party convention as formally committed supporters of a particular presidential candidate) to be selected within a roughly three-month window from early March to early June of a presidential election year (except for those delegates representing states that have received special permission to vote earlier, as noted below). In both parties, pledged delegates are chosen either in state primaries, in which party-affiliated voters cast a ballot at a traditional polling place for their favored candidate, or in caucuses, which consist of a number of public meetings around the state in which party members discuss and measure support for each of the candidates. As a practical matter, candidates must contest nearly every primary and caucus on the nomination calendar in order to collect enough delegates to win.[2]

2. Both parties grant special dispensation to four states to hold early primaries and caucuses before the rest of the nation is allowed to begin the delegate selection process. The first event on the nomination calendar is

always the Iowa caucus, held in January or February of a presidential election year, followed closely by the New Hampshire primary. In recent years, the Nevada caucus and South Carolina primary have then followed. Other states have attempted from time to time to compete with the four authorized early states by scheduling primaries and caucuses prior to the normal selection window, though they risk incurring penalties from the national party organizations by doing so—such as a severe reduction or outright elimination of their delegate seats at the national convention.

3. For both Democrats and Republicans, the number of delegates allocated to each state is based on formulas that take into account both the state's number of electoral votes and the extent to which it has supported the party's candidates in recent elections. Candidates for the nomination thus have a particular incentive to win primaries and caucuses in populous states that usually vote for their party. Democrats also award bonus delegates to states holding their primaries and caucuses in April or later in order to discourage excessive front-loading of the nomination calendar.

4. In the Democratic Party, a candidate in a state primary or caucus who receives more than 15 percent of the vote in any congressional district within the state is entitled by national party rules to gain a proportionate share of the delegates chosen in that district. Democrats also require state delegations to be evenly divided between men and women. The Republican Party, by contrast, allows states to choose proportional representation, winner-take-all allocation, or a combination thereof for awarding delegates to candidates based on the results of primary elections or caucuses. However, states holding Republican primaries or caucuses before March 15 are not permitted to employ pure winner-take-all rules (with the exception of the four designated early states).

5. Top Democratic elected officials and members of the Democratic National Committee hold automatic seats as delegates to the national convention by virtue of their leadership positions within the party, and are free to support any candidate regardless of the outcome of the primary or caucus in their home state. These "superdelegates" constituted 15 percent of all Democratic delegates in 2016. Beginning in 2020, superdelegates will not have the power to participate in the initial round of balloting at the Democratic convention if their votes could mathematically decide the outcome, though they will be able to vote in subsequent rounds if no single candidate receives a majority on the first ballot.[3]

These rules are central to the presidential nomination system; they shape the strategies adopted by candidates. Since the party reforms of the early 1970s, the most important attribute of the nomination process is that candidates compete in state contests—primaries and caucuses—in which delegates are selected by large popular electorates. The rules of delegate selection and fund-raising require candidates to obtain a broad base of popular support both within states (for delegates) and across states (for money). These considerations encourage candidates to act as early as possible to form campaign organizations and solicit support from party leaders, financial donors, and activists. While the Iowa caucus and

New Hampshire primary ostensibly mark the beginning of the electoral calendar, serious competition among candidates actually emerges many months before the voters start to select pledged delegates to the national conventions.

BEFORE THE VOTING BEGINS: THE "INVISIBLE PRIMARY"

The more people you have to convince, the more time it takes. The nomination process is very long, and early starters gain an advantage. Candidates must also raise a great deal of money from donors in order to purchase advertising and build strong campaign organizations. This, too, dictates an early start to the campaign. Anybody who is already familiar to the American public—whether an incumbent of high office or a well-known celebrity—enjoys an initial head start due to widespread name recognition, but most candidates must embark on energetic promotional efforts in order to introduce themselves to voters beyond their home states who may not have previously heard of them. In December 2006, shortly before Senator Barack Obama of Illinois announced that he would seek the presidency in 2008, only 53 percent of Americans surveyed by Gallup knew enough about Obama to express an opinion of him; this figure had increased to 87 percent by the end of 2007, reflecting the publicity received by Obama's presidential campaign over the intervening year.[4]

Among the axioms of existing conventional wisdom to bite the dust in 1972, the first post-reform election, was the notion that an early declaration of candidacy was a sign of weakness and that it therefore behooved potential contenders to postpone jumping into the race as long as they possibly could. Such coyness ultimately destroyed the chances of the initial Democratic front-runner in 1972, Senator Ed Muskie of Maine, who took too long to organize an effective campaign. This lesson was greatly reinforced in 1976 when former governor Jimmy Carter of Georgia, a virtually unknown outsider before the primaries began, parlayed narrow wins in the early states of Iowa and New Hampshire into the Democratic nomination—and, from there, the presidency.

Candidates now recognize that there is a benefit to forming their campaigns as soon as possible in order to hire capable staff, build an organizational infrastructure, raise money, attract attention from journalists, and seek support from other politicians and party activists. They hope that if they make a big splash when they enter the race, potential opponents testing the waters might be intimidated enough not to jump in themselves. As a result, unofficial signals of likely candidacies in the next election now routinely emerge during the first year of a new presidential term, with formal campaign announcements usually occurring in the first six months of the calendar year before the election.

In 2012, Barack Obama's incumbency and popularity among Democratic voters ensured that only the Republican Party would have a competitive nomination contest. Eventual nominee Mitt Romney, a former governor of Massachusetts who had previously run for the 2008 Republican nomination, formally announced his second presidential campaign on June 2, 2011, although the news was rendered somewhat anticlimactic by the fact that Romney had been behaving like a candidate in all but name—traveling to Iowa and New Hampshire, campaigning and raising money for Republican congressional and gubernatorial candidates, and releasing a book entitled *No Apology* that was highly critical of Obama's performance as president—for more than a year by the time he officially launched his 2012 campaign. In fact, Romney had barely left the campaign trail since his withdrawal from the 2008 nomination contest three years before.

At the time of his official entry, Romney joined former House speaker Newt Gingrich of Georgia, Representative Ron Paul of Texas, former governors Tim Pawlenty of Minnesota and Gary Johnson of New Mexico, and Georgia businessman Herman Cain as declared candidates for the 2012 Republican nomination. Within a few weeks, the field expanded further to include former senator Rick Santorum of Pennsylvania, former governor Jon Huntsman of Utah, and Representative Michele Bachmann of Minnesota. Governor Rick Perry of Texas was a late entrant into the race, deliberating for months before formally announcing his candidacy on August 13, 2011, but Perry's comparative delay in building a presidential campaign may have contributed to his ultimate lack of success in debating his rivals, constructing a strong field organization, and winning support from voters in early states. As Perry's chief strategist Dave Carney admitted in retrospect: "I think there are hundreds of things that we could have done differently that would [have made Perry] better prepared to run. When you have never talked to legislators and county chairmen and political activists in the early states, when you are doing that days before getting in the race, and raising money and getting up to speed on issues, clearly that's not ideal. . . . We should have, if he was going to do this, started years ago."[5]

With Obama constitutionally prohibited from seeking a third term in 2016, multiple contenders jumped into the presidential race in both parties. The first official Republican candidate was Texas senator Ted Cruz, who formally entered the nomination contest on March 23, 2015, immediately setting off a succession of other public announcements from Kentucky senator Rand Paul (April 7), Florida senator Marco Rubio (April 13), retired surgeon and conservative activist Ben Carson (May 4), former Hewlett-Packard CEO Carly Fiorina (May 4), former Arkansas governor Mike Huckabee (May 5), former Pennsylvania senator and 2012 candidate Rick Santorum (May 27), former New York governor George Pataki (May 28), South Carolina senator Lindsey Graham (June 1), former Texas governor and 2012 candidate Rick Perry (June 4), former Florida governor Jeb Bush (June 15), real estate developer and television host Donald Trump (June 16), former Louisiana governor Bobby Jindal (June 24), New Jersey governor Chris Christie (June 30), Wisconsin governor Scott Walker (July 13), Ohio governor John Kasich (July 21), and former Virginia governor Jim Gilmore (July 30).

On the Democratic side, former first lady, New York senator, U.S. secretary of state, and 2008 presidential candidate Hillary Clinton officially entered the race on April 12, 2015, though Clinton had been making preparations to mount a second bid for the White House ever since she left Obama's cabinet more than two years before. On April 30, she was joined by Vermont senator Bernie Sanders, followed by former Maryland governor Martin O'Malley on May 31, former Rhode Island governor and senator Lincoln Chafee on June 3, and former Virginia senator Jim Webb on July 7. The fact that the 2016 presidential campaign was well underway by the early summer of 2015 is demonstrated by the $130 million in funds already raised by candidates in both parties as of June 30 (see table 4.1).

The 2020 presidential campaign proceeded on an even more accelerated schedule. When former vice president Joe Biden officially joined the race for the

Table 4.1 Early Money in the 2016 Election

Democrats		Republicans	
Hillary Clinton	47.5	Ted Cruz	14.3
Bernie Sanders	15.2	Jeb Bush	11.4
Martin O'Malley	2.0	Ben Carson	10.6
Others	0.5	Marco Rubio	9.8
		Rand Paul	6.9
		Lindsey Graham	3.7
		Mike Huckabee	2.0
		Donald Trump	1.9
		Carly Fiorina	1.7
		Rick Perry	1.1
		Others	2.0
TOTAL	65.2	TOTAL	63.5

Source: Federal Election Commission, "Presidential Pre-Nomination Receipts Through June 30, 2015," https://transition.fec.gov/press/summaries/2016/tables/presidential/PresCand1_2015_6m.pdf; Donald J. Trump for President Inc. quarterly report, June 30, 2015, http://docquery.fec.gov/cgi-bin/forms/C00580100/1015464.

Note: Figures represent funds raised between January 1 and June 30, 2015, in millions of dollars.

Democratic nomination on April 25, 2019, he became a relative latecomer to a field of about 20 active contenders. Six sitting senators (Kirsten Gillibrand of New York, Kamala Harris of California, Cory Booker of New Jersey, Elizabeth Warren of Massachusetts, Amy Klobuchar of Minnesota, and Bernie Sanders of Vermont) had already announced their candidacies during a single five-week stretch between January 15 and February 19, 2019. At the time of Biden's entry, the crowded Democratic race also included six current or former members of the House of Representatives, two current or former state governors, two city mayors, and one former Cabinet official, with even more prospective candidates signaling that they, too, were likely to jump in very soon. While he was not widely considered vulnerable to a serious challenge for renomination, President Trump had also by that point attracted a Republican primary opponent in the person of former Massachusetts governor Bill Weld, who announced his candidacy on April 15.

During the long pre-primary phase, the candidates are not just raising money and hiring campaign staff. They also take the ideological temperature of their party, attempting to shape a message that will appeal to the loyal partisans who turn out to vote in state primaries and caucuses. Knowing that most of the voters in Republican primaries are philosophically right of center, leading Republicans competed with each other in 2015 and 2016 to stake out conservative positions on issues of concern to party voters. Ted Cruz took credit for leading opposition to the Obama administration's health care policies on the floor of the Senate, Marco Rubio advocated a prohibition on legal abortion without exceptions, and Donald Trump outflanked his Republican rivals on his own signature issue of immigration by promising to build a wall along the nation's southern border and force the Mexican government to pay for it. The surprising success of Bernie Sanders's left-wing challenge likewise pushed Democratic front-runner Hillary

Clinton to publicly oppose ratification of the Trans-Pacific Partnership negotiated by the Obama administration, which she had previously touted as "set[ting] the gold standard in trade agreements." Several candidates for the 2020 Democratic nomination courted liberal activists in their party during the early months of the race by endorsing proposals for universal Medicare and a "Green New Deal" intended to combat economic inequality and climate change.

Another candidate objective during the early stage of the campaign is to achieve the status of being appraised by the news media as a "serious" contender. This ordinarily requires that a candidate should have previously won at least one major election for public office and raised a competitive amount of campaign cash. In addition, journalists pay attention to signs that candidates are hiring experienced, competent staff (campaign managers, strategists and spokespeople, fund-raisers, pollsters, media consultants, speechwriters, policy analysts) and are establishing organized field campaigns in early primary states, maintaining a high level of public activity, and doing respectably in public opinion surveys—polls that everyone says "don't count," although of course they do. All this activity is monitored by members of the increasingly watchful news media, who in turn pronounce candidates to be "serious" or "not serious," with attendant consequences for the candidate's credibility with financial donors, activists, and voters.

Although objective measures of the relative standing of the candidates are scarce during the pre-primary period, the political press is constantly preoccupied with the status of the horse race—who's ahead, who's behind, who's gaining or losing support. The federal requirement that presidential candidates regularly report their fund-raising and spending totals provides one well-publicized yardstick of candidate success. Barack Obama's capacity to represent a significant challenge to Hillary Clinton for the 2008 Democratic nomination was first revealed in April 2007 with the public release of the candidates' quarterly fund-raising figures. Despite being a relative newcomer to national politics with only a little more than two years of experience in the U.S. Senate, Obama raised $25 million in contributions during the first quarter of 2007, nearly as much as Clinton, and proceeded to outraise her over the next three months, much of it from small donations via the Internet. According to media commentators, Obama's unexpected financial success soon established him as Clinton's chief rival within the party, while other candidates who were less adept at attracting donations became relegated to second-tier status.

Public endorsements by prominent party leaders such as state governors, members of Congress, and other well-known officials can also serve as an indicator of the health of a presidential campaign. In 1999, George W. Bush, then the governor of Texas, succeeded in winning the support of all of his fellow Republican governors before the voting in Iowa even began—a formidable achievement that may have dissuaded other potential candidates from jumping in the race. Eventual Democratic nominees John Kerry in 2004 and Barack Obama in 2008 benefited from the personal backing of the late Massachusetts senator Ted Kennedy, the youngest brother of John F. Kennedy and a figure who commanded considerable respect and affection among Democratic Party activists.

But if voters are in the mood for a political outsider, the guidance of veteran politicians may not matter as much to them. Donald Trump captured the Republican presidential nomination in 2016 despite receiving little support—and, in fact, provoking substantial opposition—from the traditional leaders of his party, although Trump's Republican critics failed to mobilize effectively against his nomination by uniting around a single alternative candidate (it helped Trump that his main rival in the race, Ted Cruz, was also held in low esteem by many Republican officeholders). Most top Democratic officials endorsed Hillary Clinton over Bernie Sanders in 2016, but Sanders appealed to voters by portraying himself as fighting a party "establishment" that was, in his view, improperly conspiring to deliver Clinton the nomination. Sanders found more success in gaining the public support of liberal celebrities like actors Mark Ruffalo, Kal Penn, Josh Hutcherson, Susan Sarandon, and Rosario Dawson; filmmakers Spike Lee and Oliver Stone; and musicians Killer Mike, Lil B, Diplo, and Michael Stipe.

Televised debates are another means by which candidates can distinguish themselves in the months before the primaries and caucuses begin.[6] The near ubiquity of cable news channels and Internet video outlets ensures that journalists, party activists, and engaged citizens who are interested in evaluating the candidates' debate performances firsthand now have ample opportunity to do so. Candidates who trail their rivals in name recognition or the money race can take advantage of the national stage provided by these events to attract free positive publicity that gives their campaigns a boost, but front-runners can be damaged—sometimes fatally—by a showing judged to be subpar in the watchful eyes of the news media. Attention-grabbing moments, whether to the benefit or detriment of the candidate, frequently become fodder for cable news replays and viral video clips for days afterward. As Mitt Romney's 2012 campaign manager Matt Rhoades later remarked, "It was just shocking how [the debates] shook up the race week after week and how many people were watching these things."[7]

In 2016, two leading Republican candidates suffered serious political damage from debates. Wisconsin governor Scott Walker was widely considered to be a major presidential contender after his victory in a 2012 recall election made him a national hero to conservative interest group leaders; several polls conducted in the summer of 2015 found Walker leading the Republican field in neighboring Iowa, home to the nation's first presidential caucus. But Walker found it difficult to stand out on the debate stage among a large field of candidates; after two unmemorable performances, his fund-raising efforts dried up, forcing him out of the race in September—only two months after he had jumped in. "Scott, for whatever reason, didn't connect on TV," observed one of Walker's top financial backers. "And if you can't make it on television today in national politics, you're dead."[8]

Florida senator Marco Rubio became another victim of debate-related misfortune in 2016. Rubio's third-place finish in the Iowa caucus won him positive media coverage heading into the New Hampshire primary the following week, where he was hoping to consolidate support from Republican voters who preferred a nominee other than Ted Cruz or Donald Trump, the top two finishers in Iowa. But New Jersey governor Chris Christie, desperately hoping to salvage his own presidential candidacy after a poor Iowa performance, used a debate held three days before the New Hampshire vote to launch sharp attacks on Rubio's qualifications for the office. In response to Christie's taunts, Rubio oddly repeated the same phrase—referring to "the fiction that Barack Obama doesn't know what he's doing"—four separate times, giving Christie the opportunity to claim vindication ("There it is, everybody!") for his previous assertions that Rubio could only offer the audience a "memorized 25-second speech that is exactly what his advisers gave him."[9] As cable news broadcasts, late-night comedy programs, and social media outlets seized on the "Rubio the Robot" moment, replaying it endlessly to general bafflement, Rubio's climb in the New Hampshire polls stalled. He finished fifth in the state, severely damaging his chances of winning the nomination.

The lessons of the pre-primary stage in the contemporary nomination process are clear: long before the voting begins, candidates must work to achieve personal visibility, raise money, and assemble strong campaign organizations. Visibility is important because news media coverage introduces candidates to the voters and shapes popular perceptions of the various contenders. Money is important because it buys advertising and campaign infrastructure that communicates the candidate's message to the public. Organization is important because it turns out supporters to vote in elections. A large field of candidates normally begins the election season with presidential ambitions, making the nomination system a winnowing process in which the successive hurdles of primaries and caucuses knock off more and more contenders until only one survivor remains in each party. In advance of these events, the candidates' tasks are to build financial war chests, hire talented campaign staff, command as much positive publicity as they can, and give personal attention to states voting early in the nomination calendar.

Pre-primary activities thus take up extensive time and resources in preparation for the primaries and caucuses that select delegates to the national conventions. The nomination campaign is in full swing long before the first state elections, as candidates battle each other for notice from journalists and support from party officials, interest groups, and financial contributors. This period has been dubbed the "invisible primary" in recognition of the fact that fierce competition among candidates begins well before the voting starts, profoundly shaping the choices made by voters once they enter the process.[10]

IOWA AND NEW HAMPSHIRE: FIRST IN THE NATION

Due to various accidents of history, the states of Iowa and New Hampshire have achieved what appears to be a perpetual right to hold the first two electoral events of the presidential nomination season every four years. Iowa, which selects its delegates through a series of broadly participatory local, county, and state caucuses and conventions, always votes first, early in the calendar year of a presidential election. And New Hampshire, site of the first primary election, comes next—usually about a week after the Iowa vote.[11]

The Iowa caucus is only the first stage of a delegate selection process that culminates at state party conventions several months later. Although it is the initial precinct meetings that attract media attention, candidates who do not win the caucus frequently end up with delegates from Iowa to the national convention because the field of active candidates has usually narrowed considerably by the time of the state-level conventions. Given the complicated relationship between the caucus results and the ultimate composition of Iowa's national convention delegation, it is a wonder that there is so much attention paid to the caucus. The news coverage is heavy because the voting in Iowa and New Hampshire is the gateway to a long and complex nomination process, and participants and observers very much want whatever information they can glean from the results in the first two states, if only to position themselves for the next round of events. The media need to know to whom to give special attention. Financial supporters of various candidates want to know whether it is worthwhile to continue to give or steer money to their first choices, or whether it is time to jump to other alternatives. Voters want to know which candidacies are viable, which futile.[12]

Thus the outcomes in Iowa and New Hampshire exert a massive influence on the election results in subsequent primaries and caucuses. Over and over, these two small and not entirely representative states have demonstrated the power to set some candidates on a path to the White House while forcing others to permanently abandon their presidential dreams. The following historical examples, drawn from the past five decades of post-reform nomination politics, illustrate the repeated capacity of voters in Iowa and New Hampshire to shape the electoral choices of the entire nation.

1972

In 1972 the Republican incumbent, Richard Nixon, faced only token opposition. The Democratic caucus in Iowa, in contrast, was quite important. Operating under obsolete strategic premises, presumed party favorite Senator Ed Muskie of Maine officially entered the race just three weeks before the Iowa vote. Neither Muskie nor Senator George McGovern of South Dakota, an insurgent candidate running on a left-wing and antiwar platform, invested much effort in Iowa. Muskie defeated McGovern in the caucus by a margin of 36 percent to 23 percent, with another 36 percent of Iowa Democrats remaining uncommitted to any candidate.

The surprising closeness of this result pushed Muskie into overwork and an unaccustomed public display of emotional behavior in front of the offices of the *Union Leader* newspaper in Manchester, New Hampshire.[13] When the news media analysts were finished interpreting the results of the New Hampshire primary, prior expectations that the U.S. senator from a neighboring state would win an overwhelming victory of over 50 percent completely obscured the fact that Muskie had in fact placed first once again (46 percent to 37 percent). Because his win was 4 or 5 points less impressive than expected, thereby supposedly revealing his weakness as a candidate, Muskie's support, especially financial support, began to dry up, and he withdrew from the race altogether by April 27, leaving the nomination to McGovern. The front-running Muskie campaign was nibbled to death by ducks before it had a chance to get into gear, and McGovern marched to victory despite little enthusiasm for his campaign among Democratic Party leaders. This shocking turn of events demonstrated the newfound power of the Iowa and New Hampshire results to determine presidential nominations in the post-reform era.

1976

In 1976, incumbent president Gerald Ford, who had succeeded to the office upon the resignation of Richard Nixon in 1974, faced a serious challenge for the Republican nomination from former California governor Ronald Reagan. Ford won the official Iowa straw poll on the night of the caucus, but by only a small margin (45 percent to 43 percent); both candidates ended up with 18 delegates to the national convention. Ford's subsequent victory in New Hampshire made him the front-runner for the nomination, although Reagan rallied later in the year.[14]

On the Democratic side, the candidate who focused hardest on Iowa was former governor Jimmy Carter of Georgia. Hamilton Jordan, Carter's campaign manager, put together a strategy that was exactly three events deep, requiring strong showings in Iowa and New Hampshire, followed by a careful positioning as the anti–George Wallace (i.e., racially liberal) Southern candidate in the Florida primary.[15] Though he was initially a virtual unknown outside Georgia, Carter's strategy dovetailed nicely with those of his main competitors, Senator Henry (Scoop) Jackson of Washington, who suffered from a late start, and Representative Mo Udall of Arizona, who ran a disorganized campaign. Although he finished as high as second in seven primaries in 1976, Udall came in fifth in Iowa with 6 percent of the vote, behind "uncommitted" with 37 percent of the caucus vote and Carter with 28 percent.

The next day, *New York Times* reporter R. W. Apple Jr. minimized the strong uncommitted sentiment and spun the Iowa results as a major triumph for Carter, writing that the candidate "scored an impressive victory in yesterday's Iowa Democratic precinct caucuses, demonstrating strength among rural, blue-collar, black, and suburban voters."[16] This story and other friendly coverage in the press set the stage for New Hampshire, where Carter, positioning himself as an ideological moderate in relation to his Democratic opponents, received 28 percent of the vote, good enough for a first-place finish in a large field of contenders. Despite starting the 1976 campaign with little support (or even name recognition), and despite receiving less than 30 percent of the vote in both states, Carter's victories in Iowa and New Hampshire made him the instant leader in the Democratic race, thanks in large part to the extensive media attention that he received in their wake, and he was able to ride this good fortune through the primary season to capture the nomination.

1992

A senator from Iowa, Tom Harkin, ran for president in 1992, and the other Democratic candidates quickly declared the Iowa caucus irrelevant due to the expectation that Harkin would win overwhelmingly in his home state—a judgment reporters accepted. The focus of press coverage leading up to the New Hampshire primary, then, was not the events in Iowa, but instead the problems of the presumed Democratic front-runner, Governor Bill Clinton of Arkansas. Clinton and his wife Hillary had appeared on the CBS news program *60 Minutes* immediately following the Super Bowl in January to respond to rumors of his marital infidelity, and in early February questions regarding the governor's exemption from military service during the Vietnam War made newspaper headlines around the nation. Once the leader in polls of likely New Hampshire voters, Clinton lost his advantage to former Massachusetts senator Paul Tsongas by the week before the primary, and many journalists, mindful of the adultery scandal that befell former Colorado senator Gary Hart in 1987, began to suggest that Clinton's candidacy might be doomed.[17]

The news media's death watch over the Clinton campaign was suspended when Clinton finished second in New Hampshire, receiving a better-than-expected 25 percent of the vote to Tsongas's 33 percent. Though he didn't actually win the election, an unabashed Clinton delivered what was, in effect, a victory speech on the night of the New Hampshire primary, proclaiming himself "the comeback kid"—a clever strategy that succeeded in convincing the media of his continued viability (the *New York Times* account published the following day referred to Clinton's "resilient candidacy").[18] Because journalists had their own doubts about Tsongas's credibility as a national candidate, and because the rest of the Democratic field (Harkin, Senator Bob Kerrey of Nebraska, and former California governor Jerry Brown) had failed to catch on with New Hampshire voters, Clinton was still treated as a leading contender despite his loss in the primary, and he ultimately won both the Democratic nomination and the presidency later in the year.

On the Republican side, early expectations of a non-contest were jarred when opinion columnist and former White House aide Pat Buchanan, running as a conservative protest candidate, received 38 percent of the New Hampshire vote against incumbent president George H. W. Bush, who was held to 53 percent. Just as Minnesota senator Eugene McCarthy's surprisingly close loss to incumbent president Lyndon Johnson persuaded the press that Johnson was vulnerable in 1968, Buchanan's loss to Bush focused media attention on the nation's economic recession rather than Bush's successes in foreign policy. Though Buchanan's show-ing in New Hampshire was interpreted by journalists as a sign of Bush's unpopu-larity, the incumbent's ability to win renomination was never in doubt; Bush won every primary and took the bulk of delegates from each caucus state.

The aftermath of the 1992 New Hampshire primary once again demonstrated the news media's capacity to affect election outcomes in the primary season by interpreting results in early contests against a backdrop of consensus expectations which candidates are deemed to have exceeded or failed to meet. Had Bill Clinton continued to lead in the polls during the week of the election, journalists would have considered his eight-point loss to Paul Tsongas to be a devastating defeat; the resulting bad publicity might have jeopardized Clinton's candidacy.[19] Instead, the political damage sustained by Clinton before the primary had lowered media expectations for his performance enough that analysts largely adopted the cam-paign's proffered story line of a Clinton "comeback" on election night. Just as the press treated Clinton like a winner in New Hampshire despite his loss in the actual vote, Bush endured a great deal of negative attention even after placing first in the Republican contest, because the willingness of more than a third of New Hampshire Republicans to vote against an incumbent president of their party supposedly demonstrated Bush's political weakness.

2004

The incumbency of George W. Bush precluded a contest on the Republican side in 2004. The Democrats, however, had a lively race. It produced a definitive result in Iowa that held up all the way to the nomination.

By early 2003, many political insiders saw Senator John Kerry of Massachusetts, a decorated Vietnam War veteran, as the initial Democratic front-runner.[20] However, former Vermont governor Howard Dean began to win significant support among Democratic voters during the summer and fall of 2003, thanks to his sharp attacks on the Bush administration and his status as an outsider to Washington, not con-nected with the congressional Democrats who had, according to some liberals, failed to provide effective opposition to Bush's policies. Dean's popular campaign website brought in large numbers of financial donations from citizens across the country, and he began to attract serious attention from journalists, many of whom had initially dismissed him as a second-tier candidate. By mid-January 2004, Dean was leading in polls of Democratic voters in Iowa, New Hampshire, and across the country; had secured the endorsements of the Democrats' previous presidential nominee Al Gore, Gore's 2000 primary opponent Bill Bradley, Iowa senator Tom Harkin, and several major labor unions; and was bringing in over $1 million a week in online campaign contributions. Kerry, meanwhile, had fired his first campaign manager in November 2003 and was forced to loan his campaign over $6 million from his own very deep pocket to keep it operational after several months of unsuccessful fund-raising. Conventional wisdom in Washington said that Dean was the man to beat.[21]

Under these circumstances, Kerry's victory in the Iowa caucus on January 19 shocked most political observers. Two weeks earlier, Adam Nagourney of the *New York Times* had written from Iowa that "not even the biggest boosters of . . . Mr. Kerry are saying [he has] much of a chance of winning the caucuses here."[22] But Kerry finished first with 38 percent of the vote; almost as unexpectedly, Senator John Edwards of North Carolina came in a strong second with 32 percent.[23] Dean, whose third-place Iowa finish (with only 18 percent) fell far short of expectations, suffered an instant transformation from the presumptive favorite in the race to a widespread target of derision and mockery, especially among members of the news media who may have felt embarrassment after having enormously overstated Dean's appeal.[24]

Kerry's surprise win in Iowa had a notable effect on his fortunes in the New Hampshire primary the following week. A poll conducted just before the Iowa caucus showed him running a distant third in New Hampshire, winning just 12 percent (compared to 32 percent for Dean and 23 percent for retired General Wesley Clark).[25] But the massive media publicity generated by the events in Iowa boosted Kerry (from neighboring Massachusetts) into first place while dealing Dean (from neighboring Vermont) a damaging blow. Kerry won the January 27 New Hampshire primary by capturing 39 percent of the vote, with 26 percent for Dean, 13 percent for Clark, and 12 percent for Edwards, solidifying his position as the Democrats' leading candidate. By the end of February, Kerry had virtually wrapped up the nomination, while erstwhile front-runner Dean failed to win a single primary outside of his home state.

2008

For the first time since 1952, 2008 featured nomination contests without an incumbent president or vice president running in either party. That left both races wide open, and a large field of candidates emerged on each side.

New York senator Hillary Clinton began the campaign as the widely acknowledged favorite for the Democratic nomination. Due to her eight years as first lady before entering the Senate, Clinton was well known to Democratic voters and enjoyed support from many veteran party leaders.[26] Clinton advisers initially viewed John Edwards, the Democrats' vice presidential nominee in 2004 who was making a second run for the presidency, as her most serious potential challenger.[27] But Senator Barack Obama of Illinois demonstrated a surprising ability to keep pace with Clinton in fund-raising during 2007, though he continued to trail her throughout the year in public opinion polls and endorsements from elected officials.

Strategists for Obama calculated that their candidate's chances of winning the nomination almost certainly required placing first in the Iowa caucus. A Clinton victory, they predicted, would most likely allow her to sweep the states that followed and quickly force him from the race. As a result, recalled Obama campaign manager David Plouffe, "front and center for all our considerations on spending money and time was: Would it help us win Iowa?"[28] While Edwards also devoted a great deal of attention to Iowa, campaigning energetically across the state for months before the caucuses, Obama boasted both a financial advantage and a far superior campaign organization, spending $9 million on advertising (compared to Clinton's $7 million and Edwards's $3 million) and opening 37 Iowa field offices.[29] Assuming that most party regulars would favor Clinton, Obama's campaign combined innovative technology with traditional grassroots organizing to mobilize Iowans who did not normally participate in the caucus, such as many independents and young people, an approach that the Clinton team initially viewed with a skeptical smirk. "Our people look like caucus-goers," said one Clinton adviser while surveying candidate supporters at the Iowa Democratic Party's annual dinner in November 2007, "and his people look like they are 18 [and on] Facebook," the social networking website used by the Obama campaign as a tool to target the youth vote.[30]

Polls conducted just before the caucus showed a tight three-way race, but Obama ultimately triumphed with 38 percent of the delegate vote, outdistancing Edwards at 30 percent and Clinton a whisker behind at 29 percent. Obama's strategy was vindicated by the record turnout: about 240,000 Iowans participated on the Democratic side, nearly double the 2004 figure and far exceeding the predictions of the campaigns and the press.[31] His better-than-expected showing dominated news media coverage of the caucus—the *New York Times* declared that Obama had "rolled to victory" producing a "significant setback" to Clinton—and vaulted him into strong leads in several opinion surveys conducted in New Hampshire over subsequent days, suggesting a likely repeat performance there the following week.[32]

But Hillary Clinton defied the polls to claim a narrow victory in the New Hampshire primary, winning 39 percent of the vote to 37 percent for Obama and 17 percent for Edwards. On the day before the election, Clinton had uncharacteristically displayed open emotion at a campaign appearance in a Portsmouth coffee shop; with an audible catch in her voice, she told a voter that "this is very personal for me. . . . Some of us put ourselves out there and [campaign] against some difficult odds." Footage of the incident had led the nightly news broadcasts of all three major television networks on the eve of the primary, and advisers to both Clinton and Obama believed in retrospect that the sympathy it inspired among the electorate contributed to her surprise victory.[33] The split decision between Iowa and New Hampshire set the stage for a protracted battle for delegates between Obama and Clinton that did not conclude until early June, representing the longest contested race for the Democratic nomination since 1972.

The Republican nomination race ran truer to the usual pattern, with a clear front-runner emerging in New Hampshire and virtually locking up the nomination by the following month. Senator John McCain of Arizona, the eventual nominee, began the pre-primary phase as one of the strongest potential contenders according to the news media (due to his second-place finish in the last contested

Republican nomination race eight years before), but soon suffered from lackluster fund-raising efforts and a debilitating series of shakeups among top campaign staff; as one adviser later recalled, "in July 2007 the McCain campaign was dead as dead as dead can be . . . the press kept [asking], 'When's he going to quit?'"[34] However, McCain's opponents had problems of their own. Former New York mayor Rudy Giuliani, though he initially led in most national polls due to high name recognition, took liberal positions on social issues that limited his appeal among Republican primary voters. Mitt Romney, former governor of Massachusetts, had abundant funds but faced skepticism from conservative Protestants over his Mormon faith and previous support for legalized abortion. Mike Huckabee, former governor of Arkansas and a Baptist minister, proved to be an impressive speaker and debater but found difficulty in expanding his appeal beyond his evangelical base in the South and rural Midwest. Former Tennessee senator and Hollywood actor Fred Thompson entered the race in the fall of 2007 to some fanfare but failed to ignite much voter interest in his campaign.

As he had done in 2000, McCain gave limited attention to the Iowa caucus in order to focus on the more favorable terrain of New Hampshire. After some active campaigning in Iowa, Giuliani followed suit, ultimately pulling out of New Hampshire as well in order to make a last stand in the Florida primary later in the month. This left Romney with an opportunity to place first in Iowa and coast on the resulting publicity to a second victory the following week in New Hampshire, where he was well-positioned as the former governor of a neighboring state.

Unfortunately for Romney's strategy, Huckabee upended him in the caucus straw poll by a solid nine-point margin (34 percent to 25 percent). Huckabee had little ability to capitalize on this success—the born-again Christians who served as his strongest supporters were not well-represented in the New Hampshire electorate—but Romney's loss in Iowa proved sufficiently damaging to his candidacy that New Hampshire was left open to capture by McCain, who received 37 percent of the vote there to 32 percent for Romney and 11 percent for Huckabee. Though he had a smaller campaign war chest than those of Romney and Giuliani, McCain benefited from positive media coverage in the wake of his New Hampshire victory, as well as a devoted base of popular support among fellow military veterans. He placed first by narrow margins in the crucial ensuing primaries in South Carolina (defeating Huckabee by 33 to 30 percent) and Florida (besting Romney by 36 to 31 percent), setting the stage for victories on February 5 in the large states of California, New York, Illinois, New Jersey, Missouri, and his home state of Arizona that gave him a near-insurmountable lead in the pledged delegate count.

2012

With no contest in the Democratic Party in 2012 as Barack Obama ran unopposed for renomination, public attention focused instead on the field of potential Republican challengers to the sitting president. Mitt Romney's second-place finish in the 2008 primaries had provided him with valuable name recognition and campaign experience; though some Republicans were not enthusiastically committed to another Romney candidacy, opposition to the former Massachusetts governor failed to coalesce behind a single rival. Governor Rick Perry of Texas, former House speaker Newt Gingrich, former senator Rick Santorum of Pennsylvania, and even ex–Godfather's Pizza CEO Herman Cain each experienced brief periods of forward momentum in national polls during the months before the Iowa caucus, but none of these alternatives succeeded in achieving a sustained surge in popular support among Republican leaders, activists, or voters. (Cain did not even last long enough to compete in Iowa, withdrawing from the race due to scandal before the end of 2011.)

Despite his sizable fund-raising advantage and organizational strength, Romney faced a tough battle in Iowa. The large share of evangelical Christians within the population of Republican caucus-goers rendered the state challenging terrain for his candidacy, as had been demonstrated by his loss there to the underfunded Mike Huckabee four years before. In the end, Romney finished in a dead heat with Santorum atop the Iowa vote with 25 percent apiece (a protracted recount ultimately found that Santorum had edged Romney by a margin of just 34 votes statewide). Representative Ron Paul of Texas placed third with 21 percent, followed by Gingrich at 13 percent, Perry at 10 percent, Representative Michele Bachmann of Minnesota at 5 percent, and former governor Jon Huntsman of Utah at 1 percent.

While Romney may have been temporarily humbled by narrowly losing to a rival whom he had heavily outspent (by a roughly 7-to-1 margin in Iowa, counting Super PAC expenditures on both sides), the results were not particularly unfavorable in a political sense for the former Massachusetts governor.[35] Like Huckabee before him, Santorum derived most of his popular support from strong social conservatives, who constitute a much smaller proportion of the Republican vote in New Hampshire than they do in Iowa. By denying a positive outcome to Gingrich and by severely damaging Perry's candidacy, the Iowa results failed to dislodge Romney from his position as the clear favorite in the race. He scored an easy win in the New Hampshire primary the following week (taking 39 percent of the total vote, as compared to 23 percent for Paul, 17 percent for Huntsman, 9 percent each for Santorum and Gingrich, and 1 percent for Perry), placing him firmly in the lead for the Republican nomination. Though Gingrich's subsequent victory in the South Carolina primary and Santorum's success in several later state elections kept the race unresolved until March, Romney retained his front-runner status throughout the rest of the primaries and ultimately captured the nomination with relative ease.

2016

Hillary Clinton was universally expected to mount another run for the presidency after departing the Obama administration, where she had served as its first secretary of state, in early 2013. After Vice President Joe Biden confirmed in the fall of 2015 that he would not seek to immediately succeed Obama, Clinton appeared to have a wide-open path to becoming the first female major-party presidential nominee in American history—a goal that had narrowly eluded her eight years before. Secondary candidates Martin O'Malley, Lincoln Chafee, and Jim Webb failed to catch on with voters (Chafee and Webb dropped out of the race before the Iowa caucus was even held; O'Malley folded his campaign on the night of the Iowa vote), leaving Senator Bernie Sanders of Vermont, a self-described democratic socialist who was officially a political independent, as the only significant alternative contender in the Democratic race.

Most analysts initially assumed, with some justification, that Sanders was running as a "message candidate" seeking to gain publicity for his views (and influence over the party platform) rather than as a serious rival to Clinton for the Democratic nomination. But Sanders proved unexpectedly successful at online fund-raising despite little support from the traditional network of Democratic financial donors, and his idealistic outsider persona appealed to fellow independents, young voters, and left-wing activists. Sanders began to gain ground in polls of Iowa Democrats during the final weeks before the caucus; Clinton, once the clear favorite in Iowa, ultimately prevailed in the state's delegate count by a slender margin of 49.8 percent to 49.6 percent. Sanders attracted much more positive press coverage from narrowly losing Iowa than Clinton received from narrowly winning it, giving him a further boost in the following week's primary election in New Hampshire, already a friendly neighboring state to his own Vermont. While he had established a consistent lead in New Hampshire polls prior to the Iowa vote, Sanders exceeded most news media expectations by winning the state in an outright landslide over Clinton, 60 percent to 38 percent.

Clinton soon righted her campaign once the nomination race moved to more favorable territory elsewhere in the nation; her strong advantage over Sanders among African Americans proved to be a critical asset in South Carolina, where she received 73 percent of the vote, and other southern states. However, the Iowa and New Hampshire results had revealed a limited enthusiasm for Clinton in some quarters of the Democratic Party, and Sanders's strong performance in both states helped fuel a well-funded campaign that lasted until the final set of state primaries in June. Clinton remained a heavy favorite throughout the spring to win the necessary majority of delegates to capture the nomination. But the contentious tone of the race, Sanders's increasingly pointed accusations that the Democratic National Committee had improperly "rigged" the nomination process to his disadvantage, and his belated, grudging endorsement of her general election candidacy shortly before the national convention in July all complicated the presumptive nominee's efforts to unify her party and energize its voters for the fall campaign.

While the Democratic contest in 2016 produced a few surprises en route to a widely anticipated final outcome, the Republican race resulted in the biggest upset in presidential nomination politics since Jimmy Carter emerged from national obscurity 40 years before. Real estate developer and reality television star Donald Trump, who had previously flirted with presidential candidacies in 2000 and 2012, jumped into the Republican race in the summer of 2015 to widespread astonishment and fascination. Trump's presence scrambled the strategies of the other candidates in an unusually large field that included four sitting senators (Ted Cruz of Texas, Marco Rubio of Florida, Rand Paul of Kentucky, and Lindsey Graham of South Carolina), four incumbent governors (John Kasich of Ohio, Chris Christie of New Jersey, Scott Walker of Wisconsin, and Bobby Jindal of Louisiana), plus eight other candidates led by Jeb Bush of Florida, who was both the former governor of the nation's largest swing state and the son and brother of the previous two Republican presidents.

Trump soon seized the top position in national surveys of Republican voters as a result of strong name recognition, his reputation as an outspoken critic of

Barack Obama's presidency, and a populist message that focused on restricting immigration. Despite his lead in the polls, Trump's unprecedented background, uniquely divisive behavior, and shoestring campaign organization prevented him from being universally acknowledged as the favorite in the race. But the fact that Trump was not taken seriously at first as a potential nominee may have helped him in the long run. Rather than train their attacks on Trump, most of the other candidates jostled among themselves to become the leading alternative choice while betting that the politically inexperienced and risk-taking newcomer would likely fade or implode on his own. Cruz concentrated on courting evangelical Christian activists; Kasich pursued pragmatic suburbanites; and Rubio, Bush, and Christie presented themselves as business-friendly party regulars. Meanwhile, Trump dominated the race by continuously commanding media attention, confounding his opponents by aggressively jabbing at them in debates and on Twitter—even dismissing them with demeaning nicknames ("Low-Energy Jeb" for Bush; "Lyin' Ted" for Cruz; "Little Marco" for Rubio).

The Iowa Republican caucus had proven to be friendly ground for candidates identified with the religious right, such as Mike Huckabee in 2008 and Rick Santorum in 2012. It maintained this tendency in 2016, giving Cruz a first-place finish with 28 percent of the vote. But Trump placed a strong second with 24 percent, followed by Rubio in a close third at 23 percent. Despite his ample funds and family pedigree, Bush finished in a distant sixth place with just 3 percent, severely damaging his campaign; Kasich and Christie ended the night even further behind.

According to the most widespread media interpretation of these results, a rough three-way race emerged from Iowa, with Rubio successfully establishing himself as the most viable alternative for mainstream Republicans who disliked both Cruz's brand of conservative purism and Trump's various idiosyncrasies. Despite placing third, Rubio received a great deal of positive press coverage in the wake of the Iowa vote, and he began to gain in the polls heading into the following week's primary in New Hampshire.[36] But his weak debate performance in the face of direct attacks from Christie (who viewed Rubio as a mortal threat to his own ebbing chances) stalled his momentum, and Kasich's energetic courting of New Hampshire's significant bloc of moderate Republicans dissuaded voters who were skeptical of both Trump and Cruz from coalescing as expected behind Rubio's candidacy.

Trump won easily in New Hampshire with 35 percent of the total vote, confirming that a campaign initially dismissed by critics as a novelty or publicity stunt had become a legitimate presidential contender. New Hampshire voters strengthened Trump's position in the larger national race not only by giving him a 19-point margin of victory, but also by dealing weak showings to candidates who might have otherwise posed serious threats to him in future contests. Bush finished fourth with 11.1 percent, signaling a fatally wounded campaign. Rubio finished fifth with 10.6 percent, disappointing supporters who had hoped for an upward trajectory after Iowa. And Christie, placing sixth with 7 percent, was driven immediately from the race. Kasich and Cruz, the second- and third-place finishers, survived to challenge Trump in subsequent primaries and caucuses, but both struggled to expand their popular appeal beyond the center and right ideological edges of the party, respectively—and a divided opposition merely frustrated the efforts of anti-Trump Republicans (like 2012 presidential nominee Mitt Romney, who gave a well-publicized speech in early March blasting Trump as a "fake" and a "con man") to unite behind a single alternative. Trump solidified his once-shocking position as the favorite for the nomination with victories in seven state primaries on March 1, wrapping up the race by the beginning of May.

WHAT DO THESE HISTORICAL VIGNETTES TEACH?

1. Candidates ignore Iowa and New Hampshire at their peril. This does not mean that losing Iowa and New Hampshire is sufficient to lose the nomination or that doing well is sufficient to win. It does mean that the results in both states can be a tremendous help or, more likely, a significant hindrance to every campaign.

2. This is so not because of their size or number of delegates but because of their temporal primacy: Iowa results, plus media spin, influence the results of the New Hampshire primary. These two events together, plus more media spin, shape the race as it proceeds to the remaining 48 states.

3. While winning either Iowa or New Hampshire does not ensure nomination, losing badly in both states effectively extinguishes a candidacy. Since the modern nomination system was implemented in 1972, only one eventual nominee has ever finished below third place in either Iowa or New Hampshire (John McCain in 2008, who did not campaign extensively in Iowa—in order to focus on New Hampshire—and finished fourth by less than 500 votes).[37] Over the same period, every nominee in both parties has won at least one of the first two states except for George McGovern in 1972 and Bill Clinton in 1992, whose second-place finishes were both treated like victories by the news media. With few exceptions, candidates have learned these lessons and responded by focusing intensively on Iowa and New Hampshire for months before the voting begins, knowing that they need at least one strong performance to remain plausible contenders for the nomination.

4. Political pundits tend to identify a single candidate in each party as the front-runner prior to the elections in Iowa and New Hampshire, based principally on candidates' relative fund-raising totals, positions in national polls of potential primary voters, and public support from party leaders and elected officials. Status as the widely proclaimed leading contender, however, raises expectations for that candidate's performance in the early states; as a result, receiving a lower-than-predicted share of the vote can produce substantial negative publicity. While the "invisible primary" period plays a critical role in structuring the nomination contest before the voting begins, the victories of John Kerry (on the Democratic side in 2004), Barack Obama (on the Democratic side in 2008), and John McCain (on the Republican side in 2008) over rivals who were more heavily favored going into the primary season illustrate the capacity of voters in Iowa and New Hampshire to fundamentally reorder the existing race once they make their preferences known.

STATE PRIMARIES

Candidates for presidential nominations now routinely hit the campaign trail nearly a full year before the first votes are cast. Once the events in Iowa and New Hampshire have passed, however, elections in other states follow quickly in subsequent weeks, rapidly narrowing the field to a single remaining candidate in each party. Only in rare cases does the race remain undecided for long. Each state and U.S. territory holds a primary or caucus during the winter or spring of a presidential election year in order to select that state's delegates to the national party conventions.

The national parties impose rules on this process, specifying the number of delegates allotted to each state, the time frame within which the delegates must be selected, the formulas by which candidates may be awarded delegates pledged to support them at the convention based on their relative standing with the voters, and so on. However, individual states maintain some flexibility, such as the decision whether to hold a presidential primary administered by the state government or opt for a caucus organized by the state parties. More than two-thirds of the states, selecting the bulk of the delegates in both parties, currently hold primary elections.

A more important decision than the choice between primaries and caucuses, however, is the date on which a state's elections occur. As reliably keen observers of the dynamics of presidential nominations, state politicians and party officials across the nation have largely—and correctly—concluded that states voting early in the primary season exert far more influence over the outcome than those scheduled near the end of the process, when one candidate has usually wrapped up the nomination. Over time, states have moved their presidential primaries further ahead in the calendar, hoping to have a greater say in the determination of the party nominees and therefore receive more attention from candidates—a phenomenon known as "front-loading."

In 1976, Democratic presidential primaries were spread out over a relatively long period: after New Hampshire on February 24, only five states held primaries in March, and only two held primaries in April. Twelve primaries were held more than three months after the New Hampshire primary, including contests on June 8 in the populous states of California, New Jersey, and Ohio.[38] This schedule certainly granted greater importance to early primaries because winning in February and March helped candidates receive attention and raise money for the later events. This meant that early and vigorous participation in primaries was already the only strategy available to serious presidential aspirants. Nevertheless, many of the actual delegates were selected late in the process.

As state leaders began to understand the importance of the early contests, more states moved their primaries or caucuses earlier and earlier in the spring, hoping to gain additional influence over the nominations. The 1988 election introduced the phenomenon of "Super Tuesday," when a number of states scheduled primaries on the same day near the beginning of the nomination calendar. While Super Tuesday in 1988 was principally the result of coordinated efforts among Democratic leaders in the South to increase their region's voice in the presidential nomination contest, in subsequent elections it has simply represented the collective consequence of individual states' attempts to maximize attention and clout by holding primaries or caucuses in the first week permitted by the national parties (not including the special recognition given to the four early states of Iowa, New Hampshire, Nevada, and South Carolina). As table 4.2 reveals, by 1992 state contests in both parties, but especially on the Democratic side, had

Table 4.2 The Front-Loading of the Presidential Primary Calendar, 1992–2016

	Jan.	Feb. 1–15	Feb. 16–29	March 1–15	March 16–31	April	May	June/ July
DEMOCRATS								
1992								
States	0	1	3	22	5	6	8	6
Pct Delegates	0.0	1.4	1.6	37.0	10.9	18.0	10.6	20.3
Cumul. Pct Delegates	0.0	1.4	3.0	40.1	51.0	69.0	79.7	100.0
2000								
States	1	1	0	28	3	4	9	5
Pct Delegates	1.4	0.6	0.0	65.3	5.4	9.5	11.5	6.3
Cumul. Pct Delegates	1.4	2.0	2.0	67.3	72.7	82.2	93.7	100.0
2008								
States	6	29	2	6	0	1	5	2
Pct Delegates	8.8	60.8	2.8	12.4	0.0	4.7	9.5	0.9
Cumul. Pct Delegates	8.8	69.6	72.4	84.8	84.8	89.5	99.1	100.0
2016								
States	0	2	2	22	6	8	4	7
Pct Delegates	0.0	1.7	2.2	46.8	6.9	18.5	5.8	18.1
Cumul. Pct Delegates	0.0	1.7	3.9	50.8	57.7	76.2	81.9	100.0
REPUBLICANS								
1992								
States	0	1	4	15	4	8	13	6
Pct Delegates	0.0	1.1	3.9	30.4	9.7	17.4	18.1	19.6
Cumul. Pct Delegates	0.0	1.1	4.9	35.3	45.0	62.3	80.4	100.0
2000								
States	2	3	6	21	3	2	9	5
Pct Delegates	2.4	2.1	11.6	50.0	6.0	5.6	14.3	8.0
Cumul. Pct Delegates	2.4	4.5	16.1	66.1	72.1	77.7	92.0	100.0
2008								
States	7	28	1	5	0	1	6	3
Pct Delegates	9.4	57.4	1.7	13.2	0	3.3	11.2	3.8
Cumul. Pct Delegates	9.4	66.8	68.5	81.7	81.7	85.0	96.2	100.0
2016								
States	0	2	2	26	2	9	5	5
Pct Delegates	0.0	2.2	3.3	54.1	4.1	15.5	8.2	12.6
Cumul. Pct Delegates	0.0	2.2	5.5	59.6	63.7	79.2	87.4	100.0

Source: Compiled by authors.

Note: This table includes the District of Columbia but excludes all territories of the United States not represented in the Electoral College.

become particularly concentrated in the first two weeks of March. Even so, nearly half of all pledged Democratic delegates in 1992—and 55 percent of Republican delegates—were still chosen in April, May, or June.

The rate of front-loading accelerated in subsequent elections. By 2000, fully half of the total number of Republican pledged delegates and nearly two-thirds of the Democratic delegates were selected during the first two weeks in March alone. Winning the first round of primaries was now important not merely to signal a candidate's viability or to raise money for future contests but because most of the delegates were actually chosen early in the calendar.

In 2004, the Democratic Party followed the Republicans' lead in 2000 and moved the start of the national delegate selection window forward by one month. A number of states immediately responded by rescheduling their primaries and caucuses to take advantage of the new timeline, predictably converging on the first Tuesday in February, the earliest allowable date under the revised party rules. For some observers, the traditional moniker "Super Tuesday" seemed insufficient by 2008 to convey the potential importance of this event, now including primaries or caucuses in 24 states; many in the seldom hype-averse press corps began referring instead to "Super Duper Tuesday" or "Tsunami Tuesday." Seeking to maintain their jealously guarded first-in-the-nation status, Iowa and New Hampshire responded by scheduling their elections in early January. The 2008 Iowa caucus was held only two days after the New Year, with the New Hampshire primary following on January 8.

In order to avoid future occurrences of primaries and caucuses within mere days of the holiday season, the Democratic and Republican national committees engaged in an unprecedented cooperative initiative after 2008 to standardize an election schedule for both parties. The plans enacted by the national parties for 2012 and subsequent elections called for the four early states to vote during the month of February, with the rest of the nation holding primaries and caucuses between March and June. Republicans also modified their rules to ban the use of pure winner-take-all delegate allocation before April 1, increasing the incentive for states to hold their elections later in the year. (This rule was slightly relaxed after 2012 to permit pure winner-take-all primaries and caucuses beginning on March 15.)

As table 4.2 illustrates, these party rules reforms succeeded in partially reversing the trend toward a severely accelerated calendar. Most states that had previously voted in February delayed their primaries until March beginning in 2012, though Iowa and New Hampshire still held their events in early January that year. By 2016, the parties' coordinated efforts had gained more success: Iowa and New Hampshire shared the month of February with Nevada and South Carolina, as intended, while all remaining states waited until March or later. Super Tuesday now predictably falls on the first Tuesday in March; in 2016, 11 states in each party held primaries or caucuses on March 1, the first allowable date within the national delegate selection window.[39]

But states still face the temptation to move their primaries earlier in the schedule to gain more influence and attention for themselves. California, which has usually held a June election, moved its primary to the first Tuesday in March starting in 2020. With early and absentee balloting starting weeks in advance of Election Day, Californians will begin voting for their presidential nominees at the same time as residents of Iowa and New Hampshire, unless those states respond to this perceived infringement by returning to an early January date. As a result of this shift, candidates will not be able to wait until the first contests are decided before starting to compete actively in the most populous, delegate-rich, and expensive state in the nation.

In past years, some states have scheduled early primaries in violation of party rules, risking the associated penalties but hoping to attract extra notice from candidates. For example, Michigan and Florida scheduled their 2008 primaries for January 15 and 29, respectively, in a brazen challenge to the delegate selection window approved by the national parties. The major Republican candidates competed seriously in Michigan and Florida anyway, and both states had a significant impact on the nomination contest that year. Mitt Romney's victory over John McCain in Michigan kept his campaign alive, at least temporarily, while McCain's first-place finish in Florida two weeks later ended the candidacy of Rudy Giuliani and dealt Romney a serious setback that foreshadowed his poor Super Tuesday performance and subsequent withdrawal the following week.

Because the national Democratic Party penalized Michigan and Florida by denying both states any representation at the national convention, the major 2008 candidates signed an agreement not to compete in either state. Hillary Clinton won both primaries more or less by default, though she claimed victory after the fact; in Michigan, she was the only major candidate to place her name on the ballot. As the Democratic nomination contest dragged on into the spring with Obama holding a slender but steady lead over Clinton in the overall pledged delegate count, Clinton campaign officials began to call for the Democratic National Committee to reconsider the sanctions imposed on Michigan and Florida. On May 31, the party's Rules and Bylaws Committee met in Washington to resolve the issue. The committee rejected the Clinton campaign's proposal that the Michigan and Florida delegations be restored at full strength and divided between the candidates on the basis of the January primary results, opting instead to grant each state's delegates half votes at the convention and to award 59 of the 128 pledged delegates from Michigan to Obama, even though he had not appeared on the ballot—a decision that effectively ended Clinton's already slim chances of winning the nomination.[40]

The saga of Michigan and Florida in 2008 was merely one battle in an ongoing war between state officials and national party leaders for control of the presidential nomination process. While the self-interested actions of state governments seeking power and attention by intentionally violating the scheduling requirements imposed by the national parties may inspire little sympathy from residents of more cooperative states, these actions also raise the legitimate question of whether Iowa and New Hampshire should continue to receive special dispensation under the rules of both major parties to hold the first caucus and first primary in every presidential nomination season. This issue has emerged regularly in recent years. Within the Democratic Party, representatives of labor unions and racial minorities, two key components of the party's electoral coalition, have often argued that their constituents are significantly underrepresented in the electorates of Iowa and New Hampshire, and therefore exert less influence on the outcome of Democratic nominations than they might deserve based on their share of the party's national membership.

Responding to these and similar arguments, the Democratic National Committee appointed an internal commission after the 2004 election to study the nomination sequence. The commission, co-chaired by former U.S. secretary of labor Alexis Herman and Representative David Price of North Carolina, recommended that the party continue to recognize the traditional right of Iowa to hold the first presidential caucus and New Hampshire the first primary, but that it should also allow two additional states to schedule early events before the bulk of other primaries and caucuses takes place. The DNC voted to authorize Nevada, a state with a significant union presence and Latino population, to hold a caucus after Iowa. South Carolina, a state in which a large proportion of the Democratic electorate is African American, received approval to hold the second primary of the election calendar.[41] After 2012, the Republican Party adopted a similar carve-out provision formally recognizing Nevada and South Carolina as additional early states with the right to schedule elections prior to the March opening of the national delegate selection window.

In 2016, both states exerted important influence over the nomination process. Hillary Clinton achieved victories in Nevada and South Carolina that restored positive attention to her campaign after her damaging loss to Bernie Sanders in the New Hampshire primary. As advocates of these groups had hoped, Clinton's strong support among African Americans, Latinos, and union members was decisive in both states. On the Republican side, Donald Trump carried his success in the New Hampshire primary into South Carolina, winning the state by 10 points over Ted Cruz and Marco Rubio while capturing all 50 Republican delegates. Trump performed even better in Nevada, receiving 46 percent of the caucus vote (to 24 percent for Rubio and 21 percent for Cruz) and establishing himself as the clear favorite heading into the multiple Super Tuesday primaries the following week.

How have changes in the primary calendar over time influenced the outcome of presidential nominations? In practice, front-loading has mostly worked to reduce the amount of time between the beginning of the primary season and the point at which a presumptive nominee emerges. Once the voting starts, pressure quickly builds for unsuccessful candidates to drop out of the race. Most presidential contenders only contest a handful of states before they are forced to withdraw, usually due to financial hardship as contributions dry up in the wake of early defeats. A front-loaded primary schedule simply accelerates this process, usually producing a presumptive nominee in a matter of weeks instead of months.

For example, seven Republican candidates began the 2012 primary season by competing in the Iowa caucus on January 3. One candidate, Michele Bachmann, ended her campaign immediately after finishing sixth in Iowa; two more, Rick Perry and Jon Huntsman, dropped out after the New Hampshire primary the following week. Front-runner and New Hampshire victor Mitt Romney scored another key win in the Florida primary on January 31 and took a commanding lead in the pledged delegate count with victories in multiple states on Super Tuesday, March 6. After another first-place finish in the March 20 primary in Illinois, Romney became the consensus nominee of the party, with more than 10 weeks remaining in the primary calendar.

Victorious candidates in the first events, or those who exceed media expectations for their performance, can ride the resulting "momentum" of publicity to further success in states holding primaries in the following days. At the same time, candidates who stumble early on have little opportunity in a front-loaded primary process to right their campaigns in time to prevent additional defeats that only compound their problems. The central limitation facing the advocates of front-loading is the dependable tendency of party leaders, journalists, and voters to interpret the very first events of the primary season as important evidence of the relative standing of the candidates. As long as political elites consider the results in Iowa and New Hampshire worthy of extensive attention, hyping winners and disparaging losers, the outcomes in those states will exert a strong effect on the results of subsequent primaries and caucuses, even—perhaps especially—if those elections follow closely behind. As long as voters, confronted with a field of multiple contenders within the same party who are mostly not well known to them, look to the decisions of their counterparts in other states for guidance about which candidate to support, the very first states in the electoral sequence will continue to have the loudest voice.

Over the years, states have attempted to gain influence over nominations in ways other than front-loading. One common strategy employed to attract candidate and press attention is the organization of regional primaries. Perhaps if several contiguous states with presumably similar interests coordinate their delegate selection events on a single date, they can compel candidates to show interest in whatever issues are of particular interest to that region. Such primaries have not, for the most part, been particularly successful, in part because states are unable to monopolize a date on the primary calendar. Should other states share the day, candidates may choose to campaign extensively only in the largest states within the region (say, Massachusetts in a New England regional primary) and give less attention to the smaller states.

At least one other strategy is common. States that are home to a prospective candidate may manipulate the delegate selection process in order to help the "favorite son" (or daughter). If the candidate is expected to win the state, the victory presumably provides extra publicity and more points on the delegate count scoreboard. If the candidate is worried about losing the state or failing to meet news media expectations, however, he or she may not benefit from an early home-state primary; even hinting at this may generate negative press coverage. This happened to John McCain in 2000. Arizona Republicans had moved their primary to mid-February, following New Hampshire by only a week. McCain was reported to be in favor of moving the primary back in the schedule, after the key New York and California primaries, in order to avoid the possibility of an embarrassing loss—or narrow victory—in his home state affecting results elsewhere. In this case, however, Arizona Republicans failed to respect McCain's wishes and left the date of the primary early, on February 22. McCain's fears ultimately went unrealized; he won the state easily.[42]

Thus the design of the presidential nomination process continues to be in constant flux from one election to the next. Many states, as well as both national parties, have demonstrated a great deal of willingness over the past several decades to manipulate the primary calendar for various purposes. At the root of this incessant tinkering is the unfortunate truth that most political actors and observers perceive the current nomination system to be significantly flawed and therefore in need of further reform, a topic to which we return in chapter 6.

Despite a significant degree of change over the past several decades, especially in the timing of state contests, there have been some consistent patterns across the years. "Regardless of the different nominating rules . . . there is a dynamic affecting both parties that makes early defeats devastating," observes Rhodes Cook. "No candidate in either party in recent years has mounted a successful comeback during the mop-up period."[43] What helps a candidate overcome a poor early performance? It helps to have a set of devoted supporters who are reluctant to jump to other candidates even in the wake of defeat. Candidates can also benefit from raising enough money before the voting begins to outlast disappointing outcomes in the early going. Barack Obama and Hillary Clinton enjoyed both advantages in 2008, allowing her to overcome an initial Iowa setback and him a surprising loss in New Hampshire. Bernie Sanders also received enough financial and organizational support in 2016 to stay in the Democratic race against Clinton until the end of the primary calendar in June, even though his chances of winning the nomination had long since faded.

Primaries are the battlegrounds of the nomination process, giving the news media a crucial role in how nominees are chosen. Since primary voters lack the guidance that distinct party labels provide during general elections, they tend to have weakly held preferences and limited knowledge about how the candidates differ from each other. Media reporting about who is ahead or behind, or how seriously candidates should be taken, assumes considerable importance. Therefore, a significant part of running for president includes trying to manipulate how media analysts interpret primary elections both before and after they take place. This is known as "spin control."[44] The contestant who loses but does better than expected may reap greater advantage from a primary than the one who wins but falls below expectations. It is therefore manifestly to the advantage of candidates to make modest preelection predictions and to then tout results as more favorable than anticipated once the votes are counted.

A good example of spin control was the effort of Bill Clinton's 1992 campaign to declare a victory in New Hampshire as the "comeback kid," even though he had lost the primary to Paul Tsongas.[45] The press accepted the idea of a resurgent Clinton, ignored the other candidates, and gave Tsongas little of the positive coverage a winning candidate might ordinarily receive.[46] In contrast, Bob Kerrey's decisive victory (with 40 percent of the vote) in South Dakota one week later netted him much less favorable publicity than Clinton's second-place showing in New Hampshire. Kerrey succeeded with the voters, but failed in the crucial job of spin control.

Substantial evidence exists that voters absorb opinion poll results and gather other impressions of viability which then exert considerable influence over their choice of candidates. But information on policies, character, and leadership ability is comparatively scarce and is assimilated slowly.[47] "It appears safe to conclude," John G. Geer writes, "that most primary voters do not compare the issue positions of candidates when voting."[48] One reason that primary voters do not perceive much issue distance between the candidates is perhaps because, being members of the same party, there is in fact not that much difference. Another reason may be that candidates are purposely unclear. Since it may well be advantageous for candidates to appeal differently to various audiences, they may, like Hillary Clinton or Donald Trump, appear moderate to some people and firmly liberal or conservative to others.

There are bandwagon effects in primaries, with voters jumping aboard a candidacy that seems to have achieved a popular breakthrough in the early states. Jimmy Carter rose from near obscurity in national polls, 1 percent in January 1976, to 29 percent by mid-March after his success in Iowa and New Hampshire. Gary Hart surged from 2 percent of national support early in February 1984 to 33 percent just three weeks later, in the wake of his own well-publicized upset victory in the New Hampshire primary. John Kerry was the favored candidate of 9 percent of Democrats nationwide in a *Time*/CNN poll conducted in mid-January 2004, before the Iowa caucus. After winning both Iowa and New Hampshire, Kerry soared to 43 percent in the same poll by February 6.[49] Newt Gingrich led Mitt Romney in an aggregation of national polls by 11 percentage points (32 percent to 21 percent) on December 5, 2011; six weeks later, after Romney had achieved a virtual tie in Iowa and an easy victory in New Hampshire, he had pulled ahead of Gingrich in the national vote by a comparable margin of 30 percent to 20 percent.[50]

If voters can be swept along by the sheer momentum of events, the strength of their issue preferences or of their assessments of leadership ability must be very low. On what basis, then, do citizens choose? As the nominating campaign moves along, voters develop feelings about the personalities of the candidates. In a study of primary voters in Los Angeles, California, and Erie, Pennsylvania, John Geer found that comments centered on the candidates' personalities predominated in the reasons given for voting in primaries.[51] Since much of the debate in the primary is about who among members of the same party can provide the best leadership, Geer concluded that voter concentration on candidates' personal qualities is reasonable. Others disagree. Henry E. Brady and Michael G. Hagen argued that "primaries seem to be seriously flawed by forcing voters to commit to candidates before they can learn about . . . policy positions, electability and leadership ability of those standing for the nomination. . . . American primaries force people to choose before they are ready."[52]

STATE CAUCUSES

The majority of delegates to the national party conventions are selected by means of state primary elections. In 2016, for example, 73 percent of the delegates to the Democratic convention were chosen in primaries, 15 percent were unelected superdelegates (discussed further below), and 12 percent were selected via state caucuses or conventions. For Republicans, 82 percent of convention delegates were chosen in primaries and 18 percent in caucuses. If the race is close, however, delegates chosen in caucuses can make a difference to the final outcome. It is therefore important to examine how caucuses differ from primary elections, and how these differences matter for candidate strategies and electoral results.

The party caucus is a legacy of the pre-reform presidential nomination process. Caucuses or state conventions were commonly used before 1972 to select delegates who would attend the national convention as representatives of the state party. As a result, these delegates' votes would often be influenced, and were commonly controlled outright, by party leaders and elected officials from their home states. Attempts by candidates to seek their support were usually made after these delegates were selected by state parties. The first strategic requirement for the candidate seeking to influence these delegates was an intelligence service—a network of informants who could report on which delegates were firmly committed, which were wavering, and which might be persuaded to provide second-or third-choice support. Advance reports on the opportunities offered by internal division in the state parties, the type of appeal likely to be effective in each state, and the kinds of bargains to which leaders were most amenable were also helpful. The costs of this information were high in time, money, and effort, but it was worthwhile to the serious candidate, who needed to know how to maneuver to increase support and block opponents.

After the disastrous 1968 national convention in Chicago, the Democratic Party created an internal committee, the McGovern-Fraser Commission, to propose changes to the party rules governing presidential nomination procedures. The commission recommended, and the Democratic National Committee agreed, that states be required to select delegates via a process in which all registered voters who identify as members of the party may participate. Republicans soon adopted a similar provision. Although most states have opted to satisfy these mandates by holding primary elections, several states—most notably Iowa—have retained the caucus system of delegate selection, merely opening them to all eligible party voters. The use of caucuses is most widespread among lightly populated states in the Midwest and West and within territories of the United States such as Guam and American Samoa. Today, however, the delegates selected in caucuses can no longer be said to represent the state party or its leaders. As in primaries, these delegates are pledged to support a specific candidate at the national convention, and are chosen by caucus participants to reflect their own preferences.

In general, caucuses differ from primaries in two key respects: there are often many fewer voting sites within the state—perhaps only one per county—and participation requires attending a (possibly lengthy) party meeting at a specific time, usually on a weekday evening or weekend afternoon. As a result, turnout rates for caucuses are consistently quite low, since the time and energy required of voters far exceeds that of a simple primary election. Even the Iowa caucus, the most important and heavily publicized caucus on the nomination calendar, attracted a turnout rate of only 16 percent in 2016 (compared to the 52 percent turnout rate in the following week's New Hampshire primary); in Nevada and Minnesota, only 8 percent of eligible voters attended state caucuses despite active nomination contests in both parties.[53] Concerned about the inability of some citizens to participate in person due to work requirements, family needs, or disability, the Democratic National Committee approved a rule in advance of the 2020 election requiring all states holding caucuses to accept absentee ballots.[54]

Caucus procedures vary from state to state. Some caucuses resemble simple straw polls, while others take the form of extended sessions at which a great deal of other party business is transacted. Iowa Democrats employ a unique two-stage process in which each candidate's supporters openly declare their preferences by congregating in a group to be counted by party officials. If a candidate fails to receive enough support in the first round of voting to gain at least one delegate from the precinct to the county party convention, that candidate's supporters are free to distribute themselves among other candidates for the second count, which determines the final allocation of delegates. This system benefits candidates who are popular second-choice alternatives for voters whose preferred candidate was eliminated in the first round of their precinct caucus. Later on, these county conventions choose representatives to the state party convention, which in turn selects Iowa's national convention delegation.

The nature of caucuses tends to reward candidates with extensive campaign organizations in the state that are able to mobilize voters to attend the caucus meetings and navigate their procedural complexity. In 2008, Barack Obama's campaign strategists placed special emphasis on competing in caucuses, which they believed would favor their strong grassroots organization and high level of supporter enthusiasm. "[T]he first six [Super Tuesday] states we staffed were caucus states," recalled Obama adviser Steve Hildebrand. "That was a strategic decision."[55] The Hillary Clinton campaign, in contrast, was wary of caucuses, especially after Clinton's disappointing performance in Iowa, and believed that the time commitments they require prevented the participation of working-class voters who preferred their candidate. According to one campaign aide who spoke to her on the subject, "Hillary . . . hated caucuses [because] her supporters had jobs to go to, they were waitresses and day care workers. . . . 'The caucus system skews to the wealthy!' she said."[56]

As a result, Clinton made little effort in most caucus states, openly conceding them to Obama. Her decision allowed the Obama campaign to rack up overwhelming margins among caucus delegates that effectively counteracted much of Clinton's success in larger primary states. On February 5, for example, Obama received nearly 80 percent of the vote in the Idaho caucus, winning 15 of the state's 18 pledged delegates. This net gain of 12 delegates for Obama from Idaho more than negated the 59-to-48 delegate advantage won by Clinton courtesy of her 10-point primary victory on the same day in New Jersey, where more than 50 times as many Democrats had turned out to vote. When Obama ultimately edged out Clinton in the national pledged delegate count at the end of the 2008 nomination season, the two candidates' very different approaches to party caucuses appeared in retrospect to be a potentially decisive factor in the outcome.

Eight years later, Clinton's second presidential campaign faced another difficult challenge in caucus states due to the particular enthusiasm for Bernie Sanders among some grassroots liberal activists. Candidates with particularly devoted followings, like Sanders, often perform better in caucuses than in primaries, since their relatively fervent supporters are especially willing to make the required effort to participate. Clinton narrowly won Iowa and Nevada, the first two caucuses on the nomination schedule, but Sanders swept the later caucuses in 12 other states. Clinton's weakness in caucuses did not deprive her of the 2016 Democratic nomination as it had in 2008, however, since she did better in primary elections during her second presidential campaign than she had in her first. Among Republicans in 2016, Ted Cruz's especially strong support among highly mobilized Christian conservative activists helped him win the caucuses in Iowa, Colorado, Kansas, Wyoming, Utah, Maine, and Alaska, though Donald Trump placed first in the Nevada, Kentucky, and Hawaii caucuses while Minnesota gave Marco Rubio his only statewide victory.

Caucuses' dramatically lower turnout rate and occasional tilt toward insurgent candidates, as well as the unreliable capacity of some state party organizations to run them in an efficient manner, prompted the Democratic National Committee to adopt a resolution in advance of the 2020 election officially encouraging states to abandon caucuses in favor of primary elections.[57] At least six states that held caucuses in 2016—Colorado, Idaho, Washington, Minnesota, Nebraska, and Utah—signaled plans to hold primaries instead in 2020. While the caucus system may be losing favor over time (at least in one party), its distinctive characteristics will remain an important component of the presidential nomination process as long as multiple states and territories continue to select their convention delegates via caucuses—and as long as the Iowa caucus retains its key position as the very first event on the nomination calendar.

DELEGATE ALLOCATION

Presidential nominations are decided by the state-by-state accumulation of convention delegates, not by a simple national popular vote. It is therefore worth examining the rules governing the process by which the votes of citizens are transformed into the distribution of delegates among candidates. No one pretends that primary and caucus electorates are perfect representations of the segment of the public that identifies with a particular political party or is likely to support the party's leading vote-getter. For one thing, voters are not allowed to rank their preferences, so a candidate's popularity with voters who gave their first-choice votes to others is unknown. Voter turnout is also usually much lower in primaries and caucuses than in the November election and is likely to contain a larger proportion of loyal party supporters. Even in 2016, with competitive and well-publicized nomination races in both parties, the proportion of eligible voters participating in most state primaries ranged between 20 and 35 percent, dropping to single digits in many caucuses (compared to a 60 percent national turnout rate in the November general election).[58] And the varying rules for assigning delegates to candidates can bias the results still further.

One way of converting popular votes to convention delegates is winner-take-all: whichever candidate places first receives all the delegates. Another is proportional: all candidates who reach a certain threshold—15 percent, for example—divide the delegates among themselves in accordance with their relative shares of the vote. A third is a hybrid of the first two: a candidate who receives at least 50 percent of the vote receives all of the delegates, but delegates are distributed proportionately if no single candidate wins a majority. These systems can be used to allocate delegates based on the vote across the entire state, within each congressional district, or both. In many cases, some of a state's delegates are assigned on the basis of the statewide vote totals while the rest are distributed at the level of individual districts.

Because the national Republican Party mostly leaves these decisions up to the state party organizations, allocation methods in Republican primaries can vary dramatically. In 2016, Florida Republicans used a winner-take-all system at the state level; because Donald Trump placed first in the state, he gained all 99 of Florida's pledged delegates, even though he received less than half (46 percent) of the popular vote. In California, most Republican delegates were apportioned by the winner-take-all system at the level of individual congressional districts; candidates gained three delegates for each district that they carried. In New Hampshire, Republican delegates were divided proportionally among candidates based on their shares of the statewide vote. In other states, such as Texas, some delegates were allocated statewide while others were distributed by congressional district via a complex formula specified by state party rules.

Historically, proportional allocation has not been widely used in Republican primaries; most states have apportioned delegates in a winner-take-all fashion either at the state or district level, or both in combination.[59] However, the national Republican Party now requires that all states holding primaries or caucuses before March 15 (other than the four designated early states) must use proportional allocation—although these states are still permitted the option of allowing a candidate who receives more than 50 percent of the total statewide vote to collect all the delegates from the state, a rule sometimes known as "conditional winner-take-all." Party leaders adopted this reform to discourage extreme front-loading; it can also work to prolong the nomination process by making it more difficult for a single candidate to quickly amass a commanding lead in the delegate count.

The national Democratic Party does not permit winner-take-all delegate allocation under any circumstances. Instead, it requires states to apportion most of their delegates proportionally by congressional district. The remaining share of the state's pledged delegates must be allocated proportionally based on the statewide popular vote. Democratic candidates who win at least 15 percent of the vote in a district or state are entitled to receive delegates under national party rules.

The prevalence of winner-take-all delegate allocation in their party gives Republican candidates a strategic opportunity not available to Democrats. A Republican late bloomer, by winning multiple primaries near the end of the nomination calendar, could conceivably hope to overcome a front-runner's early delegate lead. Though Ronald Reagan won no primaries until late March, for example, he almost took the 1976 nomination away from Gerald Ford by receiving all the delegates from such late-voting large states as California and Texas.

In contrast, Democratic rules requiring proportional representation make it difficult for lagging Democratic candidates to catch up in the delegate count. Even if front-runners falter, proportional representation slows their momentum only a little in the later primaries. Once Hillary Clinton fell behind Barack Obama among pledged delegates in mid-February 2008 due to Obama's success in a series of primaries and caucuses, proportional representation rules blunted her progress in making up lost ground in March and April, despite primary victories in several populous states. Bernie Sanders suffered the same challenge when trailing Clinton in the late stages of the 2016 nomination race; as Sanders aide Mark Longabaugh lamented in retrospect, "It is very, very hard to play the delegate game from behind."[60]

In fact, had winner-take-all apportionment been in place for Democrats in the largest state primaries in 2008, Clinton would have received the nomination on the strength of her victories in California, New York, New Jersey, Texas, Ohio, and Pennsylvania. Obama ultimately collected more pledged delegates than Clinton under the proportional rules that were actually in effect by doing well enough in large states to reap a significant share of their delegates while winning lopsided victories in several medium-sized primary states (such as Maryland, Virginia, and Wisconsin) and a number of small states holding caucuses where Clinton failed to compete. At the same time, the widespread use of proportional allocation in Republican primaries would have worked to the advantage of Mitt Romney's first, ultimately unsuccessful bid for the Republican nomination in 2008. Romney finished a close second or third in the populous states of Florida, Georgia, and Missouri but did not receive a single pledged delegate from any of them due to winner-take-all apportionment, while his 35 percent share of the statewide vote in California netted him only 15 of 170 delegates.

Of course, these hypothetical outcomes fail to account for the alternate strategies that the candidates would surely have pursued under different institutional rules. Because the Democratic Party currently forces all states to use proportional representation, Democratic presidential candidates face a particularly strong incentive to build active campaign organizations virtually everywhere, since they can win delegates even if they fail to place first. Successful campaigns devote a great deal of attention to the details of party procedure, identifying particular states, and even congressional districts within states, where resources should be directed to maximize the number of delegates gained. The Obama campaign was considered particularly adept on this score in 2008, especially in comparison with the less savvy Hillary Clinton operation. Clinton aide Harold Ickes later claimed that chief strategist Mark Penn—a bitter rival of his within the campaign—mistakenly thought the California primary was winner-take-all and that Clinton's likely victory there would virtually clinch the race. "How can it possibly be," Ickes asked sarcastically, "that the much vaunted chief strategist doesn't understand [Democratic Party rules requiring] proportional allocation?"[61] Assuming that the Democratic race would be effectively decided on Super Tuesday due to their candidate's strength in most of the populous states holding primaries that day, Clinton campaign officials failed to build strong organizations in caucus states or states holding elections in subsequent weeks, to her great disadvantage.

Highly competitive nomination contests are particularly valuable in illustrating the tremendous procedural complexity of the contemporary presidential primary system and the need for candidates to employ sophisticated strategic and tactical approaches in order to navigate it successfully. The process is a complicated and ever-evolving network of institutions, actors, and rules in which national and state party organizations, state legislatures and governors, candidates, interest groups, journalists, and voters all interact to produce a presidential nominee. For citizens, their degree of influence over the process mostly reflects the position of their state in the sequential series of elections occurring over the course of the primary season. Residents of states at the front of the calendar will have a choice of multiple candidates actively seeking their support; those who must wait until May or June to participate usually find that the nomination has already been effectively decided by their fellow party members elsewhere in the nation.

SUPERDELEGATES

The reforms instituted in 1972 were designed to eliminate the direct power of party officials to control the outcomes of presidential nominations. The Hunt Commission of the early 1980s, one of a succession of internal Democratic Party committees charged with proposing further reform measures, recommended that party leaders be brought back into the nomination process by granting them automatic seats as delegates at the national convention that did not require them to be pledged beforehand to support a particular candidate. The Democratic National

Committee agreed, creating delegate positions formally labeled under party rules as unpledged Party Leaders and Elected Officials (PLEO) delegates, but popularly known as "superdelegates."[62]

Who are the superdelegates? All sitting Democratic senators, representatives, and governors receive automatic delegate status, as do all members of the Democratic National Committee (including all state party chairs and vice chairs) and all current and former Democratic presidents, vice presidents, congressional leaders, and national party chairs. About 80 "add-on" superdelegate positions are also distributed among the state parties to fill however they wish; these seats are often given to state legislative leaders or mayors of large cities. Superdelegates usually number about 800, constituting less than 20 percent of all Democratic convention delegates. Typically, slightly more than half of the superdelegates are members of the DNC.

For two decades after their creation, superdelegates received little attention during the nomination process. The presumptive Democratic presidential nominee routinely emerged at some point during the spring of an election year as a result of multiple victories in primaries and caucuses, giving the superdelegates little influence over the process. But in 2008, the unusually close margin between Barack Obama and Hillary Clinton in the pledged delegate count made it clear by mid-February that the superdelegates would hold the mathematical balance of power between the two candidates. For the first time, superdelegates became big national news.

Both the Obama and Clinton campaigns devoted a great deal of energy to courting unpledged delegates, announcing each new endorsement with much fanfare as the news media—and even the general public—focused with intensifying interest on what had previously been a procedural obscurity. Many DNC members accustomed to relative anonymity were suddenly swamped with attention from journalists, campaign operatives, and voters hoping to divine or influence their choice of candidate. The nation's youngest superdelegate, a 21-year-old college student from Wisconsin named Jason Rae, was taken to breakfast by Hillary Clinton's daughter Chelsea and received telephone calls from Bill Clinton and former secretary of state Madeleine Albright on behalf of the Clinton campaign, while the Obama team dispatched Massachusetts senator John Kerry, the 2004 Democratic presidential nominee, to discuss party strategy with him.[63] Rae's status as an overnight political celebrity among his peers was cemented when he was interviewed in his dormitory room by a correspondent from *The Daily Show* on Comedy Central.

Obama ended the primary season on June 3 with a 124-vote lead over Clinton in pledged delegates (1,748 to 1,624). Though members of the news media had previously speculated that the nomination fight might continue into the summer, perhaps even to the national convention, enough previously neutral superdelegates endorsed Obama on the final day of the primaries to provide the necessary 2,142 delegates for the nomination, allowing him to claim victory in his remarks that evening. Clinton conceded the race several days later. While the superdelegates technically determined the outcome of the nomination process in 2008, in fact they merely ratified the results of the pledged delegate selection contests.

Superdelegates became controversial once more during the next competitive Democratic nomination race in 2016. As of mid-April, Hillary Clinton had received the public endorsement of 460 superdelegates compared to just 38 for Bernie Sanders, reflecting her stronger personal ties to party leaders, greater perceived electability among top Democratic officials, and status as the overwhelming favorite heading into the race.[64] But Sanders argued that this numerical imbalance merely showed how a Democratic "establishment" had systematically stacked the nomination process against his outsider candidacy. He also criticized media organizations for incorporating the public endorsements of superdelegates in their ongoing delegate counts during the nomination season, noting that superdelegates—unlike the pledged delegates selected in primaries and caucuses—were free to shift their candidate allegiances at any time before the national convention.

Clinton ultimately bested Sanders among pledged delegates by a margin of 2,205 to 1,846, meaning that the superdelegates, as in 2008, simply confirmed the victory of the candidate who won the most delegates chosen by Democratic voters. But Sanders's repeated attacks on the very existence of superdelegates (and the notably cool reception that his candidacy provoked among them) left a palpable residue of illegitimacy over the outcome in the eyes of some disappointed supporters. After the election, even many party leaders conceded the potency of these arguments. Superdelegate support for Clinton "handed [Sanders] a wedge issue," observed New Hampshire Democratic Party chair Ray Buckley. "It connected to his entire [campaign] message about the elite versus the people."[65]

In truth, the superdelegates were nearly certain to deliver the 2016 Democratic nomination to whichever candidate could claim the most support from primaries and caucuses, as they had in 2008; if Sanders had managed to finish the nomination season with the most pledged delegates, he—like Obama eight years before him—would have had a persuasive argument with which to sway party leaders: how could the Democratic Party rightfully deny the nomination to the candidate chosen by the Democratic electorate, igniting a certain firestorm just as the general election campaign began? In the end, Sanders lost the 2016 nomination because he failed to win enough support from voters, not because the superdelegates conspired against him. But if superdelegates were exceedingly unlikely to overturn the "will of the people" in practice—even as their hypothetical ability to decide a close nomination contest made the entire party vulnerable to recurrent suspicion that the nomination process was rigged in favor of elite-backed candidates—some leading Democrats started to wonder whether the existence of superdelegates was worth the trouble it seemed to be causing.

In the wake of the 2016 general election, Democratic officials considered a number of proposed reforms intended to resolve the issue, ranging from simply abolishing superdelegates altogether to sharply reducing the number of party leaders entitled to superdelegate status. In the end, the Democratic National Committee opted to maintain the existing rules governing superdelegates' eligibility, but to revoke their power to participate in the first presidential nomination ballot at the national convention unless their votes would be mathematically irrelevant to the outcome. Superdelegates therefore retain the ability to attend conventions as credentialed participants, to assist in the approval of the party platform and other responsibilities, and to help break a deadlock if no presidential candidate enters the convention with a majority of pledged delegates. But if such an unlikely event were to occur, superdelegates would still face considerable pressure to deliver the nomination to the plurality leader in the pledged delegate count, who would undoubtedly claim the mantle of popular legitimacy and argue that party "bosses" had no right to choose another candidate.

Though they have never attracted the attention that Democratic superdelegates received in 2008 and 2016, Republicans provide a small number of party leaders with automatic delegate seats. This group, which represented 7 percent of the Republican delegates in 2016, encompasses all state party chairs and members of the Republican National Committee, but (unlike the Democrats) does not include members of Congress or other elected officials. Beginning with the 2016 election, however, national party rules now require these delegates to support the candidate who placed first in their home state's primary or caucus, reducing their ability to act as independent agents at the Republican national convention—but also preventing them from producing the same degree of controversy as their Democratic counterparts.

Donald Trump's successful nomination in 2016, despite low levels of support for his candidacy among fellow Republican politicians and party officials, renewed calls in some quarters to return a form of peer review to the process of presidential selection. Critics argued that a party should not be compelled to nominate a candidate to be its national standard-bearer over the objection of its top leadership.[66] But the recurrent controversies over the proper role, and even the very presence, of superdelegates in the Democratic Party demonstrate how deeply Americans have accepted the belief that the presidential nominee must be chosen by "the people, not the bosses" in order to retain popular legitimacy. The party leaders who exercised control over nominations during previous eras of American history can now only influence the process indirectly, through public appeals to the citizens who hold the ultimate power over nominations. And in an era when trust in "career politicians" is low and demand for political outsiders is high, there is no reason to expect that voters will always defer to their judgment.

THE NATIONAL PARTY CONVENTIONS

The national party conventions are four-day events held by both major parties in the summer of a presidential election year to formally nominate candidates for president and vice president, to approve an official policy platform, and to address other internal party matters. Each party's national committee usually selects a site and date for the convention between 18 months and 2 years in advance of the event itself. Political considerations are often important in tipping the balance between competing potential host cities. Democrats chose Denver in 2008 partly because the party was seeking to increase its strength in the West and because the state of Colorado, long a Republican bastion in presidential politics, had been recently trending Democratic. Republicans chose Saint Paul, Minnesota, in 2008 in part because the Twin Cities media market encompasses large areas of the presidential swing states of Minnesota, Iowa, and Wisconsin. In 2012, the Democrats met in Charlotte to recognize North Carolina's growing electoral competitiveness, while Republicans chose Tampa in the perennial battleground state of Florida. The parties opted for populous swing states once again in 2016, with the Republicans meeting in Cleveland, Ohio, and the Democrats assembling in Philadelphia, Pennsylvania. Democrats selected Milwaukee as the site of their 2020 convention in response to the surprising results of 2016, when the key state of Wisconsin provided Donald Trump with a narrow victory after Hillary Clinton failed to make any personal appearances there; Republicans decided to hold their 2020 convention in Charlotte, where the Democrats had met eight years before.

Other considerations include the quality of the facilities, the suitability of the convention hall to television coverage, sufficient hotel and entertainment accommodations, and (for Democrats) the availability of places to meet and stay with acceptable records on the treatment of labor unions.[67] The parties often prefer to bring their publicity and their business to cities and states where the mayor and the governor are friendly members of the party, since this may give added access to (and control of) public facilities. In 2008, Colorado's Democratic governor Bill Ritter and Minnesota's Republican governor Tim Pawlenty both satisfied that objective, as did Democratic governor Bev Perdue of North Carolina and Republican governor Rick Scott of Florida in 2012—and Democratic governor Tom Wolf of Pennsylvania and Republican governor John Kasich of Ohio in 2016. In 2004, the Republicans selected New York, thanks in part to the presence of a Republican mayor, Michael Bloomberg, and governor, George Pataki. Aides to George W. Bush also wished to use the convention to emphasize the president's record on fighting terrorism by holding it in the same city as the World Trade Center attacks of September 11, 2001. Democrats, meanwhile, chose Boston as the site of their 2004 convention, which turned out to be the hometown of their nominee that year, John Kerry.

The timing of conventions varies between mid-July and early September. Since the four-year periodicity of presidential elections always coincides with the Summer Olympics, parties are careful not to schedule their conventions during the weeks when Americans are especially distracted from politics by the spectacle of international athletic competition. By tradition, the party of the sitting president holds its convention after the party of the opposition, whether or not the incumbent is seeking another term in office. In 2008, 2012, and 2016, the parties opted to schedule them in consecutive weeks, but in 2020 more than a month will separate the Democratic convention (July 13–16) from the Republican convention (August 24–27).

PARTY DELEGATES AT THE CONVENTIONS

In bygone days, presidential nominations were actually decided at the conventions, rather than months in advance by the results of primaries and caucuses. Today's conventions can therefore seem anticlimactic in comparison, with the participants holding more symbolic than substantive power. It is still valuable, however, to know something of the delegates themselves, since they represent the more engaged and committed sector of the party to which they belong. Who are they? Who do they represent? What do they believe? Repeated studies of convention delegates allow us a perspective on the changing nature of party activists. While delegates today no longer have independent influence over the choice of the presidential nominee, they still play a role in platform debates and in establishing the image the party projects to the public. If we should ever have a deadlocked convention, in which no single candidate enters with a majority of delegate votes, delegate attitudes and behavior will take on even more importance.

Each of the major parties has its own distinctive style and norms. "Republicans," Jo Freeman observes, "perceive themselves as insiders even when they are out of power, and Democrats perceive themselves as outsiders even when they are in power."[68] Republicans are also ideologically oriented, while Democrats think of themselves as members of subgroups.[69] The more varied and egalitarian Democratic Party, in Freeman's words, "has multiple power centers that compete for membership support in order to make demands on, as well as determine, the leaders."[70] For Democratic delegates, therefore, subgroup caucuses are significant reference groups. The component parts of the Republican Party, states and geographic regions and ideological factions, maintain a less robust existence outside the party structure than do the Democratic caucuses of African Americans, union members, feminists, gay rights activists, or environmentalists. Democrats go to caucuses and make demands, while Republicans "network" at receptions.[71]

The Democratic rules governing delegate selection have succeeded in increasing the proportion of racial minorities and women in attendance over the decades. But even if delegates differ somewhat by income and education, political activists are still a rather elite class. Table 4.3 reveals the differences in income between delegates and party voters for both parties in 2008, the last year for which data are available.

Educational differences between delegates and the broader universe of party identifiers were even more striking. About seven in ten delegates from both parties had college degrees, compared to one in five among rank-and-file Democrats and one in three of rank-and-file Republicans. Little had changed from 1975, when Jeane Kirkpatrick concluded, "The delegates to both conventions were an overwhelmingly middle to upper class group."[72] Summarizing the demographic composition of delegates from 1944 to 2008, table 4.4 reveals a gradual rise in the education level of delegates. But the big change evident over the same period is the four-and-a-half-fold increase in the participation of women (with the conspicuous exception of the 2008 Republican convention, which also had a particularly old group of delegates).[73] From 1972 to 1976, half of female Democratic delegates were employed in the public sector, either in government itself or in public education. This was also true of a little over a third of Democratic men. Among Republicans, somewhat more than a third of female and just under a fifth of male delegates were government employees. Over a quarter of all delegates were

Table 4.3 Income of Delegates and Party Voters in 2008 (in percentages)

	Voters	Delegates
Democrats' Income		
Less than $50,000	43	10
$50,000–$75,000	21	17
Over $75,000	26	70
Republicans' Income		
Less than $50,000	31	5
$50,000–$75,000	22	22
Over $75,000	39	66

Source: "*The New York Times*/CBS News Poll 2008 Republican National Delegate Survey," http://graphics8.nytimes.com/packages/pdf/politics/20080901-poll.pdf.

Table 4.4 Selected Delegate Surveys, 1944–2008 (in percentages)

	1944		1968		1976		1984		2004		2008	
	Dem.	Rep.	Dem.	Rep.	Dem.	Rep.	Dem.	Rep.	Dem.	Rep.	Dem.	Rep.
Sex												
Men	89	91	87	83	67	69	49	54	50	57	51	68
Women	11	9	13	17	33	31	51	46	50	43	49	32
Education												
High school or less	24	23	N.A.	N.A.	N.A.	N.A.	11	12	5	6	4	3
Some college	18	18	N.A.	N.A.	N.A.	N.A.	18	25	18	20	12	15
College graduate	12	16	10	—	21	27	20	28	24	29	26	31
More than college degree	46	41	44	34	43	38	51	35	53	44	55	50
Age												
Average age (in years)	52	54	49	49	43	48	44	51	51	53	52	56
Convention attendance												
Never attended convention before	63	63	67	66	80	78	74	69	57	55	57	58
Ideology												
Liberal	—	—	—	—	40	—	50	1	41	1	43	—
Moderate	—	—	—	—	47	45	42	35	52	33	50	26
Conservative	—	—	—	—	8	48	5	60	3	63	3	72

Sources: Barbara G. Farah, "Delegate Polls: 1944 to 1984," *Public Opinion* (August/September 1984): 44. Reprinted with permission of American Enterprise Institute for Public Policy Research; "*The New York Times*/CBS News Poll National Delegate Surveys," 2004 and 2008, http://www.nytimes.com/packages/html/ politics/20040829_gop_poll/2004_gop_results.pdf; http://www.nytimes.com/packages/html/politics/20040724poll/20040724_delegates_poll_results.pdf; http:// graphics8.nytimes.com/packages/pdf/politics/20080901-poll.pdf; http://graphics8.nytimes.com/packages/pdf/politics/demdel20080824.pdf.

Notes: 1984 figures are a combination of the CBS News poll, the *New York Times* poll, and the *Los Angeles Times* poll; the 1968 and 1976 figures come from the CBS News poll.

union members, most of them from teachers' and other public-sector unions. For women in particular, then, M. Kent Jennings concludes, "public employment is a key route to the avenues of party power."[74]

As the party traditionally favoring government, it is to be expected that Democratic delegates would come more frequently from the public sector. This may also explain why they seek higher spending on domestic programs. But there is nothing inherent in government employment that would necessarily lead to a preference for lower spending on defense or against military intervention in the Middle East or for liberal positions on social issues. For that, we must look to an ideological explanation.

Delegates are likely to represent the ideological left or right, while the bulk of the voters out in the country remain closer to the center. This pattern has occasionally resulted in the nomination of a presidential candidate who is also ideologically extreme. The classic examples were the Republicans in 1964, who selected the very conservative Senator Barry Goldwater of Arizona, and the Democrats in 1972, who chose the very liberal Senator George McGovern of South Dakota. In each case, studies found that convention delegates held political beliefs that were not shared by ordinary members of their party. In each case, the nominee lost badly in November, partially because of defections from his own party to the opposition candidate. The participant sectors of the parties were far more polarized in 1972 than they had been in the 1940s and 1950s in two directions—one party from the other at the elite level, and elites in both parties from their followers.[75]

Evidence from representative governments throughout the world demonstrates that voters have more ideologically moderate views than elected officials, who in turn are more moderate than party activists.[76] While the general public prefers smaller government and restrictions on abortion far more than Democratic elites do, it also likes environmental regulation and deficit reduction a lot more than Republican elites do. tables 4.5 and 4.6 compare the views of delegates to the Democratic and Republican national conventions in 2008 to the positions of Democratic and Republican identifiers, and to all voters. On nearly every issue, convention delegates were significantly more extreme than the rank-and-file members of their own party, and were far more so than the less ideologically oriented American electorate.

Trends in the ideological dispositions of party activists in the two parties are reflected in changes in the composition of the two delegate populations over time. Democratic delegates have become somewhat more liberal, and Republicans more conservative, reflecting the growing polarization of American political elites also seen in congressional voting behavior in recent decades.[77] The view that the major parties were essentially alike, which was never true, is even less true today. The consequences of ideological polarization, which is what we have been describing, are well known: heightened conflict and the risk of political instability. According

Table 4.5 Democratic Delegates to the Left of Rank-and-File Party Members and Public, 2008 (percentages in agreement with statements)

	All Voters	Democratic Voters	Democratic Delegates
2001 tax cuts should be made permanent	47	34	7
The United States was right to invade Iraq in 2003	37	14	2
Abortion should be permitted in all cases	26	33	58
Gay couples should be allowed to marry	34	49	55
Protecting the environment is more important than developing new energy sources	21	30	25

Source: "New York Times/CBS News Poll 2008 Democratic National Convention Delegate Survey," http://graphics8.nytimes.com/packages/pdf/politics/demdel20080824.pdf.

Table 4.6 Republican Delegates to the Right of Rank-and-File Party Members and Public, 2008 (percentages in agreement with statements)

	All Voters	Republican Voters	Republican Delegates
2001 tax cuts should be made permanent	47	62	91
The United States was right to invade Iraq in 2003	37	70	80
Abortion should be permitted in all cases	26	13	5
Gay couples should be allowed to marry	34	11	6
Protecting the environment is more important than developing new energy sources	21	9	3

Source: "New York Times/CBS News Poll 2008 Republican National Convention Delegate Survey," http://graphics8.nytimes.com/packages/pdf/politics/20080901-poll.pdf.

to the venerable theory of cross-cutting cleavages, when people agree on some issues and disagree on others, the need to call on each other for support sometimes moderates the severity of conflict at other times. By putting the same people in opposition on issue after issue, the current trend of polarization also increases mutual antagonism.

THE CONVENTION AS ADVERTISING

Party conventions were probably always seen, in part, as a means of advertisement. At the least, listening to convention speeches and talking to peers might furnish delegates with rhetoric to use in local campaigns back home. But until the age of modern media, conventions were primarily concerned with nominating candidates and other internal party activity.

Television arrived at the conventions in 1952 and transformed their role, with the help of party reforms that ended the old system of selecting nominees via deliberation and compromise. Now, conventions are for selling candidates.[78] The proceedings are planned in order to promote the presidential nominee, running mate, and party to a national audience. The unflashy business of conventions, such as putting the names of candidates before the assembled delegates and approving the party platform, is scheduled for afternoon or early evening sessions before the broadcast networks' live coverage goes on the air. Prime time is filled with speeches meant to appeal to voters, along with celebrity appearances and video productions designed to keep viewers interested.

Indeed, conventions are now judged by pundits on how well they are organized as advertisements. Any intrusion of substantive debate (such as platform disagreements) into the convention is considered a breach of unity and therefore a sign of weakness in the party. More serious still is poor entertainment. Woe to any convention such as the one in New York that renominated Jimmy Carter in 1980, in which the mechanism for releasing brightly colored balloons from the roof of Madison Square Garden malfunctioned, thus providing commentators with a handy metaphor for the incumbent president's stalled reelection bid.[79] Carter's misfortune contrasts strikingly with Barack Obama's 2008 acceptance speech spectacle, featuring a well-delivered address before a cheering crowd of 80,000 people in a football stadium followed by outdoor fireworks.

The advertising content of the conventions is influenced by the decisions of television news producers; the parties try to provide programming that they believe the networks will allow people to see, now that the parties cannot count on extensive coverage. Currently, the broadcast networks cover the conventions through their nightly news reports, their morning shows, and one-or two-hour wrap-up programs from the conventions during prime time, while cable news channels cover them live throughout the day and evening, albeit with frequent cutaways from the proceedings for analysis and punditry. Uninterrupted gavel-to-gavel coverage of convention business can now be found only on the C-SPAN cable network or via online streaming.

By using the convention as advertising, the parties hope to receive a "bounce" in the support their candidates get in the polls. Since the advent of modern public opinion research, only Lyndon Johnson in 1964 (who was already winning by a landslide) and George McGovern in 1972 (who had a disastrous convention) failed to improve in voter surveys taken immediately after their conventions. One might think that this effect would dissipate as broadcast networks reduced the amount of convention coverage and as viewers had more options than network television. But the public still appears to respond positively to the conventions, at least temporarily. In 1996, both Bill Clinton and Bob Dole received healthy bounces of several percentage points in the polls, as did George W. Bush and (especially) Al Gore in 2000.[80] The nominees in 2004, George W. Bush and John Kerry, each received a more modest convention bounce, estimated at four percentage points apiece by the *Washington Post*/ABC News poll.[81] Assessing the 2008 bounces was complicated by the back-to-back scheduling of the conventions, but both Barack Obama and John McCain did seem to receive small polling boosts from the party conclaves.[82] In 2012, Obama received a noticeable bounce of several points from his convention, though polls disagreed about whether Mitt Romney did the same.[83] Hillary Clinton and Donald Trump each received a convention bounce of roughly 4 points in 2016.[84]

How do the parties turn what once was a business meeting into advertising?

1. The layout of the convention hall itself is designed with television, not the comfort of the delegates, as the first priority. As the late Democratic media consultant Bob Squier said, "To be blunt, the room is designed to be a television set." Another Democratic media expert, Frank Greer, said in praise of one convention: "It has become clear that, as it should be, this is a convention designed and presented for TV viewers more so than for delegates on the floor. It's a chance to talk to people in their living rooms and not the delegates on the floor."[85]

2. The delegates, far from having an important role in deciding party business, have been reduced to serving primarily as extras. "Homemade" handwritten signs are constructed and distributed by party staffers to reinforce campaign themes. Not even crowd noises are left to chance: at one Republican convention, aides "arranged that, at key moments, troops of

rehearsed young people flooded onto the floor and filled the first fifty feet in front of the podium and in the aisles. They knew what to chant when, and they were standing in front of most of the delegates so they couldn't be missed by the cameras."[86]

3. Both parties try to script as much as possible of the convention, carefully orchestrating the words and images delivered from the podium and providing suggested responses to likely interview targets. Speeches are pre-approved by campaign advisers, fed into teleprompters, and timed so that signs and chants from the floor can be properly coordinated with them. Convention organizers try to present an appealing public image by attempting to contradict unfavorable stereotypes about the kinds of people who belong to their party. For example, observers at the 2004 Republican convention noted that there was a far higher proportion of members of minority groups at the speaker's podium, or providing the musical entertainment, than in the hall as delegates.[87] Similarly, the Democrats that year emphasized the U.S. Navy service of their nominee, John Kerry, in order to counter perceptions during a time of war that the party was hostile to the military. Kerry began his acceptance speech by giving a salute to the assembled delegates and telling them that he was "reporting for duty."[88]

Very little is left to chance. The parties treat their conventions as extended commercials for the presidential ticket and for the party as a whole. This is not necessarily a bad thing: many commentators have urged the networks to make available free airtime for the parties to present their messages directly to the voters during the fall campaign, not realizing that the conventions already serve that purpose (though broadcast networks have devoted progressively less time to convention coverage over the last several elections). First and foremost, the candidate wants a united party.[89] Rival candidates who are in a position to disrupt this unity may extort small advantages from the nominee, a significant strategic resource for Jesse Jackson's candidacies in the 1980s. By threatening messy floor fights over several issues, Jackson won changes to Democratic Party rules, cutting the number of superdelegates and requiring that all delegates be awarded to candidates on a proportional rather than a winner-take-all basis.

The unusually close Democratic primary contest in 2008 meant that nearly half of the delegates attending the party's national convention to nominate Barack Obama had been strong supporters of Hillary Clinton's unsuccessful presidential campaign. After the long battle of the nomination season, Obama's campaign advisers were somewhat mistrustful of both Hillary and Bill Clinton and worried about their behavior at the convention. *Newsweek* later reported "nervousness that the Clintons, with an eye on [another presidential run in] 2012, might try to steal the show, perhaps by demanding a noisy floor vote that would show how close Hillary had come to the nomination. The Obamaites figured that the Clintons could be counted on to do just enough to say that they tried to help Obama—but maybe not so much that he won in November."[90] Ultimately, both Clintons delivered well-received convention speeches that endorsed Obama without equivocation, to the great relief of both the Obama team and Democratic leaders worried about a divided party heading into the fall campaign. Nor did the Clinton faction cause Obama any procedural difficulties; during the traditional roll call of state delegations, Hillary Clinton introduced a "surprise" motion from the floor that Obama be nominated by acclamation—a stunt that was choreographed by convention planners to occur during the networks' evening news broadcasts, thus maximizing public attention.[91] With the assistance of both Clintons, Obama succeeded in convincing the news media and, by extension, the voters that the party had united around his candidacy.

Eight years later, Clinton found herself in Obama's former position as the presumptive nominee urging party unity after a hard-fought primary season, with Bernie Sanders and his supporters in the role of potential troublemakers at the Democratic convention. The Clinton campaign made contact with top Sanders aides as early as May 2016 in hopes of ensuring a peaceful convention two months later. "It was so important that we began to collaborate early and that we, at least, agreed on, at a fundamental level, whoever was going to be the nominee, we had to come together and support them," recalled Clinton campaign manager Robby Mook. Clinton strategist Mandy Grunwald explained that "we did schedule Bernie [Sanders's prime-time speech] for Monday [of convention week] with this thought in mind—that we knew we needed to consolidate and come together . . . [on] the first day so that we could have a united convention going forward."[92]

After some haggling over language in the party platform and other arrangements, the Clinton team succeeded in satisfying the concerns of Sanders and his advisers. But some Sanders supporters—both delegates on the convention floor and activists who assembled outside the hall—did not easily follow the lead of their candidate in accepting Clinton's nomination. Sharing a common interest in making Sanders appear to be a good sport who was supporting Clinton and not using the convention to inflame party divisions, staffers to both Clinton and Sanders collaborated on a real-time messaging system that allowed open dissent to be quickly identified and, if possible, hidden from view of the cameras. "When a Bernie supporter raised an anti-Clinton sign, a whip team member in the convention hall could relay the message quickly to the boiler room," reported Jonathan Allen and Amie Parnes. "The team there would send a note to Bernie and Hillary aides on the floor, who would ask the person to take it down. The flash-speed communications network would turn out to be a major factor in transforming what was a tumultuous convention inside the hall into a unified one on television."[93]

The rare moments when true spontaneity is injected into the proceedings of a modern convention usually turn out to be bad news for both the nominee and the party. In the midst of a speech in support of Mitt Romney at the 2012 Republican convention, Academy Award–winning actor and director Clint Eastwood launched into an impromptu routine in which he improvised an antagonistic conversation with an absent Barack Obama, represented by Eastwood's placement of an empty chair on the stage next to him. Romney campaign staff insisted afterward that they were unaware in advance of Eastwood's plans to ad lib at great length. Reviews in the news media were decidedly unkind—the *New York Times* described the speech as "the most bizarre, head-scratching 12 minutes in recent political convention history"; CNN called it "rambling" and "vaudevillian-like schtick"; and the *Washington Post* characterized it as "like your crabby uncle doing dinner-table comedy"—while the unexpected oddness of Eastwood's behavior made his appearance an instant viral sensation on social media, leaving Republicans deeply frustrated that the performance diverted popular attention from Romney's own acceptance address later in the evening.[94]

Because the national press corps tends to get bored when scripted proceedings go smoothly, any signs of disagreement or disorganization at a national convention will provoke a torrent of headlines. In 2016, news coverage of both conventions became preoccupied with the presence of disgruntled party members opposed to the choice of Hillary Clinton and Donald Trump as the presidential nominees. Anti-Trump activists even mounted a half-hearted attempt to install procedural roadblocks to his nomination at the Republican convention; although this rebellion soon fizzled, it received considerable press attention at the time. As Trump adviser Paul Manafort later remembered, "The Dump Trump effort was really a media effort. They didn't have any strength among delegates of significance. It was never a factor [threatening Trump's nomination]."[95] Aware of these journalistic proclivities, the nominee's campaign strategists endeavor to stage-manage the convention in such a way to prevent reporters, always on the lookout for juicy conflict, from noticing that any segment of the party is less than thrilled about the outcome.

THE VICE PRESIDENTIAL NOMINEE

After the national convention finally nominates a presidential standard-bearer, it turns to the routine task of ratifying the nominee's choice for vice president. Party nominees for president and vice president appear on the ballot together and are elected together; since 1804 a vote for one has always been a vote for the other. Presidential contenders therefore select their running mates in order to help them achieve the presidency. They look for a vice presidential candidate who is politically and personally compatible with themselves, who promises to inspire respect and enthusiasm among the electorate, who will be judged as sufficiently qualified to assume the presidential office if the need arises, and who possesses some desirable qualities that the presidential nominee lacks: in American political parlance, the running mate must "balance the ticket."

The vice president's constitutional role as the presiding officer of the Senate is mostly honorific, while the office's specific powers and responsibilities in the executive branch are subject to the will of the president and are not necessarily extensive.[96] Yet the vice presidency is the position from which presidents of the United States are most frequently drawn. Nearly one-third of our 45 presidents previously served as vice presidents. Five were later elected president in their own right, eight took office upon the death of their predecessors, and Gerald Ford succeeded because of President Nixon's resignation. American history has given us 14 good reasons—one for each vice president who ascended to the presidency—for inquiring into the qualifications of vice presidents and for examining the criteria by which they are chosen.

Historically, geographic considerations often played a large role in the selection of a vice presidential candidate. A running mate from a different region of the country was thought to broaden the appeal of the presidential nominee, while a resident of a populous, politically competitive state could potentially deliver the state to the party, thus offering an advantage in the Electoral College. The classic example of this approach is Senator John F. Kennedy's selection of Senate Majority Leader Lyndon Johnson to join him on the Democratic ticket in 1960. A liberal Catholic from Massachusetts, Kennedy needed to carry a number of southern states in order to win the election and chose Johnson, an energetic, folksy Texan, to be his ambassador to the region. Johnson spent much of his time campaigning in the South during the final weeks of the race, concentrating especially on his home state, ultimately won by the Democrats by less than 50,000 votes.[97]

This geography-based approach to vice presidential selection still seems to influence the thinking of many political pundits, who inevitably consider governors, senators, and other officials from key swing states to be likely potential candidates when speculation turns—as it inevitably does in the summer of a presidential election year—to the identity of the vice presidential nominees. Since Kennedy chose Johnson in 1960, however, most presidential candidates have not selected running mates from large or competitive states. In fact, the home states of the last three vice presidents—Dick Cheney of Wyoming, Joe Biden of Delaware, and Mike Pence of Indiana—were both already considered safe territory for their party (as was Alaska, home to 2008 Republican vice presidential nominee Sarah Palin), suggesting that contemporary presidential candidates tend to pick running mates whom they believe will help them win votes everywhere, not just within a single state or region. Hillary Clinton did appear to have geography in mind when she selected Tim Kaine of Virginia, a senator and former governor from an important battleground state, as her vice presidential candidate in 2016. But Kaine, a former chair of the Democratic National Committee who was a personable campaigner and fluent in Spanish, also seemed to bring other advantages to the national ticket besides his potential appeal among his fellow Virginians.

If the party is split by ideological differences, the selection of a running mate from a rival faction can encourage unity. In 1964, Lyndon Johnson chose a prominent liberal, Senator Hubert Humphrey of Minnesota, as his vice presidential nominee. Johnson's own credentials as a liberal Democrat had weakened from his early days as a New Deal congressman; when Kennedy picked him as vice president, he had been opposed on these grounds by labor leaders and by party officials from several of the most important urban Democratic strongholds. Gerald Ford, with his midwestern and congressional background, may have had the same thing in mind when he chose a more moderate, eastern establishment figure, Governor Nelson Rockefeller of New York, to be vice president on his elevation to the presidency. Later, threats from the right wing of the Republican Party to his own nomination chances caused Ford to dump Rockefeller and replace him for the 1976 election with the more conservative Senator Bob Dole of Kansas. Ronald Reagan, more securely tied to the Republican right wing than Ford, leaned toward the moderate side of his own party in picking George H. W. Bush in 1980. Bush, in turn, looked to the right when selecting a running mate in 1988, settling on Senator Dan Quayle of Indiana, who not only offered solid conservative credentials, but also, Bush hoped, would appeal to young people and women—two groups of voters the Republicans were targeting.[98] In 2016, Donald Trump selected Indiana governor Mike Pence, a prominent social conservative, in order to reassure Christian activists within the Republican Party of his commitment to their positions on issues of concern like abortion.

Though presidential candidates have some freedom to select running mates who differ from themselves ideologically, the issue positions of the vice presidential candidate must still be acceptable to party activists. According to later press reports, John McCain initially favored Senator Joe Lieberman of Connecticut, the 2000 Democratic vice presidential nominee who had subsequently become an independent and endorsed McCain for president, as his running mate in 2008 in order to reinforce his campaign message of bipartisanship and to bolster his appeal to independent voters and wavering Democrats. But McCain campaign aides argued that Lieberman's liberal views on social issues—as well as the fact that he was not even a Republican—would anger the party faithful, possibly leading to an open revolt on the floor of the convention. Looking back after the election, McCain's chief campaign strategist Steve Schmidt claimed that Lieberman's selection "would have been an exciting and dynamic pick . . . that would have been electrifying to the broader electorate," but that McCain "would not have been able to get him nominated through the convention . . . we would have blown up the Republican Party."[99] Similar concerns eliminated Tom Ridge, a former Republican governor of Pennsylvania and secretary of homeland security who favored legalized abortion, from consideration as well.[100] (The fact that many on the right were already suspicious of McCain's own devotion to conservative principles merely strengthened the perceived need for his running mate to be an ideologically orthodox Republican.) McCain ultimately selected Palin, who proved to be popular with party loyalists. Likewise, influential Democratic congressman Barney Frank of Massachusetts responded to rumors that Barack Obama might consider former senator Sam Nunn of Georgia as his vice presidential nominee by publicly warning Obama in June 2008 that he viewed a long-standing record of opposition to gay rights as disqualifying Nunn for a position on the Democratic ticket.[101]

Factional divisions may not necessarily be based on ideology. The long, hard-fought primary campaign between Obama and Hillary Clinton in 2008 inspired widespread speculation that the winning candidate might feel compelled to choose the loser as his or her running mate in order to heal the rift in the party. As it became increasingly clear that Obama would prevail, Clinton supporters were most vocal in calling for a "unity ticket." It appears that the Obama campaign never seriously considered Clinton as a potential vice presidential nominee, concluding that such a move was not necessary in order to win the backing of her followers in the general election. Instead, Obama cemented his reconciliation with Clinton after his victory over McCain by selecting her to be the first secretary of state in his presidential administration.

Another way to balance the ticket is to focus on experience. Presidential nominees who have served little or no time in Washington will typically select a veteran of Congress or the executive branch to reassure voters and the news media that their administration will be competent—and to help them govern successfully once in office. Jimmy Carter, a one-term former governor of Georgia, chose a popular senator, Walter Mondale of Minnesota, in 1976 to compensate for his own lack of federal experience. Similar considerations drove four other state governors to choose prominent Washingtonians as their running mates— Ronald Reagan's selection of former representative, CIA director, ambassador to China, and Republican National Committee chair George H. W. Bush in 1980,

Michael Dukakis's pick of Texas senator Lloyd Bentsen in 1988, Bill Clinton's choice of Tennessee senator Al Gore in 1992, and George W. Bush's selection in 2000 of former House Republican whip, presidential chief of staff, and secretary of defense Dick Cheney all fit this model. Barack Obama, less than four years into his first term in the Senate when nominated for the presidency in 2008, selected six-term fellow senator Joe Biden as his vice presidential candidate in part to address concerns about his own qualifications, while Donald Trump, who had never served in elective office prior to his presidential candidacy, chose Pence, a former six-term member of the House of Representatives before his election as governor of Indiana.

Presidential nominees with long careers in Washington, on the other hand, tend to prefer running mates who are notably younger or who are political "outsiders" in order to provide a fresh-faced contrast to themselves. Examples of this pattern include Richard Nixon choosing Governor Spiro Agnew of Maryland in 1968, George H. W. Bush selecting Dan Quayle in 1988, John Kerry picking first-term senator John Edwards of North Carolina in 2004, and McCain's selection of Palin in 2008. Mitt Romney's choice of Wisconsin representative Paul Ryan in 2012 represented a new spin on this approach; Ryan, though he was more than 20 years younger in age, had also served seven terms in Congress and chaired the House Budget Committee, thus supplying extensive federal government experience that Romney lacked.

Personal characteristics or reputations of potential running mates also matter. In the 2000 election, both presidential candidates had perceived deficiencies that they sought to address with their vice presidential selection. Al Gore picked the upright and conspicuously pious Joe Lieberman to offset the charge that Democrats were morally lax, while George W. Bush picked the veteran administrator Dick Cheney to address the perception that he was incurious about the workings of government. Four years later, the well-born and detached John Kerry chose John Edwards in part to benefit from Edwards's blue-collar roots and telegenic style. Barack Obama's advisers hoped in 2008 that the selection of Joe Biden would help them appeal to working-class white voters who had mostly supported Hillary Clinton over Obama in the Democratic primaries and who were being courted heavily by the McCain campaign. McCain, meanwhile, calculated that choosing Palin might attract female voters disappointed by Clinton's absence from the Democratic ticket.

Recent vice presidential candidates have sometimes been distinguished politicians who had a great deal to recommend them as holders of high office. But the assistance that they could offer their parties in winning the election was undoubtedly an important consideration in their selection. If it is impossible to find one person who combines within his or her heritage, personality, and experience all the virtues allegedly cherished by American voters, the parties console themselves by attempting to confect out of two running mates a composite image of traditional-modern, rural-urban, principled-pragmatic, experienced-outsider, energetic-wise leadership that evokes ideological, generational, and demographic loyalties among a maximum number of voters. That, at least, is the theory behind the balanced ticket.

Because the choice of a vice presidential candidate is designed to help the presidential nominee get elected, it is invariably shaped by the strategic environment at the time of the decision. A candidate who is leading in the polls may pick an unexciting but dependable running mate, while an underdog might prefer the option that offers higher risk but a potentially greater reward in the hope of changing the dynamics of the campaign. This last strategy has twice led to the selection of female nominees for the vice presidency by trailing candidates who hoped that an unorthodox running mate would transform the race. Walter Mondale's selection of Representative Geraldine Ferraro of New York in 1984 did not fit traditional patterns of ticket balancing; her views were quite similar to his own, and Mondale had served longer than Ferraro in federal office. Far behind in the polls, Mondale was hoping instead that choosing a woman would mobilize female support and invigorate his candidacy. Richard Brookhiser argues that "the best justification for Mondale's audacity, though, was that it was audacious. . . . Prudent losers remain losers. The first woman on a major party ticket might shake things up."[102] Ferraro's problems with family finances, however, proved to be an unwelcome distraction during the fall campaign, and Mondale lost the election by a wide margin.

In 2008, John McCain took a similar gamble by choosing Sarah Palin, a first-term governor of Alaska who was virtually unknown outside her home state. Palin's selection, announced on the morning after Obama's well-received acceptance speech at the Democratic convention, achieved McCain's immediate goal of catching the Obama campaign, the news media, and the American electorate by complete surprise. McCain and his aides were aware of the risk inherent in opting for a running mate with no previous experience in the national political arena, but, like Mondale, concluded that a bold vice presidential choice offered them the best hope of victory; as senior adviser Nicolle Wallace explained after the election, "We were down nine [percentage points in the polls]. We needed a game changer."[103]

Palin proved to be a charismatic campaigner, but her limited familiarity with national politics, revealed in a series of media interviews, soon became a liability. Political scientist Gerald Pomper concluded that her "ultimate effect on the election is uncertain, but it was probably harmful to McCain" because many in the public came to view her as unqualified for high office.[104] One academic study estimated that Palin's presence on the ticket cost McCain two percentage points in the popular vote, serving as an exception to the usual pattern that running mates seldom substantially affect electoral outcomes.[105] McCain's previous bouts with skin cancer and potential status as the oldest first-term president in American history made the issue of succession to the presidency more salient than usual, to Palin's further disadvantage.

If good results require noble intentions, then the criteria for choosing vice presidents leave much to be desired. Especially able politicians may become vice president because of the political advantages that they promise to bring to the campaign trail, rather than their ideal fitness for the position itself. Yet all successful vice presidential candidates must reassure the public that, regardless of whatever other qualities they may possess, they are not only capable of serving ably in the (not inherently powerful) office for which they have been nominated but are also prepared to lead the nation should circumstances require them to assume the presidency at a moment's notice. There is little sensible reason for a presidential candidate to select a running mate who inspires significant doubt on this point, though it has occasionally happened due to other considerations weighing more heavily in the mind of the nominee.

History strongly suggests that a risk-averse approach to vice presidential selection is nearly always preferable. A well-received yet unexciting choice may not win millions of votes that the presidential candidate would not have otherwise received, but an attention-grabbing yet controversial pick can, at the least, introduce unwelcome distractions in the midst of a hard-fought campaign, and perhaps even cost the ticket a degree of popular support. Candidates should also keep in mind that the presidency, should they achieve it, is an easier burden to bear with a skilled vice president to provide trusted advice and share governing responsibilities. As Hillary Clinton's 2016 campaign manager Robby Mook argues, "Any presidential candidate needs to pick someone who is going to be a great partner and helper in the job. There's actually a danger . . . in picking someone [merely] for tactical reasons."[106]

Though prospective running mates are now routinely subjected to extensive vetting by campaign staff, no presidential candidate has the time or resources to research every aspect of a prospective vice president's background. Instead, nominees have regularly turned to the pool of potential running mates who not only have been thoroughly investigated but also have extensive experience dealing with the national news media: former presidential candidates. George H. W. Bush in 1980, Lloyd Bentsen in 1988, Al Gore in 1992, Jack Kemp in 1996, John Edwards in 2004, and Joe Biden in 2008 had all been scrutinized and tested in previous presidential primaries before their selection as vice presidential running mates. None of them encountered scandal or significant bad press during the fall campaigns. Three vice presidential nominees over that period who had not been previously exposed to national journalists, Geraldine Ferraro in 1984, Dan Quayle in 1988, and Sarah Palin in 2008, ultimately brought far more than their share of turmoil with them, as did George McGovern's original running mate in 1972, Senator Tom Eagleton of Missouri, who left the ticket during the campaign after it was revealed that he had been medically treated for depression. If future presidential nominees want to play it safe in their choice of running mates, they will give special attention to this small group of prescreened possibilities.

THE FUTURE OF NATIONAL CONVENTIONS

If contemporary conventions are really only for advertisement, why do they matter at all? A comparison with the Electoral College is instructive. Ever since the early days of the republic, electors virtually always vote as they have been instructed by their states. The majority wins. Should no candidate receive a majority, electors still have no decisive say in the outcome, because under the Constitution the selection is made by the House of Representatives from among the top three finishers.

Delegates to nominating conventions, even under the current rules, are in a somewhat different position. While their votes on the nomination are (in normal years) simply a matter of registering the preferences of the voters who chose them, they also enjoy the right to vote on platforms and party rules. These votes may be important, and the delegates are free to make their own decisions. Even hand-picked delegates have the option of opposing their candidate's preferences, should they so choose.

Far more important, however, is that in the event of deadlock—if no single candidate controls a majority of delegates going into the convention—the delegates would have the responsibility of selecting the nominee. If the contest is merely close, we would expect few delegate defections, since they have been in most cases selected by candidates mainly on grounds of potential loyalty. A good test of that was the Democratic convention in 1980, when Ted Kennedy hoped to use favorable preconvention publicity to sway the convention. The hope turned out to be unrealistic. In the key test vote, delegates pledged to incumbent president Jimmy Carter stayed loyal to their candidate.

Should no single contender enter the convention with a majority, however, loyalty might matter less. Pundits often mull over this hypothetical scenario early on in the primaries, when no candidate has yet built a sizable majority in the delegate count. As we have seen, however, a deadlocked convention is not particularly likely. Such a result would almost certainly require at least three candidates to reach the convention with large numbers of delegates; if the convention is divided between only two candidates, one or the other will hold a majority of delegates, no matter how slender. Since the normal operation of primaries and caucuses, along with the well-publicized media interpretations of victory and defeat, typically reduces the field of presidential aspirants substantially in the first few weeks of the nomination race, a deadlocked convention with three or more candidates is an improbable result. This is particularly true on the Republican side, where the presence of winner-take-all primaries reduces the capacity of secondary candidates to accumulate delegates. The last convention requiring more than one delegate roll-call vote to choose a presidential nominee occurred in 1952, well before the modern system of delegate selection was established. Still, deadlock is possible, and if it happens, it will be the delegates who will have to choose the party nominee.

How would a modern, post-reform convention handle such a decision? The same rules that have made conventions rubber stamps for the candidate preferences of primary and caucus voters also would make bargaining difficult once there. In order to reach the convention, candidates would need intense factional support; delegates selected for those traits would, presumably, be ill-equipped to negotiate away their vote for the candidate to whom they were loyal. The candidates themselves, then, might be the only ones able to negotiate—and candidates fresh off the campaign trail, having endured negative ads and other attacks from each other, might not be eager to cut a deal, or even able to bring along all of their supporters if they did make a deal.

If the candidates did not resolve their differences, how else would the delegates reach a decision? Some, no doubt, would turn to factional leaders. State delegations might work together, even across candidate lines. Still others might remain unconnected, waiting until somebody else proposed a resolution. Given the enormous size of modern conventions (the Democrats seated more than 4,700 delegates in 2016, compared to the 1,100 delegates who nominated Franklin D. Roosevelt in 1932), it would be impossible for serious, one-on-one deliberation to take place without some sort of organization emerging. If not, we might expect the media to dominate the proceedings, with delegates swayed by the latest reported rumors and speculations.

Given the modern convention's lack of resemblance to a true deliberative body, it is all but certain that national party leaders would attempt to broker an agreement of some kind—for example, by uniting two contenders on a single presidential ticket—in the period between the end of the primary season and the start of the convention. A convention that assembles with the presidential nomination still unresolved would risk spinning into chaos that would jeopardize the chances of the party in the general election; at the least, it would substantially impede the ability of the eventual nominee to prepare for electoral battle with the opposition. The prospect of convention deadlock, while improbable, increases the incentives of party members to attempt to nudge trailing candidates out of the race as soon as it becomes clear that they cannot win the nomination on their own but can only act as spoilers by denying the front-runner an overall majority of delegates.

Just as the news media have interacted with political forces to produce the ratifying rather than the deciding convention, so the two have combined to give the conventions their electoral meaning. Deprived of their substantive importance beyond officially confirming the choice of party voters in primaries and caucuses, the conventions become an opportunity for campaign publicity with the party united behind a single candidate and touting his or her plethora of virtues. Without the need to worry about maneuvering to win the nomination at the convention, candidates can more carefully consider how they want to manage the presentation of themselves and their party to the public. Thus national conventions serve dual roles. In a strictly formal sense, they represent the culmination of the nomination process. In terms of their political importance, however, they are best seen as notable milestones in a general election campaign that is, by midsummer, already well underway.

5

The Campaign

■ ■ ■

AFTER THE END OF THE NATIONAL PARTY CONVENTIONS, it was once a tradition for the two presidential candidates to "relax" for a few weeks until Labor Day, when they were supposed to start their official campaigning. Nowadays, the general election campaign begins once both parties have in effect chosen their nominees, usually well in advance of the national conventions in the spring prior to the November election. Once the conventions ratify their selection, the two candidates confront the voters directly, each carrying the banner of a major political party. How do the candidates behave? Why do they act the way they do? What kind of impact do their activities have on the electorate?

For the minority of Americans who are party activists, campaigns serve as a signal to get to work. How hard they work depends in part on whether the candidates' political opinions, slogans, personalities, and visits spark their enthusiasm. Activists may sit on their hands, or they may pursue their chosen activities—making campaign donations, registering voters, phone banking, ringing doorbells—with something approaching fervor.

For the majority of the population, most of whom normally keep their distance from politics, campaigns call attention to the advent of an election. Some excitement may be generated and some diversion (as well as annoyance) provided for those who turn on the television to find that their favorite program has been preempted by political talk or who check their phone only to see a text message or voicemail exhorting them to vote. The campaign is a great spectacle. Conversation about politics increases, and some citizens become intensely invested in the race as their interest is piqued by news coverage, advertising, and mobilization efforts.

Campaigns usually do not function so much to change the minds of citizens as to activate or reinforce previous convictions. As the campaign wears on, the underlying party identification of most people rises ever more powerfully to the surface. Republican and Democratic identifiers are split further apart—polarized—as their increased awareness of party competition emphasizes the things that divide them.[1]

The substance of campaigns depends on the political context. The swiftly changing nature of the electoral environment makes it unwise for candidates to lay down all-embracing rules for campaigning that cannot meet special situations as they arise. Candidates may prepare for battle on one front and discover that unexpected developments force them to fight on another. Yet political actors must rely on some sort of theory about the probable behavior of large groups of citizens under a few likely conditions. There are too many millions of voters and too many thousands of possible events to deal with each one individually. The candidates must simplify their pictures of the political world or its full complexity will overwhelm them; the only question is whether or not their theories, both explicit and implicit, will prove helpful to them.

What kind of organization should they construct? Where should they campaign? What kinds of appeals should they make to which voting groups? How specific should they be in their policy proposals? What kind of personal impression should they seek to create or reinforce? How far should they go in attacking the opposition? How should they behave in debates with their rivals? These are the kinds of strategic questions for which presidential candidates need answers—answers that vary depending on their party affiliations, their personal attributes, whether they are in or out of office, and targets of opportunity that come up in the course of current events.

THE WELL-TRAVELED CANDIDATES

The central goals of a presidential candidate's campaign are to persuade undecided voters to back the candidate while simultaneously mobilizing supporters to vote and work on behalf of the campaign in large numbers. To this end, candidates seek to maintain a high level of visibility throughout the duration of the election season by making public appearances all over the country in order to attract positive attention from voters and the news media.

Long ago, when publicly campaigning on one's own behalf was considered undignified, presidential nominees faced the serious choice of whether to conduct a "front porch" campaign or to get out and meet the people. The first president to make a campaign speech, William Henry Harrison at Columbus, Ohio, in June 1840, was scolded for his pains: The *Cleveland Adviser* asked, "When was there ever before such a spectacle as a candidate for the Presidency, traversing the country advocating his own claims for that high and responsible station?" Now, each candidate rents an airplane and hires speechwriters, maps out an itinerary, and flies off in all directions. Veteran campaign reporter David Maraniss of the *Washington Post* describes the campaign bubble that includes the candidates, their staff, and accompanying reporters:

> "The bubble" is what surrounds the traveling road show of any presidential campaign. It includes the candidate, the staff, the press, the plane, the bus and all the electronic gear of the hustle—after all, even in the television era, someone's still got to get out there and do the job—yet it is not so much a tangible phenomenon as a metaphysical one, a way of looking at things, at once cynical and cozy, but mostly just weird. It is where you find both the real story and yet an utterly false one, a speed-blurred picture of a very large country. The bubble is addictive yet debilitating.[2]

A veteran of two lengthy campaigns in 2008 and 2016 (as well as two more as the spouse of the Democratic nominee in 1992 and 1996), Hillary Clinton recalled the sometimes disorienting life of a presidential candidate:

> The plane was our home away from home for months. . . . One day we were in Little Rock and had to get to Dallas. The plane had a mechanical issue, so they sent another one. While we were waiting on the tarmac, my staff got off the plane

to stretch their legs. I decided to close my eyes after a grueling few days. I woke up a few hours later and asked, "Are we there already?" In fact, we hadn't moved. At a certain point in a long campaign, all sense of time and space disappears. . . . Sometimes it wasn't fun at all. But it was also wonderful.[3]

There is method in the ceaseless coast-to-coast travel of the presidential candidates over the course of a campaign. Specifically, their behavior is dictated by the strategic implications of the Electoral College. Candidates know that electoral votes, allocated on a state-by-state basis, determine the outcome of the election, not the national popular vote. Except for Maine and Nebraska, which allocate electoral votes by congressional district, each state awards its entire allocation of electoral votes under the unit rule to the candidate who places first in the statewide popular vote, even if by a small margin or with less than a majority.

As a result, candidates have no incentive to spend precious time and campaign resources contesting states in which the outcome is not in doubt. Instead, they concentrate on the swing states that are considered winnable by either side. These politically competitive states are also commonly referred to as "battleground" states, reflecting their status as the centers of campaign activity by both candidates.[4] Populous swing states are especially targeted by campaigns, since their large caches of electoral votes are particularly valuable prizes.

Candidates identify potential swing states by whether they have delivered victories to both parties within recent memory, and according to the results of public opinion polls conducted during the campaign. Since the 1990s, most states in the South and interior West have voted for Republican candidates by large margins, while those in the Northeast (New England, New York, New Jersey, Maryland) and the Pacific Coast (especially California) have constituted a similarly reliable geographic base for Democrats.[5] As a result, candidates of both parties tend to ignore these sections of the country, preferring to focus their attention on states expected to be highly competitive. Over the final two months before the 2016 election, neither presidential candidate made a public campaign appearance in the safely Republican states of Alabama, Alaska, Arkansas, Georgia, Idaho, Indiana, Kansas, Kentucky, Louisiana, Mississippi, Missouri, Montana, Nebraska, North Dakota, Oklahoma, South Carolina, South Dakota, Tennessee, Texas, Utah, West Virginia, and Wyoming, or the securely Democratic states of California, Connecticut, Delaware, Hawaii, Maryland, Massachusetts, New Jersey, New York, Oregon, Rhode Island, Vermont, and Washington.[6]

Instead, Donald Trump and Hillary Clinton spent the final weeks of the 2016 campaign fighting over the minority of states deemed to hold the balance of power in the Electoral College, focusing in particular on swing states with large numbers of electoral votes such as Florida, Pennsylvania, and Virginia. On Labor Day, both candidates independently chose to campaign with their vice presidential nominees in the very same section of northeastern Ohio, composing a memorable shot for media photographers when their campaign jets sat in clear view of each other on the tarmac at the Cleveland airport.[7] Every four years, voters in politically competitive states receive frequent visits from the two candidates, their spouses and running mates, and other top political figures, and are bombarded with advertising and mobilization efforts from both sides attempting to win their support. As Barack Obama's adviser Anita Dunn recalled, "Everything in our campaign was driven by battleground states."[8]

As the campaign wears on, the candidates take repeated soundings from opinion polls and are likely to redouble their efforts in states where they believe frequent personal visits might turn the tide. The actual itinerary is made by a campaign scheduling team guided by two main rules: "Go where the polls say an appearance by the candidate can make a difference. Make it look good on television and the Internet."[9] The scheduler manages this operation so that nominees and running mates get the most value from their appearances. Thus schedulers not only arrange more candidate visits to big competitive states than to smaller, more secure states, but identify particular cities or media markets within the state where a personal appearance might be expected to pay the greatest electoral dividends.

Schedulers try to make plans in advance if possible, but arrangements can change quickly as survey results suggest increasing margins of safety in a given state or reveal new states in need of attention. Running behind in the polls in the fall of 2008, John McCain's campaign made scheduling decisions "on the fly" as strategists looked for states where McCain could possibly overcome Barack Obama's lead. The Obama campaign, for its part, capitalized on its financial advantage and favorable position during the final weeks of the campaign by targeting normally Republican-leaning states like Indiana and North Carolina that surveys indicated were within Obama's reach; this approach paid off when both states voted Democratic for president for the first time in over 30 years.

But if the polls are flawed, the candidate's travel plans will be as well. The Hillary Clinton campaign relied on what turned out to be erroneous survey data in judging Wisconsin and Michigan to be friendly territory in 2016; as a result, Clinton made no public appearances in Wisconsin during the fall campaign and only visited Michigan once evidence of a tightening race began to pile up in the final days before the election. She ultimately lost both states by narrow margins to Donald Trump, whose campaign had been quicker to recognize electoral volatility in the region and who had paid several visits to each state. Though Clinton later defended herself against claims that her campaign had "ignored" Wisconsin and Michigan, noting that she had sponsored television ads and built campaign organizations in both states, she also admitted that "if our data . . . had shown we were in danger, of course . . . I would have torn up my schedule, which was designed based on the best information we had, and camped out there."[10]

Schedulers also decide on the type of event to put onto the candidate's itinerary. The most common type of event in the weeks before a general election is the large public rally, usually held in a municipal park, sports arena, or convention center. Entertainers (usually country music stars for Republicans; pop singers, rock 'n' rollers, or hip-hop artists for Democrats), other celebrities, and prominent political figures are often enlisted to warm up the crowd before a candidate's speech. Some campaigns organize multiday excursions, with candidates traveling between appearances in key states by train, boat, or bus, in order to court additional media attention.

Candidates hold other types of events as well, visiting colleges, small businesses, and county fairs, delivering addresses to prominent interest groups such as the NAACP and the Veterans of Foreign Wars, and hosting "roundtables" and "town hall meetings" in which they respond to questions from voters. As ever, their use is dictated by campaign strategy, with positive media coverage the most important objective. In 2008, Obama advisers became concerned that their frequent use of outdoor rallies attended by large, adoring crowds confirmed the McCain campaign's criticism of Obama as possessing more glamour than substance. They quickly organized alternative events designed to show their candidate's policy-minded side.[11] But other formats have potential pitfalls of their own. A questioner at a Minnesota town hall meeting held by McCain in October 2008 told the candidate that she couldn't trust Obama because he was "an Arab," prompting McCain to quickly grab the microphone to contradict her and express his belief that his opponent was "a decent family man."[12]

Once the schedulers have booked an appearance for the candidate, the campaign's advance team moves in. Its responsibility is to ensure that the event happens without a hitch and that the candidate's message is presented to an adequately prepared press corps, ready to include the day's sound bite in their latest coverage. The advance team's responsibilities include ensuring security for the candidates, arranging housing and transportation (candidates can change vehicles a dozen times or more in one day), overseeing site setup, and providing campaign signs, buttons, and banners for the crowd. Campaign staff must make certain that the press has audio and visual access to the candidate and facilities from which to file stories, that equipment feeds are working properly, and that the visual and promotional materials on the spot evoke the campaign's theme.

But if campaign events are too scripted, the press may get bored and decide that there was little news to report. Donald Trump received more media coverage in 2016 than Hillary Clinton in part because he resisted the tradition of the pre-written "stump speech" delivered off of a teleprompter in near-identical form day after day. Trump's extemporized deviations from his prepared remarks often attracted much more daily media attention than Clinton's well-rehearsed rhetoric. Clinton later complained that "the press didn't cover 'normal' campaign speeches. What they were interested in was a steady diet of conflict and scandal. As a result, when it came to driving a consistent message, we were fighting an uphill battle."[13] Clinton received more coverage when her campaign gave advance notice that she would say something new, such as a late August speech in Nevada that accused Trump of "taking hate groups mainstream and helping a radical fringe take over the Republican Party."[14]

It is beside the point that no one knows whether this frenetic campaign activity does much good. Richard Nixon learned from his enervating experience in 1960, when he pledged to visit all 50 states and then had to follow through on his promise despite a severe illness; in his subsequent campaigns for president in 1968 and 1972, Nixon relied less on in-person campaigning and more on radio and television appearances. Nowadays, most candidates follow a strategy geared to earning coverage on local news broadcasts in key competitive states, but they benefit from the existence of national outlets as well. No matter where the candidates are, the media are likely to report on their activities, extending the reach of a candidate's message far beyond his or her immediate audience.[15]

It is the candidate's job, in this environment, to stay "on message"—that is, if the campaign theme is trust, to emphasize words such as "honesty" or "reliable" in prepared speeches and to work themes of trust into impromptu remarks to the press and public. It is also the candidate's job to deliver a speech with great enthusiasm, no matter how many times he or she has had to reuse the same lines; to avoid doing or saying anything that could be considered embarrassing; and, generally, to be "on" at all times. Presidential candidates must expect to appear before the voters live and on television throughout the campaign, knowing that a mistake can have devastating consequences.

Sheer physical endurance is required. Bob Dole, running behind in the polls in the final stages of the 1996 contest, embarked on a "96 Hours to Victory Tour," the idea being that he would not stop campaigning (except for quick naps) during the four days before the election. "Dole caught a cold, and by Monday he could barely speak," reported Evan Thomas and Peter Goldman. "But he was buoyant and cheerful, drinking a tea called Throat Coat and gaining strength from surprisingly large and lively crowds that showed up at diners and bowling alleys, high-school gyms and airport hangars, in small towns across the country. . . . Dole's plane got a flat tire on Monday afternoon, so Dole moved into [the press plane], where he dozed up front while his aides tried to hush the serenades by reporters."[16]

John McCain endured a similar final push in 2008, visiting seven states from Florida to Nevada over a 20-hour trip that ended after midnight on Election Day. Such grueling campaign schedules are potentially risky—an exhausted candidate is more likely to lose his or her temper or commit a damaging gaffe in front of the press or public—but nervous staffers often convince candidates to hold as many events as possible, fearful of the "what-if" second-guessing that would inevitably follow a narrow defeat. When Hillary Clinton caught pneumonia in September 2016, she ignored doctors' advice to take five days of rest from campaign activity; as a result, she was forced to abruptly leave a September 11 memorial event due to exhaustion.[17]

Journalists, not voters, are the immediate audience for much of what candidates do while running for the presidency. Republican campaign aide John Buckley estimated that "if you discount travel time, I'd say that the media take a third of a candidate's entire day. It's not just the news conferences, but one-on-one interviews, hotel room press briefings, radio and television shows, editorial board discussions, back-of-the-car interviews and conversations."[18] Nicolle Wallace, senior adviser to John McCain's 2008 campaign, recalled that McCain "did two to three hours of battleground [state] media [interviews] every day from the middle of August to Election Day . . . with three or four network affiliate reporters in a market and the print reporters . . . plus a satellite tour, and if we were hitting two states, he'd do that twice."[19] Hillary Clinton revealed that even time spent on the road between public events would be devoted to media outreach: "Sometimes our 'drive time' would stretch to an hour or more. To make the most of it, we would schedule radio interviews back to back."[20]

The effect of all this planning and the demands on the candidates' time mean that candidates can seem to be puppets with the campaign staff pulling the strings, ushering them from one performance to another. Indeed, candidates often complain of stress, fatigue, and sometimes confusion as they are whirled from place to place. But this view underestimates the importance of the candidate, who is ultimately responsible for communicating his or her vision to the voters and, if victorious, is also responsible for implementing it.

PERSUADING VOTERS

Political campaigns have two objectives: to persuade voters open to either candidate ("the swing vote") to support their side (or, at the very least, not to support the opposition), and to inspire their own loyalists (the "base vote") to turn out in large numbers and to work hard at persuading and mobilizing others. Sometimes these goals can conflict, as when an ideological appeal designed to motivate the party base risks alienating independent-minded swing voters. But nearly every campaign activity is designed to further one or both aims, with successful campaigns managing to find an appropriate balance between them.

As we discussed in chapter 1, most voters are not particularly open to persuasion; they align with one of the two major parties and nearly always vote for their party's nominee. The ability of a political campaign to affect whether an individual votes or not is similarly constrained. Citizens who have strong political beliefs, who follow current events closely, and who consider political participation to be an important civic duty will tend to turn out on Election Day regardless of campaign mobilization efforts, while those who don't know much and don't care much about politics will generally remain beyond the reach of even the most ambitious get-out-the-vote operations. In addition, most states require voters to have been registered for at least 30 days in order to participate in an election, further complicating the task of bringing new voters into the electoral process. Yet the success of a campaign at persuading and mobilizing key sectors of the electorate can be critical to the outcome of the election, with margins of a few thousand votes in one or two pivotal states potentially representing the difference between victory and defeat.

The fact that Republican candidates have won six of the last ten presidential elections even as self-identified Democrats continue to outnumber Republicans in the American public demonstrates that party identification, though a powerful indicator of individual voting habits, cannot by itself account for aggregate national results. Other factors besides party have been shown to influence the decisions of voters, and are thus of intense interest to campaigns and political analysts alike. Chief among these are policy issues, the job performance of the incumbent president, and personal evaluations of the candidates.

Economic Policy and Performance

On the broad range of economic affairs and "pocketbook" issues, the Democrats are usually favored as the party most voters believe will best meet their needs. Table 5.1 illustrates the persistence of this view over the decades; more often than not, Democrats have received credit as the party most likely to bring prosperity. Democrats are also usually perceived as more in touch with the material interests of regular Americans. For example, a September 2018 poll by the Pew Research Center asked Americans which party was more "concerned with people like me"; 56 percent of respondents named the Democratic Party, compared to 31 percent who cited the Republican Party.[21] A campaign in which the salient issues are economic, therefore, is more likely to aid the Democrats than the Republicans.

The Democratic Party's modern tendency has been to be "liberal" in several senses of that word. It promises something for everyone. Democrats support extensions of social welfare programs financed by the federal government, an

Table 5.1 Which Party Is Better for Prosperity? (in percentages)

	Democratic	Republican	No Opinion
1992 October	45	37	18
1996 July	42	41	17
2000 October	47	40	13
2005 September	46	41	11
2008 September	52	39	9
2012 September	51	42	7
2016 September	43	46	11

Source: Data from Gallup, "Party Images," http://www.gallup.com/poll/24655/party-images.aspx.

increased minimum wage, health care coverage for the uninsured, job training for the unemployed, additional federal funding for education, programs to protect the environment, and so on. No one is left out—not even business people, who are promised prosperity and given tax benefits, although they usually remain opposed to the additional government regulation of private industry supported by most Democratic candidates.

As a result, opinion surveys usually show that most voters tend to consider themselves closer to the Democratic than the Republican position on economic matters, and to trust the Democratic Party more than the GOP to handle domestic policy issues such as health care, education, and Social Security.[22] Democratic candidates usually seek to exploit this advantage by focusing on these topics while on the campaign trail. Yet there are limitations to this strategy. While voters say they are in favor of social programs, they do not like the spending totals that emerge from them—hence Democratic vulnerability to being tagged as serving "special interests." When voters become concerned that excessive government spending has led to inflation, large budget deficits, or high taxes, Democrats are at a disadvantage.

In order to blunt the Democratic advantage on specific economic policies, Republicans often seek to frame elections in broader philosophical terms as a choice between big government and individual freedom.[23] But because most expensive federal programs, such as Social Security and Medicare, are quite popular with voters, candidates are well advised to be vague concerning the exact types of excessive spending that they oppose. Republican presidential nominees Mitt Romney (2012) and Donald Trump (2016) attacked the Affordable Care Act, enacted in 2010 during the presidency of Barack Obama, as wasteful, ineffective, and threatening to the liberty of citizens, but quietly sidestepped Democratic countercharges that their plans to repeal "Obamacare" would result in some Americans losing their health insurance coverage.

Another potentially fruitful tactic for Republican candidates is co-optation. In 2000, Republican candidate George W. Bush proposed an initiative, later titled No Child Left Behind (NCLB), that would significantly increase federal spending on public education in exchange for implementing standardized national evaluations of student and school performance. Bush successfully positioned himself as the "education candidate" in the race, despite the traditional Democratic edge on the issue, and the enactment of NCLB was one of the major achievements of his first term in office. Bush also passed legislation that added a prescription drug benefit to the federal Medicare program—another successful attempt to contest the usual Democratic popular advantage on domestic policy matters.

In 2016, Donald Trump strategically distanced himself from traditional Republican economic principles. Portraying himself as a populist champion, Trump blasted corporate elites for sending American jobs overseas, vowed to use federal power to reduce the cost of prescription drugs, claimed that his tax cut proposal would deliver most of its benefits to the middle class, and promised to replace the Affordable Care Act with a health care plan that would "take care of everybody . . . much better than they're being taken care of now."[24] Trump's unorthodox rhetoric helped him attract strong support from blue-collar white voters, especially in small towns and rural areas in the Midwest and South, that proved to be a critical component of his electoral victory. Once in office, however, Trump's actual economic policies—with the partial exception of his willingness to impose tariffs on international trade—hewed much more closely to normal Republican practice than he had suggested before the election.[25]

While previous Democratic nominees made middle-class economic appeals a central campaign theme, Hillary Clinton departed abruptly from this pattern in 2016. Only 25 percent of Clinton's television spots focused on policy issues, including fewer than 10 percent of her campaign's negative ads, according to a study conducted by the Wesleyan Media Project. Rather than disputing Trump's credentials as an economic warrior for regular Americans, Clinton confronted her opponent on more personal grounds, characterizing him as intellectually, morally, and temperamentally unqualified for the presidency. But this line of attack was not as potent as her advisers appeared to expect. As the Wesleyan Media Project scholars observed, "In stark contrast to any prior presidential [campaign] for which we have . . . data, the Clinton campaign overwhelmingly chose to focus on Trump's personality and fitness for office . . . leaving very little room for discussion in advertising of the reasons why Clinton herself was the better choice." They concluded that Trump's unexpected strength in midwestern states like Michigan and Wisconsin may have partially reflected the fact that voters were "receiving policy-based (and specifically economically-focused) messaging from Trump" while "a lack of policy messaging in advertising may have hurt Clinton enough to have made a difference" in the outcome of the 2016 election.[26]

When voters say that economic concerns are important to their vote, they are often referring less to ideological debates over the government's proper role in domestic affairs than to the overall health of the nation's economic performance. The incumbent president tends to claim (and receive) credit from the electorate for job and wage growth in the year before the election, while tough economic times lead voters to favor a change in party control—even though the connection between economic performance and the policies of a presidential administration is complex at best. The historic Democratic advantage in the realm of economic policy stems in part from the fact that Republican presidents were in office when the Great Depression began in 1929 and during four sizable but shorter recessions in later years (1970–71, 1982–83, 1991–92, and 2008–9). But Democratic presidents have also suffered blame for poor economic conditions on their watch. After the advent of "stagflation" during the presidency of Jimmy Carter (1977–81), the Republican Party was for some time deemed the party of prosperity.

In 2008, the faltering national economy worked to the electoral benefit of Barack Obama and his fellow Democrats. Though John McCain was not the incumbent president, Obama succeeded in associating his opponent with George W. Bush's unpopular economic record in the minds of many voters while positioning himself as the candidate of change. The onset of a serious crisis threatening the financial sector in late September ensured that the nation's economic woes would dominate news coverage in the weeks before the election; McCain's chief campaign strategist admitted afterward that he realized then that McCain's chances of victory were negligible.[27]

By 2012, the American economy had returned to positive but sluggish economic growth, with the national unemployment rate declining from a peak of 10.0 percent in October 2009 to 7.8 percent three years later. The Obama reelection campaign argued that the nation was moving in the right direction thanks to the policies of the incumbent presidential administration—though Obama and his advisers, mindful of the electorate's still-considerable dissatisfaction with the state of the economy, were careful not to appear out of touch by seeming to overstate the extent of the recovery (especially after Obama made an off-the-cuff remark in a June 2012 press conference that "the private sector is doing fine," which earned him criticism for appearing too sanguine about the economic condition of the nation). For opponent Mitt Romney, the continued weakness of the economy after four years of Obama's presidency represented a convincing reason to adopt a new approach—and Romney, a former management consultant and head of a private equity firm, argued that his experience in the business world gave him valuable expertise in creating a positive economic environment. Voters ultimately sided with Obama once again, though his margin of victory in 2012 (3.9 percentage points in the national popular vote) was substantially smaller than it had been in his first election in 2008 (7.3 points).

The national economy's steady but slow expansion continued through the 2016 election. Caught awkwardly between defense of her party's existing record and a desire to promise better times to come, Hillary Clinton was careful not to criticize Obama's performance directly—but neither did she suggest that conditions were entirely satisfactory. Donald Trump had an easier and more straightforward argument: Obama and Clinton had failed to protect working Americans against economic threats from excessive immigration and foreign powers like China, and Trump's business acumen, knack for deal-making, and independence from the "swamp" in Washington meant that, in the words of his acceptance speech at the Republican national convention, "only I can fix it." By remaining in a medium state between boom and bust, the national economic climate in 2016 foreshadowed what turned out to be a very close presidential race.

Foreign Policy and Performance

While Democrats are often trusted the most on domestic economic matters, Republicans have traditionally held a corresponding advantage in the realm of foreign affairs. They are usually considered better able to manage the military, maintain American security, and conduct a war should the need arise (see table 5.2).[28] For example, George W. Bush won reelection in 2004 in part because most Americans believed that he would better lead the "war on terrorism" declared after the attacks of September 11, 2001, than his Democratic opponent, John Kerry.[29]

Table 5.2 Which Party Better Protects the Country? (in percentages)

	Republican	Democratic	No Opinion
1992 February	39	39	22
2002 September	50	31	19
2005 September	48	37	15
2008 September	49	42	9
2012 September	45	45	10
2016 September	47	40	13

Sources: "Party Best for Peace," *Gallup Poll Monthly,* February 1992; Gallup, "Party Images," http://www.gallup.com/poll/24655/party-images.aspx. 1992: "Which party is the best for peace?" After 1992: "Which political party will do a better job of protecting the country from international terrorism and military threats?"

But unsatisfactory presidential performance can temporarily weaken this advantage. As the Iraq War initiated by Bush in 2003 extended into his second term with no clear resolution in sight, public support for Bush's approach began to fade. In the election to succeed Bush in 2008, Democratic nominee Barack Obama easily prevailed over his Republican opponent John McCain while calling for withdrawing American forces from Iraq—even though McCain, a supporter of Bush's policies, could claim superior experience on military matters as a former U.S. Navy pilot, prisoner of war, and senior member of the Senate Armed Services Committee.

In 2016, Hillary Clinton emphasized her experience as secretary of state during Obama's first term to argue that she was the most qualified candidate to serve as the nation's leader. But Donald Trump attempted to build upon the usual Republican advantage on foreign policy issues by accusing Obama and Clinton of being insufficiently protective of national sovereignty, pledging instead that he would put "America first." Trump promised to increase military spending, to reduce the nation's involvement in the United Nations and NATO, and to withdraw from international agreements limiting climate change and Iranian nuclear activity. National exit polls revealed that voters believed Clinton to be better at handling foreign policy (by a margin of 53 percent to 42 percent), though respondents were more evenly split over which candidate would be the best commander-in-chief (49 percent for Clinton, 46 percent for Trump).[30] Clinton's repeated warnings during the fall campaign that Trump was too emotionally volatile to be trusted with the American military and nuclear arsenal did not, in the end, convince enough voters to deliver her an Electoral College victory.

Social Issues and the "Culture War"

What about the third great cluster of policy questions, the "social issues"—including race and gender relations, LGBT rights, abortion, school prayer, crime and drug abuse, immigration, and gun control?[31] For many years after the social revolutions of the 1960s and 1970s, conventional wisdom held that the more conservative Republicans benefited from a popular backlash to the swiftly changing national culture.[32] In 2004, for example, Republican leaders sponsored a number of state ballot referendums instituting same-sex marriage bans in order to increase the turnout of socially conservative voters, while George W. Bush publicly endorsed a constitutional amendment prohibiting same-sex marriage nationwide.

In recent years, however, Democratic leaders have become more aggressive in raising social and cultural issues that they believe mobilize their own popular base in presidential elections. Democrats adopted campaign rhetoric during the Obama years that characterized socially conservative Republican policies (such as restricting legal abortion and allowing private employers to refrain from providing contraception to employees as part of their health insurance coverage) as constituting a "war on women." The increasing support for gay rights within the American public also transformed a subject once used by Republicans to put Democrats on the defensive (as in 2004) into an issue that Democrats increasingly perceive as politically advantageous—a change personified by Barack Obama, who claimed to oppose same-sex marriage during the 2008 campaign but reversed his public position in 2012. Even gun control, an issue that Democratic presidential candidates once hesitated to emphasize because of its unpopularity among Southern and rural voters, has become a more frequently invoked cause for the party as its electoral base has shifted to northern metropolitan America. A similar change has occurred on race: while Bill Clinton publicly distanced himself from Jesse Jackson in 1992 in order to appeal to white moderates and conservatives, his wife Hillary Clinton invoked the Black Lives Matter movement protesting law enforcement's treatment of African American citizens during her own presidential campaign 24 years later.

But Republicans still perceive considerable strategic advantage in priming cultural concerns as well. Donald Trump placed the issue of immigration at center stage during the 2016 election, blaming immigrants for committing violent crimes and smuggling illicit drugs while arguing that "a country without borders is, quite simply, not a country."[33] A variety of well-publicized Trump remarks over the course of the 2016 campaign included a claim that "when Mexico sends its people [to immigrate], they're not sending their best"; a dismissal of a federal judge who had issued a ruling against a Trump business venture as suffering from a conflict of interest due to his "Mexican heritage"; and an endorsement of "a total and complete shutdown of Muslims entering the United States." Hillary Clinton responded to these comments by repeatedly accusing Trump of harboring personal prejudice and exploiting popular resentments for political gain, meaning that both major candidates focused their campaign messages on these subjects to an unusual degree in 2016.

The result was an election that uniquely activated voters' views on issues of race, gender, immigration, and "political correctness." Trump's controversial rhetoric alienated many non-white and highly educated white voters. But less educated and more culturally traditionalist whites were much less offended by Trump's positions than anticipated by the Clinton campaign, which incessantly denounced their opponent's remarks and behavior in its television advertising spots. One post-election study conducted by Brian F. Schaffner, Matthew MacWilliams, and Tatishe Nteta found that voters' racial and gender attitudes were much more closely related to their degree of support for Trump than their opinions on economic matters, and that different views on race and gender accounted for two-thirds of the partisan gap between college-educated and non-college whites in 2016.[34] Another analysis by Michael Tesler concluded that "racial attitudes were more important in 2016 that they were for Obama's elections. . . . Trump simply seems to make racial attitudes matter more in public opinion."[35] Thus the conflict between the two major parties continues over time to expand into new issue areas without resolving any of their old disagreements.[36]

Presentation of Self

In addition to party affiliation, positions on policy issues, and performance in office, some voters also base their choice of candidates on their personal impressions of the nominees. A candidate benefits from appearing trustworthy, reliable, sincere, knowledgeable, empathetic, pious, even-tempered, kind but firm, devoted to family and country, and in every way normal and presentable. To this end, a great deal of campaign activity is devoted to the portrayal of the candidate as a likable person and typical American. Candidates deliver speeches in front of backdrops draped with flags, grill hot dogs and toss footballs for the benefit of television cameras, and relate charming personal anecdotes about themselves and their families to journalists and voters. No amount of expostulation about the irrelevance of all this ordinariness as qualification for an extraordinary office wipes out the fact that candidates must try to conform to the public stereotype of goodness—a standard that is typically far more demanding of politicians than of ordinary mortals.

The unorthodox campaign of Donald Trump broke some of these long-standing rules in 2016. Trump seldom attempted to come across as a "regular person," to speak carefully in order to avoid factual misstatements, or to control his emotions in public. Most voters were alienated by Trump's behavior, but many also viewed his opponent Hillary Clinton as dishonest and unethical. As a result, the 2016 general election was contested by the two most personally unpopular nominees in modern presidential history.[37]

To be sure, the prevailing standards of normality have evolved considerably over time. Until the mid-twentieth century, all presidents—and nearly all serious contenders for the office—were white male mainline Protestants who traced their ancestry to the British Isles or northern Europe. The landslide defeat of Al Smith, the first Roman Catholic nominee for the presidency, in the 1928 election convinced many political observers that the United States would not elect a Catholic president—an assumption finally refuted by John F. Kennedy's narrow victory in 1960. (Enough anti-Catholic sentiment still existed at the time for Kennedy to find it necessary to deliver a major public address during the campaign denying that he would take orders from the pope if elected.) Other obstacles fell in subsequent elections: Jimmy Carter became the first evangelical Christian president in 1976; Michael Dukakis, the son of Greek immigrants, became the first descendant of southern or eastern Europeans to win a major-party nomination in 1988; Joe Lieberman in 2000 was the first non-Christian on a national ticket; and Mitt Romney became the first-ever Mormon presidential nominee in 2012.

The historic candidacy of Barack Obama in 2008 challenged the widespread belief that a significant fraction of white voters would never support a black candidate for president. Many African Americans initially shared this suspicion, backing Obama by large margins for the Democratic nomination only after his victory in the Iowa caucus demonstrated that he could also attract votes from whites and thus compete seriously for the presidency.[38] While Obama and his campaign staff expressed great confidence in public that his race (and foreign-sounding name) would not cost him the election, in candid moments they were far less certain. This concern intensified in March 2008 when video footage of inflammatory remarks by the pastor of Obama's church in Chicago, Reverend Jeremiah Wright, surfaced in the news media. Against the recommendations of some of his top advisers who worried that dwelling on the subject of race would be politically unwise, Obama decided to respond to the issue by delivering a televised address in Philadelphia on March 18 in which he distanced himself from his pastor's views while refusing to condemn Wright personally, calling for greater understanding and reconciliation among both black and white Americans. The speech was generally well received in the news media, largely—though not completely—defusing the Wright controversy. Though Obama's race ultimately cost him some votes in the general election, it did not turn out to be the outright barrier to the presidency that many had once imagined.[39]

Hillary Clinton's near-miss campaign in the 2008 presidential primaries, when she lost narrowly to Obama, and successful capture of the 2016 Democratic nomination raised the possibility that the historical "glass ceiling" preventing a woman from achieving the presidency might finally be shattered. Like Obama's race, Clinton's gender appears to have been a modest disadvantage with voters. But while Obama won anyway in 2008 and 2012, the 2016 election was sufficiently close that the priming of gendered attitudes and perceptions might well have shifted enough votes to deny Clinton victory in the Electoral College.[40]

The personal lives and private behavior of candidates may also become fodder for the news media and thereby influence voters' perceptions. Back in John F. Kennedy's time, reporters were aware of his extramarital affairs but evidently thought it wrong to reveal them to the public. But a major contender for the 1988 Democratic presidential nomination, former senator Gary Hart of Colorado, withdrew from the race after the press corps uncovered evidence of adultery. Bill Clinton faced similar accusations in 1992 but was able to overcome them—in part because the experience of Hart had removed some of the shock factor from the revelations.

By 2016, Donald Trump's well-chronicled history of marital infidelity did not turn out to be a major vulnerability in either the Republican primaries or general election—even among the Republican Party's popular base of culturally traditionalist evangelical Christians—although it emerged after the election that Trump had helped engineer financial payouts to multiple women with whom he had been involved in order to ensure their public silence. In October 2016, footage was leaked to the press that depicted Trump bragging in coarse terms about committing sexual assault to a reporter from the television program *Access Hollywood* during a 2005 interview. The tape received considerable media attention, after which most pundits and even many leading Republicans concluded that Trump's candidacy was fatally damaged. (Trump himself dismissed his remarks as "locker room talk" that did not reflect his actual behavior.) In the end, however, the *Access Hollywood* video did not alienate Trump supporters from their chosen candidate—to the surprise of many political analysts who assumed that Republican women, in particular, would be scandalized by the revelations.

Past use of illicit drugs is another area where public attitudes have become more forgiving, if not altogether blasé. In what seemed at the time to be an important story, Bill Clinton admitted during the 1992 campaign to having smoked marijuana while a graduate student in England in the 1960s. Though Clinton's defensive claim that he "didn't inhale" was widely mocked, his disclosure failed to outrage voters, and several candidates in subsequent elections have acknowledged previous illegal drug use without much being made of the matter. Similarly, while

Adlai Stevenson's status as the first major-party nominee to have been divorced inspired some comment when he ran in 1952 and 1956, the multiple marriages of more recent presidential contenders did not attract much notice from the press or public. The pregnancy of 2008 Republican vice presidential candidate Sarah Palin's unmarried teenage daughter caused somewhat more of a stir in the news media, though it seems to have had little effect on the decisions of voters.

It would be a painful process for candidates to remodel their entire personalities in order to comport with what they—or their campaign advisers—believe appeals best to the electorate. And, to be fair, most of the people who run for the presidency are not so far from the mark as to make this drastic expedient necessary. What the candidates actually try to do is to smooth off the rough edges, to counter what they believe are the most unfavorable impressions of specific aspects of their public image. John F. Kennedy, who in 1960 was accused of being young and immature, hardly cracked a smile in his televised debates with Richard Nixon, whereas the latter, who was said to be stiff and frightening, beamed with friendliness. Michael Dukakis, suspected of excessively pacific leanings, allowed himself to be driven around in an army tank.[41] George H. W. Bush was told to lower his voice so as to counteract the impression that he was a "wimp."[42] Bill Clinton was told to "talk straight" and avoid smiling too much—for his previous persona had come across as too slick and insincere.[43] Kennedy restyled his youthful shock of hair, and Nixon thinned his eyebrows to look less threatening. Ronald Reagan smiled and ducked when Jimmy Carter tried to portray him as a dangerous ideologue. George W. Bush compensated for his blue-blooded, Ivy League background by purchasing a ranch in Crawford, Texas, where he was frequently filmed performing physical labor and wearing a cowboy hat. Hillary Clinton emphasized her familial roles as a mother and grandmother in order to make herself seem warmer and more relatable.

The qualities that some people do not like may be interpreted favorably by others. Hubert Humphrey, the Democratic nominee in 1968, was alleged to be a man who could not stop talking. His garrulousness, however, was just another side of his detailed knowledge of public policy. He might have talked too much to suit his detractors, but the fact that he knew a lot pleased his supporters. Was Ronald Reagan amiable and charming, or was that a vacant expression on his face? Was Barack Obama idealistic and inspirational, or insincere and inexperienced? Was Hillary Clinton smart and tough, or scheming and untrustworthy? Was Donald Trump strong and passionate, or reckless and offensive? Voters may also change their opinions of political figures over time, reinterpreting strengths as weaknesses or vice versa. During his successful 2000 and 2004 campaigns, George W. Bush was widely praised for being decisive, folksy, plainspoken, and comfortable in his own skin, in contrast to his Democratic opponents Al Gore and John Kerry, who were often characterized as phony, awkward, and pedantic. As Bush's popularity began to decline markedly during his second term in office, however, his decisiveness came to be seen by many as stubbornness, and his folksiness as demonstrating a lack of gravity and engagement.

In modern elections, candidates who come across well on television hold an obvious advantage. John F. Kennedy, Ronald Reagan, Bill Clinton, and Barack Obama all owed their political success in part to their telegenic skills. Candidates now hire professional specialists who advise them on optimal communications strategy. Most commonly, consultants recommend that candidates develop a simple theme for their campaign and stick to it in prepared and unscripted remarks, debates, and advertisements—a practice known in the political world as "message discipline." As a result, candidates will typically deliver a standard stump speech many times over the course of the campaign. Journalists complain quite a lot about the repetitiousness of presidential candidates, as if campaigns should be designed mostly to keep the news media entertained. As Obama campaign manager David Plouffe recalled after the 2008 election, "The consistency of our message [of 'change'] drove the press crazy. [They thought it] was boring [and] were annoyed by it."[44]

But political consultants note that most citizens do not follow the campaign closely from one day to the next; in order for a candidate's message to take root in the minds of the public, they argue, it must be repeated over and over. In politics, veteran Republican communications strategist Frank Luntz explains, "There's a simple rule: you say it again, and you say it again, and you say it again, and you say it again, and you say it again, and then again and again and again and again, and about the time that you're absolutely sick of saying it is about the time that your target audience has heard it for the first time."[45] This predicament ranks high on the list of unsolved (and no doubt unsolvable) problems of American democracy: how to reach the relatively inattentive mass electorate without completely alienating the hyper-attentive mandarins of the news media through whom a candidate ordinarily reaches the rank-and-file voter. Donald Trump's more extemporaneous and free-wheeling approach to campaigning in 2016 helped gain him a great deal of attention from reporters, who were perpetually fascinated by the possibility that he would ad lib something memorable or controversial during his public rallies. But even Trump recognized the value of repetition, developing a collection of signature catchphrases (including "fake news," "build the wall," and "drain the swamp") that he reliably invoked to energize his audiences. As Trump aide Corey Lewandowski explained in retrospect:

> It was the same message, whether we were in Massachusetts or we were in California or we were in Minnesota or Florida . . . What are you going to do? "I'm going to make America great again." Think of that branding. . . . We just stuck on the same message the entire time. It was so [simple] and it didn't target any specific demographic. It targeted every demographic. We didn't have this notion where we have to go win evangelicals in South Carolina to be successful, we have to go win Latinos in Florida to be successful. We had the same message for everybody.[46]

Equally important, perhaps, is the desirability of appearing comfortable in delivery. Televised speeches are the major opportunities for a candidate to be seen and evaluated by large numbers of people. Barack Obama benefited greatly in 2008 from his frequent smile, calm demeanor, and glowing oratory. His opponent John McCain was consistently less polished when delivering prepared remarks, often struggling to read his speeches off teleprompter machines, and tended to resist coaching from his handlers and image consultants. McCain aides felt that their candidate fared better in spontaneous interactions with reporters and voters, which more effectively displayed his passion, humor, and penchant for "straight talk."

Mitt Romney's unsuccessful 2012 campaign offers a particularly revealing example of the dilemmas that candidates may face in deciding how to present themselves to the public. Romney operatives placed little emphasis on revealing the candidate's personal side compared to a typical presidential campaign; Romney's television advertising and stump speeches notably lacked extensive biographical content, and he rarely appeared on popular talk shows and other venues that might provide an opportunity to show his personality to voters. After the election, Romney strategist Stuart Stevens defended the decision to eschew a campaign message that focused on Romney's personal qualities, noting that "to capture the totality of him is very difficult. Whenever we would test this [in focus groups], which we did extensively, it never tested well. Voters . . . thought that at a certain point it was sort of like looking at someone's [family photo] album." Romney adviser Kevin Madden similarly recalled that the campaign "tried to make an argument that this [election] is not about . . . 'Who do you like?' But instead it was about, 'Who is going to be most competent? Who is it that can do the job? Who has the better plan for the future?'"[47] Viewing the middling state of the national economy as Obama's chief vulnerability, the Romney campaign wished to define the choice between the candidates on grounds that favored their side, concluding that a debate over which candidate had the most appealing personality would be a distraction from this objective.

After Obama's victory, however, many Romney supporters, including friends and family of the candidate himself, expressed frustration that the election had left voters without a more positive impression of Romney as a person—in part due to a well-funded series of negative advertisements from the Obama campaign and allied Super PACs portraying Romney as a ruthless corporate raider who lacked compassion for regular Americans. Kerry Healey, who had served as lieutenant governor of Massachusetts under Romney, lamented that "even at the end of the campaign, I never felt that the American people understood Mitt Romney's genuine character and that is a terrible shame." Even David Axelrod of the opposition Obama camp was surprised by the strategy, later telling the *Boston Globe*, "I questioned why they didn't spend more time and energy early defining Romney in a fuller way so people could identify with him. . . . My feeling is you have to build a candidacy on the foundation of biography. That is what authenticates your message. I was always waiting for that [to] happen."[48]

The Hillary Clinton campaign struggled with a similar challenge in 2016. Close friends and acquaintances of the candidate—who, by her own admission, was not a natural political communicator—often lamented that her empathy and charm did not come across in large public settings or on camera. Despite consultants' repeated attempts to "humanize" Clinton, however, it was difficult for them to successfully redefine a candidate who had been in the public eye for 25 years, who had built up a guarded suspicion of the news media over that time, and who was facing persistent controversies during the campaign over her tenure as secretary of state and subsequent well-compensated speeches to Wall Street interests. Many voters continued to view her in negative terms, and her reputation as a calculating and untrustworthy woman was especially damaging to her popularity.

Donald Trump's advisers faced a very different set of problems. Rather than needing to loosen up an excessively self-conscious nominee, they were faced with the difficulty of managing a candidate who was capable of saying nearly anything at any moment. Confident in his own instincts, Trump often resisted the advice of his professional staff. But his penchant for divisive remarks and posts on social media earned him considerable negative publicity, and voters often told reporters and pollsters that they wished that Trump exercised more self-discipline. At the same time, Trump's larger-than-life persona and distinctive emotional transparency—an unusual trait among politicians—helped him stand out among other Republican candidates in the 2016 primaries and attract a loyal base of popular support in the general election.

Negative Campaigning

Candidates not only cultivate positive personal images of themselves among the electorate, but also work to create unfavorable perceptions of their opponents. At various points in a campaign, there may be a temptation for the candidates or parties to let loose a stream of negative material about the other side. This may have its greatest effect very early, before the opposition can establish its own image with voters. As the *New Republic* explained in response to an outbreak of negative advertising:

> [T]he proliferation of negative ads is simply a result of the consultants' discovery that attacks make a more lasting impression on voters than positive commercials. More candidates are making the attacks personally, rather than working through stand-ins, because research shows that the ads work better that way. The surge in negative advertising has even given rise to the countertactic known as "inoculation": ads designed to answer potential negative ads even before the attacks air.[49]

Of course, the nominees of the two major parties will always differ quite substantially on public policy questions, or over the performance of an incumbent administration. Negative advertising that simply criticizes the opposition for its issue positions or record in office is a constant part of every presidential campaign. Somewhat more controversial, but often effective, is a more personal attack by a candidate or campaign on a rival—one that claims or implies that the opponent is weak, incompetent, corrupt, mentally unbalanced, dishonest, morally lax, or even unpatriotic.

Negative campaigning is hardly new to American politics, or even new to television advertising. In 1964, Tony Schwartz produced the most famous political advertisement of its era, the "daisy spot" for the Lyndon Johnson campaign, that notoriously juxtaposed an image of a girl innocently pulling petals off a flower with footage of a missile detonation and mushroom cloud. Like many effective attack ads, the "daisy spot" capitalized on a fear that already existed. Voters saw Barry Goldwater, Johnson's Republican opponent, as a man who might start a nuclear war, and the ad, although it aired only once and never mentioned Goldwater directly, gained sufficient attention to reinforce this perception.[50] Johnson's campaign also attacked Goldwater for his views on the United Nations, the Social Security Administration, and Medicare. Goldwater responded with his own negative ads, linking the Johnson administration to the "moral decay" of America as the screen filled with pictures of race riots, drug use, alcoholism, and crime. Another spot accused Johnson of corruption and voting fraud.[51]

In the commercial world, this is known as "comparative advertising." The campaign consultants' trade journal *Campaigns and Elections* regularly counsels candidates, in the words of one article title, to "Nail the Opposition."[52] This can be a risky strategy. Research has shown that voters prefer positive, informational advertising that appears to be fair.[53] "Going negative," as it is known, is not therefore a surefire solution for candidates, but it is a tool to achieve several common campaign objectives: to stigmatize or "characterize" a relatively unknown opponent, to focus the agenda of the campaign on the weaknesses of the other side, or to call attention to an embarrassing blunder on the part of the opposition.[54] Media consultants pay especially close attention to focus groups and polling results when devising negative ads because they can backfire if misused.

The 2008 McCain campaign faced a delicate problem: how to go negative against Barack Obama, the first African American major-party presidential nominee, without encountering charges of racism. McCain's advisers decided to avoid any attacks that might be construed as racial, ruling out any mention of Obama's 20-year membership in the church of the controversial Reverend Jeremiah Wright. The campaign did repeatedly attempt in October 2008 to tie Obama to (white) former 1960s radical William Ayers, with running mate Sarah Palin accusing Obama of "palling around with terrorists." However, Obama had dealt with both associations during the primary season, making such criticisms seem to be old news. In another line of attack, McCain sought support among fiscally conservative independents and Democrats by suggesting that Obama's economic views were out of the mainstream.[55] Finally, echoing Hillary Clinton's attacks during the Democratic primaries, McCain questioned whether Obama possessed sufficient knowledge, experience, and toughness to assume the presidency. "I know how the world works," declared McCain in his convention address, implying that his opponent might not.

Obama's negative strategy, in contrast, was straightforward, easy to execute, and low in risk. In speeches and ads, Obama's campaign tightly linked McCain's policies to those of the unpopular incumbent, George W. Bush. Obama frequently asserted that McCain represented a "third term" for Bush, a criticism that appeared to resonate, according to surveys revealing that many voters saw McCain and Bush as holding similar views. However, the Obama campaign was not above making personal attacks as well. As McCain's handling of the fall financial crisis became an issue (McCain announced that he was suspending his campaign to deal with the situation but played little role in crafting the congressional response), Obama's ads accused him of "erratic" behavior in what was seen by the press as an insinuation that McCain lacked the appropriate temperament for the presidency and perhaps even as a reference to McCain's age.[56] By Election Day, many voters in key states agreed with Obama's characterization of McCain as an impulsive version of George W. Bush, an image that did not bode well for his electoral fate.[57]

In the late spring and early summer of 2012, the Obama reelection campaign sought to exploit a temporary financial advantage over Mitt Romney, who had just spent most of his available funds winning the Republican nomination, by sponsoring a series of negative ads designed to create an initially unfavorable impression of Romney among undecided voters who knew little about him at the early stages of the campaign. This line of attack centered on Romney's previous career as the head of the Bain Capital private equity firm. Obama's ads characterized Romney's business dealings as leading to bankruptcies, plant closures, outsourcing, and layoffs for workers at companies acquired by Bain Capital; in one Obama-produced ad, a former employee of a shuttered company said of Romney that "he doesn't care anything about the middle-class or the lower-class people."[58]

Romney's attacks on Obama in 2012 tended to be less personal than Obama's attacks on Romney; perhaps mindful of the fact that victory required appealing to swing voters who had supported Obama in his first presidential run in 2008, the Romney campaign mostly avoided negative campaigning that questioned Obama's character. Instead, Romney made Obama's performance in office the centerpiece of his case against the incumbent, suggesting that the previous four years had confirmed that Obama was not a capable president. Romney's ads also accused Obama of hostility to private-sector entrepreneurship, of cutting Medicare benefits for senior citizens, and, perhaps most controversially, of "gutting" the work requirements in federal welfare programs—a charge hotly disputed by Democrats.

The 2016 campaign was waged in a persistently negative environment replete with fierce personal attacks. Hillary Clinton accused Donald Trump of racist and sexist behavior, argued that he would be a poor role model for the nation's children, and suggested that he was too ignorant and emotionally unsound to manage the government and command the armed forces. Trump blasted Clinton as an out-of-touch elitist who looked down on regular people; who was responsible for the deaths of four Americans killed during an attack on the U.S. consulate in Benghazi, Libya, during her tenure as secretary of state; and who deserved to be arrested and jailed for violating State Department guidelines in the use of a private email server. Unsurprisingly, both candidates ended the campaign with most Americans viewing them in decidedly unfavorable terms.

Campaign professionals maintain that there is a clear line between legitimate attacks on the record, or even the personal background, of opposing candidates, and illegitimate smears. They even argue that "comparative" ads are beneficial, because they give voters important information they otherwise might not learn. There is some justification for this view. But the line between fair and unfair is easily blurred.

Negative campaigning works best, as one might guess, when it is not answered; voters assume that charges that are not explicitly denied by the target campaign might well be true. Personal attacks ("mudslinging") are often lamented for lowering the quality of political debate and even perhaps turning citizens off from participating in politics.[59] John G. Geer argues, on the other hand, that negative advertising actually focuses more often on issues and less on personal characteristics than positive advertising does, thus providing voters with better information about their electoral choices.[60] Either way, we expect candidates in the future to turn to negative campaigning when they believe the potential benefits outweigh the risks to their own reputations for fair play and serious attention to the issues of the day.

GETTING GOOD PRESS

Although we have seen that news media coverage has a limited influence on voter opinion when the strong cue of party is present, it is still considered important for a candidate to get the most favorable treatment possible from journalists. At least, the candidates and their organizations behave as though it is important; they can and do assiduously court the reporters assigned to cover their campaign.[61] Not only do candidates and their staff attempt to placate the journalists who travel with them, but they follow their press coverage closely and complain about it if dissatisfied.[62] "A presidential campaign is an earned media campaign," explains Republican operative Danny Diaz.[63]

Because candidates seldom receive uniformly positive treatment, and because journalists view campaign flacks as obstructing their attempts to dig for the (potentially unflattering) truth, a certain degree of conflict governs the interaction between reporters and their subjects. "The message discipline required to run an effective campaign oftentimes frustrates the press," explains veteran Republican spokesman Kevin Madden. "They always want more access. Their job is to never be satisfied with the access that we're giving them. My job is to be never satisfied with the message discipline that I'm providing them. I think one of the other natural tensions is that I've never met a reporter who doesn't think they could run a better campaign. And I've never met a press secretary, including myself, who didn't think [he or she] could write a better news story."[64]

The volume and angle of press coverage may depend to some extent on how the reporters regard the campaign. If journalists find it easy or difficult to receive cooperation from campaign staff, or if they find the candidate personally likable or unlikable, their impressions may affect the tone of the stories they file. For example, Al Gore's distant relationship with the press in 2000 contributed to his campaign's problems, while George W. Bush's jocularity earned him more kindness from the news media.[65] In the 2008 campaign, both Barack Obama and John McCain were generally popular with the reporters who covered them; in 2016, however, neither Donald Trump nor Hillary Clinton inspired much affection from the press corps.

Trump, in fact, made his rocky relationship with the news media into a major theme of his campaign, complaining frequently about "fake news" and directing insults toward the press pen at his rallies as supporters jeered and shouted threats at reporters. Rather than embark on a charm offensive to inspire favorable coverage, Trump chose the unorthodox strategy of engaging in public confrontation with journalists outside the conservative media universe, even criticizing individual reporters by name at campaign events or on Twitter. His unusual approach was risky but benefited from the fact that his opponent received predominantly negative press coverage as well.

Unlike Trump, Hillary Clinton did not express open contempt for the media in the midst of the race. But she nonetheless left a clear impression among the correspondents who covered her that she regarded them with antipathy—and this attitude was largely reciprocated by reporters. Journalists constantly complained about how difficult it was to gain access to Clinton and how unresponsive her staff could be to their queries and needs. As Mark Leibovich of the *New York Times* described his experience attending an Iowa event with Clinton during the

2016 campaign, "[S]he has been largely steadfast in avoiding interviews, with a campaign team that can convey a heavy-handed preoccupation with control . . . 'What makes you so special,' a [reporter's] voice boomed out, 'that you don't have to answer the press's questions every day?'"[66]

The attempts of candidates and their aides to control the tone and content of press coverage can backfire if they are too transparently manipulative or antagonistic, as Clinton discovered in 2016 when she nearly collapsed at a September 11 memorial event in New York, forcing public disclosure that she had been suffering from a case of pneumonia. Incensed that this information had been kept secret, reporters gave more credence than they might otherwise have to unfounded rumors spread by Republicans that she was suffering from more serious health problems. After the campaign was over, Clinton became more vocal in complaining about the treatment she received from the news media, singling out the *New York Times* as viewing her with "hostility and suspicion" and accusing it of "downplaying the seriousness of Russia's meddling" in the election.[67]

Getting good press, like the rest of the campaign, has become professionalized, with media and communication staff whose responsibility is to make the candidate look as good as possible on television, in the newspapers, and on the Internet. Little things, such as timing events and announcements to meet the requirements of both morning newspapers and evening television broadcasts, or supplying reporters with access to the nominees and top campaign officials, can pay off with favorable coverage. The personalities of the candidates, and their ability to command the respect of the sometimes rather jaded men and women assigned to cover them, may count heavily. Candidates also must make the most of their opportunities in public speeches and interviews. If what they say and do "makes news," and their press aides are effective in promoting the stories, they may get notice through the desire of the media to attract customers.

Thus far, we have spoken of the news media as if they were a monolithic entity. But there are all sorts of news outlets with differing biases, needs, and audiences. A great deal of a candidate's attention is devoted to generating coverage in local newspapers and television in key electoral battlegrounds. Local reporters, who are not experienced at covering presidents and other national political figures, may ask fewer tough questions and produce more positive stories than the more skeptical and campaign-weary journalists from national publications and broadcast networks, and their coverage may have more of an influence on the impressions of voters in strategically important states. Campaign aides often claim that local news media are also more likely to emphasize substantive policy issues, while national reporters tend to be preoccupied with campaign strategy and the candidate horse race.

Finally, there is the overwhelming importance of staging the daily bit of news for the network television broadcasts, cable channels, and websites. Candidates know that they will be covered every day of the campaign, but doing and saying what? In order to seize control of the situation, they stage little dramas: a speech in front of the Statue of Liberty or on an aircraft carrier; a visit to a factory, school, church, or shopping center; dropping in "spontaneously" at diners to greet lunchtime customers. If the backdrop is right, the candidate thinks, the coverage may be too. Sometimes it is. Consultants and speechwriters, aware that only a few seconds of a speech will likely appear in news programs, craft short, memorable statements ("sound bites") reinforcing the campaign's message of the day.

Bill Clinton was the first presidential candidate to make repeated visits to television talk shows; campaign aides felt that it brought out his personality and allowed voters to connect with the candidate. Presidential candidates now routinely appear on popular programs, hoping to reach a wider audience of potential supporters. The appearances are often staged, sometimes awkwardly, to showcase a candidate's personal charm, sense of humor, or status as a "regular person." In 2004, John Kerry sought to shed his stiff public image by riding his Harley-Davidson motorcycle onto the set of the *Tonight Show* clad in a leather jacket.[68] After comedian Tina Fey's impersonation of Republican vice presidential candidate Sarah Palin became a popular hit in 2008, Palin herself appeared with Fey on *Saturday Night Live* two weeks before the election, giving the program its highest audience ratings in 14 years.[69] Nowadays, candidates frequently visit late-night comedy programs as well as daytime shows like *Ellen* and *The View*. Donald Trump hosted an episode of *Saturday Night Live* during the 2016 campaign, while Hillary Clinton pursued younger voters by making cameo appearances on *SNL*, the Comedy Central sitcom *Broad City*, and comedian Zach Galifianakis's satirical web series *Between Two Ferns*.

The overall value of these appearances is unclear. Some political commentators have criticized the practice, arguing that the hosts of popular talk shows are pushovers for the candidates and do not ask tough questions or follow up on answers the way "serious" journalists do. Instead, these critics argue, candidates should spend more time on political programs such as *This Week* and *Meet the Press*, where confrontational interviewers will make sure the candidates meet a certain standard. Proponents argue that pop-culture shows are good for the political system because they allow the candidates to reach viewers who do not regularly watch news programs and give them a chance to display a more informal, personal side of themselves to the public. Whatever the contribution these shows make to American political life, positive or negative, there is no doubt that most candidates will continue to make appearances as long as producers will invite them. The free media and direct access to voters are valuable properties, especially for candidates who shine in such situations.[70]

CAMPAIGN PROFESSIONALS

Candidates have never lacked for willing accomplices in their quest for office, but the practice of running a campaign has become thoroughly professionalized over time. Modern campaigns are typically comprised of a campaign manager, consultants, ad makers, speechwriters, pollsters, communications staff, social media and information technology specialists, fund-raisers, field organizers, interest group liaisons, and policy advisers. The paid staff surrounding a modern candidate is drawn from a population of people for whom electoral politics is a full-time career.[71]

We can get a grasp on the relationship between candidates and campaign professionals by looking closely at its initial phases. Although candidates are more typically found in the role of the suitor, it is not at all unusual for consultants to go prospecting for a candidate if they are short on business in a particular election cycle.[72] Once the initial contact has been made, the two sides bargain over a contract that, if signed, will formalize responsibility, set payment agreements, and establish general ground rules that will guide their interactions over the course of the campaign. Key resources, for both parties, are money and a winning reputation. Candidates are looking for the most successful consultant their money can buy, which generally means a firm with a strong recent win-loss record on their side of the ideological spectrum. Consultants likewise prefer potential winners over probable losers (so they can protect their record) and fat cats over lean. And neither side wants to end up with a partner who is ideologically or personally incompatible.[73]

Not surprisingly, top-flight consulting firms are besieged with offers from candidates and would-be candidates. Big-name presidential hopefuls are similarly able to pick and choose, while no-name candidates must often wait patiently until relatively late in the game and settle for whoever is left. Sometimes a prominent consultant will take on a long-shot candidate to advance a political agenda or because of a personal friendship. Even if the campaign is not generously bankrolled, the publicity attached to running a presidential campaign may lead to future business opportunities for the firm.

How powerful are the professionals within the campaign organization? The candidate-client relationship varies considerably from case to case, depending on the experience and stature of each party and the terms of the original contract. It is the candidate, all agree, who has the last word in approving the general strategy of the campaign.[74] Having done this, however, many candidates apparently prefer to absent themselves from the nitty-gritty choices that follow. One survey found that 44 percent of a population of consultants agreed that candidates generally backed off from making decisions on the priority of different campaign issues. Most "were neither very involved nor influential in the day-to-day tactical operation of the campaign."[75]

Consultants (not a shy and self-effacing group of people) will gladly tell you all about the power they enjoy—and should enjoy—as campaign strategists. The late Bob Squier, for instance, who worked for Democrats, said: "It is very possible to go through an entire campaign with a candidate, and when it is all over, they have no idea what went on. It is not to our advantage to explain to them. It is to our advantage to get them to do what we want—what's best for them—with the least amount of fuss."[76] Mitch Daniels, who became President George W. Bush's first budget director and later the governor of Indiana, sums up the consultant effect this way: "You tend not to make major gaffes, because somebody will spot them. On the other hand, you may not take very many bold actions, because someone will be very nervous."[77]

In recent years, some political consultants have become celebrities in their own right, often as a result of news media coverage portraying them as the brains behind victorious campaigns—a view that most consultants are happy to encourage. James Carville, a plainspoken Louisiana native who served as Bill Clinton's chief campaign strategist in 1992, parlayed his candidate's success in winning the presidency into a lucrative second career as a writer, speaker, and television personality, becoming sufficiently well known that he appeared in cameo roles as himself in several major Hollywood movies. Karl Rove, chief political adviser to George W. Bush and widely credited as the intellectual force behind Bush's two successful campaigns for the White House, became even more prominent a public figure than Carville. Rove was the subject of two major biographies,[78] a *Frontline* special on PBS television, and even a documentary film titled *Bush's Brain*. Barack Obama's victories in 2008 and 2012 elevated his chief strategist David Axelrod into the role of a celebrated political guru; after Obama's reelection, Axelrod announced his retirement from the electoral battlefield to found a new Institute of Politics at the University of Chicago, his alma mater. For a time after Donald Trump's upset victory in 2016, his campaign CEO Steve Bannon was credited by the Washington news media as the visionary thinker behind Trump's brand of politics—an impression Bannon himself helped to cultivate—though he departed his White House position as chief strategist only seven months into Trump's term in office after losing power struggles with other advisers in the presidential orbit.

Have consultants made presidential campaigns more ideological? Probably not. With the exception of a few ideologically motivated firms, consultants tend to be party loyalists but not issue advocates. As Larry Sabato says, "for most consultants ideology is a surprisingly minor criterion in the selection of clients."[79] The business logic of consultancy militates against an approach that would too severely limit a firm's clientele, and the game-playing logic of the campaign itself encourages the use of any strategy that will win, regardless of its ideological fit. To some consultants, elections are not a debate over policy so much as a competition between dueling corporate brands, with the candidate as the "product" being hawked to "consumers" in the electorate. For example, Republican consultant Bonnie Siegel recommends that "all messaging, website design, content and events [should be] created to complement the overall candidate brand identity," encompassing everything from the colors and fonts used in the campaign logo and social media accounts to the visual staging of candidate appearances.[80]

Has the professionalization of campaigns lowered standards of conduct in presidential elections? Even though the candidate is ultimately responsible for all campaign decisions, the use of paid staff and consultants may change the range of campaign options available and the types of strategies ultimately chosen. Consider the use of negative campaigning. "I love to do negatives," declared media consultant Bob Squier. "It is one of those opportunities in a campaign where you can take the truth and use it just like a knife to slice right through the opponent. I hate the kind of commercials that are just music and pretty pictures."[81] This bit of refreshing candor raises the possibility that the average campaign professional may in fact be different from the average politician.

Candidates are aware, of course, of most of what goes on in their name, but it is easier to sign on the dotted line and have someone else take care of your dirty business for you than to have to haul the bodies away yourself.[82] Other commentators point out that there are limits to what campaigns can say on television, limits that did not apply to old-fashioned campaigns run by thousands of semi-independent and localized party bosses, newspapers, and partisans. In the Internet age, any effort by a campaign to engage in underhanded tactics or smear the opposition can be publicized instantly across the nation. On the other hand, current campaign finance regulations encourage the growth of nominally independent Super PACs and other groups that can spread misleading information for the benefit of their favored candidate while allowing the candidate's own campaign to deny any responsibility.

Do campaign professionals undermine partisanship? There is little reason to think so. Most consultants, with rare exceptions, have strong partisan affiliations.

In fact, many have worked for party organizations, and parties provide training in electioneering skills in order to have reliably partisan professionals.[83] "Party affiliation," according to one study, "is by far the most important factor considered by consultants in selecting their clients, outweighing a candidate's electability, ideology, or financial standing."[84] As Adam Sheingate notes, shared partisan loyalties have historically served as the "bedrock upon which consultants could build the kind of 'personal handholding operation' that was critical to their business. Because candidates were unlikely to trust a consultant who did not share the same political beliefs, much less vote for the same party, the vast majority of consultants identified as partisans and restricted themselves to working only for one party or the other. This had important consequences, both for the business of politics and for the character of political competition."[85]

The way in which consultants are professionally aligned with parties, attaching themselves to one individual candidate after another as they build their careers, can be demonstrated by the employment history of Kellyanne Conway, who served as a campaign manager for Donald Trump in 2016. Conway got her start in the political consulting world by working for firms founded by prominent Republican strategists Richard Wirthlin and Frank Luntz. In 1995, she formed her own business, the Polling Company, whose professional clients included House speaker Newt Gingrich and former vice president Dan Quayle as well as a number of Fortune 500 corporations. She also served as a frequent guest on cable news and pop-culture shows like ABC's *Politically Incorrect*, hosted by comedian Bill Maher.

When Gingrich ran for the Republican presidential nomination in 2012, Conway signed on as a strategist. Though she later became well-known for her passionately loyal on-camera defenses of Trump, Conway originally worked for a Super PAC supporting Ted Cruz for president in 2016, only joining Trump's campaign after he had become the presumptive Republican nominee in July. Conway was promoted to succeed Paul Manafort as campaign manager upon Manafort's sudden resignation the following month, holding this position for the rest of the campaign. After Trump's upset victory in November, Conway moved into the government, serving as a top political adviser in the Trump White House.[86]

Policy Advisers

Everyone has advice for the would-be president. In the old days, most of the policy advice came after the general election as the victor prepared to assume office. Nowadays the advising process has been incorporated into the process of campaigning. The function of the policy adviser is no longer simply to help the future president govern but to help the candidate define and publicize the campaign's position on the issues. Campaigns do not always publish official lists of advisers, but all campaigns develop extensive contacts with academics, think tank fellows, and policy analysts who draw up position papers on specialized issues of foreign and domestic policy and help set the general ideological tone of the campaign.[87] The experts do this at least in part to position themselves to have influence on national policy if their candidate wins.

The lengthy duration of presidential campaigns means that candidates have to develop positions on major national issues more than a year in advance of the election. "If you're . . . in the policy-advising business," explains Pat Choate, an economist and policy analyst who was Ross Perot's running mate in 1996, "you must move on that time schedule."[88] Introducing a novel idea later on in the game, during the heat of the campaign, is risky, first because the candidate may gain a reputation as an opportunist or a waffler, and second because there will be no opportunity to test the new idea for technical or political feasibility, to get its rough edges smoothed out (box 5.1).

Box 5.1 ■ In the Arena: Campaign Professionals on the 2016 General Election Campaign

On Strategies for Contacting Voters

Robby Mook, Campaign Manager, Hillary for America: "We conducted an experiment over the summer with direct mail and television. . . . What we found was, with people under 40, digital and those phone calls moved favorability, moved the vote. For people over 40, it was television and direct mail. . . . For somebody under 40, we were probably spending, in terms of the budget strategy, 90 percent of our money for them on digital. But, for folks over 40, that spending skewed much more towards mail and TV."

Brad Parscale, Digital Director, Donald J. Trump for President: "We spent 50 percent of our money on digital and 50 percent on TV. That's a groundbreaking thing for a presidential campaign. . . . We knew the 14 million people we needed to win 270. We targeted them in over 1,000 different universes with exactly the things that mattered to them. We didn't let the media go to them. We went straight to them. And we spent the money on digital to do that because we couldn't compete with them on TV."

On Getting Out the Vote

Robby Mook, Campaign Manager, Hillary for America: "Our ground game was there. . . . It was there to get you that extra 1 or 2 percent that you needed. . . . When you're a campaign manager and you're staying up at night and kicking yourself and thinking what the heck could I have done, would I have had 300 field staff in Michigan instead of two? . . . because we lost by less than a point so more of that ground activity could have made a difference in those [closely contested] states, absolutely."

Brad Parscale, Digital Director, Donald J. Trump for President: "Our ground game was operated through the RNC [Republican National Committee] instead of operating more independently. The RNC was the best blessing that we had as we came out of the convention. The RNC was ready for a plug-and-play ground operation with a data-centric view. That was a huge plus for us. . . . We didn't need offices because we had an app. We didn't have to rely on old paper, door-to-door knocking. We didn't have to build offices. These are things that are significantly different between the two campaigns."

Source: Institute of Politics, John F. Kennedy School of Government, Harvard University, *Campaign for President: The Managers Look at 2016* (Lanham, MD: Rowman & Littlefield, 2017), 228, 234.

Since the candidate is expected to offer judgments on world events as they break into the news over the course of the race, every campaign will typically rely on a "little black book" with the telephone numbers of advisers in different policy areas who can be contacted during emergencies. A dramatic example of this occurred during the 2008 campaign, when a global financial crisis in September damaged the soundness of American credit markets and the overall health of the American economy. The McCain and Obama campaigns scrambled for a response to the problems as the economy and stock market slumped. Obama's economic advisers urged a cautious message of reassurance and support for a bipartisan solution to the problem, while McCain's response was more experimental. He announced that he was suspending his campaign on September 24 and called for cancellation of the first presidential debate scheduled for two days later, then returned to Washington to address the crisis. His consultations with economists, congressional lawmakers and the Bush administration, however, did not place him at the center of efforts to find a solution, which took several weeks to develop. McCain was forced to reignite his campaign after a few days and at the last minute flew to Mississippi to participate in the debate. McCain's problem was that no amount of advice would quickly solve the problem or make him the author of a solution. Obama's cautious reaction proved to be the politically more beneficial response.

Tensions between policy advisers and campaign staff complicated McCain's response and vindicated Obama's caution. Such conflicts have been a feature of presidential campaigns for decades. Campaign policy experts come in three flavors, according to Democratic policy adviser Janne E. Nolan: those who believe in the issues they are pushing, those adrenaline junkies attracted by the chance to participate in the events of a presidential campaign, and those who have attached their ambitions to a particular candidate in the hopes of achieving a position in a new administration.[89]

Policy advisers, even of the third type, are a very different breed from pollsters and media consultants. With the exception of the candidate's most senior policy coordinators, they are usually not paid. Their ties to the day-to-day campaign may be tenuous, and they all have nonpolitical careers to return to. Well-known academics may offer advice in an informal capacity to several campaigns in the same election.

Not surprisingly, there is a certain degree of tension between the "flack masters and [the] idea mongers," in the words of Republican policy adviser Richard Allen, who quips that "people in flackery don't know ideas and wouldn't know if one hit them at a great rate of speed."[90] But there may be some justification for this conflict in view of the extraordinary demands of a presidential campaign; after all, policy experts may propose ideas that prove to be unpopular with voters or easy for the opposition candidate to attack. "There's a big difference," explains Brookings Institution fellow and Democratic policy adviser William A. Galston, "between having a position paper and having a politically salable commodity."[91] As adviser John Holum observes, "if an idea can't be communicated to the public, then it won't be part of the campaign." Someone, in other words, must administer the "test of political marketability."[92]

Polling

Multimillion-dollar polling is the norm in today's presidential elections. Public opinion polls have been used in politics, in varying ways, since the 1930s,[93] but they have not always been as important in shaping campaigns as they are today.

As recently as the 1950s, most candidates still viewed polls with considerable skepticism. Some, like Harry Truman, were downright hostile. "I wonder," he said, "how far Moses would have gone if he'd taken a poll in Egypt? What would Jesus Christ have preached if he'd taken a poll in Israel? Where would the reformation have gone if Martin Luther had taken a poll? It isn't polls or public opinion of the moment that counts. It is right and wrong leadership—men with fortitude, honesty and a belief in the right—that makes epochs in the history of the world."[94] Winston Churchill, inhabiting the same political universe, said, "Nothing is more dangerous than a Gallup poll, always taking one's pulse and taking one's political temperature."[95] Like all long-lived politicians in democracies, these exemplary figures undoubtedly paid attention to their intuitions about public opinion. But intuition has now been largely replaced by more accurate methods, and it is hard to ignore these more thorough soundings of the popular will.

The first significant use of polls within a campaign organization occurred in 1960, when surveys taken by Louis Harris helped guide John F. Kennedy's campaign in key primary states. Pioneers such as Harris and George Gallup were followed in succeeding decades by hundreds of professional firms throughout the country that now make up the polling industry.[96] General nationwide public opinion polls not owned or paid for by particular candidates are now regularly taken by the Pew Research Center, Quinnipiac, Ipsos, YouGov, Rasmussen, and several national media groups: *Wall Street Journal*/NBC News, *New York Times*/CBS News, *Washington Post*/ABC News, CNN, Fox News, and Bloomberg.

Other polling operations work for political campaigns, and among these, a few are involved in all phases of presidential campaigning.[97] Campaigns conduct a constant series of polls over the course of an election season, in order to monitor the horse race in key battleground states and to collect information about the electorate's views of the candidates, issues, and national conditions. The modern pollster's role goes far beyond gathering data and analyzing trends. "There's no question that our role has changed from collector of facts to interpreter and strategist," notes Republican pollster Richard Wirthlin.[98] They ask: What should be the major campaign issues and themes, or, at least, which would be most attractive to the electorate? How should the candidate attack an opponent's record? What are the candidate's (and the opposition's) perceived strengths and weaknesses, and what can be done to exploit or minimize them? How should the candidate's issue positions or performance in office be framed in order to maximize popular appeal? The campaign pollster helps make these and a variety of other crucial decisions, such as which states to visit and which groups within the electorate to court, all subject to the candidate's approval.

The intricacies of campaign strategy often seem to fascinate the news media, if not the electorate at large. Campaign consultants may encourage this preoccupation by attempting to convince journalists of their cleverness in pinpointing particular subgroups of voters deemed critical to the construction of an electoral majority and developing a campaign message aimed at these narrow segments of the population. In 1996, Bill Clinton's campaign advisers identified "soccer moms"—white suburban women with children—as an important constituency whose support they especially courted. Political reporters wrote endless stories about this strategy, finding actual mothers of soccer-playing children to interview in order to find out what they thought about politics.[99] In subsequent elections, soccer moms were joined by other supposed social groups, including "office park dads" and "security moms," as key voting blocs, at least according to consultants and journalists.[100] There are good reasons to be skeptical of such claims. The United States is too large and diverse for any single group to be pivotal in an election, especially such specific categories as these. Individuals who share certain demographic characteristics may not agree politically, and a message crafted to appeal to one group may repel another. Still, the increasing sophistication of polling methods now allows campaigns to focus their attention on classes of undecided or persuadable voters whom they think will influence the outcome of the election.

During the summer of 2008, the Obama campaign conducted extensive polling to determine the strengths and weaknesses of the two parties' nominees, fixing on a strategy of associating opponent Republican John McCain as closely as possible with the increasingly unpopular Bush presidency. This message proved effective in attracting independent voters to Obama over the subsequent weeks of the campaign. In articulating Obama's strategy, chief strategist David Axelrod argued that America was looking for "the remedy [for the Bush administration], not the replica."[101] To this end, Obama distanced himself from "Washington insiders," as he had done with great success in his contest with Hillary Clinton during the Democratic primaries. Further, Obama's research revealed that voters did not know much about McCain, despite his previous run for the Republican presidential nomination in 2000 and subsequent prominence in national politics. Joel Benenson, the campaign's pollster, recalled, "What we knew at the start of the campaign was that the notion of John McCain as a change agent and independent voice didn't exist anywhere outside of the [Washington] Beltway."[102] The adverse environment for the GOP, limited voter knowledge about McCain, and large financial advantage made the execution of a fall campaign straightforward for the Obama high command.

Top McCain aides, in contrast, understood that they began the campaign with serious disadvantages. Chief strategist Steve Schmidt recalled: "This was a campaign that was dealt a very, very tough hand of cards. It was highly unlikely that there will ever be another campaign in our lifetimes that [will feature] a worse environment than the environment that John McCain had to run in."[103] Since no simple message was likely to bring down Obama, the McCain campaign focused instead on a series of tactical disruptions designed to throw their opponent off track and open up new opportunities for them. The main chances to introduce surprises that might shake up the race lay in the central events of the fall campaign: the vice presidential selection, the convention acceptance speeches, and the candidate debates. The McCain campaign began their disruptions with an advertisement soon known as the "celebrity" spot, which mocked Obama's trip overseas in late July by comparing him to Paris Hilton and Britney Spears, two pop culture personalities with reputations for vacuous tawdriness. The celebrity label disturbed the Obama campaign, which viewed it as a negative description that might stick to their candidate. McCain's selection of Sarah Palin as his running mate was a bold move that succeeded, in the short term, at catching both the Obama campaign and the news media by surprise, though the questions raised about her qualifications for national office ultimately caused difficulties for McCain. In the end, McCain's strategy involved high-risk tactics that sometimes backfired, helping Obama to maintain his advantage in the polls.

In 2012, polls conducted by the Romney campaign and Republican-allied Super PACs revealed that the subpar performance of the national economy during Obama's first term as president represented the incumbent's biggest political vulnerability. As Carl Forti of the pro-Romney Super PAC American Crossroads recalled after the election, "Ninety percent of [undecided voters] voted for Obama last time [in 2008]. They liked him. They just didn't like what he was doing to the country. So anything that was attacking his character or his personality was already decided in their mind. . . . It was a question of, can we prove he was not doing the job and shouldn't be given another four years?"[104] Romney strategist Stuart Stevens noted that "we always said that this [election] would be a referendum on Obama."[105] Negative ads produced by the Romney campaign thus primarily emphasized the unsatisfactory economic condition of the nation during Obama's first term in office.

Romney advisers also used survey research to determine how to present their own candidate to voters. As Stevens recalled after the election, "We polled a lot. We tested a lot. We tested four main approaches. The overall Mitt Romney Story—a combination of personal and business/public service. We tested a focus on the business record—how he created jobs and grew businesses. We tested the Romney Mass[achusetts] record—how he turned around a faltering state. And we tested the Romney Agenda as President—what he would do as President. Overwhelmingly, people wanted to know more about what he would do as President. . . . That drove us to launch our 'Day One' series of ads."[106]

For the Obama reelection campaign, polling likewise supported the strategic decision to counter Romney's attempt to frame the election as a referendum on the economic performance of the previous four years. "Obviously we weren't running in the most optimal of circumstances," acknowledged Obama strategist David Axelrod in retrospect. "But we believed that we would prosper from putting [the election] in the context of a choice."[107] Chief pollster Joel Benenson examined reams of survey data to find a rhetorical frame that worked to Obama's advantage: "Who would fight for middle class Americans? . . . People didn't think [Romney] was on their side and they didn't think he would fight for their interest."[108] This finding ended up guiding the messages conveyed in Obama's paid advertising spots and campaign stump speeches.

Kellyanne Conway, Trump's final campaign manager in 2016, explained after the election how polling data were valuable in suggesting that Trump could survive the numerous personal controversies surrounding him:

> For most of the electorate, the 70 percent or so number [in polls] that said they wanted to take the country in a new and different direction never budged. . . . [We] really focused very heavily, state by state, [on] this 23 to 28 percent of the electorate in each of those states that said they want to take the country in a new and different direction but they weren't yet voting for Donald Trump. The one thing that the undecided voters were very decided on was that they did not want to vote for Hillary Clinton. They already knew a lot about her. Ethics and veracity and truthfulness, those were qualifications, too. . . . They were being told constantly [by the Clinton campaign], "Stare at this, care about this, make this the deal breaker once and for all." They were told that five or six times a week about different things. Yet, they voted the way voters have always voted, on things that affect them, not just things that offend them.[109]

Polling also allows campaigns to decide which states to contest fiercely and which to ignore. George W. Bush's 2000 campaign discovered that Bush was competitive in the historically Democratic state of West Virginia and that he also polled strongly in Tennessee, even though the latter was the home state of Bush's opponent, Al Gore. The Bush campaign devoted time and resources to these states, initially considered safe for Gore, and carried them both—two key victories in an extremely close election. Likewise, early assumptions that Florida would not be competitive in 2000 (the state usually voted Republican, and Bush's younger brother Jeb served as its governor) were contradicted by polling results indicating a tight race, especially after Gore's selection of a Jewish running mate, Senator Joe Lieberman of Connecticut, won him significant support in the Jewish communities of South Florida. Both campaigns invested heavily in Florida in the final weeks before the election; on Election Day, the state was so closely divided between Bush and Gore that it took weeks of recounts and extensive litigation before a winner could be determined.

The electoral battleground map in 2004 closely resembled that from four years before. Once again, top campaign targets on both sides included Florida, Pennsylvania, Michigan, Wisconsin, Iowa, Nevada, and New Mexico. Both sides conducted continuous polling in each state in order to pick up the latest trends and react accordingly. While the Gore campaign had pulled its resources from Ohio in the last weeks before the 2000 election, choosing to focus on winning Pennsylvania and Florida instead, in 2004 the state remained a hard-fought battleground up until Election Day, with multiple public appearances from Bush and Kerry and their running mates, constant television advertising and campaign mobilization efforts, and a frenzy of activity by party organizations and outside groups on both sides. Initially promising polls led the Bush campaign to invest resources in the traditional Democratic strongholds of Minnesota and Oregon, while the Kerry campaign actively contested Colorado, a state Gore had conceded to Bush in 2000. Bush's running mate Dick Cheney even took an all-night airplane trip to Hawaii for a campaign appearance a few days before the election after an opinion poll suggested (falsely, as it turned out) that the state, normally a Democratic bastion, was politically competitive.[110]

In 2008, the results of state-level polling likewise determined candidate strategy, but with an additional complication: the Obama campaign's decision to decline public financing for the general election in order to spend unlimited private funds gave them a critical advantage over the McCain team. Obama capitalized on his financial edge (and overall lead in the polls) to contest several states usually conceded to the Republican candidate in presidential elections, thus forcing McCain to spend precious resources defending territory that he otherwise could have taken for granted. When polls taken in the late spring showed unexpected strength in Indiana, Obama spent money establishing an active campaign organization in the state—the first Democratic presidential nominee to do so in decades—and ultimately carried it by a small margin. North Carolina was not initially a top target (Obama made only one visit to the state between June and mid-September), but as surveys continued to suggest a competitive race, the Obama campaign redoubled its efforts there, sending the candidate to the state five times in the final month of the campaign and forcing McCain to respond with three appearances of his own.

McCain's Electoral College strategy similarly evolved in reaction to the findings of his pollsters. The campaign decided in early October to transfer resources from Michigan, normally an electoral battleground but judged by McCain advisers on the basis of survey results to be out of reach for their side, to more promising states elsewhere—a move criticized publicly by running mate Sarah Palin.[111] With Obama pulling ahead in several states that had voted for George W. Bush in 2004, including Colorado, Iowa, Nevada, and New Mexico, the McCain campaign concluded that their only chance for victory in the Electoral College required carrying a large state that had been won by John Kerry four years before. Identifying Pennsylvania as their best opportunity for an upset, McCain and Palin campaigned frequently in the state during the weeks before the election, but ultimately fell short—as they did in nearly all the battleground states.[112]

In 2016, the Hillary Clinton campaign was sufficiently confident of its standing in many perennial swing states that it ambitiously extended its list of targets to include the traditionally Republican-leaning North Carolina and Arizona. But Clinton strategists overestimated their candidate's popularity in the Midwest, giving insufficient attention to the must-win states of Michigan and Wisconsin (both narrowly carried by Trump) while investing heavily in Ohio and Iowa, which Clinton ultimately lost by decisive margins. Though Trump aides appeared to agree that their candidate was the underdog in the race, they were quicker than the Clinton team to identify her electoral vulnerability. Trump gave active attention to both Michigan and Wisconsin, even paying a visit to the normally Democratic-leaning Minnesota, another state taken for granted by the Clinton side, shortly before the election (where he ultimately lost by only 1.5 percentage points).

Why are polls and pollsters so important to campaigns? Why have they replaced party bosses and cronies of the candidate as the key decision-makers? Plenty of attention has been focused on the mistaken or misleading results of polling. Nevertheless, taken together, polls are reasonably accurate indicators of public sentiment. Thus they are a better tool for shaping campaign strategy and content than anything else now available, and this, in the uncertain universe of the presidential campaign, is all that is really necessary to make polls indispensable to the candidate.

One need only consider the information sources that used to govern campaign strategy to appreciate the significance of the advent of modern polling techniques. Nineteenth and early-twentieth-century indicators of public opinion consisted of reports from precinct captains and state party leaders, newspaper editorials and letters to the editor, crowd sizes and responses at rallies, letters to the candidate, and pure hunches. Most of these measures were unreliable. Editorials may signify the views of only a few newspaper owners; letters to the editor represent a lot of writing by a rather small number of activists; crowd responses can be manipulated, or variously interpreted; party leaders may communicate only what they think the candidate wishes to hear.

While polls themselves may be indispensable, their interpreters frequently play much larger roles in presidential politics than would seem warranted for mere keepers of statistics. George H. W. Bush, to take one example, was persuaded by pollster Bob Teeter (with the aid of strategists Roger Ailes and Lee Atwater) to adopt the get-tough strategy of his 1988 campaign.[113] The modern-day polling consultant, in the words of one practitioner, plays an instrumental role in deciding "which states to hit, where people should go, how much money should be spent where, which groups [to] target, and the kinds of money and messages [to] use."[114]

The explanation for this abdication of authority on the part of the candidates and their personal advisers lies partly in the changing nature of polling. With computer-assisted sample selection processes and polling techniques, it has been possible to increase the number of polls taken in the course of a campaign to allow daily surveys in key states for both campaigns. Moreover, the information obtained from polls has expanded greatly. Originally, opinion surveys were merely a device to measure candidate support; good pollsters would try to isolate which groups within the electorate were more and less likely to vote for the candidate. Nowadays, polls are constructed to address not just how social groups will vote (and these categories here have become progressively more precise), but why they will do so and what might change their minds. Pollsters, in other words, are asked to do more than simply report on the state of public opinion; they are routinely expected to help influence it.

Focus Groups

Focus groups have been a tool of communication and advertising research for decades; by the 1980s, they had become an integral part of campaign strategy. The ideal group consists of about 12 to 15 voters chosen from the general population to discuss the election and the candidates, usually residents of a battleground state targeted by the campaigns. A much smaller number is likely to place too much of a burden on each individual, while more than 15 or so tends to reduce each member's participation. A moderator guides the discussion, focusing on matters of interest to the campaign. Discussions are lengthy—anywhere from one and a half to three hours—so that all participants have a chance to express their feelings.

Unlike opinion polls, which depend for their validity on randomly selecting a representative cross-section of voters, focus groups are usually structured to be socially homogeneous "so that the numerous interacting demographic variables do not confuse the issues; to be most productive, all the participants must be on the same wavelength."[115] For example, focus group organizers may not place married, stay-at-home mothers in the same group as single working women because their lifestyles and goals are deemed too different, leading to excessive guardedness or even conflict among the participants.[116] "The key to focus groups is homogeneity," Democratic pollster Stanley Greenberg explains. "The more homogeneity, the more revealing."[117]

Focus-group interviewing violates most of the accepted canons of survey research. As William D. Wells of the University of Chicago Graduate School of Business says:

> Samples are invariably small and never selected by probability methods. Questions are not asked the same way each time. Responses are not independent. Some respondents inflict their opinions on others; some contribute little or nothing at all. Results are difficult or impossible to quantify and are not grist for the statistical mill. Conclusions depend on the analyst's interpretive skill. The investigator can easily influence the results.[118]

With so many defects, why have focus groups come to be so widely used in political campaigns? Part of the reason is that they are fast and relatively cheap compared to large-scale surveys. Another reason to use focus groups is to test campaign messages, ideas, or advertising spots not yet released to the general public. Participants are asked whether particular information affects their views of the candidates, and what their response would be to particular arguments. Like Hollywood movies, which can be changed if preview audiences give them poor reviews, political ads can be altered or discarded if focus groups don't like what they see.

The most important reason focus groups are employed is that they give the campaign an opportunity to probe respondents to a greater depth than in regular polls. Deeper feelings and half-formed thoughts of ordinary voters emerge, and in their own words. It is true that the group's responses cannot easily be quantified, but in the hands of a sensitive analyst, focus groups may reveal important insights. "Focus groups allow you to put flesh on the bones," Democratic pollster Mark Mellman says; they provide "a sense of texture you can't get from a poll."[119] In a June 2008 focus group observed by a reporter from the *Washington Post*, moderator Peter Hart asked a group of Pennsylvania voters a series of questions designed to elicit their personal impressions of the candidates: "What kind of neighbor would McCain or Obama be? With which man would you choose to share an hour-long commute to work? Whom would you select to carry the American flag . . . in the Olympics?"[120]

Adviser David Simas revealed after the 2012 election that focus groups allowed Obama's reelection campaign to identify the two candidates' strengths and weaknesses in the eyes of undecided voters. Simas described the typical view of Obama among this segment of the electorate as "I like the president . . . I think he's trying really hard, I think that he shares my values, but I'm concerned that things [i.e., the performance of the national economy] haven't turned around fast enough or they haven't turned around [at all]." These voters also perceived Romney as having "been successful at different things that he's done" with "technical knowledge about . . . the economy" due to his experience in the business sector. The lesson from these findings, according to Simas, was that Obama needed to make the case to swing voters that Romney's business expertise was not accompanied by sympathy for the economic plight of the average person. "In the focus groups—group after group after group after group—we would hear these undecided, independent voters say things like, 'Look, I need a guy, a president who, from the beginning to the end, his entire focus is going to be on things that grow the middle class because that's the way you grow the economy.'"[121] On the basis of these results, the Obama campaign initiated a series of television ads portraying Romney as advancing the interests of the wealthy at the expense of middle-class workers.

Hillary Clinton's 2016 campaign concluded from focus groups that Donald Trump's temperament was a major vulnerability. As Clinton strategist Mandy Grunwald explained, "When we spoke to people who disliked both [candidates]— and we know that was a swath of the electorate—two things troubled them about Donald Trump. They were that he would blow up the world and was erratic and had made reckless statements and would embarrass the United States. I don't think we ever had a focus group where somebody didn't say, 'He's going to blow up the world. I just can't do that.'"[122] These findings inspired a well-funded series of ads from the Clinton campaign attacking Trump's readiness to be commander-in-chief.

Focus groups can also be used to generate quantitative data. Using hand-held, dial-equipped boxes, participants watching an ad, speech, or debate are asked to register their reactions, positive or negative, by twisting a knob on a scale of zero to one hundred. Dial groups were used by Bill Clinton's consultants in 1992 to address his weaknesses as a candidate. While trying to figure a way out of Clinton's problems, pollster Stanley Greenberg convened a group of middle-aged white women at a hotel in Dayton, Ohio, and asked them to "dial" their reactions to prepared presentations of the candidate and the campaign. Greenberg found that Clinton scored poorly when he looked and sounded like a politician but did well when he answered questions directly and addressed certain popular issues, such as welfare reform. When presenting the results to the campaign, Greenberg superimposed a tracing of the dial readings on the video the subjects had watched, giving Clinton a blow-by-blow report on the "grades" the dial group had given his various responses.[123]

Obama advisers used dial groups to test their candidate's acceptance speech at the 2012 Democratic national convention. While the address received middling reviews from media commentators, Obama officials responded by claiming that undecided voters were, according to their research, less interested in stirring rhetoric than hearing concrete policy proposals for a second term.[124] Cable news channels now routinely convene dial groups during their coverage of televised debates, revealing the real-time reactions of undecided voters to the candidates' performance.

Television Advertising

Despite the explosion of "new media" in recent years—via the Internet and cell phones—candidates still expend considerable resources on television advertising, and the media consultants who produce the ads play a central role in crafting the message of the campaign. Television commercials remain an effective means of reaching persuadable voters and can serve a variety of purposes. They can be used to establish name recognition or to improve a candidate's personal image. They can focus on campaign issues, targeting key subgroups in the population. They can be used to capture the attention of the press. Or they can be used to attack the candidate's opponent.

After the advertisement is filmed, edited, and approved by the candidate, a schedule is prepared that is supposed to help the ad reach the right people. Every ad campaign is somewhat different and must be crafted to take account of the unique assets and deficiencies of the candidate. But amid the varying styles of each campaign, a relatively small number of tried-and-true themes have established themselves over the past several decades. These constitute the advertising consultant's tool kit, from which virtually every television campaign is built. There is the "person-on-the-street" ad, sometimes scripted and sometimes culled from actual interview footage, showing the average voter (or the average member of a targeted constituency group) endorsing the candidate's accomplishments or general integrity. The "sainthood spot" is "devoted to celebrating the candidate's life story and accomplishments." The "news-look" spot ad attempts to use the legitimacy of experts and television newscasters who relate facts about the candidate's record. The "apology" ad is used, usually out of desperation, when a liability develops that is considered so threatening to the candidate's chances of election that he or she must personally apologize to the electorate. "Cinema-verité" spots offer the audience a view into the life of the candidate as he or she is working, walking, or addressing another audience, while the older "talking head" approach (still a staple of spot ads) places the candidate directly in front of the camera so that he or she can talk personally to the audience. The "issue-position" spot defines the candidate's record on an issue of high salience to the electorate or to a key group of voters.[125]

One measure of the centrality of television advertising in the current campaign process can be found in the "back-and-forth" ad. This format begins with an excerpt from an opponent's spot ad, which is then "answered" in the second sequence, an ad within an ad. This is possible because modern technology enables campaigns to produce television ads more quickly, cheaply, and easily, and to instantaneously monitor the ads of their opponents.

Media professionals attempt to place political commercials in order to reach a targeted viewing audience. "Dissimilar kinds of people," Larry Sabato notes, "watch and listen to different sorts of programs at various times of the day."[126] A media consultant might court news programs' highly educated, well-informed audiences with information-packed ads or spots discussing issues, for example, while viewers of lighter fare might see commercials that emphasized the candidate's personality. The 2012 Obama campaign bought ads on non-political cable networks that are normally ignored by candidates, such as the Food Network and the Hallmark Channel, because research suggested that they could reach undecided voters and Democrats who might not otherwise be paying attention to the campaign.[127] Because more than 90 percent of American households now subscribe to cable, satellite, or streaming services, campaigns can exploit the multiplicity of channels to tailor messages to specific audiences (box 5.2).[128]

New Media

Modern campaigns are engaged in an ongoing technological arms race. With the advent of the World Wide Web in the 1990s, political campaigns began to view the Internet as a potentially powerful means of persuasion and mobilization. Supporters and interested voters can now access a great deal of information provided online, including biographical sketches, policy positions, lists of endorsements, press releases, video messages, and personal appearance schedules for the presidential candidate, running mate, and their families. Internet users can sign up for the candidate's mailing list and receive regular email updates from the campaign; candidates also use their websites to recruit volunteers for campaign activities like voter registration drives and phone banking.

The Internet is growing quickly as a nexus of political activity. Realizing that many Americans now consume digital media, campaigns now routinely invest heavily in maintaining an active online presence by providing streams of content to keep voters engaged while targeting specific persuasive messages to particular constituencies. The 2008 and 2012 Obama campaigns, drawing on some innovations of Howard Dean's 2004 primary campaign, pioneered new means of electronic communication, creating computer linkups of supporters, gathering

Box 5.2 ■ In the Arena: Assessing 2016 Presidential Campaign Ads

The following is a summary and text of four widely viewed 2016 campaign ads—two from the Trump campaign and two from the Clinton campaign. What is your assessment of their effectiveness and accuracy? Two were identified as particularly effective and two as quite misleading. You can view these and other campaign ads at the *New Republic* magazine's archive of 2016 ads at https://newrepublic.com/political-ad-database.

Spoiler alert: At the end of this section, we report professional analysts' verdict regarding the ads' effectiveness and accuracy.

"Two Americas: Immigration." Male narrator: In "Hillary Clinton's America, the middle class gets crushed. Spending goes up. Taxes go up. Hundreds of thousands of jobs disappear. It's more of the same, but worse. In Donald Trump's America, working families get tax relief. Millions of new jobs created. Wages go up. Small businesses thrive. The American Dream, achievable. Change that makes America great again. Donald Trump for president."

"Mirrors." Donald Trump: "I'd look her right in that fat, ugly face of hers. . . . She's a slob. . . . She ate like a pig. . . . A person who's flat-chested is very hard to be a 10. . . . Does she have a good body? No. Does she have a fat [expletive]? Absolutely." Interviewer: "Do you treat women with respect?" Trump: "I can't say that either." Text: "Is this the president we want for our daughters?"

"Change." Male narrator: "Hillary Clinton won't change Washington. She's been there 30 years. Taxes went up. Terrorism spread. Jobs vanished. But special interests and Washington insiders thrived. Donald Trump will turn Washington upside down: day one. Real change that puts Americans first. A vote for Hillary is a vote for more of the same. A vote for Donald Trump is a vote for change that makes America great again."

"Silo." Bruce Blair: "I spent many years as a nuclear missile launch officer. If the president gave the order we had to launch the missiles, that would be it. I prayed that call would never come. Self-control may be all that keeps these missiles from firing." Donald Trump: "I would bomb the s**t out of them. I want to be unpredictable. I love war." Blair: "The thought of Donald Trump with nuclear weapons scares me to death. It should scare everyone."

ANALYSIS: Researchers at the Duke University Reporters' Lab ranked "Mirrors" as the most effective Clinton ad; it was also the most widely distributed Clinton ad on the Internet. The researchers termed Trump's "Two Americas" ad series as his most effective (https://reporterslab.org/best-worst-campaign-ads-2016-election). Politifact, the fact-checking website, identified "Change" and "Silo" ads, both among the top 10 most-aired ads, as containing important exaggerations and misleading statements (http://www.politifact.com/truth-o-meter/article/2016/nov/03/10-most-aired-political-ads-fact-checked).

record online campaign contributions, and even announcing Joe Biden's selection as vice presidential nominee in August 2008 via text message. There was a clever rationale for this last initiative: the campaign collected the cell phone numbers of thousands of supporters who signed up to be notified of Obama's choice of running mate and who were later solicited for donations and volunteer work.[129]

Obama's 2012 campaign created a number of Facebook groups such as "Women for Obama," "Latinos for Obama," and "Students for Obama," whose members received regular content emphasizing the candidate's positions on such issues as contraception access, immigration reform, and college loans, respectively. The Trump campaign spent much of its budget on Internet advertising and organization in 2016 after concluding that such an approach was a more cost-effective means of reaching voters than television, given that it was being outspent by the Clinton campaign. Trump's active Twitter account—featuring a stream of unvarnished messages posted personally by the candidate—also received extensive attention and often drove the daily coverage of online journalists and cable news channels.

Social media is a valuable platform for candidates not only because it allows them to maintain constant contact with their existing supporters, but also because they can reach undecided voters via the propensity of users to "share" or "Retweet" campaign messages—which places them in the news feeds of their friends and followers as well.[130] Campaigns have discovered over time that the most effective forms of social media engagement encourage the sense of a personal connection between the candidate and voters. As the social media director for Bernie Sanders's 2016 campaign observed, "People don't want to follow a brand; they don't want to follow a company; they want to follow a person. . . . they want to have this kind of conversation with you."[131]

Social media users are also more likely to spread the word about candidates if they don't think they'll suffer a backlash for doing so. Hillary Clinton's campaign in 2016 attempted to replicate Obama's previous success in using Facebook and Twitter as a platform for mobilization, but faced more difficulty in convincing supporters to openly advocate her candidacy. As Teddy Goff, chief digital strategist for the Clinton campaign, explained after the election, "There's no cost to a person—in many parts of the country—expressing their support for President Obama. If they Tweet out their support for President Obama, that makes them look cool to their friends. . . . [But] the same was not true for [Clinton]. So we had millions of people who, when they were actually polled, expressed great enthusiasm for Secretary Clinton but perceived, and then actually experienced, a bit of social risk to them if they were going to express that [online]."[132] The Trump side, in contrast, had a much more positive view of social media; "Facebook and Twitter helped us win this," argued Trump digital director Brad Parscale.[133]

Compared to television, the Internet is also relatively unregulated with a low barrier to entry, which makes it especially fertile ground for electoral interference by hackers, phony accounts, and purveyors of misinformation. The 2016 campaign was plagued by waves of false messages created and distributed by clandestine actors, including overseas "troll farms" with ties to the government of Russia that worked on behalf of the Trump candidacy. In the wake of the election, special counsel Robert Mueller secured the criminal indictment of multiple Russian nationals and three companies that had been involved in operations designed to illegally influence the outcome—demonstrating how the rise of social media has opened a new front not only in direct communication by candidates, but also in the battle to protect the legitimacy of the electoral process.[134]

TELEVISED DEBATES

Presidential debates are major milestones in the general election season because they directly expose the candidates in verbal competition before millions of Americans. For that reason, they hold the potential to influence the public's evaluations of the candidates and thus affect the outcome of the election. Like every other aspect of presidential campaigns, candidates and their advisers approach the debates with an eye toward using the attention generated by the events to their political advantage.

The now-familiar series of debates in the fall of every election year is itself the product of strategic calculation by candidates. In 1960, Senator John F. Kennedy of Massachusetts, the Democratic nominee, issued a public challenge to his Republican opponent, Vice President Richard Nixon, to debate on television— then still a new medium of communication. By holding his own on the issues with the sitting vice president before a national audience, Kennedy hoped to overcome criticism that he was too young (he was 43) and inexperienced to assume the presidency. With the benefit of hindsight, many observers now suggest that Nixon was obviously foolish to participate. But Kennedy had placed Nixon in a difficult position, because refusing to debate would have subjected Nixon to criticism for being afraid to face his opponent. Perhaps a record of success in debates going back to high school was not irrelevant in guiding Nixon to his eventual decision to appear on television with his rival.[135] Surveys taken afterward suggest that Nixon miscalculated—that the 1960 debates helped Kennedy.[136] But if Nixon had won the election instead of losing it by a wafer-thin margin, he would hardly have been reminded of any error on his part, and his willingness to debate his opponent might instead have been portrayed as a key to his victory.

The next election in which the two major-party nominees agreed to debate each other on television was 1976, and every election since then has featured either two or three presidential debates—plus (except in 1980) a debate between the vice presidential nominees as well. Early debates frequently required each candidate to answer questions from a panel of journalists, but since the 1990s it has become common for each event to have a single moderator. Beginning in 1992, one presidential debate in each election has adopted a "town hall" format in which questions are posed to candidates by undecided voters in the audience.

Debates have regularly produced remarks or exchanges that have dominated press coverage in the ensuing days or weeks, thus exerting a measurable impact on the state of the horse race between the candidates. In 1976, incumbent president Gerald Ford left the impression that, in his opinion, Poland and Eastern Europe were not under domination at the time by the Soviet Union, a gaffe requiring a subsequent week's worth of "clarifications" from his campaign. Ronald Reagan's somewhat scattered performance in the first debate in 1984 inspired a series of negative news stories telling the public how badly he had done; a *Wall Street Journal* article suggested that perhaps the incumbent's age (73 at the time of the campaign) was catching up with him.[137] Reagan did much better in the second debate, even alluding to his previous stumbles by joking that he would "not make age an issue of this campaign: I am not going to exploit, for political purposes, my opponent's youth and inexperience."[138]

When independent candidate Ross Perot came to the first debate in 1992 armed with a set of folksy, quick one-liners, journalists judged him the surprise winner of the contest. In the "town hall" debate that year, a woman from the audience asked George H. W. Bush, the sitting president, what effect the "deficit" had had on him personally. She probably meant to say the "recession" but misspoke, and Bush did not understand her meaning. "I'm not sure I get it," Bush said, essentially confirming the message that his Democratic opponent Bill Clinton had been putting forward throughout the year: Bush was out of touch with voters and did not even acknowledge that there was economic distress in the country, much less suffer from it himself.

Though Democrat Al Gore was not a sitting president in 2000, he faced the same danger most incumbents do in presidential debates: the burden of high expectations. Gore's reputation as a disciplined, on-message speaker with an impressive command of facts and figures contrasted with Republican nominee George W. Bush's public persona as a man less interested in the details of public policy and prone to the occasional malapropism. As with the results of presidential primaries, journalists tend to designate winners and losers in debates based on which candidates exceed or fall short of expectations—a point grasped by the Bush campaign, which sought to influence these expectations before the first event by referring to their opponent as a "world-class debater" while suggesting that any performance by their own candidate that did not end in embarrassment would be a significant victory.[139]

Indeed, Bush performed solidly in the first debate with no major gaffes, while Gore's aggressive style—repeatedly interrupting Bush and moderator Jim Lehrer and sighing into his microphone at many of Bush's responses—prompted critical comments from media observers. The day before the second debate, worried campaign staffers forced Gore to watch a parody of his performance on *Saturday Night Live*, in which comedian Darrell Hammond portrayed the vice president as a condescending know-it-all who obsessively repeated the word "lockbox" (Gore's metaphor for his plan to protect Social Security and Medicare funding), who responded to a question asked of Bush as if it were his turn to speak, and who asked for the chance to deliver two closing statements.[140] According to the collective media judgment, Gore overcompensated in the next debate, at times appearing excessively deferential to Bush. Though polls showed that viewers were about evenly split over which candidate won, the debates in 2000 were ultimately a disappointment to Gore campaign staff who had hoped to use them to demonstrate their candidate's strengths, while the Bush side claimed victory since their man performed better than expected.[141]

The 2004 presidential debates reinforced the historical trend that debates, when they matter at all, usually help the challenging candidate. The first debate, on the topic of foreign policy, was generally judged as a victory for Democrat John Kerry—or, rather, a loss for George W. Bush. Media commentators focused less on the substantive content of the candidates' responses to questions than on their bearing and body language. Bush was captured several times on camera making disapproving faces while Kerry was speaking and seemed generally ill at ease and annoyed by his opponent, fidgeting at his lectern and occasionally speaking in broken sentences.[142] The second and third debates—a town hall debate and an event focusing on domestic policy—proved less eventful, although Kerry caused a stir at the final debate by mentioning Vice President Dick Cheney's daughter Mary in response to a question about same-sex marriage.[143] Overall, the debates seemed to help Kerry slightly more than Bush. Kerry improved his standing in the polls over the period that the events were held, drawing nearly even with his Republican opponent in many surveys by the middle of October.[144]

In 2008, Republican John McCain hoped to use the debates to demonstrate that his Democratic opponent Barack Obama was not up to the job of president.

McCain's advisers had coached their candidate to question Obama's mastery of foreign policy, but to do so in a way that was not overly hostile (in order to prevent the backlash suffered by Gore in 2000).[145] McCain proceeded to suggest at seven different points during the debate that Obama "doesn't seem to understand" the issue under discussion, while declining to engage Obama directly— even appearing to avoid looking at his opponent.[146] Unfortunately for McCain, this approach was interpreted by many in the news media as reflecting a dismissive contempt for Obama, and the absence of any obvious mistakes on Obama's part failed to bolster McCain's charge that his opponent lacked sufficient knowledge and experience. In the third debate, McCain cited a voter named Samuel Joseph Wurzelbacher, a plumber's assistant encountered by Obama while campaigning in Ohio, who was captured on camera raising concerns about Obama's proposal to raise taxes on those making more than $250,000 a year. Wurzelbacher, nicknamed "Joe the Plumber," became a mascot of sorts for the McCain campaign in the last days of the race, appearing frequently on television and at public events on behalf of the Republican ticket.

As the incumbent president in 2012, Obama faced Republican challenger Mitt Romney in a series of debates that turned out to be significant milestones in a close race between the two nominees. Obama entered the October 3 debate on domestic policy with a narrow lead in national and battleground-state polls, prompting some enthusiastic supporters to suggest that a strong performance by the president might seal an electoral victory. But his manner once on stage immediately struck observers as surprisingly disengaged and lethargic. Over the 90 minutes of the debate, a hesitant and often meandering Obama failed to effectively defend his record in office from a series of sharp attacks by a focused and relentless Romney. Echoing the post-debate media consensus, veteran journalist Joe Klein of *Time* described the debate afterward as "one of the most inept performances I've ever seen by a sitting President."[147] Romney, in contrast, exceeded expectations, presenting himself as a pragmatic, results-oriented leader rather than the out-of-touch right-wing multimillionaire depicted by the Obama campaign's negative advertisements. The debate produced an immediate effect on the candidate horse race; Romney gained about 4 percentage points, on average, in the national polls over the following days, bringing him into a virtual tie in the overall popular vote.[148]

The stakes were thus raised considerably for the second presidential debate, held on October 16 and employing the town hall format. It was evident from the first moments of the evening that Obama had transformed his approach. "He interrupted, he scolded, he filibustered, he shook his head," noted Peter Baker of the *New York Times* in a post-debate account, describing the newly aggressive president as "intent on redeeming himself by getting in all the points he failed to get in last time."[149] Romney performed capably once again, but Obama's much-changed demeanor dominated the post-debate analysis, and the incumbent also benefited from some important help at a key moment. After Romney accused Obama of failing to label the September 11, 2012, lethal attack on the U.S. consulate in Benghazi, Libya, as an act of terrorism for 14 full days after the incident, Obama replied that he had indeed done so the following day at the White House. The two bickered briefly about the matter before debate moderator Candy Crowley of CNN interjected, telling Romney that Obama "did, in fact, sir . . . call it an act of terror." "Can you say that a little louder, Candy?" responded Obama to laughter from the audience, prompting Crowley to repeat her statement. Democrats reveled in the exchange, viewing it as an attempt by Romney to catch Obama in a "gotcha" moment that ended up backfiring, while Republicans raised the concern that Crowley had inappropriately intervened in the proceedings on Obama's behalf.[150] Polls showed that Romney's rise in the polls was stalled by the second debate, preserving a nearly neck-and-neck national race for the rest of October.

In 2016, Donald Trump's penchant for unpredictable and combative rhetoric raised the level of public and media interest in his series of debates with Hillary Clinton. Indeed, Trump performed in a consistently aggressive manner throughout the debates. He referred to Clinton as a "nasty woman" with "hate in her heart"; interrupted her criticisms of his ties to the Russian government by yelling, "No puppet—*you're* the puppet!"; and even suggested that he would ensure her criminal prosecution and send her to jail if elected president.

Clinton differed from Trump by sticking to an approach of projecting calmness while attempting to shrug off his provocations, following the guidance of aides who urged her in a pre-debate memo to convey friendliness and unflappability to viewers: "Happy to be there! Smiling! Never rattled! You look great!"[151] But Clinton also engaged in a litany of tough attacks. She questioned Trump's honesty as a businessman, accused him of "having a long record of engaging in racist behavior," and argued that "a man you can bait with a Tweet is not a man we can trust with nuclear weapons." Journalists and audiences mostly agreed that Clinton out-debated Trump, but popular views of both candidates were already so well-formed by the fall of 2016 that few Americans changed their minds about the race as a result of this unusually rancorous sparring.

Reviewing the history of presidential debates reveals two important general rules that have endured over the years. First, the post-debate media coverage is perennially dominated by endless discussion of which candidate "won" the debate and which candidate "lost," treating the events as yet another venue for partisan competition rather than an opportunity for citizens to learn more about how the candidates differ on the issues. These perceptions of victory and defeat, about which the press usually forms a strong consensus, are likely to be based on candidates' facial expressions, tones of voice, recitation of prepared one-liners, and overall deportment rather than any substantive discussion of public policy or approaches to governing. Democratic vice presidential nominee Lloyd Bentsen earned credit from journalists for aiming a scripted zinger at his Republican counterpart Dan Quayle in their 1988 debate by cracking that "Jack Kennedy was a friend of mine, and Senator, you're no Jack Kennedy," while Mitt Romney was the target of ridicule in 2012 after responding to a question about gender inequality by claiming that he had assembled "binders full of women" as candidates for appointive positions when he served as governor of Massachusetts.

Candidates and their strategists have been forced to adapt to this perhaps superficial reality. As Obama aide Anita Dunn explains, "if you're not on offense, you're on defense [and] you will lose. It's that simple."[152] Hillary Clinton's debate prep coordinators repeated the phrases "Demeanor is the debate" and "Tone, tone, tone" to their candidate prior to her faceoffs with Trump in 2016.[153] "Civics teachers won't want to hear this," argues journalist James Fallows, a former chief speechwriter for Jimmy Carter, "but the easiest way to judge 'victory' in many debates is to watch with the sound turned off, so you can assess the candidates' ease, tenseness, humor, and other traits signaled by their body language. . . . Having candidates answer policy questions is just a way to find out what we really want to know: how they look and present themselves, how they look side by side, how they think and speak on their feet, how we feel about them when they address us in their role as potential leaders."[154] At least, that's what the media believe Americans really want to know, and press coverage of debates is framed accordingly.

The second historical pattern is that debates are more likely to hurt sitting presidents and vice presidents than their electoral opponents. Non-incumbents may gain respect simply by keeping their composure as they stand on an equal footing with an occupant of high public office, since the prior expectations for their performance tend to be more forgiving among both the news media and the general public. "Challengers win . . . debates, in many respects, when they walk on stage," argues Dunn. "For the first time, most of the time, they have the same stature as the President of the United States. Suddenly, they seem more presidential, just because they're there. Challengers also have been campaigning full time [while] presidents . . . tend to have a lot going on besides preparing for the debate."[155] This dynamic seems to have worked to the advantage of John F. Kennedy against Richard Nixon in 1960, Jimmy Carter against Gerald Ford in 1976, Ronald Reagan against Carter in 1980, Bill Clinton against George H. W. Bush in 1992, George W. Bush against Al Gore in 2000, and John Kerry against the younger Bush in 2004. In some cases, an incumbent has managed to rebound from a poor first debate by adopting a new approach in subsequent events, as Reagan did against Walter Mondale in 1984 and Obama did against Romney in 2012.

Aware of their inherent risk, candidates prepare extensively for these events, spending precious days away from the campaign trail to organize "debate camps" in which they screen video footage of themselves and their opponents, discuss optimal responses and strategies with their advisers, and engage in mock debates with stand-ins impersonating their rivals. With the election potentially hanging in the balance, no effort is spared; some campaigns even build full-scale replicas of the debate venue's stage and lighting configuration on which to hold rehearsals. The Romney campaign chose Senator Rob Portman of Ohio to portray Barack Obama in multiple practice sessions with the candidate in 2012, while Massachusetts senator and 2004 Democratic presidential nominee John Kerry stood in for Romney during Obama's debate preparation.[156] In 2016, veteran Hillary Clinton aide Philippe Reines played Donald Trump during Clinton's mock debates, while the Trump campaign opted not to employ a single stand-in for Clinton during their own practice activities.[157]

Clinton later recalled the experience of preparing for her debates with Trump:

> We would gather at noon and work late into the evening. We'd practice specific exchanges, fine-tune answers, and try to plan out dramatic "moments" that would help shape the coverage of the debate, although often the most important clashes are the hardest to predict. . . . One wrong move—one roll of the eyes or slip of the tongue—can spell defeat. In debate prep, I practiced keeping my cool while my staff fired hard questions at me. They'd misrepresent my record. They'd impugn my character. . . . The weeks that Philippe spent studying tapes of Trump . . . paid off. He knew how Trump's mind worked. . . . In the end, Trump hardly said a thing in any of the three debates that I was hearing for the first time.[158]

Televised debates are now institutionalized, occurring under the auspices of the Commission on Presidential Debates, an organization jointly founded in 1987 by both major parties. The commission normally selects the sites (usually college campuses), dates, topics, and moderators for the debates. Other decisions are resolved by negotiation between representatives of the candidates, with no detail too small to escape their notice. The length of responses to questions, the right of the opposing candidate to deliver a rebuttal or the moderator to follow up on an answer, whether the candidates stand or sit, the height of the table or podiums, the location of the clocks used to time responses, the angles of the television cameras, the use of pencil and paper for taking notes, whether candidates give opening or closing statements—all of these issues and more are the subject of careful, calculated discussion between the rival camps.[159] In 2016, the first and third debates featured the two candidates standing at matching lecterns. In the second "town hall" debate, Trump and Clinton used hand-held wireless microphones as they roamed freely around a stage, surrounded by undecided voters perched on risers. In the vice presidential debate, running mates Mike Pence and Tim Kaine sat at a single table along with the moderator.

Campaign advisers' obsessive need to plan for every contingency illustrates the strategic lens through which they view each component of the campaign. The debates are ostensibly designed to educate the public about the candidates' policy ideas and reveal the capacity of each party's nominee to govern the nation effectively; journalists and the custodians of the flame of disinterested public-spiritedness reliably treat their existence as a sacred American tradition of civic virtue and enlightenment. Yet political actors know that the news media's air of excitement on the night of a debate more accurately reflects the possibility that a candidate will shake up the race by committing a major mistake on live television in front of a large national audience. The primary goal of campaign aides is therefore to minimize the probability that their candidate's electoral fortunes are damaged by the experience.

GETTING OUT THE VOTE

As Election Day draws near, presidential campaigns increasingly concentrate their energy on identifying potential supporters within the electorate and ensuring that these voters show up at the polls. Political professionals commonly refer to these efforts as get-out-the-vote (GOTV) activities, the field campaign, or simply the "ground game" (as a complement to the "air war" of dueling television advertisements).

The personal mobilization of voters has undergone something of a resurgence in recent elections. For several decades, campaigns had increasingly relied on television—via both paid spots and free news coverage—to communicate the candidate's message and encourage voter support, viewing the comparatively complex and labor-intensive task of in-person turnout operations as a less central component of their tactical efforts. Beginning in the late 1990s, however, political parties and interest groups shifted more of their resources into field activity, taking advantage of technological advances that allowed them to target voters more precisely than before. This re-emphasis of the ground game may be partially responsible for the rise in voter turnout in presidential elections after 1996 (see table 1.2 in chapter 1).

Before contacting citizens, campaigns must first identify likely supporters; it is counterproductive, of course, to mobilize voters liable to back the opposition. Targeting efforts begin with voters who are registered members of the candidate's political party (in states permitting partisan voter registration) or who tend to participate in the party's primary elections. Voters' registration status and turnout history are matters of public record. Both parties have assembled national electronic databases of voters compiling this and other information in order to best coordinate mobilization activity; for example, a Democratic field campaign might place particular emphasis on contacting registered Democrats with a record of sporadic electoral participation in order to ensure that those voters are aware of the election date and the location of their polling place. Because the vast majority of voters who consider themselves Democrats or Republicans reliably support their party's presidential nominees, campaigns can be confident that successful mobilization of these individuals will net additional votes for their candidate.

What about voters who are registered independents, or unregistered citizens whom campaigns wish to bring into the electorate? Field organizers must look for other clues to determine the likelihood that these people, if they vote, will support their favored candidate. One approach that has recently proven popular with campaigns is the mining of available data such as demographic characteristics, interest group affiliations, magazine and catalog mailing lists, and consumer preferences, which are available for sale by corporations and marketing firms, to estimate individuals' political beliefs—a practice known as "microtargeting." For example, consultants identify hybrid car owners, subscribers to music or gourmet cooking magazines, married couples with different last names, and Sierra Club members as likely Democratic supporters, while sport-utility vehicle drivers, readers of *Golf Digest* or *Field and Stream*, and bourbon connoisseurs are expected to prefer Republican candidates. Campaigns use this information not only to determine which voters should be contacted by field staff, but also what messages might prove especially persuasive in winning their support.[160]

The most common forms of voter contact are the telephone (whether by live volunteers at campaign phone banks or via automated "robocalls" that play prerecorded messages), direct mail, text messaging, and in-person door-to-door canvassing. Research by political scientists Alan Gerber and Donald Green has demonstrated that the latter approach is by far the most effective at increasing voter turnout, though it is also the most costly.[161] Both the 2004 Bush campaign and the 2008 and 2012 Obama campaigns placed particular emphasis on voter mobilization through preexisting social networks, believing that contact by friends, neighbors, coworkers, and fellow parishioners was more likely to stimulate a wavering voter's electoral participation than a knock at the door by a stranger.[162]

Bush's field operation in 2004 was, at the time, widely considered the most effective in decades, setting standards for data collection, voter targeting, and coordination of staff and volunteer activities. But the Obama campaigns in 2008 and 2012 appear to have built voter contact and turnout networks that were unprecedented in modern American politics. Obama field staff gave volunteers the opportunity to assume additional organizational responsibilities designed to increase their commitment and attachment to the campaign. A reporter who witnessed the building of the Obama campaign's infrastructure in Ohio described how one volunteer was recruited by a paid field organizer to a leadership position in the Obama ground operation:

> After Glenna had proven her reliability and effectiveness, Ryan asked her for another special one-on-one meeting where he invited her to formally agree to become [a "Neighborhood Team Leader"]. He spelled out all of an NTL's responsibilities before allowing her to accept it and even gave her a binder spelling it all out in writing: She would work with him to recruit other team members such as coordinators for canvassing, phone banking and data management. Her team would be responsible for connecting with *all* of the Democratic and undecided voters within their "turf." Other volunteers who stepped forward in her area would not be managed by campaign staff, but by Glenna's team. As team leader, Glenna would report results to Ryan a couple [of] times per week and would be held accountable for meeting specific goals by certain deadlines.[163]

The Obama campaigns also benefited from technological innovations. They merged voter lists with financial donation records, email addresses and cell phone numbers, and information provided by field staff and online activists to create an integrated database of supporters and targeted voters. This operation allowed officials at the campaign headquarters to access real-time data on mobilization efforts in key states all over the country. On Election Day, Obama volunteers stationed in polling places sent names of voters to the campaign via electronic device as they signed in, allowing campaign field offices to target their get-out-the-vote operations in the final hours of the election to those supporters who had yet to appear at the polls.[164]

In 2012, the Obama technology team built a massive electronic architecture that "unified what Obama for America [the campaign organization] knew about voters, canvassers, event-goers, and phone-bankers, and it did it in real time," according to a post-election profile by *The Atlantic*.[165] The campaign used this information to send targeted communications to voters with specific demographic or ideological profiles: young, single professional women might receive campaign mailings and online messages emphasizing Obama's support for legalized abortion and contraception access, for example, while Latinos would be notified of the candidate's policies on immigration and public education.[166]

The increasing prevalence of early voting and voting by mail in a number of states over the past several elections (see chapter 1) has had a profound impact on the campaign ground game. In these states, getting voters to the polls is an activity consuming several weeks rather than a single day. Campaigns seek to bank as many votes as possible by encouraging their supporters to vote early or by absentee ballot; this practice also allows mobilization drives to focus more precisely on those who have yet to vote. The rise of early voting also affects the candidates' strategies; rather than wait until the week before the traditional November election date to make their final pitches to voters, candidates must recognize that voting begins in some states as early as the third week in September. "We start having Election Day right around the corner," noted Obama campaign manager David Plouffe in mid-September 2008. Early voting "fundamentally changes two things: timing and budgets," observes Republican strategist Mike DuHaime. "You need to close the deal earlier for some voters, and Election Day can be spread out over weeks. That means your get-out-the-vote costs are more than ever."[167]

Like television ads and candidate appearances, campaigns concentrate their voter mobilization efforts in the politically competitive battleground states where either party has a chance to win. Residents of these states may well receive dozens of phone messages, regular in-person visits, and a steady stream of mailings from the candidates, parties, and interest groups over the final weeks of the campaign. Voters located in states deemed safe for one side or the other, by contrast, tend to see little direct evidence of a presidential election in their neighborhoods or mailboxes. While some may feel envious of the special attention lavished on the denizens of battleground states, others are undoubtedly just as content to be left in relative peace for the duration of the campaign.

CAMPAIGN BLUNDERS

Once an election is over, the losing side is routinely subjected to endless second-guessing by the news media and by its own putative supporters, with its defeat often blamed on strategic mistakes made over the course of the campaign—especially if the candidate lost by a narrow margin or squandered a previous lead in the polls. For example, the decision of New York governor Thomas E. Dewey, the Republican nominee in 1948, to mute the issues and campaign on empty platitudes in the final weeks of the race was blamed in retrospect for snatching defeat from the jaws of victory.[168] A more vigorous campaign, it was said, would have taken the steam out of Democratic incumbent Harry Truman's feisty comeback effort and would thus have ensured Dewey's election. Perhaps. What we know of the 1948 election suggests that it provoked a higher degree of voting on the basis of economic class than any of the elections that succeeded it.[169] A slashing attack by Dewey, therefore, might have polarized the voters even further. This would have increased Truman's margin of victory, since there were many more people with low than with high incomes. Had the election gone the other way—and a handful of votes in a few states would have done it—we would have heard much less in retrospect about Dewey's strategic blunders and much more about Truman's lack of popularity.

Democratic nominee Michael Dukakis declared that the 1988 presidential campaign would be about "competence, not ideology." But he did not campaign competently, failing to answer the barrage of charges George H. W. Bush's campaign made in its attempt to introduce Dukakis, unfavorably, to the mass of American voters who had never heard of him. The list of Dukakis's campaign errors, real and alleged, was a long one, and the should-haves and should-not-haves were legion. When asked in one debate what he would do if his wife were raped and murdered—a question, one must observe, that candidates are not usually asked—Dukakis took it not as a signal to pour out his emotions, an act he viewed with distaste, but as an opportunity to discuss the kinds of governmental policies that might cut down on rapes and murders. This, according to the consensus media interpretation, showed that he lacked emotion and was heartless.

Over and over again, Dukakis told his campaign advisers that he would not engage in mudslinging no matter what the provocation. Presumably this eminently desirable position was seen as a source of weakness.[170] "How many times do I have to tell you?" an aide heard him say. "That's not me." Candidate Dukakis was also governor of Massachusetts and felt he should abide by a pledge to the citizens of that state to spend several days a week doing the job. He might have done better had he put himself into the campaign full-time.[171] There were other faults. Dukakis failed to answer questions about national defense, which is, after all, a major presidential responsibility. He did not intervene to decide how to halt damaging internal squabbles in his campaign team. Almost from the beginning, the organization of the campaign was poor in that phones were not answered, supplies were not provided, and activities were not coordinated.[172] By the following year, Dukakis had learned how to blame himself. "I have reluctantly come to the conclusion," he admitted, "that if they throw mud at you, you've got to throw it back."[173]

No campaign is without its faults. Consider the 2000 election, ultimately decided by a Supreme Court ruling after several weeks of recounts and lawsuits over the treatment of ballots in the state of Florida. In the view of most observers, including many bitter Democrats, Al Gore gave away the election by failing to emphasize the economic prosperity of the nation under the Clinton administration. Gore's debate performances were roundly criticized, as was his low-key, uninspiring public persona, for costing him the race. Yet Gore finished first in the national popular vote, and probably would have won the electoral vote as well if not for a flawed, confusing ballot design in one Florida county that apparently led many votes intended for Gore to be counted instead for third-party candidate Pat Buchanan. Had Gore prevailed in the Florida recount, he would have been credited for running an effective campaign instead of facing accusations of political incompetence.

George W. Bush, by contrast, was seen in retrospect as a particularly skilled candidate. His chief strategist, Karl Rove, was often labeled a political "genius." But a different outcome in Florida would have forced Bush and Rove to return to Texas as failures. Rove sent Bush to campaign in California during the weekend before the 2000 election, on the theory that a visit by the candidate to a state considered safe for the Democrats would inspire a flurry of news stories about how confident the Bush campaign was of victory. Late-deciding voters, Rove argued, would interpret this coverage as a sign that Bush was going to prevail in the election and would eagerly jump on the bandwagon of a likely winner, producing a self-fulfilling prophecy. This was almost certainly a misguided strategy that would have led to endless second-guessing in Republican circles had Bush, not Gore, lost the election by a few hundred votes in Florida.

Criticism of John Kerry's campaign after his own narrow loss to Bush in 2004 seemed to combine the widely identified mistakes of Gore in 2000 (stiff, elitist, overly programmed, unappealing candidate) with those of Dukakis in 1988 (personal weakness, failure to respond to attacks from the opposition). Yet Kerry competed effectively with the allegedly more popular Bush throughout the entire campaign, and came within a single state of winning the presidency. Bush enjoyed not only the usual advantages of incumbency, but had seen his job approval rise to near-record levels after the terrorist attacks of 2001. His risky strategy—again, primarily masterminded by Rove—of advocating strongly conservative policies in order to mobilize the Republican base ultimately alienated a majority of independent voters and nine out of every ten Democrats, leaving little electoral margin for error. Bush's slim victory also deprived him of the ability to claim a broad popular mandate for his ambitious policy agenda. The centerpiece of his second-term domestic program, partial privatization of the Social Security system, quickly foundered in Congress, and further deterioration of the conditions in U.S.-occupied Iraq led directly to significant Democratic gains in the 2006 and 2008 elections. A more centrist, conciliatory approach to governing during his first term might well have given Bush a more decisive victory in 2004, and would have better preserved his political standing in the face of subsequent adversity.

John McCain's campaign in 2008 was commonly portrayed in the news media as undisciplined, disorganized, and prone to dramatic, attention-grabbing stunts. While this characterization contained some truth, McCain was also the decided underdog in the race, trailing Barack Obama in most polls from the early summer onward, and had little chance of prevailing if the election became a referendum on the policies or performance of the unpopular incumbent Bush administration. Under these circumstances, a strategy of playing it safe would have meant near-certain defeat. Instead, McCain and his advisers favored risky moves that, while they stood a good chance of backfiring, also had the potential to transform the race enough to allow a possibility for victory.

Perhaps the biggest gamble made by McCain was his choice of running mate. The campaign planned to announce the vice presidential candidate on the day after the conclusion of the Democratic national convention, in order to draw media attention away from Obama's acceptance address and minimize the traditional post-convention "bounce" in the polls for the Democrats. McCain's initial favorites for the position, independent Senator Joe Lieberman of Connecticut and former governor Tom Ridge of Pennsylvania, were opposed by senior campaign aides who warned that both men's liberal social views would be unacceptable to party activists.[174] The day before the choice was to be made public, McCain settled on Governor Sarah Palin of Alaska, concluding that Palin's political history—as a reform candidate, she had successfully challenged an incumbent governor of her own party two years before—complemented his own. In addition, McCain hoped that the selection of a female running mate might draw support from disgruntled women who had backed Hillary Clinton in the Democratic primaries. (With an eye toward courting these voters, the original version of Palin's stump speech contained an explicit tribute to Clinton, which was quickly dropped after Republican audiences routinely booed any mention of her name.)

The Palin selection certainly generated a great deal of attention, though not in the way the McCain campaign hoped. Although her introduction to the national stage was mostly positive, including a well-received speech at the Republican national convention, less flattering stories soon emerged. A rocky series of interviews with evening news anchors Charles Gibson of ABC and Katie Couric of CBS suggested that Palin was insufficiently informed about national issues. Reports also surfaced that Palin, a self-styled "hockey mom" with a regular-gal persona, had spent more than $150,000 of Republican party money on a new wardrobe for herself and her family in the weeks after her selection as running mate.[175] By the end of October, the press had picked up on evidence of growing tension between Palin and campaign staff, creating further distractions in the final days before the election.[176] Ultimately, though Palin proved popular with the Republican base, her presence on the ticket failed to improve McCain's position in the race, in part because her selection undercut McCain's argument that Obama was insufficiently prepared to serve as president. According to one national survey conducted shortly before the election, 59 percent of voters considered Palin to be unqualified for the vice presidency.[177]

For John McCain in 2008, the use of bold moves, such as the selection of Palin, was not necessarily an irrational strategy, given his status as the trailing candidate. The problems for him emerged mostly in their flawed execution, which contradicted one of the central messages of his candidacy—that McCain, not his opponent Barack Obama, was experienced and dependable. With a steady lead in the polls throughout most of the fall and superior financial and organizational resources, Obama could afford to take a low-risk approach, making his campaign appear to sail along smoothly while McCain flailed about.

In 2012, Mitt Romney's ultimately unsuccessful campaign attracted more than its share of second-guessing from pundits and frustrated supporters alike, especially since many Republicans expected by Election Day that the former Massachusetts governor would defeat Obama. Romney was faulted for a supposedly stiff and awkward public persona, for ineffectively disputing the Obama campaign's portrayal of him as a heartless plutocrat who had shipped American jobs overseas during his previous career in the field of private equity, and for failing to craft an appealing campaign message to attract the votes of key groups such as Latinos and young people. The inopportune surfacing in mid-September 2012 of what became known as the "47 percent" video (in which Romney, speaking at a private fund-raising event, dismissed the "47 percent of the people . . . who are dependent upon government . . . who pay no income tax" because "I'll never convince them that they should take personal responsibility and care for their lives") served as a distraction that reinforced Obama's line of attack on Romney as a candidate whose policies tilted toward the economic interests of the wealthy. Finally, the press viewed Romney's campaign organization as logistically and technologically inferior to the Obama team. While Obama received universal admiration for the sophistication of his data analysis and voter mobilization infrastructures, for example, the Romney campaign maintained a flawed internal polling operation that incorrectly predicted victory in key battleground states heading into the election; in addition, Romney's electronic get-out-the-vote database, code-named ORCA, crashed disastrously on the morning of Election Day, leaving the campaign without key intelligence about the status of their voter turnout effort.[178]

Had Romney managed to defeat Obama by a narrow margin, however, critics would have instead emphasized mistakes made by the incumbent. Most notably, Obama's strikingly poor performance in the first televised debate, which led to a significant shift in public support from Obama to Romney as measured by published news media surveys and the candidates' own polling, would have been seen in retrospect as the central turning point in the race. By some accounts, Obama (who seemed to hold his opponent in personal contempt) had been overconfident in advance of the debate, dismissing the concerns of his advisers that a well-prepared Romney could easily put him on the defensive and keep him there.[179] After the first debate, Obama aides convinced their candidate to adopt a more effective approach for future events by alerting him that another weak showing could cost him the election.[180]

More than any other recent contest, the 2016 election illustrates the ways in which the assessment of campaign blunders is colored in retrospect by the outcome. A prior consensus among reporters, commentators, and political elites in both parties held that Hillary Clinton was the prohibitive favorite over Donald Trump. While journalists did not view Clinton as a gifted political communicator or inspirational figure, they credited her as an effective fund-raiser running an even-keeled, highly professional campaign with ample strategic acumen. The Trump effort, in contrast, was almost universally portrayed as a thoroughly incompetent operation suffering from a divisive and impulsive candidate, a small staff of inexperienced and perpetually squabbling advisers, a severe financial and organizational disadvantage, and a series of highly damaging public crises. After the *Access Hollywood* video featuring Trump's lewd remarks about women surfaced in early October, Trump's chances of winning were near-universally downgraded to negligible; Republican National Committee chair Reince Priebus even attempted to convince Trump to drop out of the race for the good of the party.[181] Reflecting the conventional wisdom of the moment, Fareed Zakaria of the *Washington Post* argued that the Trump campaign was "the most poorly resourced, undisciplined, chaotic campaign in modern political history."[182]

Once it became clear on the night of the election that Trump was in position to claim a majority of electoral votes via unexpected victories in the pivotal states of Pennsylvania, Michigan, and Wisconsin, however, the tone of media coverage reversed in an instant. Analysts blasted the Clinton campaign for paying insufficient attention to these states, reflecting an apparent overreliance on flawed survey data. Pundits also blamed Clinton for failing to excite Democrats to turn out for her at the same rate that they mobilized for Obama, and for repelling white working-class voters, who flocked to Trump in heavy numbers. Clinton's months-old comments at a New York fund-raiser referring to some Trump supporters as a "basket of deplorables [who are] racist, sexist, homophobic, xenophobic, Islamophobic, you name it" attracted sharp criticism in retrospect for exhibiting elitism and contempt, as did a campaign message that abandoned the traditional Democratic emphasis on economic opportunity in favor of aiming relentless, but insufficiently potent, attacks on Trump's personal behavior. As Democratic pollster Anna Greenberg observed in retrospect:

> You can test a whole set of arguments against Donald Trump [in polls and focus groups] and always the top attacks on him had to do with temperament. But you can have things that test well but don't move people to vote. Obviously we don't know if it would have been different if she had a more consistent economic message, but I think it's hard to win without it.[183]

Meanwhile, a Trump campaign that had been widely viewed as a strategic and tactical disaster earned sudden new respect after the candidate's shocking victory. In particular, the Trump team was praised for effectively using social media to target potential supporters, as well as for recognizing key electoral opportunities in the small-town Midwest. Even the recurrent controversies that Trump stirred up during the campaign appeared afterward to be a powerful means of dominating daily news coverage, preventing Clinton from attracting popular attention for her own proposals. A candidate who had been a widespread laughingstock in Washington for nearly the entire length of the campaign immediately transformed in the eyes of many into a political savant with his finger on the pulse of the electorate.

The fact that every presidential election ends with one winner and one loser ensures that popular interpretations of the results will likely exaggerate the perceived cleverness of one side and the supposed haplessness of the other. In truth, electoral outcomes are only partially the product of the strategic and tactical battle between the candidates and their advisers; moreover, which campaign maneuvers are master strokes and which are ineffective or damaging missteps can be difficult to determine in the heat of the battle. The 2016 Trump campaign demonstrated that various types of behavior that were commonly assumed to disqualify a candidate from consideration for the presidency—from his snide dismissal of critic John McCain's service as a prisoner of war to his vulgarity-laced bragging about committing assault against women—were, though they were somewhat damaging, not fatal to his presidential ambitions in a race with an unpopular opponent and a broad demand for political change. The ever-shifting electoral climate, and the swiftly evolving larger culture within which it lies, ensures that what may seem at first like iron laws of politics turn out to be much less reliable than they appear.

FORECASTING THE OUTCOME

As an election draws closer, popular interest increasingly focuses on attempts to predict the outcome. Thanks to the modern news media's constant fascination with the candidate horse race, opinion polls are plentiful during the months before an election. Television pundits also devote extensive attention to the results of these surveys, speculating in great detail about the meaning of any apparent trends in the levels of support for each candidate.

Most widely reported polls, such as those conducted by the major newspapers and television networks, consist of a national sample of roughly 1,000 respondents selected by dialing telephone numbers at random or drawing upon samples of Americans recruited online. Pollsters screen respondents for their likelihood to vote, asking them if they are registered, if they are paying attention to the campaign, and if they have voted in past elections. They then ask which candidate the respondent would support if the election were held that day. Researchers often collect other information, such as age, race, sex, and party identification, in order to draw conclusions about the standing of candidates among various social groups in the electorate.

Many people are distrustful of poll results because of the relatively small sample size of most surveys. They wonder how the opinions of the thousand or so potential voters interviewed in any particular poll can accurately represent the views of the more than 100 million Americans who vote in a presidential election. This, by and large, is a false issue. The laws of statistics confirm that a sample of this size chosen at random will almost always be broadly representative of the larger population from which it is drawn. Pollsters commonly report "margins of error" along with their results, which represent the interval within which 95 of every 100 samples could be expected to fall due to chance if the population were sampled repeatedly—usually about 4 or 5 percentage points for a standard media poll. In other words, if Candidate A is "really" ahead of Candidate B by 10 percentage points in the total American voting population, a poll of 1,000 randomly sampled voters might easily find a 9- or 12-point gap. But it would be extremely unlikely for the poll to report incorrectly that Candidate B is in the lead simply due to random error in the sampling of respondents.[184]

When polls turn out to be wrong, the cause is much more likely to be systematic bias in either the means by which interview subjects are sampled or in their likelihood to respond to the survey than chance error under random selection. The two most famous mistakes in the history of presidential election polling illustrate the dangers of poor methodology. In 1936, the *Literary Digest* magazine mail survey predicted a victory for the Republican presidential nominee, Kansas governor Alf Landon.[185] When Democratic incumbent Franklin D. Roosevelt was overwhelmingly reelected, carrying every state except Maine and Vermont, the *Digest* became a laughingstock and soon thereafter went out of business. The magazine had sent out millions of postcards to people who had telephones asking them how they intended to vote; only 2.3 million people returned their postcards out of 10 million recipients, and those who responded disproportionately tended to be economically well-off. So the *Digest* drew its responses from a group in the population more likely to vote Republican and completely missed the larger number of poorer people who were going to vote Democratic.[186]

In 1948, the Gallup, Roper, and Crossley polls all predicted that the Republican nominee, Governor Thomas E. Dewey of New York, would unseat President Harry Truman. Truman's victory on Election Day was so unexpected that the early edition of the *Chicago Tribune* the following morning famously featured the headline "Dewey Defeats Truman." A committee of social scientists convened after the election found that the pollsters had stopped taking surveys too early in the campaign (missing what may have been a late surge for Truman), that they sometimes "corrected" pro-Truman results due to disbelief in their initial findings, and that the quota system then used to sample respondents introduced serious systematic biases into the data that could only be corrected by moving to a method of random selection.[187]

Modern pollsters try to remain vigilant against possible sources of bias in their surveys. If nobody answers the telephone when they first call, they try again the next day, if possible. (Pollsters usually prefer to conduct surveys during weekday evenings, when respondents are most likely to be available to answer their questions.) Researchers polling in an area with a significant Latino population will attempt to hire bilingual interviewers, lest they fail to take the preferences of Spanish-speaking voters into account. The vast majority of those contacted refuse to answer altogether, and this proportion is increasing over time. As long as Republicans and Democrats are equally reticent about sharing their political opinions with telephone interviewers, this tendency will not skew the results, although low response rates make it more difficult for pollsters to achieve their target sample size.

Different pollsters employ different methods, occasionally producing inconsistent results. For example, most survey organizations employ a screen for likely voters, excluding from their reported results the preferences of poll respondents whom they believe are unlikely to vote. These screens vary in composition and degree of strictness. Some voters will claim to be undecided between the candidates, especially well in advance of the election. Pollsters differ in their eagerness to push these respondents into declaring a preference. Particular surveys may or may not ask about third-party candidates, who usually perform better in preelection polls than they do in the election itself.

When an election is not very close, polls can misstate the final outcome by a few points without much notice. But in a very narrow contest—as most recent presidential elections have turned out to be—such errors can produce a great deal of shock. In 2012, Mitt Romney awoke on Election Day expecting to defeat Barack Obama, due in part to optimistic predictions made by his own campaign's polling team; he was sufficiently confident of the outcome to prepare a victory address in advance, but did not draft a concession speech until after learning late in the evening that he had indeed lost the election.[188] Strategist Eric Fehrnstrom later acknowledged that the Romney camp "genuinely believed that we were on the march . . . and this was going to be a plus-300 electoral [vote] victory for Mitt Romney. That was not spin. Our opinions were informed by the polling that was done."[189] If anything, the major polls understated Obama's actual victory margin (which equaled 3.9 percentage points in the national popular vote, as compared to a margin of 0.7 points in the final RealClearPolitics polling average, 1.5 points in the HuffPost aggregation, and 2.7 points in the FiveThirtyEight forecast); contradicting Republican expectations, the national exit poll found a six-point Democratic advantage in party identification nationwide—only one point lower than in 2008.

Of course, presidential elections in the United States are not decided by direct popular vote. In 2016, polls suggesting that Hillary Clinton would receive more popular support than Donald Trump were confirmed by the final results, in which Clinton received more than 2.8 million more total votes than Trump nationwide. But a systematic polling error in several midwestern states had misinformed both consumers of media-sponsored surveys and the Clinton campaign itself about the true state of the race in a number of states, especially in the Midwest, by consistently underestimating Trump's strength. As these states began to report their vote totals on the night of the election, consensus expectations of a comfortable Clinton victory turned first to uncertainty and then, finally, to stunned recognition of a Trump upset.

In the wake of the 2016 shock, pollsters scrambled to determine what went wrong. They settled on a combination of factors, but focused in particular on the overrepresentation in battleground state surveys of well-educated citizens (who supported Clinton over Trump at high rates) at the expense of less-educated white voters (who broke overwhelmingly for Trump). Some pollsters had not compensated by "weighting" their survey results by the educational attainment of their respondents (i.e., making statistical corrections to account for this discrepancy). As Nate Cohn of the *New York Times* later reported:

> At least three key types of error have emerged as likely contributors to the pro-Clinton bias in pre-election surveys. Undecided voters broke for Mr. Trump in the final days of the race, or in the voting booth. Turnout among Mr. Trump's supporters was somewhat higher than expected. And state polls, in particular, understated Mr. Trump's support in the decisive Rust Belt region, in part because those surveys did not adjust for the educational composition of the electorate—a key to the 2016 race. . . . The tendency for better-educated voters to respond to surveys in greater numbers has been true for a long time. What's new is the importance of education to presidential vote choice. Mrs. Clinton led Mr. Trump by 25 points among college-educated voters in pre-election national polls, up from President Obama's four-point edge in 2012.

This made it a lot more important to weight by education. In the past, it barely mattered whether a political poll was weighted by education—which is probably part of why so many didn't do so. The education issue doesn't just explain why polls were tilted toward Mrs. Clinton—it also helps explain why the state polls fared so much worse than national polls. Most national polls were weighted by education, even as most state polls were not.[190]

In 2000, another presidential election that ultimately produced a split decision between the national popular vote and Electoral College result, uncertainty over the outcome extended far beyond the preelection telephone surveys of potential voters to encompass the exit polls used by television networks to forecast the state-by-state results on the night of the election. Exit polls are surveys of actual voters in key precincts who are asked about their vote choice as they leave their polling place. These polls are not based on random samples of the entire voting population, and are subject to both sampling bias (since voters at some precincts are more likely to be sampled than others, and those who vote early or via absentee ballot will not be sampled at all) and response bias (since some voters may be more willing to respond to a news media survey at their polling place than others). But the news media find exit polls useful, both for projecting state results on election night before all the votes are actually counted, and for drawing preliminary conclusions about the demographic and ideological composition of the electorate in a given year.

Exit polls had occasionally caused problems before 2000. In 1980, NBC declared a landslide victory for Ronald Reagan over Jimmy Carter on the basis of decisive survey results nearly three hours before polling places closed on the West Coast. Many believed that this announcement depressed turnout, as westerners who hadn't already voted decided not to bother, and thus affected the outcome of more competitive local races in those states.[191] In 1996, several television networks incorrectly projected a Democratic victory in a U.S. Senate race in New Hampshire based on exit polls showing a five-point margin between the candidates; the declared "winner" ultimately lost by three percentage points.[192]

The events of election night in 2000 turned out to be utterly disastrous. Television networks pronounced Democrat Al Gore the winner in Florida on the basis of erroneous exit polls shortly after voting ended in most (though not all) of the state. Several hours later, as Republican George W. Bush pulled ahead in the reported vote returns, the networks retracted their Florida projections. As Bush clung to a small lead in the early hours of the morning, networks then called the state—and therefore the election as a whole—for the Texas governor, though within hours Gore had drawn even on the strength of late-reporting Miami-area precincts, requiring yet another retraction as it became clear that the winner could not be determined at least until all absentee votes were tallied. Thus began a weeks-long battle over the counting of Florida ballots that ended only when the U.S. Supreme Court halted all recounts in mid-December by a 5–4 vote, effectively handing the presidency to Bush.

The embarrassing performance of the television networks in 2000 prompted some post-election soul-searching among journalists. Joan Konner, former dean of Columbia University's Graduate School of Journalism, was a member of an independent commission formed by CNN after the 2000 election debacle to examine the problem. She found that "among the obvious failings were an emphasis on speed over accuracy in reporting; excessive competition [among networks] and the pressure to come in first; outdated technology; human error; a flawed polling and projection system; and, finally, overconfidence in the system and in the polls themselves."[193] It is troubling in retrospect that the networks did not exercise more caution when reporting results based on exit polls with known sampling and response biases. Surely few viewers would remember afterward which network was the first to project the outcome in any given state; the damaged credibility resulting from an incorrect prediction far outweighs any "credit" gained from the aggressive declaration of winners and losers.

The television networks' newfound election-night patience was immediately put to the test in 2004. Exit polls conducted on Election Day for a consortium of news media clients initially indicated an Electoral College victory for John Kerry. By mid-afternoon, the poll results had leaked onto the Internet, even affecting the performance of the stock market.[194] Displaying a relative abundance of caution, however, the networks declined to make projections in close states based purely on the exit polls. As Democrats who had been reveling in the leaked poll numbers looked on in horror, the polls were proven wrong again as the actual vote returns came in. By the end of the evening, enough actual votes in key states had been counted to declare Bush the winner once again.

In general, observers should treat the findings of any single poll with a certain dose of skepticism, especially if they are counterintuitive or out of line with other surveys. When multiple polls are in agreement, consumers can be much more confident in the results; when individual polls differ, the truth is often somewhere in the middle. Online polling aggregators—such as the website FiveThirtyEight, founded in 2008 by former professional baseball statistician Nate Silver—engage in sophisticated meta-analyses of survey results, with the goal of improving the accuracy and confidence of election projections by drawing upon evidence from multiple polling sources. While these estimates cannot fully compensate for the flaws of the individual polls on which they are based—like most analysts, FiveThirtyEight predicted a likely Clinton victory in 2016—they help interested citizens avoid the common practice of selectively cherry-picking polls that favor their preferred candidate while ignoring those with less emotionally reassuring results.

Predicting presidential elections is largely a matter of satisfying curiosity. It is a great game among political experts and other interested parties to guess who will win, and we look to the polls for indications of the signs of the times. But keeping the existence of statistical uncertainty and potential sources of error in mind is always well-advised when consuming the results of public surveys.

COUNTING THE VOTE

How votes are counted—how efficiently and how accurately—becomes important mostly when elections are very close. This issue therefore became significant in the aftermath of the 2000 election. On election night, it appeared that the Democratic candidate, Al Gore, led the Republican candidate, George W. Bush, very narrowly in popular votes nationwide, and that the candidates were virtually tied in the Electoral College. The outcome of the entire election depended on the popular vote in Florida, a state in which serious problems immediately emerged in the administration and mechanics of voting and vote counting.

Each Florida county had its own ballot type and format, and in at least one populous county the ballot was designed in a way that caused voters to be confused about how to indicate their preferences, probably to Gore's disadvantage.[195]

In numerous locations, ballots were cast that could not be counted by the machinery available to produce an automatic count, and disagreements therefore arose about whether, and how, these ballots could be counted by hand. The Bush and Gore campaigns appealed to the Florida judiciary to resolve these issues, but the Florida Supreme Court's ruling was preempted by a 5–4 decision of the U.S. Supreme Court along ideological lines to take jurisdiction and to halt the ongoing manual recount of ballots, effectively awarding the official popular vote in the state to Bush by a 537-vote margin (2,912,790 to 2,912,253). As a result, Bush received Florida's 25 electors and won the election with 271 total electoral votes—one more than a majority.[196]

The legal issues raised by the conduct of the 2000 election and the *Bush v. Gore* court decision have continued to resonate in subsequent years, judging from the volume of commentary generated in law journals and elsewhere.[197] The relevant political issues are somewhat easier to identify:

1. The winner in the Electoral College actually lost the national popular vote in 2000 for the first time since 1888, but constitutional rules governing the outcome were so well settled that there was no serious claim that Bush's entitlement to the presidency was in any way impaired by the fact that Gore had received more total votes. Indeed, Bush not only assumed office without difficulty but was free to interpret his mandate to govern without much concern for the circumstances of his victory. The 2000 election (and another split outcome in 2016) renewed calls from some quarters for the reform or abolition of the Electoral College, but these proposals received, as usual, only limited support among the members of Congress and state legislators who would need to initiate any change in the present system of presidential selection (see chapter 6 for further discussion of this issue).

2. The entire topic of election administration continues to require thorough ventilation. Different states administer elections differently; there are several kinds of machinery used for recording and counting ballots, each with technical imperfections; standards for uniformity in how ballots are judged to be valid are themselves not uniform; and ballots in different localities differ in their contents and design.[198] There may be systematic flaws that deprive different subgroups in the population of equal access to the ballot or equal treatment in the counting of their votes.[199] In an age when close national elections are common, these subjects deserve considerable public attention.

3. There had previously been a widespread tacit assumption that votes in presidential elections were counted more or less as cast, with electoral results reliably reflecting voter intent. The slovenly performance of the state of Florida in 2000 in accurately and efficiently determining the voting preferences of its citizens suggested that this assumption was wrong— and not only in Florida. As a matter of political strategy, one presidential candidate, Governor Bush, strenuously worked to prevent Florida ballots that did not register a preference on the automatic machinery from being counted at all. Impartial studies after the fact by news organizations established that he needn't have worried; if they had been counted, he would have won anyway.[200] The spectacle of a candidate for public office going to court to attempt to deprive voters of their vote is nonetheless worth contemplating.

The voting equipment at issue in the Florida recount was the Votomatic punch-card ballot, then in widespread use (about 30 percent of the national electorate voted via punch-card technology in 2000). The Votomatic system required voters to use a stylus to detach perforated squares from a cardboard ballot corresponding to their preferred candidates. Punch-card ballots were popular with county and state election administrators because they were inexpensive to use and could be counted quickly by machine. However, many voters found the perforations, called *chads*, difficult to remove completely, leaving partially dislodged chads that left voter intent unclear even under human inspection. "Hanging" chads remained attached to the ballot by only one of four corners, "swinging" chads by two corners, and "dimpled" chads were not detached at all but appeared to have been unsuccessfully pierced by the voter. The varying standards adopted by different Florida counties for how completely the chad needed to be removed in order to constitute a valid vote provided the evidentiary basis for the Supreme Court majority's finding that the manual recounts underway in December 2000 violated the Equal Protection Clause of the Fourteenth Amendment.

Subsequent research demonstrated that punch-card systems produced unusually large rates of undervotes, or ballots that failed to register a vote for any candidate, and that the proportion of undervotes was disproportionately high in precincts with large populations of racial minorities and low-education voters, though the specific mechanism for this was not fully understood. In places where punch-card systems were replaced by other types of voting equipment, the proportion of undervotes declined regardless of the racial or educational profile of the voting population.[201] Punch-card ballots also produced non-trivial rates of overvotes, which occur when a voter—whether by accident or confusion—selects more than one candidate for a single-member office, thus voiding his or her vote.

In the wake of the controversy surrounding the 2000 election, Congress enacted the Help America Vote Act (HAVA), which married Democratic concerns about uncounted votes with Republican concerns about voter fraud. In addition to providing almost $4 billion in federal funding for the purchase and implementation of modern voting systems by state election administrators, HAVA required the creation of statewide voter registration lists and that persons registering to vote supply a driver's license number or social security number, set requirements for disabled access to voting equipment, and established a voter's right to cast a provisional ballot in the event that his or her name does not appear on the registration rolls. The legislation also required states to establish uniform standards for counting valid votes.[202]

The combination of the debacle in Florida and the funding provided by HAVA virtually eliminated punch-card ballots from American elections; by 2008, only a few counties in Idaho were still employing the technology.[203] A number of states replaced them with electronic voting systems, which use computer touchscreens to register voter preferences; the results are saved on memory cards that are processed once the polls close. While the touchscreen machines are user-friendly and can eliminate over-votes by preventing voters from choosing more than one candidate for each office, some voters and watchdog groups have remained suspicious that they are vulnerable to fraud via surreptitious reprogramming. Even if electronic systems simply malfunction, a recount is impossible unless the machines also provide paper backup. For this reason, a growing number of states and localities require electronic systems to provide a "paper trail" of voter preferences, while other jurisdictions, after adopting touchscreen machines in the wake of the 2000 election, subsequently abandoned them in favor of optical scan equipment. The proportion of the American electorate using electronic voting systems rose from 12 percent in 2000 to 38 percent by 2006, but then decreased to 28 percent by 2016 as concerns spread over their potential risks.[204]

Optical scan systems require voters to fill in an oval or connect a line corresponding to their favored candidate on a machine-readable paper ballot. They have become the most prevalent form of voting technology in the United States, used by states and counties representing more than 60 percent of the national electorate in 2016. Optical scan equipment is popular because votes can be counted automatically by machine, yet a physical ballot remains that can be examined manually if the scanner malfunctions. Optical scan machines can also prevent overvotes by automatically rejecting any ballot with two or more candidates selected for a single-member office.

Yet optical scan systems have their limitations. Some voters fail to follow instructions—placing a checkmark in the oval beside a candidate's name or circling it instead of coloring it in, for example, which may render their preference unreadable by the scanning machine—or make ambiguous marks that leave their intent unclear. In the 2008 election for U.S. senator from Minnesota, Republican incumbent Norm Coleman and Democratic challenger Al Franken were separated by a sufficiently small margin in the initial tally to trigger a manual recount of every optical scan ballot in the state, with a special panel of judges authorized to resolve disputes. This procedure, carried out in a series of public hearings attended by the press and representatives of the candidates, revealed the capacity of some voters to cast ballots that defied easy interpretation:

> Some ballots presented little difficulty; in one instance, a voter had clearly filled in the bubble beside Coleman's name but had accidentally, or in a moment of indecision, touched his pencil tip in Franken's bubble, leaving a small dot. The judges gave the vote to Coleman. Other ballots provoked long, absurdist exchanges. One ballot—from Beltrami County—became locally famous. The voter had filled in the bubble for Franken but had printed "Lizard People" in the write-in area. After a few minutes of discussion, Marc Elias, a lawyer for Franken, spoke up. "My argument would be this 'Lizard People' is not a genuine write-in," Elias said. "In other words, [it] is not a person."
>
> "Do we know that for sure?" one of the judges asked. . . . The judges voted to have the ballot tossed out.[205]

It should be recalled that despite intense division over the 2000 presidential result, at no point did a crisis develop. Armies did not mobilize. Tanks did not rumble in the streets. There was never a moment when the politicians responsible for the flow of events could not refer to valid laws stipulating what they were supposed to do. Though the problematic punch-card equipment primarily responsible for the Florida controversy has now disappeared from American voting booths, no system can completely eliminate inaccuracy or the possibility of a contested election outcome. For the foreseeable future, close elections will no doubt stimulate careful attention to election procedures from experts and others with legal training. Greater oversight of election administration and the adoption of better voting technology may reduce the likelihood that another presidential election will be decided by the courts on the basis of disputed results.

PART III

Issues

In the concluding chapters, we discuss issues of public policy raised by the way in which Americans conduct their presidential elections. There are always complaints about election processes, as there are about nearly every aspect of American politics. Our discussion attempts to deal with some of the more long-lasting and widely held criticisms. We attempt also to place presidential elections into the broader context of the American political system, asking whether and how these elections serve the purposes of democracy.

6

Appraisals

■ ■ ■

REFORM UPON REFORM

In 1968, the Democratic Party endured a season of turmoil: its incumbent president, Lyndon Johnson, withdrew his candidacy for another term; a leading candidate to succeed him, Senator Robert Kennedy of New York, was assassinated; and its national convention was conducted amid extraordinary uproar. In that convention, delegates chose Vice President Hubert Humphrey, who had not competed in a single primary election, to be the Democratic nominee for the presidency. In the aftermath of Humphrey's loss to Richard Nixon in the general election, a party commission on reform of the presidential nomination process—the McGovern-Fraser commission, as it was called—was constituted and a year later unveiled proposals for changing nomination procedures. The most important reform measure instituted by the Democratic Party upon the recommendation of the McGovern-Fraser commission was a new requirement forcing states to choose national convention delegates via primary elections or caucuses in which all party voters are eligible to participate.

While the presidential nomination system created by the McGovern-Fraser reforms is, in a broad sense, still in place five decades later, a series of successor commissions designed to address remaining—or, in some cases, newly emerging—perceived flaws in the process has continued to make frequent further changes to Democratic nomination procedures. The Hunt commission, formed after the 1980 election, created the position of "superdelegates" in order to allow Democratic Party leaders a vote at the national convention. The Fowler commission, created in 1985, lowered the popular vote threshold required for a candidate to receive pledged delegates in a state primary or caucus from 20 percent to 15 percent. The Herman-Price commission of 2005 responded to concerns that the electorates of Iowa and New Hampshire were insufficiently diverse by authorizing the states of Nevada and South Carolina to hold additional early elections before the opening of the national delegate selection window. Sometimes, these commissions have opted to reverse or modify the reforms instituted by their predecessors—such as the Democratic "Change Commission" of 2009–2010, which responded to concerns over the potentially decisive role of superdelegates in the 2008 primaries by increasing the number of pledged delegates at the national convention.[1]

Controversy over superdelegates arose again in 2016. Though Hillary Clinton won a majority of pledged delegates chosen via primaries and caucuses, Bernie Sanders supporters were incensed by the overwhelming support she received from superdelegates (602 for Clinton to 47 for Sanders, according to a final tally by the Associated Press), which they saw as evidence that the nomination process was unfairly stacked against their candidate.[2] Supporters of Sanders reportedly harassed and even issued death threats against Clinton superdelegates.[3] The party created yet another commission, the "Unity and Reform Commission," in the wake of Clinton's general election defeat to examine the nomination process once again. After more than a year of study and deliberation, the Democratic National Committee approved reducing the role of superdelegates in future national conventions. Beginning in 2020, superdelegates are now banned from voting on the first presidential nomination ballot unless one candidate already has a clear majority of delegates and would receive the nomination anyway. Superdelegates may still participate in subsequent roll call votes if no candidate wins a majority on the first ballot.[4]

The Republican Party, too, has undergone significant change over the years. The widespread adoption of presidential primaries as a means of selecting state convention delegates to comply with McGovern-Fraser requirements after 1968 revolutionized the Republican nomination process as well. More recently, the national Republican Party has initiated its own internal reforms gaining additional control over nomination procedures, despite its traditional reluctance to intrude on the autonomy of its state party organizations. In 2012, the national GOP for the first time mandated that states follow national delegate selection rules. The Republican National Committee attempted to coordinate its nomination contest calendar with that of the Democrats and to penalize state delegations that failed to adhere to its new calendar and delegate selection procedures. The state parties in Florida, Michigan, and Arizona failed to comply and instead moved their contests to January. The Republican National Committee inflicted the punishment only on Florida, but still allowed its winner-take-all procedure, which also violated the new rules, to determine the state's delegate allocation.

The Republican National Committee revised its national rules once again after the failure of its previous efforts in 2012. Penalties for state noncompliance were stiffened: states would lose at least two-thirds of their delegates if they ignored the 2016 rules. The RNC reaffirmed its 2012 schedule guidelines, allowing four states—Iowa, New Hampshire, Nevada, and South Carolina—to vote early but imposing the two-thirds delegate reduction penalty for other states that moved their contests before March 1. To further shorten the primary calendar, states were required to complete their delegate selection at least 45 days before the 2016 National Convention, which would be moved from around Labor Day to midsummer. The RNC also acted to restrict the number of candidate debates during the primaries, which had grown to an unwieldy 26 in the 2012 contest. A national party committee would select debate venues and moderators, and candidates who failed to comply with the national party's schedule would be barred from all party-authorized debates.[5]

Thus both national parties in recent years have enacted, and constantly revised, elaborate regulations and procedures to "improve" their presidential nomination processes. It is fair to say that for much of the past 50 years, change has been in the air.

Previous chapters have incorporated the results of these reforms into the description we have given so far, concentrating on features of the presidential nomination process as it exists at present and on the political consequences that flow from the system as it is now organized. Some of these features have been part of the landscape of American politics for a generation or more; others are newer, and the changes they may bring about lie mostly in the future. Nevertheless, if there is one certainty about presidential elections, it is that the means of selecting party nominees is subject to continuous pressure for change.

In this chapter we appraise some of these changes and proposals for future change of the American party system and its nomination and election procedures. Because of the rapid reforms of the past few years, some of the impetus behind these suggested adjustments has slackened, while other items seem likely to be pursued with renewed vigor. Past solutions lead to future problems, encouraging new ideas to enter the agenda and old ones to depart. As time goes on, moreover, old concerns become outdated and new ones take their place.

Under the party system of the 1950s and 1960s, for instance, with conservative Democrats and liberal Republicans limiting policy agreement within their respective parties, the cry went out for greater party discipline. Too little ideological unity was widely blamed for the lack of consistent party policy positions across a wide range of issues. How, it was then argued, could voters make a meaningful choice if the two parties did not offer internally consistent and externally clashing policy views? Today, complaints about the party system are far more likely to take the opposite position, as studies document record levels of partisan polarization in congressional floor voting and growing disagreement between Democrats and Republicans in the electorate.[6] We now often hear concern about the negative consequences of excessive polarization between the parties, coupled with a new set of suggested reforms intended to reverse this trend.

In the same way, reforms stressing mass participation in party affairs have in due course been succeeded by measures emphasizing the benefits of elite experience—and vice versa. After the McGovern-Fraser reforms abolished the power of party leaders to directly control presidential nominations by shifting the responsibility for selecting delegates to primary and caucus voters, some critics lamented the elimination of peer review in the process. The Democratic National Committee responded to this concern by creating superdelegates in the 1980s to give leaders some influence in the case of a close nomination race, only to face a more recent popular backlash fueled by accusations that party elites might consider contravening the preferences of "the people." Scrambling to maintain popular legitimacy, the national Democratic Party swiftly moved after both the 2008 and 2016 elections to impose further limitations on superdelegates' power. Thus the preoccupations of one era give way to those of its successors.

The reforms that have led to a transformation of the parties over the course of the past half-century mostly emerged from two schools of thought, which for purposes of discussion we wish to treat as distinct entities. The first movement we call *policy government*; the second we refer to as *participatory democracy*. Advocates of policy government urged strengthened parties, not as the focus of organizational loyalties so much as vehicles for the promulgation of policy. For them, a system with two parties separated by sharply contrasting issue positions was a desirable end. Participatory democrats urged "openness" and "participation" in the political process and advocated weakening traditional party organizations and strengthening candidates, factions, and their ideological concerns.

While the two sets of reformers appeared to disagree about whether they wanted parties to be strong or weak, this came down to a difference in predictions about the outcome of the application of the same remedy, for both in the end prescribed the same thing: more ideology as the tie that binds voters to elected officials and less loyalty to political parties as organizations.

THE POLITICAL THEORY OF POLICY GOVERNMENT

Policy government reform had its antecedents at the turn of the twentieth century in the writings of Woodrow Wilson, James Bryce, and other passionate constitutional tinkerers who founded and breathed life into the academic study of political science. The descendants of these thinkers elaborated a series of proposals through the years that were embodied in a coherent general political theory. This theory contains a conception of the proper function of the political party, evaluates the legitimacy and the roles of Congress and the president, and enshrines a particular definition of the public interest.[7] Over time, we seem to be achieving an approximation of the party cohesion that these reformers of yesteryear wanted, and so it is worthwhile to attend to the pros and cons of the debate their proposals brought about.

This group of party reformers suggested that democratic government requires political parties that (1) make policy commitments to the electorate, (2) are willing and able to carry them out when in office, (3) develop alternatives to government policies when out of office, and (4) differ sufficiently to "provide the electorate with a proper range of choice between alternatives of action."[8] They thus come to define a political party as "an association of broadly like-minded voters seeking to carry out common objectives through their elected representatives."[9] In a word, parties exist to stand for policy.

Virtually all significant party relationships are, in this view, mediated by policy considerations. The electorate at large—not merely political activists—is assumed to be motivated by policy positions and officeholders conscious of mandates granted by voters to pursue a specific agenda. Policy discussion among party members is expected to create widespread agreements upon which party discipline will then be based. Special interest groups are to be resisted, accommodated only as the overall policy commitments of party permit. The weaknesses of parties and the disabilities of governments are seen as stemming from failure to develop and support satisfactory programs of public policy. Hence we refer to this theory of party reform as a theory of policy government. This theory holds "that the choices provided by the two-party system are valuable to the American people in proportion to their definition in terms of public policy."[10] It differs from the participatory brand of party reform (which we address later) in that policy reformers believed themselves to be revitalizing party organizations, whereas participatory democrats were likely to be indifferent to party organization.

Opponents of policy reform believed that democratic government in the United States requires that parties first and foremost undertake the minimization of conflict between contending interests and social forces.[11] We call them supporters of *consensus government*. For consensus government advocates, the ideal political party is a mechanism for accomplishing and reinforcing adjustment and compromise among the various interests in society to prevent severe social conflict. Whereas policy government advocates preferred parties that operate "not as mere brokers between different groups and interests but as agencies of the electorate," supporters of consensus government saw the party as an "agency for compromise," in dramatic contrast to the current polarization of American politics. Opponents of party reform through policy government held that "the general welfare is achieved by harmonizing and adjusting group interest."[12] In fact, they sometimes went so far as to suggest that "the contribution that parties make to policy is inconsequential so long as they maintain conditions for adjustment."[13] Thus the theory of the political party upheld by critics of the policy reform position was rooted in a notion of consensus government. Advocates of policy government behaved as if problems of consensus, of gaining sufficient agreement to govern, had already been solved or did not need to be solved. Believing that there was no problem of stability, they concentrated on change. Their critics downplayed policy not because they believed it unimportant but because maintaining the capacity to govern was, to them, more important than any particular policy. Distrusting the consequences of polarization and fearing instability, they were less concerned with enhancing the system's impulses to change.

A basic cleavage between advocates of policy government and advocates of consensus government may be observed in their radically opposed conceptions of the public interest. From the perspective of consensus government, the public interest is defined as whatever combination of measures emerges from the negotiations, adjustments, and compromises made in fair fights or bargains among conflicting interest groups. There are no external criteria by which policies can be measured in order to determine whether or not they are in the public interest. As long as the process by which decisions are made consists of intergroup bargaining, within certain specified democratic, constitutional "rules of the game," outcomes are therefore in the public interest.

According to advocates of policy government, the public interest was a discoverable set of policies that represents "something more than the mathematical result of the claims of all the pressure groups."[14] Some overarching notion of the public interest, they argued, was necessary if we were to resist the unwarranted claims of "special interest" groups. While this suggests that there are in principle criteria for judging whether a policy is in the public interest, apart from the procedural test applied by supporters of consensus government, these criteria were never clearly identified. This would not present great difficulties if policy government advocates did not demand that an authoritative determination of party policy be made and that party members be held to it. But information about the policy preferences of members is supposed to flow upward, and orders establishing and enforcing final policy decisions are supposed to flow downward in a greatly strengthened pyramid of party authority. Without criteria of the public interest established in advance, however, party leaders or commentators can define the public interest in any terms they may find convenient.

Over time, the party system has evolved to more closely resemble that envisioned by the advocates of policy government, shedding some previous attributes that were prized by the supporters of consensus government. American parties were once conceptualized as "big tents" that contained a variety of internal factions divided along ideological, social, geographic, and policy-related lines, and that maintained a federalist power structure open to influence from a number of sources. While this state of affairs regularly led to internal disagreements and presented challenges to leaders attempting to manage a diverse party coalition, it also permitted the representation of multiple views and interests, and allowed for policy moderation, bipartisan cooperation, and compromise among differently situated actors to occur at regular intervals.

The post-1968 reforms of the presidential nomination process were one of many developments that empowered ideologically motivated activists and interest groups within the party organizations and officeholding ranks. These changes were cheered by most proponents of policy government, who wished the parties to become both more internally unified and more externally differentiated so that voters were presented with a stark choice between two very distinct policy agendas at election time. This goal, at least, was achieved. While only 50 percent of Americans agreed in a 1992 Gallup survey that there were "important differences between Republicans and Democrats on issues that matter to you," compared to 47 percent who responded that the parties were "pretty much the same," by 2014 the share of respondents perceiving the parties as very different outnumbered dissenters by nearly a two-to-one ratio (64 percent to 35 percent).[15]

Because presidential nominees dominate the process of platform writing at the national conventions, play the most visible role in defining the positions of the party in the minds of the mass public, and (if elected) hold the most influence of any single figure over the policy-making process at the federal level, the theory of policy government has in practice led to an arrangement in which the candidate who happens to emerge from the complex and occasionally chaotic nomination system gains an ability to define the positions and reputation of the party at large. The growing power of congressional leaders, financial donors, and (especially in the Republican Party) ideological media has also sharpened party discipline over time. Individual members of Congress are less free than they once were to take positions at odds with their national party, even if doing so better aligns them with the prevailing public opinion in their home states and districts.

The nationalization of American politics has accelerated polarization by endangering the electoral fortunes of ideological moderates in both parties. Metropolitan coastal Republicans and Southern or rural Democrats, once the leaders of each party's centrist bloc, have both become endangered species in Congress, threatened in party primaries by more ideologically orthodox challengers and in general elections by increasingly formidable candidates of the opposite party.[16] The evolution of the American party system toward the more philosophically coherent parties envisioned by the advocates of policy government has made each party less internally factionalized than it once was and has given voters a choice of dramatically different alternatives in national, state, and local elections. Victorious candidates claim that their electoral success represent a "mandate" on behalf of the party's principles, and victorious parties more frequently act as a bloc on the floor of Congress to minimize the influence of the minority party.[17] But the rise of policy government has also failed to produce a more consistently functional or popular style of governing, nor has it bolstered public confidence in political parties, leaders, or the political system as a whole. Throughout the twenty-first century, Congress has remained severely divided along party lines, with few examples of substantive bipartisan cooperation.

It is not at all clear whether this increasing importance of party ideology has been good for the parties, much less the nation itself. Several policies implemented by the George W. Bush, Barack Obama, and Donald Trump administrations via party-line votes in Congress proved unpopular with the public, demonstrating that narrow election victories do not actually confer broad mandates to execute a comprehensive issue agenda. Bush's popularity ratings dropped steadily in his second term as the U.S. war in Iraq suffered significant setbacks. In 2006, voters communicated their disapproval of his performance in office by turning control of both houses of Congress over to the opposition Democrats. Congressional Republicans lost a number of seats in liberal and moderate northern constituencies, where voters registered their strong objections to the policies of the ruling GOP.

Similar results in 2008 ushered in Democratic dominance of Congress and the presidency under Obama. In turn, the new president's pursuit of a liberal policy agenda increased the electoral vulnerability of moderate Democrats from the South and West who, in adopting policy positions, faced an unappetizing choice between satisfying either their party leaders or their constituents. Obama's declining popularity led to heavy losses for these Democrats in the 2010 midterm elections, giving control of the House of Representatives back to the Republican Party for the remainder of his presidency while further increasing the extent of ideological polarization and partisan rancor within Congress.

During the 2016 campaign, Donald Trump positioned himself as both an outsider to Washington and an unorthodox, economically populist Republican. But once elected, Trump pursued a strongly conservative agenda across a range of issue domains while maintaining his sharp-edged and divisive political style. His major domestic policy initiatives—attempting to repeal Obama's 2010 national health care law, enacting major tax cuts targeted toward corporations and wealthy individuals, and pursuing the construction of a wall along the southern border of the United States—were unpopular with the public, and he made little effort to reach out to Democratic legislators or voters. As a result, Republicans lost control of the House of Representatives in 2018, representing the fourth consecutive midterm election in which Americans expressed their dissatisfaction with the president by electing a wave of opposition party members to one or both chambers of Congress.

Are parties that take relatively extreme positions more "responsible" or "accountable" to the ideologically inconsistent American electorate than parties that allow for greater flexibility on issues? Reforms that reinforce party polarization risk offering voters a clear choice—but between two unpalatable options. To a large extent, advocates of policy government have succeeded in implementing their goals, but the results may have proven less popular—and less conducive to a well-functioning political system—than they foresaw.

An even more fundamental barrier to the effective implementation of policy government lies in the distinctive institutional structure of the United States. With a constitution that allows for divided party control of the government, with procedural features like the Senate filibuster that grant obstructive power to the opposition even during periods of single-party rule, and with frequent elections that offer the constant opportunity for today's minority to become tomorrow's majority, the emergence of party polarization has produced long periods of policy inertia, deepening party rancor, and recurrent moments of crisis (such as the extended government shutdowns of 1995–96, 2013, and 2018–19). As long as presidents or the leaders of the opposition view the pursuit of partisan advantage or ideological purity as a more appealing goal than partnership or compromise, the drift toward policy government will continue to be, at best, a very mixed blessing.[18]

REFORM BY MEANS OF PARTICIPATORY DEMOCRACY

The second type of reform movement we identify as participatory democracy. The efforts of those who advocate participatory democracy and who have attempted to make the Democratic Party the vehicle of this approach to government have met with considerable success over the past 50 years, as the history of presidential nomination reform attests.[19] The more recent advent of the Tea Party movement subjected the Republican Party to participatory demands as well. Here we wish to contemplate the theory of politics that underlies this position. Ordinarily, participatory democrats criticize the American political system in two respects. First, they argue that elections have insufficient impact on policy outcomes of the government. These critics perceive too weak a link between public policy and what they believe to be the desires of electoral majorities. Second, there is the critique of the electoral process itself, which argues that policy does not represent what majorities want because undemocratic influences determine election results. These criticisms are simple-minded in one sense and cogent in another. They are simple-minded in that they ignore the immense problems that would have to be overcome if we were truly serious about transforming America or any large, diverse population into a participatory democracy. They are cogent in that responsiveness to majorities on questions of policy is a fundamental value that gives legitimacy to democratic government. The connection between such criticism and the legitimacy of government makes it important to deal at least briefly with some of the issues and problems that should be raised (and usually are not) by judgments of this fundamental nature.

The first and obvious question to ask is whether the criticisms are based on fact. Is the American system unresponsive to the policy desires of a majority of its citizens? Unfortunately, there is no unambiguous way to answer this question. If we focus our attention, for example, on the mechanics of the policy process, we find what appears to be government by minorities. In some policy areas, a great number of people and interests, organized and unorganized, may have some influence on the final product. But fewer individuals may be involved in areas dealing with other problems and policies, some of which will be of a specialized nature, of limited interest, and so on. Even members of Congress do not have equally great influence over every decision: committee jurisdictions, seniority, special knowledge, party, and individual reputation all combine to weigh the influence of each member on a different scale for each issue.

So we must conclude that if we adopt direct participation in, and equal influence over, the policy decisions of our government (the decisions that "affect our lives") as the single criterion of democracy, then our system surely fails the test. So, we might note, does every contemporary government of any size known to us, possibly excepting two or three rural Swiss cantons.

Another approach might focus on public opinion as an index of majority desires. Using this standard, a quite different picture emerges. Policy decisions made by the government mostly have the support of popular majorities. Where this is not true, the apparent lack of "responsiveness" may have several causes, not all of them curable: (1) conflicts between majority desires and intractable situations in the world (e.g., a hypothetical desire for peace in the Middle East); (2) public attitudes favoring certain sets of policies that may be mutually incompatible (such as the desire for low taxes, generous benefits, and balanced budgets); or (3) clear, consistent, and feasible majority desires that are ignored by the government because the desires are unconstitutional or antithetical to enduring values of the political system, to which leaders are more sensitive than popular majorities. Surveys, for example, have from time to time revealed majorities in favor of constitutionally questionable repressive measures against dissenters and the press.

Criticisms of the popular responsiveness of presidential elections are more difficult to assess. American electoral politics does respond to the application of resources such as money that are arguably undemocratic and that cause the influence of different actors to be weighed unequally. In a truly democratic system, it could be argued, the system would respond to votes and only votes. All methods of achieving political outcomes other than registering preferences by voting would be deemed illegitimate. As we have indicated, however, money, incumbency, energy and enthusiasm, popularity, name recognition, ability, and experience are all valuable assets within the structure of American politics. Is this avoidable? Should we attempt to eradicate the influence of these resources?

Political resources and the people who possess them are important primarily because campaigns are important. Campaigns are important because the general public needs to be alerted to the fact that an election is near. Partisans must be mobilized, the uncommitted convinced, perhaps even a few minds changed. Resources other than votes are important because—and only because—numerical majorities must be mobilized.

American politics responds to diverse resources because many citizens abstain from active participation and are hard to reach by campaigners. Sometimes this is described as political apathy. Why is political apathy widespread? Perhaps it is because the system presents the citizenry with no real alternatives from which to choose. Yet voting participation in presidential elections seems to rise and fall without much regard for either the ideological distance between candidates of the major parties or the level of popular trust in the political system.

Some explain the existence of political apathy by arguing that the public has been imbued with a "false consciousness" that blinds them to their "real" desires and interests. They would participate if they knew better. This explanation is traditionally seized on by the enlightened few to deny value to the preferences of the ignorant many. The people, we are told, are easily fooled; this testifies to their credulity. They do not know what is good for them; this makes them childlike. But when the people cannot trust their own feelings, when their desires are alleged to be unworthy, when their policy preferences should be ignored because they are not "genuine" or "authentic," or there are not enough of them, they are being deprived of their humanity as well. What is left for the people if they are held to have no judgment, wisdom, feeling, desire, and preference? Such an argument would offer little hope for democracy of any sort, for it introduces the most blatant form of inequality as a political "given": a structured, ascribed difference between those who know what is "good" for themselves and those who must be "told." No doubt it is true that much of the time we do not know (without the advantage of perfect foresight) what is best for us. But that is not to say that others know better, that our consciousness is false but theirs is true. Persons who make the "false consciousness" argument do not believe in democracy.

A more hopeful and less self-contradictory explanation of political apathy might note that throughout American history a substantial number of citizens have not wished to concern themselves continually with the problems and actions of government. Many citizens prefer to participate on their own terms, involving themselves when they feel like it with a particular issue area or problem. These citizens' participation is necessarily sporadic and narrower than that of the voter interested in all public problems and actively involved in general political life. Many other citizens are more interested in their own personal problems than in any given public policy issue.[20] These citizens meet their public obligations by going to the polls at fairly regular intervals, making their selections on the basis of their own criteria, and then mostly withdrawing from active engagement in politics until the next election. In the intervals, unless they themselves are personally affected by some policy proposal, most of these citizens may wish to be left alone. Given the complexity of issues and the uncertainty surrounding the claims of candidates, citizens may arrive at their voting decisions by asking themselves a simple, summary question: Are things (the domestic economy, world affairs) better or worse than they were? This is perhaps a reasonable way to make a choice in the voting booth, but it does not offer much future policy guidance to political leaders.[21]

Discussions of political apathy may say more about the values of the participants than about the ostensible objects of their interest. Those observers who approve of existing institutions are likely to view apathy as relatively benign; they believe people do not participate because they are satisfied or genuinely indifferent. Those who disapprove of existing institutions naturally find the defect in the institutions themselves; they believe people do not participate because they are denied the opportunity or because they rightly feel ineffectual. Observers who view individuals as capable of regulating their own affairs see these individuals as deciding case by case whether it is worth the time and effort to participate. Projecting the investigator's preferences onto citizens does not seem to us a useful way of learning why this or that person chooses to participate in political life. As political scientists and citizens, we think self-government an ideal so valuable that we would not impose our own views on those who decide they have better things to do.

Studies have from time to time shown unfavorable citizen attitudes toward the political system, a phenomenon sometimes called "alienation." As we argued earlier in this book, these attitudes do not explain low rates of voting participation; persons who score high in these unfavorable attitudes have been shown to participate at about the same rate as the nonalienated.[22] So we surmise that a great many citizens who do not vote abstain because they are concerned with other things important to them, like earning a living or painting a picture or cultivating a garden, and not because they feel it is so difficult to influence outcomes. In short, for them, politics is peripheral. Given the secondary importance of politics in many people's lives, making it easier to vote does increase turnout. But even lowering barriers to participation does not reduce abstention from voting to zero or anything like zero.

Consider a society in which all citizens were as concerned about public matters as the most active. Such a society would not require mobilization: all who were able to would vote.[23] The hoopla and gimmickry associated with political campaigns would have little effect: this citizenry would already know the records of the parties and the candidates and, presumably, would make reasoned choices on this basis. Should such an active society be the goal of those whose political philosophy is democratic? This question should not and cannot be answered without first addressing the problem of how such a society could be achieved.

Without attempting to be comprehensive, a few difficulties merit some specific comment. First and foremost, building political knowledge and engaging in political activity can take a great deal of time. Yet most American citizens work for a living and have a demanding family life. They lack the opportunity, even if they had the temperament and training, to engage continually in politics. To the degree that representative institutions—political parties, legislatures, elected executives—are disregarded in favor of more direct modes of activity, the majority of the people will be without the means through which they can most effectively make their will felt. In short, to impose requirements of direct participation on those desiring a voice in decisions would be to ensure that the incessant few rather than the sporadic many would rule: thus the 1960s slogan "power to the people" really proposed to replace a representative few, who were elected, with an unrepresentative few, who were self-activated.

In the age of global connectivity, the prospect of participatory democracy seems, according to some proponents, to lie closer than ever to realization. The prospect of citizens debating and voting on policy referendums or party platforms from the convenience of their own smartphones is, in their view, popular rule in its purest form. By cutting the costs of information-gathering and allowing virtual, rather than physical, participation, the Internet has inspired visions of revolutionary change in the relationship among citizens, parties, and government.[24]

Yet technological advances have had mixed effects to date on the quality of public discourse and the performance of public institutions. Social media platforms have indeed allowed more people to participate in political debate, though not always with enlightening or constructive results. The emerging opportunities for political engagement offered by the digital realm risk encouraging superficial or purely expressive forms of activism that do not actually improve the nation's civic health. As the political scientist Eitan D. Hersh warns, online tools that primarily offer instant emotional gratification rather than a more serious and enduring investment in a political cause can lead to "a degraded form of politics that caters to the voyeurism of news junkies and the short attention spans of slacktivists . . . that takes the form of partisan fandom, the seeking of cheap thrills, and amateurs trying their hand at a game. . . . [W]hen politics is something one does for fun rather than out of a profound moral obligation, the citizen who does not find it fun has no reason to engage."[25] Thus the very real opportunities that the online world provides for some citizens to become easily informed and mobilized must be weighed against the associated costs that may result in the disaffection of others.

Such tradeoffs are not new. The reforms of the party nomination process instituted 50 years ago held the promise of bolstering the popular legitimacy of the parties by guaranteeing interested citizens control over the selection of their presidential nominees. By requiring the parties to be internally democratic, the argument went, these reforms would improve the representation of the American people in their government.

But by making it possible for candidates to capture the presidential nomination of a major party without winning the support of leading politicians or other party professionals, these reforms also occasionally produced nominees who lacked the qualities necessary to achieve political success. George McGovern, the first Democratic nominee after reforms were implemented in 1972, turned out to be very unpopular with the larger electorate, depriving the American people of a choice between two appealing options in the general election. Jimmy Carter (Democratic nominee in 1976) and Donald Trump (Republican nominee in 2016), two subsequent "outsider" nominees who inspired little enthusiasm among the traditional leaders of their party, were nonetheless able to win election to the presidency. But both Carter and Trump immediately found it difficult to govern effectively, and their performance in office quickly alienated a majority of the public. The "empowerment" of voters via reforms to the nomination process has not ensured the selection of either broadly attractive candidates or well-qualified potential presidents, raising the question of how much these changes indeed furthered the cause of representative democracy. Yet the ideal of popular rule as the guiding principle of internal party affairs remains strongly held among many activists, and (as the Democrats have discovered during their recent battles over superdelegates) any suggestion that popular passions should be tempered by professional expertise reliably provoke accusations of elitism, corruption, and injustice.

In his well-known work, the philosopher Jürgen Habermas has argued that the only way to make a democracy legitimate, for it to be considered a true democracy worthy of support, is for it to approximate the conditions of what he calls "an ideal speech situation." Every person would be equally interested and active. Each would have equal rights, money, information, and all other resources necessary for effective participation.[26] What could be wrong with such an ideal? Nothing at all, we think. If it were to be realized in practice in a very diverse society, however, it might lead to surprising results.

A diverse society may lead to the expression of diverse values. Individualists, for example, adhere to the ideal of equality of opportunity so that people can be different, and some may consequently end up with more resources than others. This expresses a different equality from that postulated by Habermas. Other people may prefer a more patriarchal or hierarchical set of values in which different people occupy different statuses. Amplifying still other voices might well lead to the more frequent public expression of intolerant or incendiary sentiments. Thus it is helpful to consider whether democracy is only about equality or whether it may be about enabling people who hold different values to live together peaceably.

Thus there are practical difficulties with a theory that requires high levels of participation or demands a great deal of knowledge and interest in political life. We raise this issue not because we are opposed in principle to the idea of an active, participatory, democratic society. By persuasion and political education, the majority of our citizens might indeed be convinced that the quality of our shared existence could be improved through more continuous devotion to public activity. This is quite different from arguing that the rules of the game should be changed to reduce the influence of those who at present lack the opportunity or desire to be active. Efforts to implement ideal goals when the preconditions and the means of achieving these goals do not exist are self-defeating. Actions that, in the name of participatory democracy, restrict the ability of most of the people to have their political say are not as democratic as advertised.

SOME SPECIFIC REFORMS

Comprehensive reforms of the political system, when they occur, always ride in on tides of strong feeling. But thoughtful citizens may find it instructive to consider the consequences of the best-laid plans in a more dispassionate and analytical manner. Once these consequences have had an opportunity to manifest themselves, however, a new generation of reform may be in order. After all, practically everything that political reformers object to now was once somebody's favorite reform.

We suspect that the achievement of many—but not all—of the common objectives of reformers would be detrimental to their aims and to those of many others. Let us consider, for example, three specific reforms of governmental machinery that are frequently advocated to make the parties more internally democratic and more responsive to popular will. Reformers often advocate a variety of changes to the nomination process, changes to party convention procedures, and modification or abolition of the Electoral College. We address each of these topics in turn.

The Nomination Process

In order to evaluate the strengths and weaknesses of the current presidential nomination process, it would be helpful to suggest a set of goals that most Americans might accept as desirable and important.[27] The following six standards appear to meet this test: any method for nominating presidential candidates should (1) help secure vigorous competition between the parties, (2) maintain some degree of cohesion and agreement within each party, (3) produce nominees who are likely to win voter support, (4) lead to the choice of nominees who are reasonably well-qualified, (5) lead to the acceptance of the nominees as legitimate, and (6) result in officeholders who are capable of generating support for public policies they intend to pursue. We first look at some suggested alternatives to the current nominating system.

The most common nomination reform proposal would replace the sequential series of state primaries and caucuses now in place with a national direct primary election held on a single date in the spring of a presidential election year. Advocates of this reform argue that a national primary would be more equitable than the current system, which gives disproportionate influence to states voting earliest in the calendar. Iowa and New Hampshire, two small and not entirely representative states, hold particular sway in determining the presidential nominees of both parties every four years, while the frequent emergence of a presumptive nominee soon after the first primaries occur often renders later elections in more populous states irrelevant to the outcome.

Defenders of the current system counter that there is an advantage in allowing two small states to vote first. Candidates competing in Iowa and New Hampshire must engage in "retail politics," building support by making frequent personal appearances and winning the backing of party activists. As Everett Carll Ladd argues:

> By leading off, manageable little Iowa and New Hampshire enable less well-known and well-heeled candidates to gain attention through presenting their wares to real people in real election settings. If a candidate with moderate resources, and previously lacking a national reputation, manages to impress a fair number of voters in these small states, isn't this laboratory experience of some considerable interest to the country?[28]

This merely points to a more general problem of financing national primary elections. It is quite probable that 10 or even 20 candidates might compete in a true, 50-state, national primary. In a year when there is no incumbent president in the race, it is not hard to imagine a crowd of challengers in both parties hustling all over the United States campaigning in such an election. It would take, of course, enormous amounts of money. The parties could hardly be expected to show favoritism and so could not finance these candidates. The pre-primary campaign, therefore, would assume enormous importance and would be exceedingly expensive. Nationwide challengers would need access to very large campaign war chests. It would help if they were already well known. They would also have to be quite sturdy physically.

We know that voters often find it difficult to distinguish among candidates of the same party, especially when these candidates are not previously familiar to them. Voters in a national primary could be expected to make evaluations by knowing one or two of the candidates' names in favorable or unfavorable contexts, liking or not liking their looks, identifying or not identifying with their ethnic or racial characteristics, attending to their treatment in the press, responding to television advertisements and social media memes, or relying on some other means of differentiation having nothing whatever to do with ability to do the job, or even with their policy positions. Since patents on policy positions are not available, it is reasonable to suppose that more than one candidate would adopt roughly the same set of positions, virtually eliminating any important substantive differences between them.

A national primary would present another potential complication: in a field of multiple candidates, no single individual would be likely to receive a majority of the votes. Under current party rules, candidates must win support from a majority of delegates to be nominated; the Democratic Party's insistence on proportional allocation of delegates virtually ensures that a potential nominee must receive close to a majority of the popular vote. The establishment of a national primary would therefore increase the likelihood of a deadlocked convention—or, at least, a flurry of deal-making by candidates after the primary to provide one contender the necessary number of delegates. It is hard to see how this alternative would better reflect the will of the voters than the current system.

Of course, the parties could amend their rules to grant the presidential nomination to the first-place winner of the national primary, regardless of whether that candidate gained a majority of the total vote. This measure would allow for the possibility that a candidate could win the nomination despite receiving support from just 20 or 30 percent of the party's voters—a much less democratic outcome than we now have, since who knows how the rest of the electorate might have distributed itself if it had known what the rank order of the candidates was going to be? Another possibility would be for the top two finishers to contest a second 50-state runoff election after the first primary and before the general election. The party might end up with a good candidate, of course, if there was anything left of that candidate to give to the party in the general election campaign, which would follow. Then the poor candidate, if elected, would have to find the energy to govern. By following this procedure, the United States might effectively restrict the presidency to the candidacies of wealthy athletes.

We are concerned that the widespread use of direct primaries encourages prospective candidates to pursue campaigns stressing personal publicity in ways that can emphasize superficiality over substance. The current system also provides for no peer review—that is, consideration of those aspects of fitness of candidates to hold office that can best be observed by colleagues who actually know them personally, who have themselves a heavy investment of time and energy in making the government work, and who know that they may have to live at close quarters with the results of their deliberations. Other politicians may make public endorsements or argue the relative merits of various contenders, of course, but primary voters are under no obligation to pay attention. The victories of outsiders Jimmy Carter and Donald Trump in the 1976 Democratic primaries and 2016 Republican primaries, respectively, are striking examples of primary voters' willingness to ignore clear signals from the leaders of their own party.

It is difficult to persuade activists who participate only casually in politics, and those who tend to do so only when moved by a great issue or charismatic figure of the day, that the intensity of their feelings does not confer a sweeping mandate. These feelings, no matter how worthy, do not make occasional participants more worthy than party veterans. They do not bestow a special moral status on latecomers to politics, as compared with people who are already active. Those less motivated by "hot" contemporary issues or specific personalities cannot be excluded on grounds of their moral inferiority from decision-making in the presidential nomination process.

The great virtue of state-by-state sequential primaries is, of course, that they provide a means—supplemented by polls—of gauging the popularity of various candidates and their effectiveness in conducting themselves under challenging circumstances. We believe that as long as there are many things we demand of a president—intelligence as well as popularity, integrity as well as speaking ability, private virtue as well as public presentability—we ought to foster a selection process that provides a mixture of devices for screening according to different criteria. The mixed system we advocate is not perfect, of course, but it is greatly superior to the unmixed non-blessing of the single national primary.

Regional primaries have sometimes been suggested as a halfway house between a single national primary and a multitude of state primaries. One form merely requires that all states holding presidential primaries schedule them for one of four sanctioned dates, spaced a month apart, and that all candidates on a list prepared by the Federal Election Commission appear on the ballot. A second proposal would group states into geographic regions. All states within a given region that choose to have a primary would be required to hold it on the same day, on the second Tuesday of a month between March and July.[29]

Under the regional primary system candidates would not have to campaign in as many distant places at nearly the same time; this would save them money and effort. Since each election would encompass a large geographic area, however, the need to campaign earlier, to be better known at the start, and to have more money with which to begin would be even greater than it is now. The major advantage of regional primaries, assuming they were spaced about one month apart, as in one plan, would be that both politicians and people could reconsider their earlier choices in the light of the latest information. Yet if delegates were pledged to candidates, their flexibility as bargainers—in the event they were needed at the national conventions—would still be diminished. In addition, the predilection of the media to simplify complex phenomena would mean that voters in states allocated later dates would have their choices severely constrained by the results of earlier primaries. For this reason, it is possible that conflicts among states may doom the entire enterprise.

Responsible political analysts and advocates must face the fact that party identification for most people provides the safe cognitive anchorage around which political preferences are organized. Set adrift from this anchorage, as they are when faced with an intraparty primary election, most voters have little to guide their choices. Name recognition, clever advertising, verbal gaffes, debate exchanges, the adoption of an attention-grabbing persona or slogan—all have turned out to be decisive factors in presidential primaries. Given the conditions of popular interest and participation that prevail, we question whether primary electorates are always well-equipped to make decisions about the direction of the party.

What is more, a nomination process dominated by primaries gives the news media great—possibly too much—influence. Their extensive impact over the outcome of presidential nominations was illustrated in a dramatic way in the spring of 1987, when the initial front-runner for the 1988 Democratic nomination, former senator Gary Hart of Colorado, suddenly fell victim to publicity calling attention to a close personal relationship that he was pursuing with a woman who was not his wife, ultimately leading to his withdrawal from the race. This episode of intensive negative commentary caused many thoughtful journalists to express concern about the extraordinary influence of the news media in the nomination process. Some journalists felt that they and their colleagues were unable to do justice to the special circumstances of the private lives of public figures, and that even public figures have rights to privacy in those areas of life that have little to do with the performance of public duties. Others argued that the way people behave in private is bound to affect the way they do their public chores, and that voters have the "right to know" about information that might affect their evaluations of their leaders. Under the current nomination system, these debates over proper journalistic practices have inevitable implications for which candidates are advantaged or disadvantaged in party primaries—surely a serious responsibility for the press to shoulder, whether or not reporters and commentators are conscious of bearing it.

Not long ago, when there was something like peer review in the nomination process, other politicians who were influential in the process and who knew the candidates could make assessments about the suitability of presidential hopefuls for office. Perhaps they would be forgiving in cases of bad temper, laziness, big-otry, slowness of wit, vindictiveness, duplicity, stubbornness, chronic pettiness, marital infidelity, substance abuse, or any of the other infirmities and imperfec-tions that afflict human beings. Or perhaps not. At least, it was possible for rea-sonably well-informed judgments to be made about the qualities of candidates by people who knew something about what these qualities were.

Today, when presidential nominations are determined by primary electorates, we must ask: What do these electorates know of the human qualities of the can-didates? Typically, very little. But virtually all of what they do know comes via the news media. So journalists have had thrust on them far greater responsibilities to tell what they know and to find out whether what they suspect is true or not.

So we must wonder whether attention to any candidate's possible flaws of character ought not to be compared more conscientiously against flaws that some of the others may have. Surely, if these are qualities of candidates, they will also be qualities of the presidents these candidates might become. But it is hard to predict just how these qualities will work in any given presidency. There is no foolproof method for making sensible inferences from private behavior about the conduct of public office. Can we suppose that a lazy candidate will be a lazy president? Possibly. Still, some candidates hate campaigning but love governing and may be mediocre at delivering a stump speech but superb at negotiating a legislative compromise.

What is worse, the opposite may be true, and a gifted campaigner may turn out to be an incompetent president. Equally serious difficulties may be in store for those who attempt to make inferences about the conduct of the presidency from knowledge of candidates' personalities, sexual behavior, drinking habits, relations with their family members, and so on.

So what are ordinary citizens to do? Ignore information that might be rele-vant to our primary vote if we knew about it? Attend to information about can-didates even though it may be irrelevant to their conduct of the presidency? If we could tell in advance the difference between relevant and irrelevant information, it would help. But mostly we cannot, nor can the journalists who must decide what to report and what not to report. As long as primary elections and, there-fore, the votes of citizens matter as much as they currently do, the only hope of achieving informed choices is by means of publicly available information. Thus it is understandable that journalists usually choose disclosure over the protection of candidates' private lives—with serious implications for voters' perceptions of the various contenders and, therefore, their choices in the voting booth.[30]

The presidential nomination process continues to evolve even without the imposition of comprehensive reforms by the federal government or national par-ties. Front-loading of the nomination calendar as the result of individual states' decisions to schedule their primaries and caucuses earlier in the season has resulted in what increasingly resembles a quasi-national primary on the first permissible date for most states to hold elections; in 2016, about half the states voted by March 10. As long as the national parties allow Iowa, New Hampshire, and a few other states to vote before the rest of the nation, however, these early states will continue to hold a disproportionate influence over nominations, winnowing the field of candidates and structuring the choices faced by voters in subsequent pri-maries. At the same time, front-loading has increased the need for candidates to raise large amounts of money and build extensive campaign organizations prior to the start of the primaries, in order to have the capacity to capitalize on favorable press coverage as a result of strong performances in Iowa and New Hampshire. During and after every nomination, complaints arise from various corners about the complexity or unfairness of the current system, but widespread agreement on a preferred alternative presidential selection procedure—much less the power to actually implement it—remains far from being realized.

The Decline of the National Convention

High on the list of practices that in the past were regarded as objectionable was the private gathering of party leaders in the "smoke-filled room" to select a presidential nominee. Some likened this to a political opium den where a few irresponsible party bosses, hidden from public view, secretly determined the destiny of the nation.[31] Yet it is difficult to see who, other than the party's leaders, should have been entrusted with the delicate task of finding a candidate to satisfy a majority of delegates. If head-on clashes of strength on the convention floor could not resolve the question, the only alternatives were continued deadlock, anarchy among scores of leaderless delegates splitting the party into rival factions, or some process of accommodation.

National conventions no longer pick presidential nominees; they merely ratify the work of primaries and caucuses. But let us suppose that some national convention in the future must choose a nominee because no single candidate enters with support from a majority of delegates. Would we require that a smoke-free successor to the smoke-filled room be abolished and with it all behind-the-scenes negotiations? All parleys would then be held in public, before the delegates and millions of television viewers. Could the participants resist spending their time scoring points against each other in order to impress the folks back home? Bargaining would not be taking place because the participants would not really be communicating with one another. No compromises would be possible; if they were attempted, leaders would be accused by their followers of selling out to the other side. Once a stalemate existed, breaking it would be practically impossible, and the party would probably disintegrate into warring factions.

An extensive system of state primaries in which delegates are more or less compelled to vote for the candidate to whom they are pledged has led to the eclipse of negotiation processes without any formal action of a convention. This was the case even in the hotly contested 2008 Democratic nomination contest. Hillary Clinton, trailing narrowly in pledged delegates at the end of the primaries, recognized the impossibility of productive negotiations with delegates pledged to Barack Obama. She conceded the race in June, well before the national convention. In 2016, Bernie Sanders continued to contest the Democratic nomination until shortly before the convention, but Clinton's nomination was foreordained by the caucus and primary results. Since delegates cannot change their positions except by direction of the candidate to whom they are pledged, there is little point in bringing party leaders together for private conferences; the party is at the mercy of the candidates themselves.

Although the Democratic Party provides for hundreds of party leaders and elected officials to attend the national convention with voting rights as unpledged superdelegates, post-2016 rules changes prevent them from acting as a decisive force in the convention's first presidential nomination ballot. Since no Democratic presidential nomination has gone to a second ballot since 1952, it is far from obvious whether these individuals could, under any circumstances, effectively exercise independent influence over the identity of the party's presidential nominee. Most of the time, a single candidate wins decisively among pledged delegates chosen in state elections, making the preferences of the relatively small proportion of superdelegates irrelevant to the outcome. The concept of a "democratic" nomination process has taken hold so completely in the years since the party reforms of the 1970s that an attempt by the party's own popularly elected officials to independently influence the outcome, even in a case in which public sentiment is evenly divided, would be guaranteed to raise widespread charges of unfairness and even tyranny. Party leaders are likely to calculate that uniting around even a potentially flawed candidate provides a greater chance of winning in November than risking a damaging intraparty battle that could continue even beyond the convention itself.

Normally, party officials view the convention as an opportunity to aid party unity in a variety of ways. It provides a forum in which initially disunited fragments of the national party can come together and find common ground as well as a common nominee. The platform helps in performing this function. In order to gain a majority of electoral votes, a party must appeal in some way to most major population groups. Since these interests do not always want the same thing, it is necessary to compromise and, sometimes, to evade issues that would lead to drastic losses of support.

Reformers' concerns with party platforms stem primarily from two assumptions: first, that there is a significant demand in the electorate for more clear-cut differences on policy; second, that elections are likely to be a significant source of guidance on individual issues to policy makers. Yet both these assumptions are either false or highly dubious. As we have seen, leaders in both parties are further apart than are ordinary citizens on a wide range of issues.[32] Issue polarization is most pronounced among the politically active. When party platforms spell out clear and important differences between the parties on policy, it usually reflects a desire of party leaders to please the most vocal activists rather than demands from the electorate.

Some critics objected to the weight that parties historically placed on picking an electable nominee, rather than the "best candidate" regardless of popularity. This objection is not compatible with the democratic notion that voters should decide who is best for them and communicate this decision in an election. Only in dictatorial countries does a set of leaders arrogate unto themselves the right to determine who is best regardless of popular preferences. Unpopular candidates can hardly win free elections. Unpopular presidents can hardly secure the support they need to accomplish their goals. Popularity can be regarded as a necessary element for obtaining consent in democratic politics.

Although popularity is normally a necessary condition for nomination, it should not be the only condition. The guideline for purposes of nomination should be to nominate the best of the popular candidates. But "best" is a slippery word. A great deal of what we mean by "best" in politics is "best for us" or "best represents our policy preferences," and this can hardly be held up as an objective criterion. What is meant by "best" in this context are such personal qualities as experience, intelligence, and decisiveness. Nevertheless, it is not at all clear that an extremely conservative voter would prefer a highly intelligent liberal candidate to a moderately intelligent conservative. Personal qualities clearly are subject to discount based on the compatibility of interests between voters and candidates.

For some critics, the defect of conventions lies not only in their poor performance in nominating candidates but also in their failure to become a sort of "superlegislature," enforcing the policy views of the platform on party members in the executive branch and Congress. But how could either party retain a semblance of unity if the stakes of convention deliberations were vastly increased by converting the platform into an unbreakable promise of national policy? If one believes that an increase in heated discussion necessarily improves the chances of agreement, then the problem solves itself. Experience warns us, however, that airing sharp differences, particularly when the stakes are high, is likely to decrease agreement.

The fact that platforms are not binding permits a degree of unity necessary for the delegates to stay put long enough to agree on a nominee. By vastly increasing the number of delegates who would bitterly oppose platform decisions and possibly leave the convention, a binding platform would jeopardize the legitimacy of the convention's nominating function. Paradoxically, in such circumstances, it would be difficult to resist the temptation to make the platform utterly innocuous in order to give offense to no one at all.

Even so, platforms do have a far from negligible impact on public opinion. Platform planks are enacted as governmental policy slightly more than half the time.[33] Programs favored by the public, according to opinion polls, are twice as likely to be enacted if they also appear in party platforms.[34] When large majorities favor programs, both parties are likely to put them in their platforms; when the public is somewhat more divided and important constituencies object, the parties are capable of going against popular majorities. Thus Republican platform planks on welfare and economic issues and Democratic provisions on labor unions and affirmative action tend to run counter to majority opinion.[35] The question of whom the parties are for, special or general constituencies, is resolved by going for the majority when it is substantial and modifying that position when it conflicts with special party concerns.

Even though they no longer have a role other than as advertising, the superiority of the traditional, decision-making national conventions to presidential selection by alternative means is clear. Only the convention permits us to realize in large measure all of the six goals—party competition, some degree of internal cohesion, candidates attractive to voters, qualified candidates, acceptance of nominees as legitimate, and a connection between winning the nomination and governing later on—that we postulated earlier would commonly be accepted as desirable.

The Electoral College

In 2000, the candidate who received the most votes failed to become president for the first time in 112 years. Then it happened again in 2016. Many Democrats viewed George W. Bush's victory over Al Gore and Donald Trump's triumph over Hillary Clinton as illegitimate. In 2000, their objections were based primarily on the controversy over the counting of votes in Florida and the active role of the

Supreme Court in halting recounts, not the rare discrepancy between the popular and electoral vote. Complaints about that discrepancy were more widespread in 2016, in part because Clinton's national popular margin over Trump (2.1 percentage points) was much larger than Gore's margin over Bush (0.5 points). In 2016, charges of illegitimacy were also based on the efforts of the Russian government to influence the election on Trump's behalf via email hacking and social media manipulation. While advocates of electoral reform renewed their efforts in the wake of the 2000 and 2016 elections, the absence of strong public pressure for modifying or abolishing the Electoral College hindered their cause, leaving the institution intact for future elections.

Even so, debate over the merits of the current procedure for selecting presidents continues in some quarters, and from time to time a state or group of states will consider changing its method of allocating electoral votes. In 2004, a Colorado ballot initiative would have repealed the state's winner-take-all apportionment of electors in favor of proportional allocation; the measure was rejected by a two-to-one margin. Three years later, a bill allocating electors by congressional district passed the North Carolina legislature but was quietly killed at the urging of national Democratic officials worried about starting a state-level vote allocation war with the Republican Party. Fourteen states—including California, New York, Illinois, New Jersey, and Washington—and the District of Columbia have joined a national compact of states pledging to cast their electoral votes for the winner of the nationwide popular vote; the compact would take effect once states casting a majority of electoral votes chose to participate. In that case, the current system would effectively be replaced by a simple national popular election without the need for a constitutional amendment. However, the only states voting to join the compact so far have been those in which Democrats control both the state legislature and governorship, leaving the effort still short of a national majority.

The Electoral College as it is now constituted, with each state casting as many electoral votes as it has senators and representatives while awarding electors to candidates on a winner-take-all basis, provides an advantage to two groups of states. It yields a modest benefit to very small states, since the Constitution provides that each state elects two senators regardless of population. This means that the 10 smallest states, with 3 percent of the total voters in the 2016 presidential election, maintain voting weight in the Senate equal to the 10 largest states, home to 50 percent of the voters in 2016. The small states' disproportionate share of senators guarantees them slight overrepresentation in the Electoral College as well. After the 2010 census, the 7 states casting 3 electoral votes each had a ratio of 331,472 or fewer residents per electoral vote, while every state with 13 or more electoral votes had a ratio of 607,972 or more residents per electoral vote.

But the near-universal use of the unit rule method of allocating electoral votes to candidates works to the advantage of larger states that are politically competitive. Candidates who win a narrow majority in California alone receive more electoral votes (55) than they would by carrying all of the 14 smallest states plus the District of Columbia (52); they can, mathematically, carry California by one vote and not receive any votes in those 14 states and do a bit better in the Electoral College. This encourages presidential candidates to focus their campaign efforts on competitive states with large numbers of electoral votes.[36] In fact, large states are somewhat more likely to be closely divided between the parties, while smaller states are more commonly dominated by one party or the other.

Nearly all electoral reform proposals fall into three basic categories. One would abolish the Electoral College outright and weigh individual votes equally everywhere in a simple national popular election. The second option would retain the Electoral College but abolish the unit rule in favor of proportional allocation of electoral votes within states. A third possibility also retains the current apportionment of the Electoral College but allocates one electoral vote to the plurality vote winner in each congressional district and two electoral votes to the winner in each state.[37]

Allowing a majority (or plurality) of voters to choose a president in a simple national popular election has a great deal to commend it. This is the simplest method of all; it would be most easily understood by the greatest number of people; it is the reform plan favored by the majority of Americans (65 percent of respondents in one 2018 poll reported preferring a national popular vote to the Electoral College),[38] and it comes closest to reflecting intuitive notions of direct popular sovereignty through majority rule.

How would abolishing the Electoral College affect presidential elections? Under the current system, candidates focus their campaign resources on politically competitive states, especially on the populous swing states that cast large numbers of electoral votes. In a national popular election, candidates would concentrate more on mobilizing high voter turnout in states that already supported them, hoping to gain a lopsided popular margin within their party's geographic base. The emphasis would not be on which candidate was going to carry a state but by how many votes he or she was going to win.[39] Small states do not gain influence under this alternative, however, because even those dominated by one party are not populous enough to provide large numbers of votes. Replacing the Electoral College with a direct popular election thus mostly benefits medium-sized and large one-party states at the expense of two-party states.

Some advocates of reform criticize the current system for encouraging presidential candidates to focus on courting the residents of swing states while giving less attention to voters elsewhere in the nation. A few critics consider this strategic consequence of the Electoral College to be undemocratic because it supposedly sends a message to voters in noncompetitive states that they lack a significant voice in the outcome of presidential elections.[40] However, no clear evidence exists that voters in battleground states exhibit more political efficacy than their counterparts in safe party states. In fact, many Americans are largely unaware of the degree of partisan competitiveness in their home states and show little interest in the details of campaign tactics. Because candidates would still target certain populations or geographic areas more than others even under a system of direct popular election, the abolition of the Electoral College would by no means guarantee that voters in each state would receive equal attention from presidential campaigns.[41]

The role of third parties under the direct popular election alternative is also unclear. The current system disadvantages minor parties by requiring candidates to place first in a state in order to receive electoral votes; while the presence of a third-party or independent candidate may deny the first-place finisher a majority of the popular vote, it is much less likely to produce deadlock in the Electoral

College. For example, no candidate received a national popular majority in 1948, 1960, 1968, 1992, 1996, 2000, or 2016, yet in each case one of the major-party contenders gained a majority of electoral votes and thus assumed the presidency. On one hand, instituting a majority requirement in a direct popular election would frequently force the House of Representatives to choose the president; on the other, the prospect of a candidate assuming the presidency with a small plurality of the vote also seems undesirable. Consequently, the Electoral College reform amendment that passed the House in 1969 provided for a runoff election between the top two finishers if no candidate secured at least 40 percent of the popular vote in the initial round of voting.[42]

The first effect of this provision would be to increase the influence of splinter parties. If a satisfactory major-party candidate is going to have a second chance to win the office anyway, there is an incentive for any sizable organized minority to contest the first election on its own. That the runoff would likely be used if it were provided for is suggested by 1992, when there was a fairly strong third-party candidate, Ross Perot, in the race. A fourth candidate would have needed only 6 or 7 percent of the national total to keep either major-party candidate from having the required 40 percent (Clinton won with 43 percent, although he received 69 percent of the electoral vote).[43] Once this becomes even a plausible expectation, there is an incentive for various intense minorities to put up their own candidates, and visions of an evangelical Christian party, an African American party, a labor party, a peace party, an environmentalist party, a right-to-life party, a farmers' party, and so on, appear. Whereas one of the strong points of the present system is that it enforces a compromise by penalizing all minorities that will not come to terms, the direct election system could well encourage a continental European situation, in which numerous groups contest the first election and then recombine for the second; at the least, severe changes would be worked on the present system.[44] Should such a result occur in the future, the simplicity, ease of comprehension, and inherent majoritarian rightness of the direct election solution would quickly disappear.

Another proposal is seen by some reformers as an acceptable middle option between the current system and outright abolition of the Electoral College.[45] Under this measure, the Electoral College is retained but the unit rule is repealed. Instead, the electoral vote in each state is divided among the candidates according to their relative shares of the state's popular vote.

The widespread implementation of proportional allocation would encourage candidates to concentrate their energy on the very biggest states, since only in states with large numbers of electoral votes would campaign activity be likely to influence the popular vote outcome enough to affect the distribution of electors among the candidates. Other states would receive attention to the extent that one or the other candidate was deemed within reach of the numerical threshold necessary to gain an additional elector. The candidates would largely ignore small states because the share of electoral votes allocated to each party in those states would tend to be highly predictable and relatively insensitive to marginal changes in the state's popular vote.[46]

Under the unit rule, candidates who fall short of a popular majority can still win the presidency by gaining sufficiently broad support to place first in states casting at least 270 electoral votes. But proportional allocation would make it very difficult for a plurality winner in the popular vote to gain an electoral majority. As a result, presidential elections would be decided by the House of Representatives with some regularity, as the Constitution provides when no single candidate receives a majority in the Electoral College. (Under this provision, the House must choose among the top three finishers in the electoral vote, and each state delegation casts one vote regardless of size.) Even in 1996, when Democratic incumbent Bill Clinton received a near-majority, 49.2 percent of the national popular vote (to 40.7 percent for Republican nominee Bob Dole and 8.4 percent for Reform Party candidate Ross Perot), Clinton would have been denied a victory in the Electoral College under proportional allocation, giving the House, then controlled by the opposition Republicans, the opportunity to select the next president. As a result, though the proportional allocation alternative is superficially more "democratic" than the winner-take-all system now in place, elections would be decided by Congress so frequently (requiring only a very close election or a moderately strong third-party candidate) that the presidency would be frequently dependent on the actions of the legislative branch, under a procedure that gives disproportionate weight to small states—not the voters.[47]

A third reform, the congressional district plan, has been proposed as still another "compromise" between the status quo and more radical change. Under this measure, each state allocates two electoral votes to the statewide winner and one electoral vote to the candidate placing first in each House district within the state. Maine and Nebraska, the only states in which the unit rule is not currently in effect, employ this alternative means of apportioning electoral votes to presidential candidates.

Advocates of this proposal argue that its implementation would encourage candidates to contest politically competitive congressional districts within noncompetitive states, thus significantly expanding the electoral battleground. But most House districts are dominated by one of the major parties and are therefore unlikely to be targets for presidential campaigns. One study found that only about 10 percent of the national electorate resides within competitive congressional districts inside safe party states and would therefore benefit from the widespread adoption of the district plan.[48]

The most predictable consequence of the district plan would be the introduction of a consistent partisan bias to the Electoral College. Under the unit rule, the Electoral College does not systematically favor either party; the Republican advantage deriving from the overrepresentation of small, rural states is usually balanced out by the more efficient distribution of Democratic voters across states. Because the proportion of Republican-leaning House seats perennially outweighs the share of districts favoring Democrats—due to the existence of urban supermajority districts with large numbers of "wasted" Democratic votes—the universal adoption of the district plan would work to the dependable advantage of the GOP. Republican candidates would have prevailed in the Electoral College in 1960, 2000, 2012, and 2016 under the district plan despite Democratic victories in the national popular vote, while Jimmy Carter would have won a bare electoral majority in 1976 (270 to 268), despite receiving nearly 1.7 million more votes nationwide than his opponent, Gerald Ford.

Since the goals of electoral reform are supposedly to make the system more "fair" and "democratic," it is hard to see the advantage of an alternative that

(1) increases the likelihood that the less popular candidate nationwide wins the election; (2) provides no more guarantee against deadlock than the present system (third-party candidate George Wallace in 1968 received 45 electoral votes under the unit rule, but would have received 58 under the district plan); (3) preserves the winner-take-all method; (4) fails to produce a significant expansion of the electoral battleground; and (5) systematically favors one party over the other.

Table 6.1 shows electoral outcomes under the unit rule and the three alternative plans for selected presidential elections since 1960. The elections of 1964, 1972, 1976, 1980, 1984, 1988, 2004, and 2008 would have come out the same way under all the plans for counting votes we have been considering. Of those, however, only 1976 and 2004 featured a close margin in the national popular vote. Had proportional allocation been in place, the 1992, 1996, 2000, and 2016 elections would all have been decided by the House of Representatives. Bill Clinton (in 1992 and 1996), George W. Bush (in 2000), and Donald Trump (in 2016) would still have won under the district plan, but the format would have given Mitt Romney the presidency in 2012, despite his four-point loss in the popular vote.

Table 6.1 Outcomes under the Unit Rule and Three Alternatives, Selected Elections, 1960–2016

Year	Unit Rule	No.	Popular Vote	%	Proportional Allocation	No.	District Plan	No.
2016	*Trump wins*		*Clinton wins*		*Winner unclear*		*Trump wins*	
	Trump	305	Clinton	48.2	Clinton	268	Trump	290
	Clinton	233	Trump	46.1	Trump	267	Clinton	248
					Others	3		
2012	*Obama wins*		*Obama wins*		*Obama wins*		*Romney wins*	
	Obama	332	Obama	51.1	Obama	278	Obama	264
	Romney	206	Romney	47.2	Romney	258	Romney	274
			Others	1.7	Others	2		
2008	*Obama wins*		*Obama wins*		*Obama wins*		*Obama wins*	
	Obama	364	Obama	52.9	Obama	287	Obama	301
	McCain	174	McCain	45.6	McCain	251	McCain	237
			Others	1.5				
2004	*Bush wins*		*Bush wins*		*Bush wins*		*Bush wins*	
	Bush	286	Bush	50.7	Bush	278	Bush	317
	Kerry	252	Kerry	48.3	Kerry	259	Kerry	221
					Others	1		
2000	*Bush wins*		*Gore wins*		*Winner unclear*		*Bush wins*	
	Bush	271	Bush	47.9	Bush	263	Bush	288
	Gore	267	Gore	48.4	Gore	262	Gore	250
			Others	3.7	Others	13		
1996	*Clinton wins*		*Clinton wins*		*Winner unclear*		*Clinton wins*	
	Clinton	379	Clinton	49.2	Clinton	267	Clinton	345
	Dole	159	Dole	40.7	Dole	224	Dole	193
	Perot	0	Perot	8.4	Perot/Others	47	Perot	0

(continued)

Table 6.1 (*continued*)

Year	Unit Rule	No.	Popular Vote	%	Proportional Allocation	No.	District Plan	No.
1992	*Clinton wins*		*Clinton wins*		*Winner unclear*		*Clinton wins*	
	Clinton	370	Clinton	43.0	Clinton	236	Clinton	323
	Bush	168	Bush	37.4	Bush	197	Bush	215
	Perot	0	Perot	18.9	Perot	105	Perot	0
1976	*Carter wins*		*Carter wins*		*Carter wins*		*Carter wins*	
	Carter	297	Carter	50.1	Carter	273	Carter	270
	Ford	241	Ford	48.0	Ford	263	Ford	268
			Others	1.9	Others	2		
1968	*Nixon wins*		*Nixon wins*		*Winner unclear*		*Nixon wins*	
	Nixon	302	Nixon	43.4	Nixon	235	Nixon	290
	Humphrey	191	Humphrey	42.7	Humphrey	225	Humphrey	190
	Wallace	45	Wallace	13.5	Wallace	78	Wallace	58
1960	*Kennedy wins*		*Kennedy wins*		*Kennedy wins*		*Nixon wins*	
	Kennedy	303	Kennedy	49.7	Kennedy	270	Kennedy	252
	Nixon	220	Nixon	49.6	Nixon	261	Nixon	280
	Others	14	Others	0.7	Others	6	Others	5

Note: Results in the unit rule column assume that all electoral votes in a state are allocated to the candidate placing first in the state popular vote. These figures differ from the actual electoral vote in several years, due to electors who violated their pledges in 1960, 1968, 1976, 2000, 2004, and 2016, as well as the congressional district-based allocation now used by two states that produced split results in Nebraska in 2008 and Maine in 2016. "Winner unclear" denotes scenarios in which no candidate receives a majority of electoral votes. The House of Representatives would then select the president from among the three candidates receiving the most electoral votes, with each state casting one vote.

Under the present Electoral College system, there has been no time since 1876 when any splinter group has been able to make good on a threat to throw the election into the House of Representatives. Even in 1948, Harry Truman won an Electoral College majority despite sizable threats from both a third (Henry Wallace, Progressive) and a fourth (Strom Thurmond, States Rights) party. Only twice in the past century—in 2000 and 2016—has the winner of the popular vote not become president. On the other hand, a direct election plan that required a 40 percent plurality might well have forced a runoff in 1968 and 1992. Proportional allocation would have caused deadlocks in four recent elections, and the district plan would have thrown the election to the popular vote loser not only in 2000 and 2016, but in 1960 and 2012 as well. In view of their likely effects, it is curious that many reformers have supported such changes to the procedure of electing presidents.

Underlying all these arguments, of course, is the premise that most structural reforms "tend" to shift influences in certain ways. There may well be situations of social polarization that alternative electoral mechanisms by themselves cannot paper over. But while we have argued that there is no perfect system, from the standpoint of the professed goals of most reformers, there is one minor change that would aid them. Under the present plan, the actual electors who make up the Electoral College are in fact free to vote for whomever they wish. These electors are usually party loyalists who are chosen in each state by party leaders. As an almost invariable rule, they vote for the winner in their state, but abuses are possible, and three within memory come to mind.

First, the unpledged electors chosen by citizens in Mississippi and Alabama in 1960 decided for whom they would vote only well after the election, treating the preferences of citizens as advisory, not mandatory. This clearly thwarts popular control. Second, this liberty allowed the racial segregationist governor of Alabama, George Wallace, to hope that he could run for president, create an electoral deadlock, and then bargain with one of the other candidates after the election for policy concessions in exchange for the support of the Wallace electors. (Wallace did follow through with a third-party run in 1968, but failed to win enough electoral votes to affect the result.) Third, a total of seven electors—five Democrats from Washington and Hawaii, and two Republicans from Texas— refused to support their party nominees in 2016, scattering their votes among other public figures; if the outcome had been closer in the Electoral College, such mischief could have had national consequences. An amendment making the casting of electoral votes automatic would dispel such dangers in the future.

A final device deserves consideration, the creation of a private commission set up by the Twentieth Century Fund (now the Century Foundation) some years ago. It came up with a proposal for a National Bonus Plan, which would award 102 electoral votes en bloc (two for each state plus the District of Columbia) to the plurality winner of the nationwide popular vote. This plan would make it highly probable that no president could be elected who did not get the most votes. An additional feature is that candidates would be encouraged to get as many votes as they could, even in states where they were sure to lose, because these would add on to the candidate's national popular total.[49] The Bonus Plan would guard against a minority president, preserve the form and the spirit of the constitutional structure, and do all this without encouraging splinter parties.

In our form of government, "majority rule" does not operate in a vacuum but within a system of checks and balances. The president, for example, holds a veto power over laws enacted by Congress. If the veto is exercised, a two-thirds vote of each house is required to override it. Treaties must be ratified by two-thirds of the Senate, and amendments to the Constitution must be proposed by two-thirds of Congress or of the state legislatures and ratified by three-fourths of the states. Presidential appointments, in most important cases, must receive senatorial approval. The Supreme Court passes upon the constitutionality of legislative and executive actions. And of course there is impeachment, a political check on the presidency available to Congress. Involved in these political arrangements is the hope that the power of one branch of government will be counterbalanced by certain "checks" from another, the result being an approximate "balance" of forces.

In our view, it is not necessarily a loss to have slightly different majorities preponderant in different institutions, but it is definitely a loss to have the same majority preponderant in both political branches while other majorities are frozen out. In the past, the Electoral College had its place within this system. Originally designed to check popular majorities from choosing presidents unwisely, the Electoral College later on provided a check on the overrepresentation of rural states in the legislative branch by giving extra weight to the big-state constituencies of the president.

PARTY PLATFORMS AND PARTY DIFFERENCES

Having reviewed some of the major changes proposed by party reformers, let us return to consider their key argument. Parties, reformers have claimed, have historically been inadequately ideological and insufficiently representative. The voters have not been offered clear enough choices, and the parties, once in office, have not responsibly carried out the promises made in their platforms. We argue that American parties do indeed differ—more so today than in the past—and that much of the time, they respond to changes in voter and activist sentiment. Recent surveys of partisan voters and studies of congressional voting indicate the issue contrast between the parties is now stark. We believe that the solutions offered by reformers have in the past often led to unsatisfactory consequences, and that proposals for further reform should therefore be considered with skepticism.

Party platforms written by the presidential parties should be understood not only as ends in themselves but as means to obtaining and holding public office. It would be strange indeed if a party understood that policies such as Social Security and unemployment compensation were enormously popular and yet refused to incorporate them into its platform.[50] This would have to be a party of ideologues who cared solely about their own ideas and not about winning elections. Nor would it profit them much because they would not get elected and would never be in a position to do something about their ideas. Sooner or later, at least in a political system like the United States, ideologues have to make the choice between pleasing themselves and winning elections.

Even when the major political parties were in the hands of moderate leaders, there were clear differences between the doctrines espoused by the two parties, and these were reflected in party platforms. Now the differences are abundantly clear. The case for party reform used to rest on the assumption that American political parties were nearly identical, that this was confusing and frustrating to American voters, and that it was undesirable to have a political system where parties did not disagree sharply. Today, we are in position to judge whether greater party polarization indeed produces superior representative democracy.

Imagine for a moment that the two parties were in total and extreme disagreement on every major point of public policy, even more so than they now are. One party would limit American military power to our borders; the other would intervene in every tense situation across the globe. One group would go all-out to improve productivity; the other would put environmental values first. One group would abolish Social Security; the other would expand it drastically. One group would raise tariffs; the other would repeal them. Obviously one consequence of having clear-cut parties with strong policy positions would be that the costs of losing an election would skyrocket. If parties were forced to formulate coherent, full-dress programs and were forced to carry them out "responsibly," and in full, then people who did not favor these programs would have little recourse (until the next election). Clearly their confidence in a government whose policies were so little to their liking would suffer, and indeed they might feel strongly enough about preventing these policies from being enacted to do something drastic, like leaving the country or not complying with governmental regulations or, in an extreme case, seeking to change the political system by impeachment or by force.

The presidency of Republican Ronald Reagan may give pause to liberal reformers. Though Reagan's campaign rhetoric was too general to alarm voters, in many respects he played the part of the responsible-party president who proposed and attempted to carry out a wide-ranging program designed to modify, if not to undo completely, the efforts of his Democratic predecessors. There was no mistaking his thrust—less domestic government and more money for defense. Reagan to some extent succeeded, at least early in his administration, in carrying out his campaign promises. If the results did not meet with universal approval, citizens cannot say they were not informed as to the direction the candidate would take in the event he was elected.

Or consider the performance in office of George W. Bush, who promised to change the climate of partisanship in Washington and to be "a uniter, not a divider" but who in fact wielded his razor-thin majority in Congress in energetic pursuit of conservative initiatives. Bush was installed in office by a ruling of the Supreme Court that halted the counting of votes in Florida and awarded him the state's electoral votes. Later investigations indicated that had the votes all been counted, Bush would have won, very narrowly, in the Electoral College, but owing to the popular votes in other states, Bush became president without winning the popular vote nationwide. The election overall yielded an outcome that was closely split between the major parties. Yet Bush, so long as his party controlled both houses of Congress, made few concessions to the middle ground expressed in the net result.

Barack Obama followed Bush's example. On the night of his election in 2008, he proclaimed that "we have never been just a collection . . . of red states and blue states. We are, and always will be, the United States of America." But like Bush, Obama governed by his party's agenda and not toward the political middle ground. His presidency resulted in little bipartisan legislation alongside record levels of partisan polarization in congressional voting and public opinion concerning the performance of the chief executive. Although Donald Trump also suggested during his successful 2016 campaign that he took a more populist approach to economic policy than other Republicans, his presidency, too, turned out to be highly partisan and ideologically orthodox. Most recent presidents have performed in accord with the "responsible government" model, effectively dividing Washington and the public while doing so.

If the goals of party reform—both policy government and participatory democracy—were to give citizens better choices and improve popular trust in the parties and the government, it is fair to ask after several decades of experience whether such goals are indeed being met. If the opening of the nomination process to popular rule was intended to bolster the sensitivity of the political system to the preferences of citizens, it is fair to ask who is representing the millions of Americans who prefer moderation and compromise to ideological extremity and procedural gridlock. Ideally, policy making would occur in the presence of enthusiastic party activists, determined and skillful leaders, and broad public consent. These are not always available, but they sometimes are. When they are not, perhaps it is wise to make the achievement of incremental improvements possible but revolutionary changes not too easy.[51]

7

American Parties and Democracy

■ ■ ■

OVER THE PAST HALF CENTURY, a new sort of American political system has come into being. Among its features are high degrees of mass participation in formerly elite processes such as the nomination of presidential candidates, the replacement of political parties with the news media as primary organizers of citizen action and legitimizers of public decisions, the rise in the influence of media-approved and media-sustained interest groups, and the decline of interest groups linked to party organizations. Certain sorts of political activity are easy in a system structured in this way: simple voting, for example, in which alternatives are few and clear-cut. However, complex and deliberative decision-making, in which various alternatives are compared one after the other, contingencies are weighed and tested tentatively, second and third choices are probed for hidden consensuses, or special weight is given to intensity of likes and dislikes, is extremely difficult in such a system. Therefore, much influence flows into the hands of those who structure alternatives in the first place—self-starting candidates and the news media.

But the need for organizations to do the job of the parties continues. For presidential elections, we have observed the replacement of the convention with primary elections as the most significant part of the process and the rise of party activists who are more ideological and sometimes more extreme than the rest of the population.[1] Partisanship now correlates increasingly with ideological issue advocacy, and polarization is prevalent among partisans in the public and in government.

Because the American political system has moved toward a role for political parties that stresses their activities as policy advocates, it seems to us important to give some attention to the implications of this trend for democratic government. Our argument makes two main points. The first is that it is necessary for parties of advocacy in a democracy to receive mandates on public policy from popular majorities of convinced believers in their programs, but that this condition is not met in America because of the ways in which electorates actually participate in elections and conceive of public policy.

Our second point is that in view of the actual disposition of attitudes toward public policy in the electorate as compared with party elites, the fact that we have entered into an era marked by parties of advocacy poses some significant and largely unaddressed problems for American democracy. This is because it is not the policy preferences of the bulk of the electorate that are being advocated.

Moreover, the implementation of policy through government requires the sort of institutional support that parties can orchestrate only if they have some permanency and are not required to give birth to themselves anew every four years to nominate a candidate, and then wither away.

ELECTIONS AND PUBLIC POLICY

Uncoerced and competitive elections aid in making the political system open and responsive to a great variety of people and groups in the population. But elections do not unerringly transmit the issue preferences of electorates to leaders or confer mandates on leaders with regard to specific policies. The fortunes of the parties rise and fall over time without necessarily reflecting the underlying views of the broader electorate, while the increasing frequency in recent decades of divided government—different parties held the presidency and at least one chamber of Congress for 38 of the 52 years between 1968 and 2020—makes the interpretation of electoral results as the product of voters' expressed ideological preferences even more difficult.

Consider the series of events between 1992 and 2018. Bill Clinton won the 1992 presidential election by a decisive margin but received only 43 percent of the popular vote. In 1994, Republicans won a landslide election that gave them control of both houses of Congress, yet both Clinton and the Republican congressional majority that opposed him were returned to power in 1996. In 2000, George W. Bush assumed the presidency even though his main opponent, Al Gore, won more popular votes. Bush's narrow popular and electoral vote victory in 2004 was followed by massive Republican losses in 2006 that delivered control of Congress to the Democrats. In 2008, Democratic nominee Barack Obama won a popular vote majority by a relatively sizeable margin, though 46 percent of voters supported his Republican opponent, John McCain. Obama's successful campaign was built around the popular but vague theme of "change," which capitalized on popular dissatisfaction with the Bush presidency as much as support for any of Obama's own policy proposals.

Obama's narrow 2012 reelection victory resulted in great part from his successful negative campaign against Mitt Romney and did not demonstrate widespread public backing for the president's agenda. The Democratic Congress in place during Obama's first two years in office was replaced by a Republican House in 2010 and a Republican Senate as well in 2014. Donald Trump was elected president in 2016, despite losing the popular vote, but started his term with Republican control of both congressional chambers. In the 2018 midterms, however, Democrats recaptured a majority in the House of Representatives. Even in a landslide, winners can sensibly claim only a temporary, equivocal mandate. And in any case, elections that are clear-cut are rare.

It is easy to be cynical and expect too little from elections or to be euphoric and expect too much from them. A cynical view would hold that the United States was ruled by a power elite—a small group outside the democratic process. Under these circumstances, the ballot would be a sham and a delusion. What difference can it make how voting is carried on or who wins if the nation is actually governed by other means? In contrast, a euphoric view, holding that the United States is ruled as a mass democracy with equal control over decisions by all or most citizens, would enormously magnify the importance of the ballot. Through the act of casting a ballot, it could be argued, a majority of citizens would determine major national policies. What happens at the polls would not only decide who occupies public office; it also would determine the content of specific policy decisions. In a way, public office would then be a position of weakness because the power of decision in important matters would be removed from the hands of its occupants.

A third type of political system, in which numerous minorities compete for shares in policy making within broad limits provided by free elections, has more complex implications. It suggests that balloting is important but that it often does not, and sometimes should not, determine individual policy decisions. The ballot guides and constrains public officials, who are free to act within fairly broad limits subject to their anticipations of the responses of the voters and—this is important in a separation of powers system—to the desires of other active participants.

It is evident that the American political system is of this third type. Public officials do make major policy decisions, but elections matter because they determine which of the two main competing parties holds public office. In a competitive two-party situation such as exists in American presidential politics, the lively possibility of change provides an effective incentive for political leaders to remain in touch with followers.

Voters as a whole do not share the clarifying ideological preferences of today's partisan activists. The electorate does not transmit coherent policy preferences to elected officials with a high degree of reliability. There are few clear mandates in our political system because elections are fought on so many issues and in so many incompletely overlapping constituencies. Often the same voters elect candidates to Congress and to the presidency who disagree on public policies. Thus, even if mandates could be identified, they might well be impossible to enact because of inconsistency in the instructions issued to officials who must agree on legislation.[2]

Presidential elections are not single-issue referendums. The relationship between presidential elections and policies is a great deal subtler than the relations between the outcomes of referendums and the policies to which they pertain. In principle, the American political system is designed to work like this: Two teams of politicians, one in office, the other seeking office, both attempt to get enough votes to win elections. In order to win, they go to various groups of voters and, by offering to pursue policies favored by these groups, or by suggesting policies they might come to favor, hope to attract their votes. If there were only one office-seeking team, its incentive to respond to the policy preferences of groups in the population would diminish; if there were many such teams, all on a more or less equal footing, the chances that any one of them could achieve a sufficient number of backers to govern would diminish. Hence a two-party system might be regarded as a kind of compromise between the goals of responsiveness and effectiveness.

The proponents of a different theory, now much in vogue among ideologically driven partisan elites, would say that elections give the winning party a mandate to carry out the policies proposed during the campaign. Only in this way, they maintain, is popular rule through the ballot meaningful. A basic assumption in this argument is that the voters (or at least a majority of them) approve of all or most of the policies advocated by the victorious candidate. No doubt this is plausible, but not in the sense intended because, as we have seen, a vote for a presidential candidate is often an expression of a party habit: particular policy directions are therefore not necessarily meant by the vote. Indeed, citizens may be voting not for a candidate but rather against his or her opponent, or against a past president, saying, in effect, no more of this but not necessarily more of the other party's policies. For example, Donald Trump was elected president in 2016 even as a majority of voters consistently told pollsters that they opposed the construction of a wall along the nation's southern border with Mexico, which had been Trump's signature policy proposal during the campaign.[3]

Most voters in the United States are not very ideologically oriented. They do not seek to create or to adopt systems of thought in which issues are related to one another in some highly consistent manner. Caring about more than one value, sometimes they prefer a strong government here and a weak one there, or want just not to decide at the present time. Thus voters can hardly be said to transmit strong preferences for a uniform stream of particular policies by electing candidates to public office.

Other basic objections may also be raised to the idea that our elections are designed to confer mandates on specific public policies. First, the issues debated in the campaign may not be the ones in which most voters are interested. Campaign issues may be ones that interest the candidates or that, for tactical reasons, they want to stress, or that interest segments of the press. There is no clear reason to believe that any particular issue is of great concern to voters just because it gets publicity. Time and again, voting studies have demonstrated that what appear to be the major issues of a campaign turn out not to be significant for most of the electorate. Some frequent issues on the stump are simply not the topics of public controversy. In recent elections, nobody was for welfare fraud or large budget deficits, everybody was for a strong economy and successful military operation, and nobody favored crime.[4] Other campaign issues, such as the "war on women" argument aimed at the GOP by Democrats in 2012 or the Republican proposal for a constitutional amendment prohibiting same-sex marriage in 2004, are merely attempts to engage and energize particular segments of the electorate.

A second reason why voting for a candidate does not necessarily signify approval of that candidate's policies is that candidates pursue many policy interests at any one time with widely varying intensity, so that they may collect support from some voters on one issue and from other voters on another. It is possible for a candidate to get 100 percent of the votes and still have every voter opposed to most of the candidate's policies, while also having every one of those policies opposed by most of the voters.

Assume that there are four major issues in a campaign. Make the further, quite reasonable, assumption that the voting population is distributed in such a way that people who care intensely about one major issue support the victorious candidate for that reason alone, although they differ with that candidate mildly on the other three issues. Thus voters who are deeply concerned about the problem of defense against terrorism may vote for candidate Jones, who prefers a less militaristic solution, rather than Smith, who espouses a doctrine that requires an aggressive response. This particular group of voters disagrees with Jones strong support for farm price supports, on the overall size of government, and on national health insurance, but they do not feel strongly about any of these matters. Another group, meanwhile, believes that farmers, the noble yeomanry, are the backbone of the nation, and that if they are prosperous and strong, everything else will turn out all right. So they vote for Jones, too, although they prefer an ambitious anti-terrorism policy and disagree with Jones's other policies—and so on for other groups of voters. Lucky Jones ends up with all the votes, yet each of Jones's policies is preferred by less than a majority of the electorate. Since this is possible in any political system where many issues are debated or otherwise up for grabs at election time, it is hard to argue that our presidential elections give unequivocal mandates on specific policies to the candidates who win.[5]

People vote for many reasons not directly connected with issues. They may vote on the basis of party loyalty alone. Party habits may be accompanied by a general feeling that Democrats are better for the common citizen or that Republicans will keep us safe, or vice versa—feelings too diffuse to tell us much about specific issues. Some people vote on the basis of a candidate's personality, or "image." Others follow a friend's recommendation. Still others may be thinking about policy issues but may completely misperceive where the candidates stand. It is ordinarily impossible to distinguish the votes of these people from those who know, care, and differentiate accurately among the candidates on the basis of issues. We do know, however, that strongly issue-oriented voters are usually in a minority, while those who cast their ballots with other things in mind are generally more numerous. Voters, if asked, may say they want to move government in a more liberal or conservative direction, but desires of this sort are quite often inconsistent with those same voters' stated positions on specific policy matters.[6]

Even if there is good reason to believe that a majority of voters do approve of several policies supported by the victorious candidate, the mandate may be difficult or impossible to carry out. Consider the recent difficulties of achieving and pursuing a presidential mandate. George W. Bush, the popular vote loser in 2000, could hardly claim a mandate then, nor did his narrow victory in 2004 indicate popular approval for his major domestic policy initiative of 2005, the creation of private Social Security accounts, which failed even to receive a vote in Congress that year. Public disapproval of Bush's management of the Iraq War and the federal response to Hurricane Katrina helped Democrats win back Congress in 2006 and take the presidency while increasing their legislative majorities in 2008. Barack Obama encountered similar reversals after his first two years in office that featured Democratic control of national government and ambitious new laws for economic stimulus and health care reform. Donald Trump's attempt to repeal "Obamacare" in 2017 failed in public opinion and the GOP-controlled Congress. Rejection of an incumbent administration does not necessarily entail a thorough mandate for the alternative policies of the successor, as Ronald Reagan and Bill Clinton found out, and as Obama discovered as well. All three entered office in the midst of economic problems that ousted the party of their predecessor from the White House; their elections represented an expression of voters' general dissatisfaction with the performance of the previous regime, rather than widespread enthusiastic endorsement of their own initiatives.

Leaving aside all the difficulties about the content of a mandate, there is no accepted definition of what size electoral victory gives a president special popular sanction to pursue any particular policy. Would a 60 percent victory be sufficient? What about 51 percent or 52 percent, or cases such as 1992, 1996, 2000, and

2016, in which the winner receives less than half the votes cast? And is it right to ignore the multitudes who do not vote and whose preferences are not directly registered? We might ignore the nonvoters for the purpose of this analysis if we were sure they were divided in their preferences between candidates in nearly the same proportions as those who do vote. There is now reason to believe that this is more or less true.[7] But we cannot be sure this is always the case. In practice, this problem is easily solved. Whoever wins the presidential election under our current rules—which means winning in the Electoral College, not necessarily the popular vote—is allowed to pursue whatever policies he or she pleases, within the very important constraints imposed by the checks and balances of the rest of the policy-making institutions (notably Congress) in the political system. This, in the end, is all that a "mandate" is in American politics.

Opinion polls and focus groups may help the politician gauge policy preferences, but there are always lingering doubts as to their reliability. It is not certain in any event that they tell the political leader what that leader needs to know. People who really have no opinion but who care only a little may be counted equally with those who are intensely concerned. Many people giving opinions may have no intention of voting for some of the politicians who heed them, no matter what. The result may be that a politician will get no visible support from a majority that agrees with him or her, but instead will get complaints from an intense minority that disagrees. The people who agree with the politician may not vote, while those who differ may attempt retribution at the ballot box—as single-issue interest groups are reported to do. Those voters who are pleased may be the ones who would have voted for the public official in any case. The correlations that are made showing that support comes disproportionately from certain economic or social groups do not explain why some people, often a substantial minority, possessing these self-same characteristics vote the opposite way.

Let us turn the question around for a moment. Suppose a candidate loses an election. What does this signify about the policies he or she should have espoused? If one or two key issues were widely debated and universally understood, the election might tell the candidate a great deal. But this is seldom the case. More likely, there were many issues, and it was difficult to separate out those issues that did from those that did not garner support for the opponent. Perhaps the election was decided on the basis of personal images or some events in the economic cycle or a military engagement—factors that may not have been within anyone's control. Losing candidates may always feel that if they continue to educate the public to favor the policies they prefer, they will eventually win. Should a candidate lose a series of elections, however, the party would undoubtedly try to change something—policies, candidates, organization, maybe all three—in an effort to improve its fortunes.

How do winning candidates appraise an election? What does this event tell officeholders and their parties about the policies they should pursue when in office? Some policy positions undoubtedly were rather vague, and specific applications of them may turn out quite differently from what the campaign promised. Others may founder on the rock of practicality; they sounded fine, but they simply cannot be carried out. Conditions change and policies that seemed to make sense a few months before turn out to be irrelevant. Democrats may want to spend more on domestic programs and Republicans to cut taxes, but huge deficits endanger both policies. As the time for putting policies into practice draws near, the new officeholders may discover that the policies generate a lot more opposition than when they were merely campaign oratory. And those policies that are pursued to the end may have to be compromised considerably in order to get the support of other participants in the policy-making process. Nevertheless, if they have even a minimal policy orientation, newly elected candidates can try to carry out a few of their campaign proposals, seeking to maintain a general direction consonant with the approach that may have contributed (though they cannot be entirely certain) to their election.

The practical impossibility in our political system of ascertaining mandates in some objective sense is one important reason why it is so difficult for parties successfully to fulfill their function as policy advocates. It is, however, entirely possible for parties claiming a mandate to adopt policies that have little or no support in the general population. It is to the exploration of this possibility that we now turn.

PARTIES OF ADVOCACY VERSUS PARTIES OF INTERMEDIATION

The presidential election process in the United States has undergone a major transformation. As late as 1952, a president of the United States could, and with good reason, dismiss a prospective victory in the New Hampshire primary by the now little-remembered Senator Estes Kefauver of Tennessee as "eye-wash." Now primaries select most convention delegates and, combined with media spin, determine the outcome of the nomination process.[8]

Behind the shift in the role of primary elections lie shifts in the roles of political activists and changes in the powers and the significance of the news media. We believe that these changes and other changes that we have discussed—the ways in which television and digital media emphasize the personalities of individual candidates, the growing importance of political money in primary elections, the explosion of non-candidate controlled spending in the general election, the vast increase in the number of primaries, and the new rules for converting votes into delegates—add up to a fundamental redefinition of the place of the national political parties in our public life. One way to characterize this redefinition is to say that the conception of parties as agents of consensus government has faded. If we are right, then more and more we can expect candidates and party leaders to raise divisive issues and to emphasize party differences rather than paper them over, in an effort to mobilize adherents to their side of the argument rather than appeal to the masses of people in the uncommitted middle. This was called gratifying the "base" in the George W. Bush administration, and the Obama and Trump presidencies have followed a similar course.

Ideological activists are now favored by the rules of the game. In the early days of pre-primary activity, the people who become most active are apt to be those who have the most spare time, the most ideological commitment, and the most enthusiasm for one candidate above all others. Since the rules are now written to encourage activity at an earlier and earlier date, in order to raise campaign funds for the primaries and as a necessary condition for being taken seriously by the news media, it follows that activists will have more to say about the eventual outcome of the nomination process.[9] Party officials in the various states, in contrast, who in decades past preferred to wait until they could see a majority forming, under the new rules of the game must ally themselves with one or another active candidate early in the process or forfeit their influence. This applies even to the Democratic high officeholders who get automatic seats at the convention and make up about 15 percent of the total number of delegates. By the time their peculiar skills and interests in majority building might be needed—for instance, at a convention—it is too late for them to steer the process: most of the delegate positions will have been filled by the enthusiasts for particular candidates who won in the various primaries and caucuses.

We can therefore ask how the emerging structure of presidential election politics helps and hinders political parties in performing the tasks customarily allotted to them in the complex scheme of American democracy. In essence, we believe that the parties have been greatly strengthened in their capacities to provide advocacy and weakened in their abilities to provide intermediation or later to facilitate implementation in the political system (i.e., governing). Consensus among party activists is now achieved at the expense of increasing dissension within government. Thus party platforms become ever more internally consistent, while government finds it increasingly difficult to relate revenues to expenditures. The national debt burgeoned during the George W. Bush, Obama, and Trump presidencies, as partisan advocacy of tax cuts (for Bush and Trump) or spending programs (for Obama) triumphed over the more difficult governance problem of budget management.

Advocacy is strengthened because the rules of the game offer incentives to party leaders and candidates who are able to attract personal followings on an ideological basis. What is lost, in our view, is a capacity to deliberate, weigh competing demands, and compromise so that a variety of differing interests each gain a little. This loss would not be so great if the promise of policy government—to select efficacious programs and implement them successfully—were likely to be fulfilled in performance. But, on the record so far, this is doubly doubtful.

It is doubtful because for many of the problems that form the basis of political campaign discussion—economic growth, crime, poverty, terrorism—there are no known, sure-fire solutions. And second, even if we knew what to do about more of our problems, it is improbable, given the ways in which various forces in our society and responsibilities in our constitution are arranged, that presidents alone could deliver on their promises.

This last dilemma is especially poignant for candidates who speak to a very wide spectrum of issues. Were they elected, then program implementation would require support in Congress, the bureaucracies, state and city governments, and elsewhere. The ability of such policy-oriented candidates to gain the agreement of others depends on many factors that typically are neither discussed nor understood in election campaigns. Yet gaining the agreement of others is part of making policies work. Policy government might enhance the legitimacy of government if it increased the effectiveness of programs, but the insensitivity of its advocates to the needs for consensus makes that unlikely. Under these circumstances, neither policy goals nor consensus, advocacy nor intermediation, are likely to be served.

Two changes account for the decline in the vital function of intermediation by parties. First, a candidate for the presidency no longer needs to build up a mosaic of alliances with interest groups and party leaders. Instead, through the miracle of the mass media (especially television and the Internet), presidential candidates can reach every home and touch every heart and claim the allegiance of followers based on ideological or stylistic affinity rather than concrete bargains. The 2008 Obama campaign, touting an attractive "hope and change" pitch, is an example of successful "affinity politics." Donald Trump's celebrity career before his 2016 candidacy is yet another example. This is the first sense in which parties have been diminished in their capacity to mediate between the desires of ordinary citizens and the policies of government: candidates no longer need parties to reach voters.

In a second sense, parties are losing the capacity to mediate between leaders and followers because the formal properties of plebiscitary decision-making simply by voting, such as occurs in primary elections, leave little room for a bargaining process to occur. Contingent choices are impossible to express in primary elections straightforwardly through the ballot. Thus a candidate who is acceptable to a sizable majority but is the first choice of only a few systematically loses out under the current primary-driven rules to candidates who might be unacceptable to most voters but secure in their control over a middle-sized fraction (20 to 30 percent, depending on how many candidates play the game) of first-choice votes.

In this sense we can say that "participatory" democracy, as the American party system now practices it, undermines "deliberative" democracy. As more and different people have won the right to participate in the nomination process by voting in primaries, the kinds of communications they have been able to send to one another have not correspondingly been enriched. Participants can vote, but they cannot bargain. They can make and listen to speeches, but they cannot discuss or deliberate.

We have no way of knowing whether the democratic paradox of participation swallowing up deliberation has had the net effect of turning citizens away from political parties. It is in any event true that by a variety of measures—propensity of voters to decline to identify with a political party, direct expressions of disapproval of parties, active participation in party organizations—political parties, like so many other institutions of American society, suffered substantial losses in public confidence after the 1960s. In our view, the most promising way for parties to regain this confidence would be to avoid factional candidates and not only to nominate and elect good candidates but also to help them govern.

What is objectionable about policy government? What could be wrong with so intuitively attractive an idea? Governments must make policies. Surely candidates should be judged, in part at least, on their policy preferences, as well as on indications of their ability to perform when in office. Has there not been, in the past, too much obfuscation of issues and too little candor in speaking one's mind? Obviously our society needs more, rather than less, discussion of issues, and greater, rather than less, clarification of alternatives. But most people do not want parties that make extreme appeals by taking issue positions far from the desires of the bulk of the citizenry.[10] Perhaps people feel safer if their parties give them a choice, but they do not want losing to be a catastrophe. This may be why they see no great difficulty in electing a president of one party and a Congress of another.[11]

It is one thing to say that policy options have been insufficiently articulated and quite another to create conflict and develop disagreements where these did not exist before. Political activists in the United States are more ideological and polarized than at any time since studies were first conducted in the 1930s, and possibly since the 1890s or even the Civil War. Should ordinary citizens be compelled to choose from policy alternatives that appeal to these activists, or are they entitled to select from a menu closer to their tastes? The question is not whether there will be issues, for inevitably there must be, but who will set the agenda for discussion and whether this agenda will primarily reflect differences in the general population or those among elites. Thus one objection to a party of advocacy is that it imposes on the great majority of people preferences to which the majority is largely indifferent or opposed.

The rationale behind parties of advocacy leads to plebiscitary democracy. If it is not only desirable for all citizens to vote in general elections but also for them to choose candidates through preelection primaries, it must be even more desirable for them to select governmental policies directly through referendums. Instead of rule by special interests or cliques of congressmen, the public's interest would supposedly be expressed by the public.

Experience with initiatives and referendums at the state level, however, suggests that this is not quite how things work in practice. Without measures for limiting the number of referendums voters may face at a given election, citizens are swamped by the necessity of voting on dozens of items. Elites, not the people, determine the selection and wording of referendums. And how they are worded is of course extremely important. Money—to arrange for the signatures on petitions to get referendums on the ballot and to sponsor television advertising campaigns for the purposes of swaying voters—becomes more meaningful than ever. The public is faced with a bewildering array of proposals, all sponsored by special interests seeking a way around the state legislature. To learn what is involved in a single seemingly innocuous proposal takes hours of study. To understand 20 or more per election is unduly onerous. Are citizens better off guessing or following the guidance of media figures or advertising campaigns instead of trying to choose a legislator or a party to represent their interests?[12]

To take a famous case, were citizens or legislators better qualified to understand that Proposition 13 in California (passed in 1978) would not only keep property taxes down, which it was advertised to do, but would also, by depriving localities of resources, centralize control at the state level over many areas of public policy, which no one wanted? Were citizens of California, where referendums abound, wise to vote at widely separated intervals for so many mandatory expenditures that the state legislature struggled to mobilize resources to meet new needs?[13]

After a few decades of severe internal difficulty, when confidence in virtually all national institutions has suffered repeated blows, the need for consensus-building parties seems more clear than ever. Ideological parties might be desirable for a people homogeneous in all ways except the economic, but can a very large multiracial, multiethnic, multireligious, multiregional, multiclass nation such as the United States sustain itself when its main agents of political action—the parties—strive to exclude rather than include, to sharpen rather than dull the edge of controversy?

It is even doubtful that the rise of parties of advocacy leads to a more principled politics. If principles are precepts that must not be violated, when contrary principles are firmly embedded in the programs of opposing parties, one person's principles necessarily become another's fighting words. A few principles, such as those enshrined in the Bill of Rights, may be helpful, indeed essential, in establishing boundaries beyond which governmental action may not go. But too many principles thwart the cooperative government required by the design of the Constitution. As being a Democrat increasingly requires adherence to litmus-tested liberal positions and a Republican to litmus-tested conservative positions, cross-cutting cleavages—organizing people who support one another on some issues while opposing on others—are bound to diminish. With officeholders opposing each other on more issues, and with more issues defined as moral issues, political passions are liable to rise—and so, we suppose, will negative campaigning and popular disapproval of government and of politicians.

Compromise, of course, can also be a curse. If everything were bargainable, including basic liberties, no one would feel safe—and, indeed, no one would be. Similarly, if candidates cared everything about winning and nothing about how they win, if they were not restrained by internal norms or enforceable external expectations, elections would become outrages.

Parties without policies would be empty; parties fixated on only a narrow band of policies are dangerous. Without the desire to win elections, not at any cost but as a leading motive, there is no reason for politicians to pay attention to the people who vote. Winning requires a widespread appeal. Thus the desire to win can lead to moderation, to appeals to diverse groups in the electorate, and to efforts to bring many varied interests together. This is why we prefer parties of intermediation to parties of advocacy. Parties of advocacy do not sustain themselves well in government. They fail to assist political leaders in mobilizing consent for the policies they adopt, and this widens the gap between campaign promises and the performance of government. This, we believe, has too often become the fate of our parties as they now exist.

Because so many of the rules of presidential election politics are changing, we cannot say with a high degree of assurance how parties, candidates, and voters will adapt to the new incentives, regulations, and technological innovations that are continuously introduced. We are confident only in asserting that the adaptations they make will be of enormous consequence in determining the ultimate capacity of the American political system to sustain the fascinating and noble experiment in self-government begun on this continent more than two hundred years ago.

Appendix A

Vote by Groups in Presidential Elections, 1984–2016 (in percentages)

■ ■ ■

	1984		1988	
	Mondale (D)	Reagan (R)	Dukakis (D)	Bush (R)
National	40	59	45	53
Sex				
Men	37	62	41	57
Women	44	56	49	50
Race				
White	35	64	40	59
Black	90	9	86	12
Latino	62	37	69	30
Education				
Not high school graduate	50	50	56	43
High school graduate only	39	60	49	50
Some college	38	61	42	57
College graduate	41	58	37	62
Postgraduate	–	–	48	50
Income				
Under $15,000	55	45	62	37
$15,000–$29,999	42	57	50	49
$30,000–$49,999	40	59	43	56
$50,000 and over	30	69	37	62
Labor union household	53	46	57	42
Age				
Under 30 years	40	59	47	52
30–44 years	42	57	45	54
45–59 years	40	60	42	57
60 years and over	39	60	49	50

(continued)

	1984		1988	
	Mondale (D)	**Reagan (R)**	**Dukakis (D)**	**Bush (R)**
Religion				
White Protestant	27	72	33	66
Catholic	45	54	47	52
Jewish	67	31	64	35
Marital status				
Married	38	62	42	57
Unmarried	47	52	53	46
Party Identification				
Democratic	74	25	82	17
Republican	7	92	8	91
Independent	36	63	43	55
Region				
East	47	53	49	50
Midwest	41	58	47	52
South	36	64	41	58
West	38	61	46	52

	1992			1996		
	Clinton (D)	**Bush (R)**	**Perot (I)**	**Clinton (D)**	**Dole (R)**	**Perot (I)**
National	43	38	19	49	41	8
Sex						
Men	41	38	21	43	44	10
Women	45	37	17	54	38	7
Race						
White	39	40	20	43	46	9
Black	83	10	7	84	12	4
Latino	61	25	14	72	21	8
Education						
Not high school graduate	54	28	18	59	28	11
High school graduate only	43	36	21	51	35	13
Some college	41	37	21	48	40	10
College graduate	39	41	20	44	46	8
Postgraduate	50	36	14	52	40	5

(*continued*)

	1992			1996		
	Clinton (D)	Bush (R)	Perot (I)	Clinton (D)	Dole (R)	Perot (I)
Income						
Under $15,000	58	23	19	59	28	11
$15,000–$29,999	45	35	20	53	36	9
$30,000–$49,999	41	38	21	48	40	10
$50,000 and over	39	44	17	44	48	7
Labor union household	55	24	21	59	30	9
Age						
Under 30 years	43	34	22	53	34	10
30–44 years	41	38	21	48	41	9
45–59 years	41	40	19	49	41	9
60 years and over	50	38	12	48	44	7
Religion						
White Protestant	33	47	21	36	53	10
Catholic	44	35	20	53	37	9
Jewish	80	11	9	78	16	3
Marital status						
Married	40	41	20	44	46	9
Unmarried	51	30	19	57	31	9
Party Identification						
Democratic	77	10	13	84	10	5
Republican	10	73	17	13	80	6
Independent	38	32	30	43	35	17
Region						
East	47	35	18	55	34	9
Midwest	42	37	21	48	41	10
South	41	43	16	46	46	7
West	43	34	22	48	40	8

	2000			2004	
	Gore (D)	Bush (R)	Nader (G)	Kerry (D)	Bush (R)
National	48	48	2	48	51
Sex					
Men	42	53	3	44	55
Women	54	43	2	51	48
Race					
White	42	54	3	41	58
Black	90	8	1	88	11
Latino	67	31	2	56	43

(*continued*)

	2000			2004	
	Gore (D)	Bush (R)	Nader (G)	Kerry (D)	Bush (R)
Education					
Not high school graduate	59	39	1	50	49
High school graduate only	48	49	1	47	52
Some college	45	51	3	46	54
College graduate	45	51	3	46	52
Postgraduate	52	44	3	55	44
Income					
Under $15,000	57	37	4	63	36
$15,000–$29,999	54	41	3	57	42
$30,000–$49,999	49	48	2	50	49
$50,000 and over	45	52	2	43	56
Labor union household	59	37	3	59	40
Age					
Under 30 years	48	46	5	54	45
30–44 years	48	49	2	46	53
45–59 years	48	49	2	48	51
60 years and over	51	47	2	46	54
Religion					
White Protestant	34	63	2	32	67
Catholic	49	47	2	47	52
Jewish	79	19	1	74	25
Marital status					
Married	44	53	2	42	57
Unmarried	57	38	4	58	40
Party Identification					
Democratic	86	11	2	89	11
Republican	8	91	1	49	48
Independent	45	47	6	6	93
Region					
East	56	39	3	56	43
Midwest	48	49	2	48	51
South	43	55	1	42	58
West	48	46	4	50	49

Source: Data for 1952–1980 from the final preelection Gallup survey, as summarized in *Gallup Poll Monthly* 374 (November 1996), pp. 17–20. Data for 1984–2004 from *New York Times* exit polls, as summarized in Marjorie Connelly, "How Americans Voted: A Political Portrait," *New York Times*, November 7, 2004, sec. 4, p. 4; "Exit Polls," MSNBC, available at http://www.msnbc.msn.com/id/5297138.

	2008	
	Obama (D)	McCain (R)
National	53	46
Sex		
Men	49	48
Women	56	43
Race		
White	43	55
Black	95	4
Latino	67	31
Education		
No high school	63	35
High school graduate only	52	46
Some college	51	47
College graduate	50	48
Postgraduate	58	40
Income		
Under $15,000	73	25
$15,000–$30,000	60	37
$30,000–$50,000	55	43
$50,000 and over	49	49
Labor union household	59	39
Age		
Under 30 years	66	32
30–44 years	52	46
45–64 years	50	49
65 years and over	45	53
Religion		
White Protestant	34	65
Catholic	54	45
Jewish	78	21
Marital status		
Married	47	52
Unmarried	65	33
Party Identification		
Democratic	89	10
Republican	9	90
Independent	52	44
Region		
East	59	40
Midwest	54	44
South	45	54
West	57	40

Source: CNN.com, "Election Center 2008," http://www.cnn.com/ELECTION/2008/results/polls/#USP00p1.

	2012	
	Obama (D)	Romney (R)
National	51	47
Sex		
Men	45	55
Women	55	44
Race		
White	39	59
Black	93	6
Latino	71	27
Education		
No high school	64	35
High school graduate only	51	48
Some college	48	49
College graduate	47	51
Postgraduate	55	42
Income		
Under $50,000	73	25
$50,000–$100,000	60	37
$100,000 and over	44	54
Labor union household	58	40
Age		
Under 30 years	60	37
30–44 years	54	45
45–64 years	47	51
65 years and over	44	56
Population of Area		
Large city	69	29
Small city	58	21
Suburbs	48	50
Small town	42	56
Rural	37	61
Religion		
White Protestant	30	69
Catholic	50	48
Jewish	69	30
Marital status		
Married	42	56
Unmarried	62	35
Party Identification		
Democratic	92	8
Republican	7	93
Independent	45	50

Source: CNN.com, "Election Center 2012," http://www.cnn.com/election/2012/results/race/president.

	2016	
	Clinton (D)	Trump (R)
National	48	46
Sex		
Men	41	52
Women	54	41
Race		
White	37	57
Black	89	8
Latino	66	28
Asian	65	27
Education		
High school or less	46	51
Some college	43	51
College graduate	49	44
Postgraduate	58	37
Income		
Under $50,000	53	41
$50,000–$100,000	46	49
$100,000 and over	47	47
Labor union household	51	42
Age		
Under 30 years	55	36
30–44 years	51	41
45–64 years	44	52
65 years and over	45	52
Population of Area		
Urban area	60	34
Suburban area	45	49
Rural area	34	61
Religion		
Protestant	39	56
Catholic	46	50
Jewish	71	23
Marital status		
Married	44	52
Unmarried	55	37
Party Identification		
Democratic	89	8
Republican	8	88
Independent	42	46

Source: CNN.com, "Exit Polls," https://www.cnn.com/election/2016/results/exit-polls.

Appendix B

Voter Turnout in Presidential Elections, by Population Characteristics, 1984–2016

■ ■ ■

	1984			
	Persons of Voting Age (in thousands)	Persons Reporting They Voted (in thousands)	Percent Reporting They Voted	Percent Reporting They Did Not Vote
Total	169,963	101,878	59.9	40.1
Men	80,327	47,354	59.0	41.0
Women	89,636	54,524	60.8	39.2
White	146,761	90,152	61.4	38.6
Nonwhite	23,202	11,726	50.5	49.5
18–24 years old	27,976	11,407	40.8	59.2
25–34 years old	40,292	21,978	54.5	45.5
35–44 years old	30,731	19,514	63.5	36.5
45–64 years old	44,307	30,924	69.8	30.2
65 years and older	26,658	18,055	67.7	32.3
Nonsouth	112,376	69,183	61.6	38.4
South	57,587	32,695	56.8	43.2
Under 9 years of school	20,580	8,833	42.9	57.1
9–11 years of school	22,068	9,798	44.4	55.6
12 years	67,807	39,773	58.7	41.3
More than 12 years	59,508	43,473	73.1	26.9

(continued)

	1984			
	Persons of Voting Age (in thousands)	Persons Reporting They Voted (in thousands)	Percent Reporting They Voted	Percent Reporting They Did Not Vote
Employed	104,173	64,213	61.6	38.4
Unemployed	7,389	3,247	44.0	56.0
Not in labor force	58,401	34,418	58.9	41.1

Source: US Bureau of the Census, *Current Population Reports*, Series P-20, no. 405 (March 1986).

Note: Voting age population defined as civilian noninstitutional population (including noncitizens) aged 18 years and over.

	1988			
	Persons of Voting Age (in thousands)	Persons Reporting They Voted (in thousands)	Percent Reporting They Voted	Percent Reporting They Did Not Vote
Total	178,098	102,224	57.4	42.6
Men	84,531	47,704	56.4	43.6
Women	93,568	54,519	58.3	41.7
White	152,848	90,357	59.1	40.9
Nonwhite	25,250	11,867	47.0	53.0
18–24 years old	25,569	9,254	36.2	63.8
25–34 years old	42,677	20,468	48.0	52.0
35–44 years old	35,186	21,550	61.3	38.7
45–64 years old	45,862	31,134	67.9	32.1
65 years and older	28,804	19,818	68.8	31.2
Nonsouth	117,373	69,130	58.9	41.1
South	60,725	33,094	54.5	45.5
Under 9 years of school	19,145	7,025	36.7	63.3
9–11 years of school	21,052	8,698	41.3	58.7
12 years	70,033	38,328	54.7	45.3
More than 12 years	67,878	48,173	71.0	29.0
Employed	113,836	66,510	58.4	41.6
Unemployed	5,809	2,243	38.6	61.4
Not in labor force	58,453	33,471	57.3	42.7

Source: US Bureau of the Census, *Current Population Reports*, Series P-20, no. 440 (October 1989).

Note: Voting age population defined as civilian noninstitutional population (including noncitizens) aged 18 years and over.

	1992			
	Persons of Voting Age (in thousands)	Persons Reporting They Voted (in thousands)	Percent Reporting They Voted	Percent Reporting They Did Not Vote
Total	185,684	113,866	61.3	38.7
Men	88,557	53,312	60.2	39.8
Women	97,126	60,554	62.3	37.7
White	157,837	100,405	63.6	36.4
Nonwhite	27,847	13,461	48.3	51.7
18–24 years old	24,371	10,442	42.8	57.2
25–34 years old	41,603	22,120	53.2	46.8
35–44 years old	39,716	25,269	63.6	36.4
45–64 years old	49,147	34,399	70.0	30.0
65 years and older	30,846	21,637	70.1	29.9
Nonsouth	122,025	76,276	62.5	37.5
South	63,659	37,590	59.0	41.0
Under 9 years of school	15,391	5,406	35.1	64.9
9–11 years of school	20,970	8,638	41.2	58.8
12 years	65,281	37,517	57.5	42.5
More than 12 years:				
1 to 3 years of college	46,691	32,069	68.7	31.3
4 or more years of college	37,351	30,236	81.0	19.0
Employed	116,290	74,138	63.8	36.2
Unemployed	8,263	3,820	46.2	53.8
Not in labor force	61,131	35,908	58.7	41.3

Source: US Bureau of the Census, Current Population Reports, Series P-20, no. 466 (April 1993).

Note: Voting age population defined as civilian noninstitutional population (including noncitizens) aged 18 years and over.

	1996			
	Persons of Voting Age (in thousands)	**Persons Reporting They Voted (in thousands)**	**Percent Reporting They Voted**	**Percent Reporting They Did Not Vote**
Total	193,651	105,017	54.2	45.8
Men	92,632	48,909	52.8	47.2
Women	101,020	56,108	55.5	44.5
White	162,779	91,208	56.0	44.0
Nonwhite	30,872	13,809	44.7	55.3
18–24 years old	24,650	7,996	32.4	67.6
25–34 years old	40,066	17,265	43.1	56.9
35–44 years old	43,327	23,785	54.9	45.1
45–64 years old	53,721	34,615	64.4	35.6
65 years and older	31,888	21,356	67.0	33.0
Nonsouth	125,571	69,467	55.3	44.7
South	68,080	35,550	52.2	47.8
Under 9 years of school	13,986	4,188	29.9	70.1
9–11 years of school	21,002	7,099	33.8	66.2
12 years	65,208	32,019	49.1	50.9
More than 12 years:				
1 to 3 years of college	50,939	30,835	60.5	39.5
4 or more years of college	42,517	30,877	72.6	27.4
Employed	125,634	69,300	55.2	44.8
Unemployed	6,409	2,383	37.2	62.8
Not in labor force	61,608	33,335	54.1	45.9

Source: US Bureau of the Census, *Current Population Reports*, Series P-20, no. 504 (August 1997).

Note: Voting age population defined as civilian noninstitutional population (including noncitizens) aged 18 years and over.

	2000			
	Persons of Voting Age (in thousands)	Persons Reporting They Voted (in thousands)	Percent Reporting They Voted	Percent Reporting They Did Not Vote
Total	202,609	110,826	54.7	45.3
Men	97,087	51,542	53.1	46.9
Women	105,523	59,284	56.2	43.8
White	168,733	95,098	56.4	43.6
Nonwhite	33,876	15,728	46.4	53.6
18–24 years old	26,712	8,635	32.3	67.7
25–34 years old	37,304	16,286	43.7	56.3
35–44 years old	44,476	24,452	55.0	45.0
45–64 years old	61,352	39,301	64.1	35.9
65 years and older	32,764	22,152	67.6	32.4
Nonsouth	130,774	72,385	55.4	44.6
South	71,835	38,441	53.5	46.5
Under 9 years of school	12,894	3,454	26.8	73.2
9–11 years of school	20,108	6,758	33.6	66.4
12 years	66,339	32,749	49.4	50.6
More than 12 years:				
1 to 3 years of college	55,308	33,339	60.3	39.7
4 or more years of college	47,960	34,526	72.0	28.0
Employed	133,434	74,068	55.5	44.5
Unemployed	4,944	1,734	35.1	64.9
Not in labor force	64,231	35,023	54.5	45.5

Source: US Bureau of the Census, *Current Population Reports*, Series P-20, no. 542 (February 2002).

Note: Voting age population defined as civilian noninstitutional population (including noncitizens) aged 18 years and over.

	2004			
	Persons of Voting Age (in thousands)	Persons Reporting They Voted (in thousands)	Percent Reporting They Voted	Percent Reporting They Did Not Vote
Total	215,694	125,736	58.3	41.7
Men	103,812	58,455	56.3	43.7
Women	111,882	67,281	60.1	39.9
White	176,618	106,588	60.3	39.7
Nonwhite	39,076	19,148	49.0	51.0
18–24 years old	27,808	11,639	41.9	58.1
25–34 years old	39,003	18,285	46.9	53.1
35–44 years old	43,130	24,560	56.9	43.1
45–64 years old	71,015	47,326	66.6	33.4
65 years and older	34,738	23,925	68.9	31.1
Nonsouth	138,506	82,224	59.4	40.6
South	77,188	43,512	56.4	43.6
Not high school graduate	33,293	10,132	30.4	69.6
High school graduate only	68,545	35,894	52.4	47.6
Some college	58,913	38,922	66.1	33.9
College graduate	36,591	26,579	72.6	27.4
Postgraduate	18,352	14,210	77.4	22.6
Employed	138,831	83,250	60.0	40.0
Unemployed	7,251	3,362	46.4	53.6
Not in labor force	69,612	39,124	56.2	43.8

Source: US Bureau of the Census, *Current Population Reports*, Series P-20, no. 556 (March 2006).

Note: Voting age population defined as civilian noninstitutional population (including noncitizens) aged 18 years and over.

	2008			
	Persons of Voting Age (in thousands)	Persons Reporting They Voted (in thousands)	Percent Reporting They Voted	Percent Reporting They Did Not Vote
Total	225,499	131,144	63.6	36.4
Men	108,974	60,729	61.5	38.5
Women	116,525	70,415	65.7	34.3
White	183,169	109,100	64.4	35.6
Black	26,528	16,133	64.7	35.3
Hispanic	30,852	9,745	49.9	50.1
Asian	10,455	3,357	47.6	52.4
18–24 years old	26,263	12,515	48.5	51.5
25–34 years old	40,240	19,501	57.0	43.0
35–44 years old	41,460	22,865	62.8	37.2
45–54 years old	44,181	27,623	67.4	32.6
55–64 years old	33,896	23,071	71.5	28.5
65–74 years old	20,227	14,176	72.4	27.6
75 years and over	17,231	11,344	67.8	32.2
Nonsouth	143,097	83,608	64.3	35.7
South	82,402	47,536	62.6	37.4
Not high school graduate	30,204	9,076	39.3	60.7
High school graduate only	70,427	35,866	54.9	45.1
Some college	63,780	41,477	68.0	32.0
College graduate	40,850	29,330	77.0	23.0
Postgraduate	20,238	15,425	82.7	17.3
Civilian labor force	152,707	90,715	65.2	34.8
Unemployed	9,521	4,642	54.7	45.3
Not in labor force	72,792	40,429	60.3	39.7

Source: US Bureau of the Census, *Population Division, Education & Social Stratification Branch* (July 2009).

Note: Voting age population defined as civilian noninstitutional population (including noncitizens) aged 18 years and over.

	2012			
	Persons of Voting Age (in thousands)	**Persons Reporting They Voted (in thousands)**	**Percent Reporting They Voted**	**Percent Reporting They Did Not Vote**
Total	235,248	132,948	61.8	38.2
Men	113,243	61,551	59.7	40.3
Women	122,005	71,397	63.7	36.3
White	173,466	107,846	62.2	37.8
Black	26,915	17,183	66.2	33.8
Hispanic	23,329	11,188	48.0	52.0
Asian	9,033	4,331	47.9	52.1
18–24 years old	29,878	11,353	41.2	58.8
25–44 years old	80,770	39,942	57.3	42.7
45–64 years old	82,087	52,013	67.9	32.1
65–74 years old	24,162	17,182	73.5	26.5
75 years and over	18,352	12,459	70.0	30.0
Nonsouth	148,180	84,415	62.5	37.5
South	87,068	48,533	60.7	39.3
Not high school graduate	29,206	8,297	38.3	61.7
High school graduate only	70,579	34,402	52.6	47.4
Some college	67,652	41,601	64.2	35.8
College graduate	44,436	31,192	75.0	25.0
Postgraduate	23,374	17,457	81.3	18.7
Civilian labor force	153,666	88,674	63.4	36.6
Unemployed	11,091	5,111	51.9	48.1
Not in labor force	81,582	44,275	58.9	41.1

Source: US Bureau of the Census, *Population Division, Education & Social Stratification Branch* (May 2013).

Note: Voting age population defined as civilian noninstitutional population (including noncitizens) aged 18 years and over.

	2016			
	Persons of Voting Age (in thousands)	Persons Reporting They Voted (in thousands)	Percent Reporting They Voted	Percent Reporting They Did Not Vote
Total	245,502	137,537	56.0	44.0
Men	118,488	63,801	53.8	46.2
Women	127,013	73,735	58.1	41.9
White	157,395	100,849	64.1	35.9
Black	30,608	17,119	55.9	44.1
Hispanic	38,990	12,682	32.5	67.5
Asian	14,881	5,043	33.9	66.1
18–24 years old	29,320	11,560	39.4	60.6
25–44 years old	83,698	40,994	49.0	51.0
45–64 years old	83,799	51,668	61.7	38.3
65–74 years old	28,832	20,219	70.1	29.9
75 years and over	19,852	13,095	66.0	34.0
Nonsouth	153,529	87,015	56.7	43.3
South	91,973	50,522	54.9	45.1
Not high school graduate	27,488	6,990	25.4	74.6
High school graduate only	71,322	33,774	47.4	52.6
Some college	69,935	42,296	60.5	39.5
College graduate	49,526	34,364	69.4	30.6
Postgraduate	27,231	20,113	73.9	26.1
Civilian labor force	157,748	90,329	57.3	42.7
Unemployed	6,869	3,081	44.8	55.2
Not in labor force	87,753	47,208	53.8	46.2

Source: US Bureau of the Census, "Voting and Registration in the Election of November 2016," May 2017, https://www.census.gov/data/tables/time-series/demo/voting-and-registration/p20-580.html.

Note: Voting age population defined as civilian noninstitutional population (including noncitizens) aged 18 years and over.

Selections from the Democratic and Republican Party Platforms, 2016

■ ■ ■

DEMOCRATIC PLATFORM

Economic Policy

"The system is not working when we have a rigged economy in which ordinary Americans work longer hours for lower wages, while most new income and wealth goes to the top one percent. Republican governors, legislatures, and their corporate allies have launched attack after attack on workers' fundamental rights to organize and bargain collectively. . . . We believe that Americans should earn at least $15 an hour and have the right to form or join a union and will work in every way we can—in Congress and the federal government, in states and with the private sector—to reach this goal. . . . Democrats will make it easier for workers, public and private, to exercise their right to organize and join unions. . . . We will fight to secure equal pay for women, which will benefit all women and their families . . . We will fight every effort to cut, privatize, or weaken Social Security, including attempts to raise the retirement age, diminish benefits by cutting cost-of-living adjustments, or reducing earned benefits. . . . We will put Americans to work . . . We will build 21st century energy and water systems, modernize our schools, and continue to support the expansion of high-speed broadband networks. . . . Donald Trump may talk tough, but he has consistently outsourced his own products. American workers deserve better."

Education

"Democrats believe that in America, if you want a higher education, you should always be able to get one: money should never stand in the way. . . . Democrats will allow those who currently have student debt to refinance their loans at the lowest rates possible. . . . We will continue to crack down on for-profit schools that take millions in federal financial aid—often as their principal source of revenue—and then exploit students and burden them with debt rather than educating them. . . . Democrats will invest in early childhood programs like Early Head Start and provide every family in America with access to high-quality childcare and high-quality preschool programs. . . . We support democratically governed, great neighborhood public schools and high-quality public charter schools, and we will help them disseminate best practices to other school leaders and educators."

Environment and Energy

"Climate change is an urgent threat and a defining challenge of our time. . . . While Donald Trump has called climate change a 'hoax,' 2016 is on track to break global temperature records once more. . . . Democrats share a deep commitment to tackling the climate challenge; creating millions of good-paying middle class jobs; reducing greenhouse gas emissions more than 80 percent below 2005 levels by 2050; and meeting the pledge President Obama put forward in the landmark Paris Agreement . . . Democrats reject the notion that we have to choose between protecting our planet and creating good-paying jobs. . . . We are committed to getting 50 percent of our electricity from clean energy sources within a decade, with half a billion solar panels installed within four years and enough renewable energy to power every home in the country. . . ."

Abortion

"Democrats are committed to protecting and advancing reproductive health, rights, and justice. We believe unequivocally, like the majority of Americans, that every woman should have access to quality reproductive health care services, including safe and legal abortion—regardless of where she lives, how much money she makes, or how she is insured. . . . We will continue to oppose—and seek to overturn—federal and state laws and policies that impede a woman's access to abortion, including by repealing the Hyde Amendment."

Gay Rights

"Democrats believe that LGBT rights are human rights and that American foreign policy should advance the ability of all persons to live with dignity, security, and respect, regardless of who they are or who they love. We applaud President Obama's historic Presidential Memorandum on International Initiatives to Advance the Human Rights of Lesbian, Gay, Bisexual, and Transgender Persons, which combats criminalization, protects refugees, and provides foreign assistance."

Terrorism and National Security

"Democrats will protect our country. . . . We will use all the tools of American power, especially diplomacy and development, to confront global threats and ensure war is the last resort. . . . Democrats will seek an updated Authorization for Use of Military Force (AUMF) that is more precise about our efforts to defeat ISIS and that does not involve large-scale combat deployment of American troops. . . . We reject Donald Trump's vilification of Muslims. . . . We reject Donald Trump's suggestion that our military should engage in war crimes, like torturing prisoners or murdering civilian family members of suspected terrorists. . . . Donald Trump would overturn more than 50 years of American foreign policy by abandoning

NATO partners . . . and embracing Russian President Vladimir Putin instead. We believe in strong alliances and will deter Russian aggression, build European resilience, and protect our NATO allies. . . . Democrats are committed to preventing the spread of nuclear, chemical, and biological weapons and to eventually ridding the planet of these catastrophic weapons."

Health Care

"Democrats believe that health care is a right, not a privilege, and our health care system should put people before profits. Thanks to the hard work of President Obama and Democrats in Congress, we took a critically important step toward the goal of universal health care by passing the Affordable Care Act. . . . Americans should be able to access public coverage through a public option, and those over 55 should be able to opt in to Medicare. . . . Democrats will fight any attempts by Republicans in Congress to privatize, voucherize, or 'phase out' Medicare as we know it. We will fight until ACA's Medicaid expansion has been adopted in every state [and] cap the amount Americans have to pay out-of-pocket every month on prescription drugs."

Immigration

"Democrats believe we need to urgently fix our broken immigration system—which tears families apart and keeps workers in the shadows—and create a path to citizenship for law-abiding families who are here . . . we will defend and implement President Obama's Deferred Action for Childhood Arrivals and Deferred Action for Parents of Americans executive actions to help DREAMers, parents of citizens, and lawful permanent residents avoid deportation. . . . Democrats will not stand for the divisive and derogatory language of Donald Trump. His offensive comments about immigrants and other communities have no place in our society."

REPUBLICAN PLATFORM

Economic Policy

"Government cannot create prosperity, though government can limit or destroy it. . . . Republicans consider the establishment of a pro-growth tax code a moral imperative. More than any other public policy, the way government raises revenue has the greatest impact on our economy's performance. . . . American businesses now face the world's highest corporate tax rates. That's like putting lead shoes on your cross-country team. . . . We need better negotiated trade agreements that put America first. . . . We cannot allow foreign governments to limit American access to their markets while stealing our designs, patents, brands, know-how, and technology. . . . Instead of facilitating change, the current Administration and its agents at the National Labor Relations Board are determined to reverse it. . . . They have outlawed alternatives to unions even when they were favored by the workers. . . . Minimum wage is an issue that should be handled at the state and local level."

Education

"American education has, for the last several decades, been the focus of constant controversy, as centralizing forces from outside the family and community have sought to remake education in order to remake America. They have done immense damage. . . . After years of trial and error, we know the policies and methods that have actually made a difference in student advancement: Choice in education; building on the basics; STEM subjects and phonics; career and technical education; ending social promotions; merit pay for good teachers; classroom discipline; parental involvement; and strong leadership by principals, superintendents, and locally elected school boards. . . . To ensure that all students have access to the mainstream of American life, we support the English First approach and oppose divisive programs that limit students' ability to advance in American society."

Environment and Energy
"The Democratic Party's energy policy can be summed up in a slogan currently popular among its activists: 'keep it in the ground.' Keeping energy in the earth will keep jobs out of reach of those who need them most. . . . We support the development of all forms of energy that are marketable in a free economy without subsidies, including coal, oil, natural gas, nuclear power, and hydropower. . . . Poverty, not wealth, is the gravest threat to the environment, while steady economic growth brings the technological advances which make environmental progress possible. . . . The environment is too important to be left to radical environmentalists. They are using yesterday's tools to control a future they do not comprehend. The environmental establishment has become a self-serving elite, stuck in the mindset of the 1970s. . . . We firmly believe environmental problems are best solved by giving incentives for human ingenuity and the development of new technologies, not through top-down, command-and-control regulations that stifle economic growth and cost thousands of jobs."

Abortion
"We support a human life amendment to the Constitution and legislation to make clear that the Fourteenth Amendment's protections apply to children before birth. . . . We oppose the use of public funds to perform or promote abortion or to fund organizations, like Planned Parenthood, so long as they provide or refer for elective abortions or sell fetal body parts rather than provide healthcare. We will not fund or subsidize healthcare that includes abortion coverage. . . . We support the appointment of judges who respect traditional family values and the sanctity of innocent human life."

Gay Rights
"Our laws and our government's regulations should recognize marriage as the union of one man and one woman and actively promote married family life as the basis of a stable and prosperous society. For that reason . . . we do not accept the Supreme Court's redefinition of marriage and we urge its reversal . . . We oppose government discrimination against businesses or entities which decline to sell items or services to individuals for activities that go against their religious views about such activities."

Terrorism and National Security
"After nearly eight years of a Democratic Commander-in-Chief who has frequently placed strategic and ideological limitations and shackles on our military,

our enemies have been emboldened and our national security is at great risk. . . . We are the party of peace through strength. . . . We must move from a budget-based strategy to one that puts the security of our nation first. . . . We support lifting the budget cap for defense and reject the efforts of Democrats to hold the military's budget hostage for their domestic agenda. . . . A Republican administration will restore our nation's credibility. We must stand up for our friends, challenge our foes, and destroy ISIS. . . . Foreign aid must serve America's interests first. . . . We face a dangerous world, and we believe in a resurgent America."

Health Care
"Any honest agenda for improving healthcare must start with repeal of the dishonestly named Affordable Care Act of 2010: Obamacare. . . . It imposed a Euro-style bureaucracy to manage its unworkable, budget-busting, conflicting provisions. . . . To simplify the system for both patients and providers, we will reduce mandates and enable insurers and providers of care to increase healthcare options and contain costs. . . . To guarantee first-rate care for the needy, we propose to block grant Medicaid and other payments and to assist all patients, including those with pre-existing conditions, to obtain coverage in a robust consumer market. . . . We will empower individuals and small businesses to form purchasing pools in order to expand coverage to the uninsured. We believe that individuals with preexisting conditions who maintain continuous coverage should be protected from discrimination. . . . Consumer choice is the most powerful factor in healthcare reform."

Immigration
"Our immigration system must protect American working families and their wages, for citizens and legal immigrants alike, in a way that will improve the economy. . . . America's immigration policy must serve the national interest of the United States, and the interests of American workers must be protected over the claims of foreign nationals seeking the same jobs. . . . Illegal immigration endangers everyone, exploits the taxpayers, and insults all who aspire to enter America legally. We oppose any form of amnesty for those who, by breaking the law, have disadvantaged those who have obeyed it."

Notes

■ ■ ■

CHAPTER 1: VOTERS

1. Anthony King, *Running Scared: Why America's Politicians Campaign Too Much and Govern Too Little* (New York: Martin Kessler, 1997).

2. See Bruce Cain, John Ferejohn, and Morris Fiorina, *The Personal Vote: Constituency Service and Electoral Independence* (Cambridge, MA: Harvard University Press, 1987), 13; and Leon D. Epstein, *Political Parties in Western Democracies* (New York: Praeger, 1967), 43.

3. See Richard W. Boyd, "Decline of U.S. Voter Turnout: Structural Explanations," *American Politics Quarterly* 9 (April 1981): 133–59. Switzerland, the other low-turnout democracy, also has frequent elections and referendums; see David Butler and Austin Ranney, eds., *Referendums around the World: The Growing Use of Direct Democracy* (Washington, DC: AEI Press, 1994). In *Running Scared*, Anthony King argues that the U.S. pattern of frequent elections has important consequences for governing.

4. See Steven J. Rosenstone and John Mark Hansen, *Mobilization, Participation, and Democracy in America* (New York: Macmillan, 1993), 178–79.

5. Raymond E. Wolfinger, David P. Glass, and Peverill Squire, "Predictors of Electoral Turnout: An International Comparison," *Policy Studies Review* 9 (Spring 1990): 551–74, at 555, based on vote validated data from the 1980 National Election Studies.

6. Ibid., 146–50. Americans do least well on "trust in government" questions, but respond much more positively to questions about their efficacy (rejecting such statements as "people like me have no say in what the government does") and to questions asking if a political party expresses their point of view.

7. A summary of these trends is a central topic in Steven E. Schier and Todd E. Eberly, *American Government and Popular Discontent: Stability without Success* (New York: Routledge, 2013) and in their forthcoming *How Trump Happened* (Lanham, MD: Rowman & Littlefield, 2020). See also Marc J. Hetherington, *Why Trust Matters: Declining Political Trust and the Demise of Political Liberalism* (Princeton: Princeton University Press, 2006) and Marc J. Hetherington and Thomas J. Rudolph, *Why Washington Won't Work: Polarization, Political Trust and the Governing Crisis* (Chicago: University of Chicago Press, 2015).

8. Peverill Squire, Raymond E. Wolfinger, and David P. Glass, "Residential Mobility and Voter Turnout," *American Political Science Review* 81 (March 1987): 45–84.

9. Orley Ashenfelter and Stanley Kelley Jr., "Determinants of Participation in Presidential Elections," *Journal of Law and Economics* 18 (December 1975): 695–733. The prospect of partisan manipulation of purge laws by politicians seeking to disenfranchise likely supporters of the opposition has become an area of concern among some government watchdog groups over the past several years; see Jonathan Brater et al., "Voter Purges: A Growing Threat to the Right to Vote," Brennan Center for Justice, New York University, July 20, 2018, https://www.brennancenter.org/publication/purges-growing-threat-right-vote.

10. Figure from Drew DeSilver, "U.S. Trails Most Developed Countries in Voter Turnout," Pew Research Center, May 21, 2018, http://www.pewresearch.org/fact-tank/2018/05/21/u-s-voter-turnout-trails-most-developed-countries. See also Harold G. Gosnell, *Why Europe Votes* (Chicago: University of Chicago Press, 1930); Raymond E. Wolfinger and Steven J. Rosenstone, *Who Votes?* (New Haven, CT: Yale University Press, 1980); G. Bingham Powell Jr., "American Voter Turnout in Comparative Perspective," *American Political Science Review* 80 (March 1986): 17–43; and Glenn E. Mitchell and Christopher Wlezien, "The Impact of Legal Constraints on Voter Registration, Turnout, and the Composition of the American Electorate," *Political Behavior* 17 (June 1995): 179–202.

11. This is presumably pegged to completion of the harvest in the colonial Northeast.

12. Stanley Kelley Jr., Richard E. Ayres, and William G. Bowen, "Registration and Voting: Putting First Things First," *American Political Science Review* 61 (June 1967): 359–79, at 374–75.

13. Stephen Knack and James White, "Election-Day Registration and Turnout Inequality," *Political Behavior* 22 (March 2000): 29–44. Not all of this difference can be explained by registration laws, however; see Benjamin Highton, "Easy Registration and Voter Turnout," *Journal of Politics* 59 (May 1997): 565–75.

14. California Secretary of State Alex Padilla, "Historical Vote by Mail (Absentee) Ballot Use In California," September 2018, https://www.sos.ca.gov/elections/historical-absentee.

15. Figures from Michael P. McDonald, United States Elections Project, http://www.electproject.org/early_2016.

16. Brennan Center for Justice, New York University, "Criminal Disenfranchisement Laws Across the United States," December 2018, https://www.brennancenter.org/criminal-disenfranchisement-laws-across-united-states.

17. McDonald, United States Elections Project, http://www.electproject.org/2016g. See also Michael P. McDonald and Samuel L. Popkin, "The Myth of the Vanishing Voter," *American Political Science Review* 95 (December 2001): 963–74, which argues that the much-lamented decline in electoral turnout rates after the 1960s was largely due to the growth of the ineligible population.

18. Paul E. Meehl, "The Selfish Voter Paradox and the Thrown-Away Vote Argument," *American Political Science Review* 71 (March 1977): 11–30.

19. The classic statement of this view is that of Anthony Downs, whose best effort is: "The advantage of voting per se is that it makes democracy possible. If no one votes, then the system collapses because no government is chosen. We assume that the citizens of a democracy subscribe to its principles and therefore derive benefits from its continuance; hence they do not want it to collapse. For this reason they attach value to the act of voting per se and receive a return from it." Downs, *An Economic Theory of Democracy* (New York: Harper, 1957), 261–62. See also John A. Ferejohn and Morris P. Fiorina, "The Paradox of Not Voting: A Decision Theoretic Analysis," *American Political Science Review* 68 (June 1974): 525–46; and William H. Riker and Peter C. Ordeshook, "A Theory of the Calculus of Voting," *American Political Science Review* 62 (March 1968): 25–42. For a perspective critical of turnout explanations based on rational calculations of voters' personal utility, see Donald P. Green and Ian Shapiro, *Pathologies of Rational Choice Theory* (New Haven, CT: Yale University Press, 1994), 47–71; and Raymond E. Wolfinger, "The Rational Citizen Faces Election Day," in *Elections at Home and Abroad: Essays in Honor of Warren E. Miller*, eds. M. Kent Jennings and Thomas E. Mann (Ann Arbor: University of Michigan Press, 1994), 71–91. Wolfinger quotes Gary Jacobson: "It's the California model; people vote because it makes them feel good" (p. 84).

20. See Rosenstone and Hansen, *Mobilization, Participation, and Democracy in America*, 23, 156–58.

21. Kay Lehman Schlozman, Sidney Verba, and Henry E. Brady, "Participation's Not a Paradox: The View from American Activists," *British Journal of Political Science* 25 (January 1995): 1–36, at 32.

22. Jan E. Leighley and Jonathan Nagler, *Who Votes Now? Demographics, Issues, Inequality, and Turnout in the United States* (Princeton: Princeton University Press, 2013).

23. This is one of the most venerable and most secure generalizations in the entire literature of voting behavior studies. See Angus Campbell, Philip E. Converse, Warren E. Miller, and Donald E. Stokes, *The American Voter* (New York: Wiley, 1960), 120–34; and Warren E. Miller and J. Merrill Shanks, *The New American Voter* (Cambridge, MA: Harvard University Press, 1996), 117–50. For variations on this interpretation, see Arthur S. Goldberg, "Social Determination and Rationality as a Basis of Party Identification," *American Political Science Review* 63 (March 1969): 5–25; Morris P. Fiorina, *Retrospective Voting in American National Elections* (New Haven, CT: Yale University Press, 1981), 89–90; Donald Green, Bradley Palmquist, and Eric Schickler, *Partisan Hearts and Minds: Political Parties and the Social Identities of Voters* (New Haven, CT: Yale University Press, 2004); Larry M. Bartels, "Partisanship and Voting Behavior, 1952–1996," *American Journal of Political Science* 44 (January 2000): 35–50, argues that "[i]n the current political environment, as much or more than at any other time in the past half-century, 'the strength and direction of party identification are facts of central importance' in accounting for the voting behavior of the American electorate" (p. 44; quotation from Campbell et al., *The American Voter*, 121).

24. William H. Flanigan and Nancy H. Zingale, *Political Behavior of the American Electorate*, 8th ed. (Washington, DC: CQ Press, 1994), give findings on the timing of voters' decisions: "In all recent elections the independents and weak partisans were more likely to make up their minds during the campaign, while strong partisans characteristically made their decisions by the end of the conventions" (p. 162). A study of voters who waited until the last two weeks before the election to choose a candidate found that "late deciders . . . are less interested in the political outcome, less subject to conventional political forces, and far less predictable than other voters." J. David Gopoian and Sissie Hadjiharalambous, "Late-Deciding Voters in Presidential Elections," *Political Behavior* 16 (March 1994): 55–78, at 76.

25. Earlier research did not differentiate among the various sorts of independents and characterized the entire population of independents as comparatively uninvolved in politics, less interested, less concerned,

and less knowledgeable than party identifiers. These generalizations hold better for the truly nonpartisan subset of "pure" independents (i.e., people who do not "lean" toward one party or the other). See Campbell et al., *The American Voter*, 143; Bernard Berelson, Paul F. Lazarsfeld, and William N. McPhee, *Voting* (Chicago: University of Chicago Press, 1954), 25–27; and Bruce E. Keith, David B. Magleby, Candice J. Nelson, Elizabeth Orr, Mark C. Westlye, and Raymond E. Wolfinger, *The Myth of the Independent Voter* (Berkeley: University of California Press, 1992), 65–67.

26. Berelson, Lazarsfeld, and McPhee, *Voting*, 215–33; John R. Zaller, *The Nature and Origins of Mass Opinion* (New York: Cambridge University Press, 1992). George Belknap and Angus Campbell state that "for many people Democratic or Republican attitudes regarding foreign policy result from conscious or unconscious adherence to a perceived party line rather than from influences independent of party identification." Belknap and Campbell, "Political Party Identification and Attitudes toward Foreign Policy," *Public Opinion Quarterly* 15 (Winter 1951–52): 601–23, at 623. See also Robert Huckfeldt, Paul E. Johnson, and John Sprague, "Political Environments, Political Dynamics, and the Survival of Disagreement," *Journal of Politics* 64 (February 2002): 1–21.

27. Many voting studies contain substantial discussions of this subject. For a recent summary, see Edward S. Greenberg, ed., *Political Socialization* (New York: Aldine Transaction, 2009). V. O. Key, *Public Opinion and American Democracy* (New York: Knopf, 1961), 293–314, sums up in these words: "Children acquire early in life a feeling of party identification; they have sensitive antennae and since they are imitative animals, soon take on the political color of their family" (p. 294). See also Fred I. Greenstein, *Children and Politics* (New Haven, CT: Yale University Press, 1965), chapter 4. In a later work, Paul R. Abramson presents an interesting discussion of this familial link and the forces that later play against it; see *Generational Change in American Politics* (Lexington, MA: Lexington Books, 1975), esp. chapters 3 and 4. See also Richard G. Niemi and M. Kent Jennings, "Issues and Inheritance in the Formation of Party Identification," *American Journal of Political Science* 35 (November 1991): 970–88.

28. "People are more likely to associate with people like themselves—alike in political complexion as well as social position." Berelson, Lazarsfeld, and McPhee, *Voting*, 83. An important recent study of the polarization resulting from this tendency is Lilliana Mason, *Uncivil Agreement: How Politics Became Our Identity* (Chicago: University of Chicago Press, 2018). See also Robert Huckfeldt and John Sprague, "Networks in Context: The Social Flow of Political Information," *American Political Science Review* 81 (December 1987): 1197–216.

29. Paul F. Lazarsfeld, Bernard Berelson, and Hazel Gaudet, *The People's Choice* (New York: Duell, Sloan and Pearce, 1944), 16–28.

30. Green, Palmquist and Schickler, *Partisan Hearts and Minds*.

31. Alan I. Abramowitz and Steven Webster, "The Rise of Negative Partisanship and the Nationalization of U.S. Elections in the 21st Century," *Electoral Studies* (March 2016): 12–22.

32. Angus Campbell and Homer C. Cooper, *Group Differences in Attitudes and Votes* (Ann Arbor: University of Michigan Press, 1956); Julian L. Woodward and Elmo Roper, "Political Activities of American Citizens," *American Political Science Review* (December 1950): 872–75; Key, *Public Opinion and American Democracy*, 99–120, 121–81; Berelson, Lazarsfeld and McPhee, *Voting*, 54–76; Robert Axelrod, "Where the Votes Come From: An Analysis of Electoral Coalitions, 1952–1968," *American Political Science Review* 66 (March 1972): 11–20; Axelrod, "Presidential Election Coalitions in 1984," *American Political Science Review* 80 (March 1986): 281–84; Robert A. Jackson and Thomas M. Carsey, "Group Components of U.S. Presidential Voting Across the States," *Political Behavior* 21 (June 1999): 123–51; Miller and Shanks, *The New American Voter*, 212–82; Gary Miller and Norman Schofield, "The Transformation of the Republican and Democratic Party Coalitions in the U.S.," *Perspectives on Politics* (September 2008): 433–50. See also table 2.3.

33. See Earl Black and Merle Black, *Politics and Society in the South* (Cambridge, MA: Harvard University Press, 1987); Raymond E. Wolfinger and Michael G. Hagen, "Republican Prospects: Southern Comfort," *Public Opinion* 8 (October/November 1985): 8–13; Earl Black and Merle Black, *The Rise of Southern Republicans* (Cambridge, MA: Harvard University Press, 2002); David Lublin, *The Republican South: Democratization and Partisan Change* (Princeton: Princeton University Press, 2004); and Byron E. Shafer and Richard Johnston, *The End of Southern Exceptionalism: Class, Race, and Partisan Change in the Postwar South* (Cambridge, MA: Harvard University Press, 2006). For an account explaining how these changes made an impact on Congress, see Nelson W. Polsby, *How Congress Evolves: Social Bases of Institutional Change* (New York: Oxford University Press, 2004).

34. See C. Vann Woodward, *The Strange Career of Jim Crow* (New York: Oxford University Press, 1966); and Woodward, *Origins of the New South* (Baton Rouge: Louisiana State University Press, 1951).

35. Nicholas Lemann, *The Promised Land* (New York: Knopf, 1991), 6.

36. James Q. Wilson, *Negro Politics* (Glencoe, IL: Free Press, 1960); Nancy Weiss, *Farewell to the Party of Lincoln* (Princeton: Princeton University Press, 1983), esp. 209–35; Eric Schickler, *Racial Realignment: The Transformation of American Liberalism, 1932–1965* (Princeton: Princeton University Press, 2016). Republican presidential nominee Barry Goldwater, who opposed the Civil Rights Act of 1964,

intensified the Democratic loyalties of black voters, who voted Democratic at about a two-to-one rate from the 1930s until 1960 and at an eight-to-one rate from 1964 onward. See Edward G. Carmines and James A. Stimson, *Issue Evolution: Race and the Transformation of American Politics* (Princeton: Princeton University Press, 1989).

37. George H. Mayer, *The Republican Party, 1854–1966*, 2nd ed. (New York: Oxford University Press, 1967), 221–71.

38. Jessica L. Lavariega Monforti, "Inevitable Change: A New Look at Cubans and Cuban-Americans," in *Minority Voting in the United States*, eds. Kyle J. Kreider and Thomas J. Baldino (Santa Barbara, CA: Praeger, 2015), 270–91.

39. See David Hackett Fischer, *Albion's Seed: Four British Folkways in America* (New York: Oxford University Press, 1989), 17; Steven Erie, *Rainbow's End: Irish-Americans and the Dilemmas of Urban Machine Politics, 1840–1985* (Berkeley: University of California Press, 1988), 25–28; Duane Lockard, *New England State Politics* (Princeton: Princeton University Press, 1959); Robert A. Dahl, *Who Governs? Democracy and Power in an American City* (New Haven, CT: Yale University Press, 1961), 33–51, 216–17; Elmer E. Cornwell, "Party Absorption of Ethnic Groups: The Case of Providence, R.I.," *Social Forces* 38 (March 1960): 205–10; and J. Joseph Huthmacher, *Massachusetts People and Politics* (Cambridge, MA: Harvard University Press, 1959), 118–26.

40. Samuel Lubell, *The Future of American Politics* (New York: Harper, 1951), 129–57; Willi Paul Adams, *The German-Americans: An Ethnic Experience*, translated and adapted by LaVern J. Rippley and Eberhard Reichmann (New York: Max Kade German-American Center, 1993).

41. Drew DeSilver, "The Politics of American Generations: How Age Affects Attitudes and Voting Behavior," Pew Research Center, July 9, 2014, http://www.pewresearch.org/fact-tank/2014/07/09/the-politics-of-american-generations-how-age-affects-attitudes-and-voting-behavior. For more on political socialization, see M. Kent Jennings and Laura Stoker, "Of Time and the Development of Partisan Polarization," *American Journal of Political Science* 52 (July 2008): 619–35.

42. David A. Hopkins, "Youthful Donkeys and Elderly Elephants: Roots of the New Generation Gap," paper presented at the Annual Meetings of the American Political Science Association, Boston, MA, August 29–September 1, 2018.

43. A notable study developing the implications of this notion is Downs's classic, *An Economic Theory of Democracy*.

44. Alan I. Abramowitz, *The Disappearing Center: Engaged Citizens, Polarization, and American Democracy* (New Haven, CT: Yale University Press, 2010).

45. Alan I. Abramowitz and Kyle L. Saunders, "Ideological Realignment in the U.S. Electorate," *Journal of Politics* 60 (August 1998): 634–52; Marc J. Hetherington, "Resurgent Mass Partisanship: The Role of Elite Polarization," *American Political Science Review* 95 (September 2001): 619–31.

46. See Hazel Gaudet Erskine, "The Polls: The Informed Public," *Public Opinion Quarterly* 26 (Winter 1962): 669–77; Hadley Cantril and Mildred Strunk, *Public Opinion, 1935–46* (Princeton: Princeton University Press, 1951). In light of this and later work, Philip E. Converse was able to conclude: "Surely the most familiar fact to arise from sample surveys in all countries is that popular levels of information about public affairs are, from the point of view of the informed observer, astonishingly low." Converse, "Public Opinion and Voting Behavior," in *Handbook of Political Science*, eds. Fred I. Greenstein and Nelson W. Polsby (Reading, MA: Addison-Wesley, 1975), volume 4, 75–169, at 79. See also Michael X. Delli Carpini and Scott Keeter, *What Americans Know about Politics and Why It Matters* (New Haven, CT: Yale University Press, 1996); and Philip E. Converse, "Assessing the Capacity of Mass Electorates," *Annual Review of Political Science* 3 (June 2000): 331–53.

47. Campbell et al., *The American Voter*, 182; Converse, "Public Opinion and Voting Behavior."

48. Campbell et al., *The American Voter*, 264. Zaller, *The Nature and Origins of Mass Opinion*, confirms these findings. He shows that the greater the level of political awareness, the more likely people are to possess "cueing messages" that help them filter out information contrary to their existing viewpoint on a given issue. Thus greater awareness results in an increasing ratio of ideologically consistent to inconsistent considerations governing opinion formation. This means that more aware liberals, for example, are more likely to support liberal positions (pp. 100–101). The implications for partisan change are clear: political awareness leads to stability in issue preferences and discourages change. Political inattentiveness, conversely, leads to unstable issue preferences and is therefore more likely to lead to partisan change.

49. Philip E. Converse, "Information Flow and the Stability of Partisan Attitudes," *Public Opinion Quarterly* 26 (Winter 1962): 578–99; Zaller, *The Nature and Origins of Mass Opinion*, 252–53.

50. Keith et al., *The Myth of the Independent Voter*.

51. Arthur H. Miller, Warren E. Miller, Alden S. Raine, and Thad A. Brown, "A Majority Party in Disarray: Policy Polarization in the 1972 Election," *American Political Science Review* 70 (September 1976): 753–78, at 760. See also Jeane Kirkpatrick, "Representation in the American National Conventions:

The Case of 1972," *British Journal of Political Science* 5 (July 1975): 265–322; and Kirkpatrick, *The New Presidential Elite* (New York: Russell Sage Foundation, 1976).

52. Erika Franklin Fowler, Travis N. Ridout, and Michael M. Franz, "Political Advertising in 2016: The Presidential Election as Outlier?" *The Forum* 14 (December 2016): 445–69.

53. Gary C. Jacobson, *The Electoral Origins of Divided Government* (Boulder, CO: Westview Press, 1990), 125. For a detailed discussion of the relationship between presidential popularity and economic performance, see Richard A. Brody, *Assessing the President: The Media, Elite Opinion, and Popular Support* (Stanford, CA: Stanford University Press, 1991), 91–103; for a study of the effects of economic conditions on presidential vote choice, see Richard Nadeau and Michael S. Lewis-Beck, "National Economic Voting in U.S. Presidential Elections," *Journal of Politics* 63 (February 2001): 159–81.

54. Marjorie Connelly, "How Americans Voted: A Political Portrait," *New York Times*, November 7, 2004, sec. 4, 4.

55. Campbell et al., *The American Voter*, 148.

56. V. O. Key Jr., with the assistance of Milton C. Cummings Jr., *The Responsible Electorate: Rationality in Presidential Voting, 1936–1960* (Cambridge, MA: Harvard University Press, 1966). This was the finding that led Key to his famous remark: "The perverse and unorthodox argument of this little book is that voters are not fools" (p. 7).

57. Charles H. Franklin, "Issue Preferences, Socialization and the Evaluation of Party Identification," *American Journal of Political Science* 28 (August 1984): 459–75.

58. The degree of aggregate stability in the electorate over time, and the sensitivity of the overall distribution of party identification to the performance of incumbent officeholders, is a matter of some dispute among scholars. See Donald Green, Bradley Palmquist, and Eric Schickler, "Macropartisanship: A Replication and Critique," *American Political Science Review* 92 (December 1998): 883–99; and Robert S. Erikson, Michael B. MacKuen, and James A. Stimson, "What Moves Macropartisanship? A Reply to Green, Palmquist, and Schickler," *American Political Science Review* 92 (December 1998): 901–12.

59. Janet M. Box-Steffensmeier and Renee M. Smith, "The Dynamics of Aggregate Partisanship," *American Political Science Review* 90 (September 1996): 567–80.

60. Franklin, "Issue Preferences, Socialization, and the Evaluation of Party Identification," 474.

61. Fiorina, *Retrospective Voting in American National Elections*, 84.

62. Donald R. Kinder and D. Roderick Kiewiet, "Sociotropic Politics: The American Case," *British Journal of Political Science* 11 (April 1981): 129–61; Douglas A. Hibbs Jr., with the assistance of R. Douglas Rivers and Nicholas Vasilatos, "The Dynamics of Political Support for American Presidents among Occupational and Partisan Groups," *American Journal of Political Science* 26 (May 1982): 312–32.

63. Converse, "The Nature of Belief Systems in Mass Publics"; Philip E. Converse and Gregory B. Markus, "Plus Ça Change: The New CPS Election Study Panel," *American Political Science Review* 73 (March 1979): 18–30. In view of the resistance to change of individual voters and the fact that nevertheless in aggregate there are changes, it is worth considering the idea that change occurs through processes by which old voters are replaced by new. V. O. Key Jr. also supported a mobilization-of-new-voters interpretation in "A Theory of Critical Elections," *Journal of Politics* 17 (February 1955): 3–18. Kristi Andersen, *The Creation of a Democratic Majority, 1928–1936* (Chicago: University of Chicago Press, 1979), argues that "the surge in the Democratic vote in 1932 and 1936 came primarily from newly mobilized groups" (p. 69): those who came of political age in the 1920s but did not vote until 1928, 1932, or 1936, and those who came of age between 1928 and 1936. On the other side, see the intriguing arguments for opinion change by individual voters in Robert S. Erikson and Kent L. Tedin, "The 1928–1936 Partisan Realignment: The Case for the Conversion Hypothesis," *American Political Science Review* 75 (December 1981): 951–62.

64. Donald R. Kinder, "Diversity and Complexity in American Public Opinion," in *Political Science: The State of the Discipline*, ed. Ada W. Finifter (Washington, DC: American Political Science Association, 1983), 389–425, at 410 (including footnote; emphasis in original).

65. Pew Research Center, "2016 Party Identification Detailed Tables," September 13, 2016, http://www.people-press.org/2016/09/13/2016-party-identification-detailed-tables.

66. See Martin P. Wattenberg, *The Decline of American Political Parties, 1952–1996* (Cambridge, MA: Harvard University Press, 1998).

67. Keith et al., *The Myth of the Independent Voter*, 13.

68. Pew Research Center, "Trends in Party Identification, 1939–2014," April 7, 2015, http://www.people-press.org/interactives/party-id-trend. Partisan independents—leaners—vote their party preferences less frequently than strong party identifiers but more frequently than weak party identifiers, and pure independents do not vote very much at all. See Keith et al., *The Myth of the Independent Voter*, 47–51, 68.

69. Samara Klar and Yanna Krupnikov, *Independent Politics: How American Disdain for Parties Leads to Political Inaction* (New York: Cambridge University Press, 2016).

70. Converse, "The Role of Belief Systems in Mass Publics"; Kinder, "Diversity and Complexity in American Public Opinion"; Green, Palmquist, and Schickler, *Partisan Hearts and Minds*.

71. Connelly, "How Americans Voted"; CNN, "Election Center 2008: Exit Polls," http://www.cnn.com/ELECTION/2008/results/polls/#USP00p1.

72. CNN, "Election Center 2016: Exit Polls," https://www.cnn.com/election/2016/results/exit-polls.

73. Larry M. Bartels, "The Irrational Electorate," *Wilson Quarterly*, Autumn 2008, https://wilsonquarterly.com/quarterly/fall-2008-the-glory-and-the-folly/the-irrational-electorate.

CHAPTER 2: GROUPS

1. For an elaboration of this argument, see Matt Grossmann and David A. Hopkins, *Asymmetric Politics: Ideological Republicans and Group Interest Democrats* (New York: Oxford University Press, 2016).

2. CNN, "Election Center 2008: Exit Polls," http://www.cnn.com/ELECTION/2008/results/polls/#USP00p1; "Election Center 2012: Exit Polls," http://www.cnn.com/election/2012/results/race/president; "Election 2016: Exit Polls," https://www.cnn.com/election/2016/results/exit-polls.

3. This table is an adaptation and update of the work of Robert Axelrod's research on the electoral coalitions of the parties. See Robert Axelrod, "Where the Votes Come From: An Analysis of Electoral Coalitions, 1952–1968," *American Political Science Review* 66 (March 1972): 11–20; Axelrod, "Communication," *American Political Science Review* 68 (June 1974): 717–20; Axelrod, "Communication," *American Political Science Review* 72 (June 1978): 622–24; Axelrod, "Communication," *American Political Science Review* 76 (June 1982): 393–96; and Axelrod, "Presidential Election Coalitions in 1984," *American Political Science Review* 80 (March 1986): 281–84.

4. Harold W. Stanley, William J. Bianco, and Richard G. Niemi, "Partisanship and Group Support over Time: A Multivariate Analysis," *American Political Science Review* 80 (September 1986): 969–76.

5. *Gallup Poll Monthly* 374 (November 1996): 17–20.

6. Marjorie Connelly, "How Americans Voted: A Political Portrait," *New York Times*, November 7, 2004, sec. 4, 4.

7. Axelrod, "Communication," June 1982, 395; Axelrod, "Presidential Election Coalitions in 1984"; Connelly, "How Americans Voted."

8. Antonio Gonzalez and Steven Ochoa, "The Latino Vote in 2008: Trends and Characteristics," William C. Velasquez Institution, Los Angeles, 2009, http://www.wcvi.org/data/election/wcvi_nov2008nationalanalysis_121808.pdf.

9. Secular Student Alliance, "Rise of the Godless," March 1, 2009, http://www.secularstudents.org/godless.

10. David A. Hopkins, *Red Fighting Blue: How Geography and Electoral Rules Polarize American Politics* (New York: Cambridge University Press, 2017).

11. See Raymond A. Bauer, Ithiel de Sola Pool, and Lewis Anthony Dexter, *American Business and Public Policy* (New York: Atherton Press, 1963), 323–99, esp. 373. A similar argument is made in John R. Wright, "PACs, Contributions, and Roll Calls: An Organizational Perspective," *American Political Science Review* 79 (June 1985): 400–14.

12. Richard L. Berke, "Trade Vote Effect May Ebb Over Time," *New York Times*, November 23, 1993, sec. 1, 23; R. W. Apple Jr., "Unions Faltering in Reprisals against Trade Pact Backers," *New York Times*, February 21, 1994, A1.

13. Marjorie Connelly, "Portrait of the Electorate: Who Voted for Whom in the House," *New York Times*, November 13, 1994, sec. 1, 24.

14. See Seymour M. Lipset, Paul F. Lazarsfeld, Allen H. Barton, and Juan Linz, "The Psychology of Voting: An Analysis of Political Behavior," in *Handbook of Social Psychology*, ed. Gardner Lindzey (Cambridge, MA: Addison-Wesley, 1954).

15. Angus Campbell, Philip E. Converse, Warren E. Miller, and Donald E. Stokes, *The American Voter* (New York: Wiley, 1960), 483–94.

16. Everett Carll Ladd, "The Brittle Mandate: Electoral Dealignment and the 1980 Presidential Election," *Political Science Quarterly* 96 (Spring 1981): 1–25, at 16.

17. Connelly, "How Americans Voted"; CNN, "Election Center 2012: Exit Polls"; CNN, "Election 2016: Exit Polls."

18. Karen M. Kaufmann, "Culture Wars, Secular Realignment, and the Gender Gap in Party Identification," *Political Behavior* 24 (September 2002): 283–307, at 291.

19. Herbert F. Weisberg, "The Demographics of a New Voting Gap: Marriage Differences in American Voting," *Public Opinion Quarterly* 51 (Autumn 1987): 335–43; Eric Plutzer and Michael McBurnett, "Family Life and American Politics: The 'Marriage Gap' Reconsidered," *Public Opinion Quarterly* 55 (Spring 1991): 113–27; Laura Stoker and M. Kent Jennings, "Political Similarity and Influence Between Husbands and Wives," in *The Social Logic of Politics*, ed. Alan S. Zuckerman (Philadelphia: Temple University Press, 2005), 51–74.

20. Barbara Norrander and Clyde Wilcox, "The Gender Gap in Ideology," *Political Behavior* 30 (December 2008): 503–23, at 521.

21. Kathleen A. Frankovic, "Sex and Politics: New Alignments, Old Issues," *PS: Political Science and Politics* 15 (Summer 1982): 439–48; Karen M. Kaufmann and John R. Petrocik, "The Changing Politics of American Men: Understanding the Sources of the Gender Gap," *American Journal of Political Science* 43 (July 1999): 864–87.

22. Kaufmann, "Culture Wars."

23. Pamela Johnston Conover and Virginia Sapiro, "Gender, Feminist Consciousness, and War," *American Journal of Political Science* 37 (November 1993): 1079–1099; Carole Kennedy Chaney, R. Michael Alvarez, and Jonathan Nagler, "Explaining the Gender Gap in U.S. Presidential Elections, 1980–1992," *Political Research Quarterly* 51 (June 1998): 311–39.

24. Indeed, some of the most vocal groups have no membership at all and exist only as lobbying organizations. See Jeffrey M. Berry, *Lobbying for the People: The Political Behavior of Public Interest Groups* (Princeton: Princeton University Press, 1977), 186; and Robert D. Putnam, *Bowling Alone: The Collapse and Revival of American Community* (New York: Simon and Schuster, 2000), 49–64.

25. Rush Limbaugh, "EIB Numbers Shooting Through the Roof: 26 Million and Climbing," April 27, 2017, https://www.rushlimbaugh.com/daily/2017/04/27/eib-audience-numbers-shoot-through-the-roof-26-million-and-growing/; "Why Americans Are Mad: An Interview with Rush Limbaugh," *Policy Review* 61 (Summer 1992): 47; "Behind the Bestsellers," *Publishers Weekly*, October 4, 1993, 14.

26. "Corporate Political Action Committees Are Less Oriented to Republicans Than Expected," *Congressional Quarterly*, April 8, 1978, 849–54; Theodore J. Eismeier and Philip H. Pollock III, *Business, Money and the Rise of Corporate PACs in American Elections* (New York: Quorum Books, 1988), 79–96.

27. Thomas J. Rudolph, "Corporate and Labor PAC Contributions in House Elections: Measuring the Effects of Majority Party Status," *Journal of Politics* 61 (February 1999): 195–206; Gary C. Jacobson, *The Politics of Congressional Elections*, 6th ed. (New York: Longman, 2004), 63–75; Federal Election Commission, "PAC Contributions to Candidates, 1993–2009," http://www.fec.gov/press/press2010/20100406Pary_Files/2contribhistory2009.pdf.

28. Edwin M. Epstein, "Corporations and Labor Unions in Electoral Politics," *Annals of the American Academy of Political and Social Science* 425 (May 1976): 49.

29. Ibid., 50. For more on PACs, see Kevin Coroneos, "PACing a Punch: The Rise in Power of Super PACs and the 2016 Election," *Political Analysis* 16 (December 2015): article 3; David Petechuk, *American Politics Today: PACs, Super PACs and Fundraising* (Eldorado Ink, 2016); Conor M. Dowling and Michael G. Miller, *Super PAC!: Money, Elections and Voters after Citizens United* (New York: Routledge, 2016).

30. Memorandum Opinion on Motion for Preliminary Injunction, *Carey v. FEC* (2011), at 13.

31. *Citizens United v. FEC* (2010), at 50.

32. *McCutcheon et al. v. FEC* (2013), at 40.

33. These and other 2016 totals cited in this section are from Opensecrets.org, "2016 Presidential Race," https://www.opensecrets.org/pres16.

34. Niv M. Sultan, "Election 2016: Trump's Free Media Kept Cost Down, But Fewer Donors Provided More of the Cash," Opensecrets.org, April 13, 2017, https://www.opensecrets.org/news/2017/04/election-2016-trump-fewer-donors-provided-more-of-the-cash.

35. Opensecrets.org, "2012 Presidential Race," https://www.opensecrets.org/pres12.

36. This issue is also about money, mainly restricting the amount of money litigants can extract from business enterprises.

37. There are, of course, numerous ways of gaining access to public officials, but participation in their original selection is the primary avenue of access used by political parties. Our interpretation of parties is based on a rich literature: for example, Pendleton Herring, *The Politics of Democracy: American Parties in Action*, rev. ed. (New York: W. W. Norton, 1965); V. O. Key Jr., *Politics, Parties and Pressure Groups*, 5th ed. (New York: Crowell, 1964); Anthony Downs, *An Economic Theory of Democracy* (New York: Harper, 1957); Leon D. Epstein, *Political Parties in the American Mold* (Madison: University of Wisconsin Press, 1986); and a burgeoning literature on state and local political party organizations. See especially David B. Truman, *The Governmental Process* (New York: Knopf, 1971), 262–87; Malcolm E. Jewell and Sarah M. Morehouse, *Political Parties and Elections in American States*, 9th ed. (Washington, DC: CQ Press, 2001); David R. Mayhew, *Placing Parties in American Politics* (Princeton: Princeton University Press, 1986); and Larry J. Sabato and Bruce Larson, *The Party's Just Begun: Shaping Political Parties for America's Future*, 2nd ed. (New York: Longman, 2002).

38. See John F. Bibby, "Party Renewal in the National Republican Party," in *Party Renewal in America*, ed. Gerald M. Pomper (New York: Praeger, 1980), 102–15; and Cornelius P. Cotter and John F. Bibby, "Institutional Development of Parties and the Thesis of Party Decline," *Political Science Quarterly* 95 (Spring 1980): 1–27.

39. Herbert McClosky, Paul J. Hoffman, and Rosemary O'Hara, "Issue Conflict and Consensus among Party Leaders and Followers," *American Political Science Review* 54 (June 1960): 406–27; Jeane Kirkpatrick, "Representation in the American National Conventions: The Case of 1972," *British Journal of Political Science* 5 (July 1975): 265–322. Differences between the party elites have increased substantially since 1972; see Warren E. Miller and M. Kent Jennings, *Parties in Transition: A Longitudinal Study of Party Elites and Party Supporters* (New York: Russell Sage Foundation, 1986); and Marc J. Hetherington, "Resurgent Mass Partisanship: The Role of Elite Polarization," *American Political Science Review* 95 (September 2001): 619–31.

40. For varying assessments of mass polarization, see Morris P. Fiorina and Samuel J. Abrams, *Disconnect: The Breakdown in Representation in American Politics* (Norman: University of Oklahoma Press, 2012), and Alan I. Abramowitz, *The Disappearing Center: Engaged Citizens, Polarization and American Democracy* (New Haven, CT: Yale University Press, 2010).

41. The Supreme Court gives the national convention the right to regulate standards for admission to it, even overriding enactments of state legislatures on the subject of primary elections, and in this important respect national standards can be imposed on state party organizations. See *Cousins v. Wigoda*, 419 U.S. 477 (1975) and *Democratic Party of the U.S. et al. v. LaFollette et al.*, 450 U.S. 107 (1981). See also Nelson W. Polsby, *Consequences of Party Reform* (New York: Oxford University Press, 1983).

42. Paul S. Herrnson, "National Party Organizations at the Dawn of the Twenty-First Century," in *The Parties Respond: Changes in American Parties and Campaigns*, 4th ed., ed. L. Sandy Maisel (Cambridge, MA: Westview Press, 2002), 47–78.

43. Gregory Koger, Seth Masket and Hans Noel, "Partisan Webs: Information Exchange and Party Networks," *British Journal of Political Science* 39 (July 2009): 633–53.

44. Herbert F. Weisberg and David C. Kimball, "Attitudinal Correlates of the 1992 Presidential Vote," in *Democracy's Feast: Elections in America*, ed. Herbert F. Weisberg (Chatham, NJ: Chatham House, 1995), 104.

45. Institute of Politics, Kennedy School of Government, Harvard University, *Campaign for President: The Managers Look at 2016* (Lanham, MD: Rowman & Littlefield, 2017), 53.

46. Tara Golshan, "Did Jill Stein Voters Deliver Donald Trump the Presidency?" *Vox*, November 11, 2016, https://www.vox.com/policy-and-politics/2016/11/11/13576798/jill-stein-third-party-donald-trump-win.

47. See Dean Lacy and Quin Monson, "The Origins and Impact of Votes for Third-Party Candidates: A Case Study of the 1998 Minnesota Gubernatorial Election," *Political Research Quarterly* 55 (June 2002): 409–37.

48. Daniel Mazmanian argued that third-party candidates do best in years in which there is an intensely conflictual issue on the political agenda, suggesting that focusing discontent and raising issues are, for these candidates, functions most profitably performed in unison. Mazmanian, *Third Parties in Presidential Elections* (Washington, DC: Brookings Institution, 1974), 28.

49. See Paul R. Abramson, John H. Aldrich, Phil Paolino, and David W. Rohde, "Third-Party and Independent Candidates: Wallace, Anderson, and Perot," *Political Science Quarterly* 110 (Fall 1995): 349–67.

CHAPTER 3: RULES AND RESOURCES

1. The unit rule is not prescribed in the Constitution or by federal law. Instead, it is the result of individual state action that provides, in all states except Maine and Nebraska, that electors for party nominees are grouped together and elected en bloc on a "general ticket," such that a vote for one elector is a vote for all the electors on that ticket, with a plurality vote electing all electors for the state.

2. Campaign visit figures from National Popular Vote, "Two-Thirds of Presidential Campaign Is in Just Six States," November 2016, https://www.nationalpopularvote.com/campaign-events-2016.

3. Important legislation affecting money in politics includes the Federal Election Campaign Act of 1971, the Federal Election Campaign Act Amendments of 1974 (2 USC 431), and, more recently, the Bipartisan Campaign Reform Act of 2002 (Pub. L. No. 107–155, 116 Stat. 81).

4. Federal Election Commission, "Statistical Summary of 24-Month Campaign Activity of the 2015–2016 Election Cycle," March 23, 2017, https://www.fec.gov/updates/statistical-summary-24-month-campaign-activity-2015-2016-election-cycle.

5. Ibid.

6. Herbert E. Alexander and Anthony Corrado, *Financing the 1992 Election* (Armonk, NY: M. E. Sharpe, 1995), 44–46.

7. Jodi Kantor and Nicholas Confessore, "Leading Role in Obama '08, But Backstage in '12," *New York Times*, July 15, 2012, A1.

8. Michael Cornfield, "Game-Changers: New Technology and the 2008 Presidential Election," in *The Year of Obama: How Barack Obama Won the White House*, ed. Larry J. Sabato (New York: Longman, 2009), 217.

9. Michael Toner, "The Impact of Federal Election Laws on the 2008 Presidential Election," in *The Year of Obama*, ed. Larry J. Sabato, 153–54.

10. Sam Stein and Jason Cherkis, "The Inside Story of How Bernie Sanders Became the Greatest Online Fundraiser in Political History," *Huffington Post*, June 28, 2017, https://www.huffingtonpost.com/entry/bernie-sanders-fundraising_us_59527587e4b02734df2d92c1.

11. Jonathan Allen and Amie Parnes, *Shattered: Inside Hillary Clinton's Doomed Campaign* (New York: Crown, 2017), 303.

12. Alexander and Corrado, *Financing the 1992 Election*, 69. See also Charles T. Royer, ed., *Campaign for President: The Managers Look at 1992* (Hollis, NH: Hollis Publishing Company, 1994), 83–84.

13. Richard Stevenson and Glen Justice, "Bush Took In $130.8 Million in Political Contributions in 2003," *New York Times*, January 8, 2004, A21.

14. "Obama Campaign Reveals Biggest Fundraisers around Election Day," CNN, March 2, 2013, http://politicalticker.blogs.cnn.com/2013/03/02/obama-campaign-reveals-biggest-donors-around-election-day.

15. Paul Blumenthal, "Obama Bundlers Raiser $55.5 Million for President's Re-Election," *Huffington Post*, October 15, 2011, http://www.huffingtonpost.com/2011/10/15/barack-obama- bundlers-55-million-dollars-re-election_n_1011877.html.

16. Shane Goldmacher, "Clinton Has Built the Biggest Big-Money Operation Ever," *Politico*, October 15, 2016, https://www.politico.com/story/2016/10/clinton-has-built-the-biggest-big-money-operation-ever-229831.

17. Federal Election Commission, "Public Funding of Presidential Elections," https://www.fec.gov/introduction-campaign-finance/understanding-ways-support-federal-candidates/presidential-elections/public-funding-presidential-elections.

18. Susan Page and Jill Lawrence, "White House Hopefuls, Activists Are Stirring," *USA Today*, February 8, 2006, 5A.

19. Center for Responsive Politics, "2016 Outside Spending, by Super PAC," https://www.opensecrets.org/outsidespending/summ.php?cycle=2016&chrt=V&disp=O&type=S.

20. Federal Election Commission, "Statistical Summary of 24-Month Campaign Activity of the 2015–2016 Election Cycle."

21. Libby Watson, "How Political Megadonors Can Give Almost $500,000 with a Single Check," Sunlight Foundation, June 1, 2016, https://sunlightfoundation.com/2016/06/01/how-political-megadonors-can-give-almost-500000-with-a-single-check.

22. Center for Responsive Politics, "2016 Outside Spending, by Race," https://www.opensecrets.org/outsidespending/summ.php?cycle=2016&disp=R&pty=N&type=A.

23. Brian Feldman, "15 Hours of Awkward, Uncut Ted Cruz Footage Was Uploaded to YouTube (by Ted Cruz)," *New York*, December 2, 2015, http://nymag.com/intelligencer/2015/12/ted-cruz-raw-and-uncut.html.

24. For a perspective critical of the alleged effects of campaign money on the political system, see Elizabeth Drew, *The Corruption of American Politics: What Went Wrong and Why* (Secaucus, NJ: Birch Lane Press, 1999).

25. See Edwin M. Epstein, "Corporations and Labor Unions in Electoral Politics," *Annals of the American Academy of Political and Social Science* 425 (May 1976): 33–58.

26. Herbert E. Alexander, *Financing the 1980 Election* (Lexington, MA: Lexington Books, 1983), 109.

27. Jim Rutenberg, "Nearing Record, Obama's Ad Effort Swamps McCain," *New York Times*, October 18, 2008, A1.

28. Kathleen Hall Jamieson, ed., *Electing the President, 2012: The Insiders' View* (Philadelphia: University of Pennsylvania Press, 2013), 145.

29. Ibid., 38.

30. Niv M. Sultan, "Election 2016: Trump's Free Media Helped Keep Cost Down, But Fewer Donors Provided More of the Cash," Center for Responsive Politics, April 13, 2017, https://www.opensecrets.org/news/2017/04/election-2016-trump-fewer-donors-provided-more-of-the-cash.

31. Philip Bump, "Assessing a Clinton Argument That the Media Helped to Elect Trump," *Washington Post*, September 12, 2017, https://www.washingtonpost.com/news/politics/wp/2017/09/12/assessing-a-clinton-argument-that-the-media-helped-to-elect-trump.

32. Herbert E. Alexander, "Financing the Parties and Campaigns," in *The Presidential Election and Transition, 1960–61*, ed. Paul T. David (Washington, DC: Brookings Institution, 1961), 119.

33. Robert G. Boatright, "Campaign Finance in the 2008 Election," in *The American Elections of 2008*, eds. Janet Box-Steffensmeier and Steven E. Schier (Lanham, MD: Rowman & Littlefield, 2009), 137–60, at 139.

34. Federal Election Commission, "Presidential Pre-Nomination Campaign Disbursements, March 31, 2012," http://www.fec.gov/press/bkgnd/pres_cf/pres_cf_odd_doc/presdisbursm42012.pdf.

35. Federal Election Commission, "Presidential Pre-Nomination Campaign Disbursements Through June 30, 2016," https://transition.fec.gov/press/summaries/2016/tables/presidential/PresCand2_2016_18m.pdf.

36. Roger Simon, "Turning Point," *U.S. News and World Report*, July 19, 2004, 34–75.

37. Edward Wyatt, "Clark Ending His Campaign after Poor Showing in South," *New York Times*, February 11, 2004, A25.

38. Michael Falcone, "Clinton Is Out $13 Million She Lent Campaign," *New York Times*, December 23, 2008, A16.

39. Philip Bump, "For What He Spent Per Delegate, Jeb Bush Could Have Bought 24 Trump Tower Apartments," *Washington Post*, July 20, 2016, https://www.washingtonpost.com/news/the-fix/wp/2016/07/20/how-much-each-republican-candidate-raised-for-every-vote-won.

40. For the details on the Forbes campaign, see Anthony Corrado, "Financing the 1996 Elections," 143–45; and William G. Mayer, "The Presidential Nominations," in *The Election of 1996: Reports and Interpretations*, ed. Gerald M. Pomper et al. (Chatham, NJ: Chatham House, 1997), 36–56.

41. John C. Green and Nathan S. Bigelow, "The 2000 Presidential Nominations: The Cost of Innovation," in *Financing the 2000 Election*, ed. David B. Magleby (Washington, DC: Brookings Institution, 2002), 55; Howard Kurtz and Ben White, "Forbes Signals He Will Withdraw," *Washington Post*, February 10, 2000, A6.

42. Mark Preston, "Romney Spending $85,000-Plus a Day on TV Ads," CNN, November 13, 2007, http://www.cnn.com/2007/POLITICS/11/13/romney.ads/index.html.

43. This information is now continuously available to the public on various websites such as Political Money Line, http://www.fecinfo.com.

44. *Buckley et al. v. Valeo et al.*, 424 U.S. 1 (1976). See also Daniel D. Polsby, "Buckley v. Valeo: The Special Nature of Political Speech," *Supreme Court Review*, 1976, 1–43.

45. Raymond J. La Raja, "Richer Parties, Better Politics? Party-Centered Campaign Finance Laws and American Democracy," *The Forum* 11 (October 2013): 313–33, at 314–15.

46. Adam Liptak, "Supreme Court Blocks Ban on Corporate Political Spending," *New York Times*, January 21, 2010, A1.

47. Institute of Politics, Kennedy School of Government, Harvard University, *Campaign for President: The Managers Look at 2016* (Lanham, MD: Rowman & Littlefield, 2017), 65.

48. See William L. Rivers, "The Correspondents after 25 Years," *Columbia Journalism Review* 1 (Spring 1962). "In 1960," he says, "57 percent of the daily newspapers reporting to the *Editor & Publisher* poll supported Nixon, and 16 percent supported Kennedy. In contrast, there are more than three times as many Democrats as there are Republicans among the Washington newspaper correspondents; slightly more than 32 percent are Democrats, and fewer than 10 percent are Republicans" (p. 5). See also S. Robert Lichter and Stanley Rothman, "Media and Business Elites," *Public Opinion* 4 (October/November 1981): 42–46, 59–60; and S. Robert Lichter, Stanley Rothman, and Linda S. Lichter, *The Media Elite* (Bethesda, MD: Adler and Adler, 1986).

49. Pew Research Center, "The State of the News Media, 2004: An Annual Report on American Journalism," May 23, 2004, http://people-press.org/reports/display.php3?ReportID=214. See also Lars Willnat and David H. Weaver, "The American Journalist in the Digital Age: Key Findings," School of Journalism, Indiana University, May 2014, http://archive.news.indiana.edu/releases/iu/2014/05/2013-american-journalist-key-findings.pdf.

50. Michael J. Robinson, "Just How Liberal Is the News? 1980 Revisited," *Public Opinion* 5 (February/March 1983): 55–60.

51. For a definitive, though fictitious, commentary, see Nathanael West, *Miss Lonelyhearts* (New York: Harcourt, Brace, 1933).

52. See Richard Brody and Catherine R. Shapiro, "A Reconsideration of the Rally Phenomenon in Public Opinion," in *Political Behavior Annual*, vol. 2, ed. Samuel Long (Boulder, CO: Westview Press, 1989); John E. Mueller, "Presidential Popularity from Truman to Johnson," *American Political Science Review* 64 (March 1970): 18–34; Kenneth N. Waltz, "Electoral Punishment and Foreign Policy Crises," in *Domestic Sources of Foreign Policy*, ed. James N. Rosenau (New York: Free Press, 1967), 263–93; and Richard A. Brody, *Assessing the President: The Media, Elite Opinion, and Popular Support* (Stanford, CA: Stanford University Press, 1991).

53. Amos Tversky and Daniel Kahneman, "Rational Choice and the Framing of Decisions," *Journal of Business* 59 (1986): 251–78.

54. Aaron Wildavsky and Karl Dake, "Theories of Risk Perception: Who Fears What and Why," *Daedalus* 119 (Fall 1990): 41–60; Aaron B. Wildavsky, *But Is It True? A Citizen's Guide to Environmental Health and Safety Issues* (Cambridge, MA: Harvard University Press, 1995); Christopher J. Bosso, "Setting the Agenda: Mass Media and the Discovery of Famine in Ethiopia," in *Manipulating Public Opinion: Essays on Public Opinion as a Dependent Variable*, eds. Michael Margolis and Gary A. Mauser (Pacific Grove, CA: Brooks/Cole, 1989), 153–74.

55. Joanne M. Miller and Jon A. Krosnick, "News Media Impact on the Ingredients of Presidential Evaluations: Politically Knowledgeable Citizens Are Guided by a Trusted Source," *American Journal of Political Science* 44 (April 2000): 301–15.

56. John R. Zaller, *The Nature and Origins of Mass Opinion* (New York: Cambridge University Press, 1992), 6–16.

57. See Theodore H. White, *The Making of the President, 1960* (New York: Atheneum, 1961), 333–38. Corroborative testimony is given by Benjamin C. Bradlee, *Conversations with Kennedy* (New York: Norton, 1975). On Barry Goldwater's press relations, see Charles Mohr, "Requiem for a Lightweight," *Esquire*, August 1968, 67–71, 121–22.

58. Timothy Crouse, *The Boys on the Bus* (New York: Random House, 1973), 189–90; Theodore H. White, *The Making of the President, 1972* (New York: Atheneum, 1973), 251–68. See also Jules Witcover, *The Resurrection of Richard Nixon* (New York: Putnam, 1970); and Joe McGinniss, *The Selling of the President, 1968* (New York: Trident Press, 1969).

59. Daron R. Shaw and Brian E. Roberts, "Campaign Events, the Media and the Prospects of Victory: The 1992 and 1996 U.S. Presidential Elections," *British Journal of Political Science* 30 (April 2000): 259–89.

60. Project for Excellence in Journalism, "Winning the Media Campaign," October 22, 2008, http://www.journalism.org/2008/10/22/winning-media-campaign/; Pew Research Center Journalism Project, "Winning the Media Campaign 2012," November 2, 2012, http://www.journalism.org/2012/11/02/winning-media-campaign-2012.

61. Thomas E. Patterson, "News Coverage of the 2016 General Election: How the Press Failed the Voters," Harvard University, December 7, 2016, https://shorensteincenter.org/news-coverage-2016-general-election.

62. Frank Luther Mott, *The News in America* (Cambridge, MA: Harvard University Press, 1952), 110; Edwin Emery and Henry L. Smith, *The Press and America* (Englewood Cliffs, NJ: Prentice Hall, 1954), 541ff.

63. Dave D'Alessio and Mike Allen, "Media Bias in Presidential Elections: A Meta-Analysis," *Journal of Communication* 50 (September 2000): 133–56, at 148–49.

64. Pew Research Center Journalism Project, "Winning the Media Campaign 2012."

65. Philip Rucker, "'I Would Be Your President': Clinton Blames Russia, FBI Chief for 2016 Election Loss," *Washington Post*, May 3, 2017, https://www.washingtonpost.com/politics/hillary-clinton-blames-russian-hackers-and-comey-for-2016-election-loss/2017/05/02/e62fef72-2f60-11e7-8674-437ddb6e813e_story.html.

66. Nate Silver, "The Comey Letter Probably Cost Clinton the 2016 Election," *FiveThirtyEight*, May 3, 2017, https://fivethirtyeight.com/features/the-comey-letter-probably-cost-clinton-the-election.

67. Aaron C. Weinschenk and Costas Panagopoulos, "The Dynamics of Voter Preferences in the 2016 Presidential Election," *The Forum* 16 (April 2018): 123–35, at 134.

68. Pew Research Center Journalism Project, "The 2016 Presidential Campaign—A News Event That's Hard to Miss," February 4, 2016, http://www.journalism.org/2016/02/04/the-2016-presidential-campaign-a-news-event-thats-hard-to-miss.

69. David L. Vancil and Sue D. Pendell, "The Myth of Viewer-Listener Disagreement in the First Kennedy-Nixon Debate," *Central States Speech Journal* 38 (1987): 16–27. See also James N. Druckman, "The Power of Television Images: The First Kennedy-Nixon Debate Revisited," *Journal of Politics* 65 (May 2003): 559–71.

70. Adam Nagourney, "Antiwar Stance Buoys Howard Dean in Iowa," *New York Times*, March 29, 2003: B12.

71. *Fox News Sunday*, June 12, 2011, transcript at http://www.foxnews.com/on-air/fox-news-sunday/print/transcript/tim-pawlenty-defends-his-economic-plan-attacks-obamneycare.

72. Adam Sorensen, "Tim Pawlenty's ObamneyCare Wimp Out," *Time*, December 7, 2011, http://content.time.com/time/specials/packages/article/0,28804,2101344_2100819_2100815,00.html.

73. Philip Rucker, "Rick Perry Says His Remarks on Immigration Were 'Inappropriate,'" *Washington Post*, September 28, 2011, https://www.washingtonpost.com/politics/rick-perry-says-his-remarks-on-immigration-were-inappropriate/2011/09/28/gIQAr25t5K_story.html.

74. Kevin Hechtkopf, "Rick Perry Fails to Remember What Agency He'd Get Rid of in GOP Debate," CBS News, November 10, 2011, http://www.cbsnews.com/news/rick-perry-fails-to-remember-what-agency-hed-get-rid-of-in-gop-debate.

75. C. Anthony Broh, "Horse Race Journalism," *Public Opinion Quarterly* 44 (Winter 1980): 514–29.

76. John Sides and Lynn Vavreck, *The Gamble: Choice and Chance in the 2012 Presidential Election* (Princeton: Princeton University Press, 2014).

77. Thomas E. Patterson, *Out of Order* (New York: Vintage Press, 1993); Joseph N. Capella and Kathleen Hall Jamieson, *Spiral of Cynicism: The Press and the Public Good* (New York: Oxford University Press, 1997); Stephen J. Farnsworth and S. Robert Lichter, *The Nightly News Nightmare: Media Coverage of Presidential Elections, 1988–2008*, 3rd ed. (Lanham, MD: Rowman & Littlefield, 2011).

78. Joshua Gillin, "John Kasich Calls Out Donald Trump's '1.8 Billion Worth of Free Media,'" *PolitiFact*, March 20, 2016, https://www.politifact.com/truth-o-meter/statements/2016/mar/20/john-kasich/john-kasich-calls-out-donald-trumps-18-billion-wor.

79. Institute of Politics, *Campaign for President: The Managers Look at 2016*, 51.

80. Lisa Richwine, "Republican Debate Sets TV Record with 24 Million Viewers," Reuters, August 7, 2015, https://www.reuters.com/article/us-usa-election-ratings/republican-debate-sets-tv-record-with-24-million-viewers-idUSKCN0QC20520150807.

81. Katy Tur, *Unbelievable: My Front-Row Seat to the Craziest Campaign in American History* (New York: Dey St., 2017), 100.

82. Milwaukee Republican Presidential Town Hall with Ted Cruz, CNN, March 29, 2016, transcript at http://cnnpressroom.blogs.cnn.com/2016/03/29/full-rush-transcript-sen-ted-cruz-cnn-milwaukee-republican-presidential-town-hall.

83. Institute of Politics, *Campaign for President: The Managers Look at 2016*, 181.

84. See the list of most popular websites as measured by Alexa at http://www.alexa.com/topsites/countries/US.

85. Brian Patrick Byrne, Matan Gilat, Jishai Evers, and E. J. Fox, "The Drudge Report: How Drudge Influenced 2015," *Vocativ*, January 4, 2016, https://www.vocativ.com/265619/the-drudge-report-report-the-definitive-guide-to-how-drudge-influenced-2015.

86. Jamieson, ed., *Electing the President, 2012*, 57.

87. See, e.g., Tim Craig and Michael D. Shear, "Allen Quip Provokes Outrage, Apology," *Washington Post*, August 15, 2006, A01; Michael D. Shear, "'Macaca Moment' Marks a Shift in Momentum," *Washington Post*, September 3, 2006, C01.

88. "Full Transcript of the Mitt Romney Secret Video," *Mother Jones*, September 19, 2012, http://www.motherjones.com/politics/2012/09/full-transcript-mitt-romney-secret-video.

89. Michael D. Shear and Michael Barbaro, "In Video Clip, Romney Calls 47% 'Dependent' and Overly Entitled," *New York Times*, The Caucus blog, September 17, 2012, http://thecaucus.blogs.nytimes.com/2012/09/17/romney-faults-those-dependent-on-government.

90. David Corn, "The Story behind the 47 Percent Video," *Mother Jones*, December 31, 2012, http://www.motherjones.com/politics/2012/12/story-behind-47-video.

91. Philip Rucker, "Romney: '47 Percent' Remarks Were 'Completely Wrong,'" *Washington Post*, October 5, 2012, http://www.washingtonpost.com/politics/decision2012/romney-47-percent-remarks-were-completely-wrong/2012/10/05/a346beaa-0ed8-11e2-a310-2363842b7057_story.html.

92. Jamieson, ed., *Electing the President, 2012*, 66–67.

93. Issie Lapowsky, "Eight Revealing Moments from the Second Day of Russia Hearings," *Wired*, November 1, 2017, https://www.wired.com/story/six-revealing-moments-from-the-second-day-of-russia-hearings.

94. Nelson W. Polsby, "The Democratic Nomination," in *The American Elections of 1980*, ed. Austin Ranney (Washington, DC: American Enterprise Institute, 1981), 37–60; and *The Gallup Opinion Index*, Report No. 183, December 1980, 51. For other examples, see Nelson W. Polsby, *Congress and the Presidency*, 4th ed. (Englewood Cliffs, NJ: Prentice Hall, 1986), 73; and Brody, *Assessing the President*.

95. Institute of Politics, Kennedy School of Government, Harvard University, *Campaign for President: The Managers Look at 2012* (Lanham, MD: Rowman & Littlefield, 2013), 199.

96. Christopher H. Achen and Larry M. Bartels have argued that when voters believe that conditions are worsening, they respond by punishing incumbents at the polls, even if public officials could not possibly be responsible for the causes of distress (such as a drought, or a series of shark attacks that ruined the vacation season for New Jersey resort towns in the summer of 1916). See Achen and Bartels, *Democracy for Realists: Why Elections Do Not Produce Representative Government* (Princeton: Princeton University Press, 2016).

97. Howard S. Bloom and H. Douglas Price, "Voter Response to Short-Run Economic Conditions: The Asymmetric Effect of Prosperity and Recession," *American Political Science Review* 69 (December 1975): 1240–54. For a more recent discussion of the relationship between economic performance, other events, and presidential popularity, see Brody, *Assessing the President*, 91–132; and Samuel Kernell, *Going Public: New Strategies of Presidential Leadership*, 4th ed. (Washington, DC: CQ Press, 2006).

98. Much of the material in this section is adapted from Nelson W. Polsby, *Political Promises: Essays and Commentary on American Politics* (New York: Oxford University Press, 1974), 156–59.

99. Ross K. Baker, "The Second Reagan Term," in *The Election of 1984: Reports and Interpretations*, ed. Gerald M. Pomper (Chatham, NJ: Chatham House, 1985), 150.

CHAPTER 4: THE NOMINATION PROCESS

1. Much of the historical discussion of the nomination process in this chapter is drawn from our own observations via the mass media, the personal observations of one of us who attended the Democratic National Conventions of 1960, 1968, 1972, and 1980, and the Republican National Conventions of 1964 and 1980, and a classic set of basic texts on American parties and elections, including Moisei Ostrogorski, *Democracy and the Party System in the United States* (New York: Macmillan, 1910); Charles Edward Merriam and Harold Foote Gosnell, *The American Party System: An Introduction to the Study of Political Parties in the United States*, rev. ed. (New York: Macmillan, 1929); Peter H. Odegard and E. Allen Helms, *American Politics: A Study in Political Dynamics* (New York: Harper & Brothers, 1938); Pendleton Herring, *The Politics of Democracy: American Parties in Action*, rev. ed. (New York: W. W. Norton, 1965); E. E. Schattschneider, *Party Government* (New York: Farrar and Rinehart, 1942); D. D. McKean, *Party and Pressure Politics* (Boston: Houghton Mifflin, 1949); V. O. Key Jr., *Politics, Parties and Pressure Groups*, 5th ed. (New York: Crowell, 1964); Edward McChesney Sait and H. R. Penniman, *Sait's American Parties and Elections*, 4th ed. (New York: Appleton-Century-Crofts, 1948); Austin Ranney and Willmoore Kendall, *Democracy and the American Party System* (New York: Harcourt Brace, 1956); William Goodman, *The Two-Party System in the United States* (Princeton: Van Nostrand, 1960); and Gerald M. Pomper, *Nominating the President: The Politics of Convention Choice*, 2nd ed. (Evanston, IL: Northwestern University Press, 1966). Other texts on party organization and presidential nominations that a student might find useful include Samuel J. Eldersveld, *Political Parties in American Society* (New York: Basic Books, 1982); Joel L. Fleishman, ed., *The Future of American Political Parties* (Englewood Cliffs, NJ: Prentice Hall, 1982); Howard Reiter, *Selecting the President* (Philadelphia: University of Pennsylvania Press, 1985); William J. Crotty and Gary C. Jacobson, *American Parties in Decline* (Boston: Little, Brown, 1980); Gerald M. Pomper, *Elections in America: Control and Influence in Democratic Politics*, rev. ed. (New York: Longman, 1980); Nelson W. Polsby, *Consequences of Party Reform* (New York: Oxford University Press, 1983); Everett Carll Ladd Jr., with Charles D. Hadley, *Transformations of the American Party System*, 2nd ed. (New York: Norton, 1978); Leon D. Epstein, *Political Parties in the American Mold* (Madison: University of Wisconsin Press, 1986); Austin Ranney, *Curing the Mischiefs of Faction: Party Reform in America* (Berkeley: University of California Press, 1975); William G. Mayer, ed., *In Pursuit of the White House: How We Choose Our Presidential Nominees* (Chatham, NJ: Chatham House, 1996); and Marty Cohen, David Karol, Hans Noel, and John Zaller, *The Party Decides: Presidential Nominations before and after Reform* (Chicago: University of Chicago Press, 2008).

2. See Gary D. Wekkin, *Democrat versus Democrat* (Columbia: University of Missouri Press, 1984); see also *Tashjian v. Republican Party of Connecticut*, 107 S. 544 (1986); Bruce E. Cain and Megan Mullin, "Competing for Attention and Votes: The Role of State Parties in Setting Presidential Nomination Rules," in *The Parties Respond: Changes in American Parties and Campaigns*, ed. L. Sandy Maisel (Boulder, CO: Westview Press, 2002), 99–120.

3. Boris Heersink, "The DNC Voted to Strip Superdelegates of Their Powers. Will It Matter for 2020?" *Washington Post*, September 4, 2018, https://www.washingtonpost.com/news/monkey-cage/wp/2018/09/04/the-dnc-voted-to-strip-superdelegates-of-their-powers-will-it-matter-for-2020.

4. Frank Newport and Joseph Carroll, "Key Election Trends from 2007," Gallup Organization, December 28, 2007, http://www.gallup.com/poll/103495/election-summary.aspx.

5. Institute of Politics, Kennedy School of Government, Harvard University, *Campaign for President: The Managers Look at 2012* (Lanham, MD: Rowman & Littlefield, 2013), 62–63, 66.

6. David A. Hopkins, "Televised Debates in Presidential Primaries," in *The Routledge Handbook of Primary Elections*, ed. Robert G. Boatright (New York: Routledge, 2018), 307–19.

7. Institute of Politics, *Campaign for President: The Managers Look at 2012*, 108.

8. Patrick Healy and Alexander Burns, "Scott Walker Ends His 2016 Presidential Run," FirstDraft blog, *New York Times*, September 21, 2015, https://www.nytimes.com/politics/first-draft/2015/09/21/scott-walker-quits-2016-presidential-race.

9. "Transcript of the New Hampshire GOP Debate, Annotated," *Washington Post*, February 6, 2016, https://www.washingtonpost.com/news/the-fix/wp/2016/02/06/transcript-of-the-feb-6-gop-debate-annotated.

10. Cohen et al., *The Party Decides*, argue that the "invisible primary" is in fact the key period for determining nomination outcomes, with party leaders steering support to their favored candidates during this time that is of immense assistance in winning the subsequent primaries and caucuses.

11. Citizens and politicians in these states seem to care deeply about their status as first in the nation and guard it jealously. Indeed, when Arizona began to consider challenging New Hampshire by scheduling an early primary for 1996, Senator Phil Gramm was widely criticized in New Hampshire for seeming to approve of that attempt; see "Rocky Start in Granite State Knocks Gramm Off Balance," *Washington Post*, February 26, 1995, A18. Our discussion of Iowa and New Hampshire borrows freely from Nelson W. Polsby, "The Iowa Caucuses in a Front-Loaded System: A Few Historical Lessons," in *The Iowa Caucuses and the Presidential Nominating Process*, ed. Peverill Squire (Boulder, CO: Westview Press, 1989), 149–62.

12. Indeed, Henry E. Brady and Richard Johnston argue that the main educational effect of the entire primary process for voters is to inform them about candidate viability. See "What's the Primary Message? Horse Race or Issue Journalism," in *Media and Momentum: The New Hampshire Primary and Nomination Politics*, eds. Gary R. Orren and Nelson W. Polsby (Chatham, NJ: Chatham House, 1987), 127–86.

13. As Muskie later recalled, "That previous week . . . I'd been down to Florida, then I flew to Idaho, then I flew to California, then I flew back to Washington to vote in the Senate, and I flew back to California, and then I flew into Manchester and I was hit with this [attack]. I'm tough physically, but no one could do that." Theodore E. White, *The Making of the President, 1972* (New York: Atheneum, 1973), 81–82.

14. "Ford's 1976 Campaign for the GOP Nomination," *1976 Congressional Quarterly Almanac* (Washington, DC: CQ Press, 1976), 900.

15. Elizabeth Drew wrote of Carter: "Early successes and surprises were big elements in Carter's plan. . . . The basic idea was to show early that the southerner could do well in the North and could best Wallace in the South. . . . He visited a hundred and fourteen towns in Iowa, beginning in 1975 (and his family made countless other visits)." Drew, *American Journal: The Events of 1976* (New York: Random House, 1977), 143–44, 466–67. See also Jules Witcover, *Marathon: The Pursuit of the Presidency, 1972–1976* (New York: Viking Press, 1977), 14.

16. R. W. Apple Jr., "Carter Defeats Bayh by 2-1 in Iowa Vote," *New York Times*, January 20, 1976, A1. This was not the first time in 1976 that Apple had puffed Carter. Elizabeth Drew's diary of January 27, 1976 reported: "A story by R. W. Apple Jr., in the *Times* last October saying that Carter was doing well in Iowa was itself a political event, prompting other newspaper stories that Carter was doing well in Iowa, and then more news magazine and television coverage for Carter than might otherwise have been his share." Drew, *American Journal*, 6.

17. R. W. Apple Jr., "Democrats' Hopes Fade as Front-Runner Slips," *New York Times*, February 11, 1992, A22.

18. Robin Toner, "Bush Jarred in First Primary; Tsongas Wins Democratic Vote," *New York Times*, February 19, 1992, A1.

19. Writing when Clinton was still neck-and-neck with Tsongas in New Hampshire opinion polls, R. W. Apple Jr. of the *New York Times* predicted that a Clinton loss would be "terribly damaging" (Apple, "Democrats' Hopes Fade"). By the time of the primary, Clinton had reduced media expectations to such an extent that his second-place showing was considered surprisingly strong.

20. Adam Nagourney, "In the First Mile of a Marathon, Kerry Emerges as a Front-Runner," *New York Times*, February 26, 2003, A14.

21. See, e.g., David S. Broder, "Dean Still Standing after Foes Take Shots," *Washington Post*, January 5, 2004, A06.

22. Adam Nagourney, "In Democratic Pack, the Race Is on for No. 3 and Maybe No. 4," *New York Times*, January 6, 2004, A18.

23. For an in-depth narrative of the events surrounding the 2004 Iowa caucus, see Roger Simon, "Turning Point," *U.S. News and World Report*, July 19, 2004, 34–75.

24. See Howard Kurtz, "Reporters Shift Gears on the Dean Bus," *Washington Post*, January 23, 2004, C01; and Kurtz, "Trailing in the Media Primary, Too," *Washington Post*, January 29, 2004, A01.

25. Ceci Connolly, "Senator Enjoys Political Renewal," *Washington Post*, January 28, 2004, A13.

26. Barbara Norrander, "Democratic Marathon, Republican Sprint: The 2008 Presidential Nominations," in *The American Elections of 2008*, eds. Janet Box-Steffensmeier and Steven E. Schier (Lanham, MD: Rowman & Littlefield, 2009), 35.

27. Joshua Green, "The Front-Runner's Fall," *Atlantic*, September 2008, 64–74.

28. Roger Simon, "Relentless: Amid the Corn," *Politico*, August 25, 2008, http://www.politico.com/news/stories/0808/12722.html.

29. Norrander, "Democratic Marathon, Republican Sprint," 42.

30. Simon, "Amid the Corn."

31. Dan Balz, Anne E. Kornblut, and Shailagh Murray, "Obama Wins Iowa's Democratic Caucuses," *Washington Post*, January 4, 2008, A01.

32. Adam Nagourney, "Obama Takes Iowa in a Big Turnout," *New York Times*, January 4, 2008, A1.

33. Roger Simon, "Relentless: Lost in Hillaryland," *Politico*, August 25, 2008, http://www.politico.com/news/stories/0808/12721.html.

34. Bill McInturff, McCain chief pollster, quoted in *Electing the President, 2008: The Insiders' View*, ed. Kathleen Hall Jamieson (Philadelphia: University of Pennsylvania Press, 2009), 84–85.

35. Peter Cook and Greg Giroux, "Romney's Tie Costs $75 a Vote to Santorum's $10," *Bloomberg Business*, January 5, 2012, http://www.bloomberg.com/news/articles/2012-01-05/ romney-s-iowa-tie-cost-75-a-vote-to-santorum-s-10.

36. Becket Adams, "Media Declares Rubio's Third Place Finish the Real Victory of the Iowa Caucus," *Washington Examiner*, February 2, 2016, https://www.washingtonexaminer.com/media-declares-marco-rubios-third-place-finish-the-real-victory-of-the-iowa-caucus; Alex Isenstadt, "GOP Establishment Rallies behind Rubio," *Politico*, February 2, 2016, https://www.politico.com/story/2016/02/marco-rubio-gop-establishment-new-hampshire-2016-218641.

37. If voters opting to remain uncommitted are counted, Bill Clinton actually finished fourth in the 1992 Iowa caucuses, which were uncontested that year due to the candidacy of Iowa senator Tom Harkin.

38. Richard M. Scammon and Alice V. McGillivray, *America at the Polls* (Washington, DC: Congressional Quarterly, 1988), 585.

39. For a wealth of information on the past, present, and future scheduling of presidential primaries and caucuses, see the Frontloading HQ website maintained by political scientist Josh Putnam at http://frontloading.blogspot.com.

40. Ultimately, the Michigan and Florida delegations were seated in full at the Democratic convention, after Clinton's concession meant that they would not affect the outcome of the nomination contest. See Barry C. Burden, "The Nominations: Rules, Strategies and Uncertainty," in *The Elections of 2008*, ed. Michael Nelson (Washington, DC: CQ Press, 2009), 39.

41. Chris Cillizza and Zachary A. Goldfarb, "Democrats Tweak the Primary Calendar," *Washington Post*, July 23, 2006, A04.

42. B. Drummond Ayres Jr., "McCain Rethinks the Arizona Primary," *New York Times*, February 7, 1999, A20.

43. Rhodes Cook, "In '88 Contest, It's What's Up Front That Counts," *Congressional Quarterly Weekly* Report, August 23, 1986, 1997–2002, at 2002.

44. Further discussion can be found in *Media Politics: The News Strategies of Presidential Campaigns*, ed. F. Christopher Arterton (Lexington, MA: Lexington Books, 1984).

45. Charles T. Royer, ed., *Campaign for President: The Managers Look at 1992* (Hollis, NH: Hollis Publishing Company, 1994), 79–80; Peter Goldman, Thomas M. DeFrank, Mark Miller, Andrew Murr, and Tom Mathews, *Quest for the Presidency, 1992* (College Station: Texas A&M University Press, 1994), 132–35, 144–49.

46. See Tom Rosenstiel, *Strange Bedfellows* (New York: Hyperion, 1993), 136.

47. Henry E. Brady and Michael G. Hagen, "The 'Horse-Race' or the Issues: What Do Voters Learn from Presidential Primaries?" paper presented at the Annual Meetings of the American Political Science Association, August 1986. See also Brady and Johnston, "What's the Primary Message?" in *Media and Momentum*, eds. Orren and Polsby, 127–86.

48. John G. Geer, "Voting in Presidential Primaries," paper presented at the annual meeting of the American Political Science Association, August 30–September 2, 1984, 6.

49. Poll results compiled by the Polling Report, http://www.pollingreport.com/wh04dem.htm.

50. Data from the poll aggregation website Huffington Post Pollster, http://elections.huffingtonpost.com/pollster/2012-national-gop-primary.

51. Ibid., 15–21.

52. Brady and Hagen, "The 'Horse-Race' or the Issues," 38–39.

53. Turnout data from Michael P. McDonald, United States Election Project, http://www.electproject.org/2016P.

54. Democratic National Committee, "DNC Passes Historic Reforms to the Presidential Nomination Process," August 25, 2018, https://democrats.org/press/dnc-passes-historic-reforms-to-the-presidential-nominating-process.

55. Roger Simon, "Relentless: Looking Like Whiny Babies," *Politico*, August 25, 2008, http://www.politico.com/news/stories/0808/12720.html.

56. Ibid.

57. Democratic National Committee, "DNC Passes Historic Reforms to the Presidential Nomination Process."

58. Turnout data from McDonald, United States Election Project, http://www.electproject.org/2016P. This pattern has held steady over time. See Austin Ranney, "Turnout and Representation in Presidential Primary Elections," *American Political Science Review* 66 (March 1972): 21–37, for the years 1948 to 1968; Austin Ranney, *Participation in American Presidential Nominations, 1976* (Washington, DC: American Enterprise Institute, 1977), 20, and James Lengle, *Representation in Presidential Primaries: The Democratic Party in the Post Reform Era* (Westport, CT: Greenwood Press, 1981), 10, for 1976; and Ranney, *American Elections of 1980*, 353, 364, for 1980. By 2000, turnout in primaries had dropped to 18 percent, while 51 percent of the voting-age population turned out in the general election. "Report: Turnout in Primaries 2nd

Lowest in Past 40 Years," *Seattle Times*, September 1, 2000, A5 (citing a report by the Center for the Study of the American Electorate). Turnout in 2004 was high on the Democratic side compared to previous years in states voting early in the process, such as New Hampshire, but dropped off considerably once Kerry became the presumptive nominee. Republican primary turnout was uniformly low in 2004, since President George W. Bush ran unopposed for renomination. See Anne E. Kornblut, "Democratic Turnout Seen So-So, Despite Party Assertions," *Boston Globe*, March 10, 2004, A3.

59. A comprehensive online resource for state delegate allocation rules and other nomination procedures is the Green Papers, http://www.thegreenpapers.com.

60. Institute of Politics, Kennedy School of Government, Harvard University, *Campaign for President: The Managers Look at 2016* (Lanham, MD: Rowman & Littlefield, 2017), 103.

61. Karen Tumulty, "The Five Mistakes Clinton Made," *Time*, May 8, 2008, http://www.time.com/time/politics/article/0,8599,1738331,00.html.

62. Thomas E. Mann, "Elected Officials and the Politics of Presidential Selection," in *The American Elections of 1984*, ed. Austin Ranney (Durham, NC: Duke University Press), 100–128, at 103–105. See also David E. Price, *Bringing Back the Parties* (Washington, DC: CQ Press, 1984); Glenn, "Front-Loading the Race," 333; and Dennis W. Gleiber and James D. King, "Party Rules and Equitable Representation: The 1984 Democratic National Convention," *American Politics Quarterly* 15 (January 1987): 107–21.

63. Greg J. Borowski, "Superdelegates Feel the Heat," *Milwaukee Journal Sentinel*, February 11, 2008, A1.

64. Mark Murray and Marianna Sotomayor, "How Do Superdelegates Work? Here's What You Need to Know," NBC News, April 11, 2016, https://www.nbcnews.com/politics/first-read/how-do-superdelegates-work-here-s-what-you-need-know-n554136.

65. Ezra Klein, "Was the Democratic Primary Rigged?" *Vox*, November 14, 2017, https://www.vox.com/policy-and-politics/2017/11/14/16640082/donna-brazile-warren-bernie-sanders-democratic-primary-rigged.

66. See Charles Lane, "If the GOP Had Superdelegates, We Might Not Be in This Trump Mess," *Washington Post*, June 8, 2016, https://www.washingtonpost.com/opinions/in-praise-of-superdelegates/2016/06/08/530234f0-2d8e-11e6-9b37-42985f6a265c_story.html; Jeff Greenfield, "Why We Need Those 'Anti-Democratic' Superdelegates," *Politico*, May 28, 2016, https://www.politico.com/magazine/story/2016/05/why-we-need-those-anti-democratic-superdelegates-213921.

67. David Mark, "Convention Cities Ready Bids for '04," *Campaigns and Elections*, August 2002, 30.

68. Jo Freeman, "The Political Culture of the Democratic and Republican Parties," *Political Science Quarterly* 101 (Fall 1986): 327–56, at 328. See also Byron Shafer, "Republicans and Democrats as Social Types: or, Notes toward an Ethnography of the Political Parties," *Journal of American Studies* 20 (1986): 341–54.

69. Matt Grossmann and David A. Hopkins, *Asymmetric Politics: Ideological Republicans and Group Interest Democrats* (New York: Oxford University Press, 2016).

70. Freeman, "The Political Culture of the Democratic and Republican Parties," 329.

71. Ibid.

72. Kirkpatrick, "Representation in the American National Conventions: The Case of 1972," *British Journal of Political Science* 5 (July 1975): 265–322, at 285.

73. Barbara G. Farah, "Delegate Polls: 1944 to 1984," *Public Opinion* 7 (August/September 1984): 43–45.

74. M. Kent Jennings, "Women in Party Politics," prepared for the Russell Sage Foundation Women in Twentieth-Century American Politics Project, Beverly Hills, CA, January 1987, 11–12.

75. For extensive documentation, see Ladd, *Transformations of the American Party System*. See also Everett Carll Ladd Jr. and Charles D. Hadley, "Political Parties and Political Issues: Patterns in Differentiation Since the New Deal," Sage Professional Paper, American Politics Series, Beverly Hills, CA, 1973, 4–11; Herbert McClosky, Paul J. Hoffman, and Rosemary O'Hara, "Issue Conflict and Consensus among Party Leaders and Followers," *American Political Science Review* 54 (June 1960): 406–27; and Jeane Kirkpatrick, "Representation in the American National Conventions," 304.

76. John D. Huber and G. Bingham Powell Jr., "Congruence between Citizens and Policymakers in Two Visions of Liberal Democracy," *World Politics* (April 1994): 291–326; Torben Iversen, "Political Leadership and Representation in West European Democracies: A Test of Three Models of Voting," *American Journal of Political Science* 38 (February 1994): 45–74. An important early work is Maurice Duverger, *Political Parties: Their Organization and Activity in the Modern State* (London: Methuen, 1954).

77. Nolan McCarty, Keith W. Poole, and Howard Rosenthal, *Polarized America: The Dance of Ideology and Unequal Riches* (Cambridge, MA: MIT Press, 2006).

78. For the best analysis of the role of the modern convention, see Byron E. Shafer, *Bifurcated Politics* (Cambridge, MA: Harvard University Press, 1988); see also Polsby, *Consequences of Party Reform*, 75–78.

79. See Joe Foote and Tony Rimmer, "The Ritual of Convention Coverage in 1980," in *Television Coverage of the 1980 Presidential Campaign*, ed. William C. Adams (Norwood, NJ: Ablex, 1983).

80. Evan Thomas and Peter Goldman, "Victory March: The Inside Story," *Newsweek Special Election Issue*, November 18, 1996, 88–90, 97–98; Robert E. Denton Jr., "Five Pivotal Elements of the 2000 Presidential Campaign," in *The 2000 Presidential Campaign: A Communication Perspective*, ed. Robert E. Denton Jr. (Westport, CT: Praeger, 2002), 9–10.

81. Richard Morin and Dan Balz, "Bush Support Strong after Convention," *Washington Post*, September 10, 2004, A01.

82. Steven E. Schier and Janet Box-Steffensmeier, "The General Election Campaign," in *The American Elections of 2008,* ed. Janet Box-Steffensmeier and Steven E. Schier (Lanham, MD: Rowman & Littlefield, 2009), 61.

83. See Nate Silver, "Split Verdict in Polls on Romney Convention Bounce," FiveThirtyEight, September 2, 2012, http://fivethirtyeight.blogs.nytimes.com/2012/09/03/sept-2-split-verdict-in-polls-on-romney-convention-bounce/; and "Polls Find Hints of Obama Convention Bounce," September 7, 2012, http://fivethirtyeight.blogs.nytimes.com/2012/09/07/ sept-7-polls-find-hints-of-obama-convention-bounce.

84. Mona Chalabi, "Trump or Clinton: Who Got the Biggest Post-Convention Poll Bounce?" *The Guardian*, August 3, 2016, https://www.theguardian.com/us-news/2016/aug/03/trump-clinton-unpopularity-2016-election-prediction-winner.

85. Christopher Madison, "The Convention Hall and the TV Screen," *National Journal Convention Special*, July 23, 1988, 1950.

86. Rosenstiel, *Strange Bedfellows*, 224.

87. James Bennet, "Bush's New Vantage Point, from an Island of a Stage," *New York Times*, September 3, 2004, P3.

88. Jim VandeHei and John F. Harris, "Kerry: 'America Can Do Better,'" *Washington Post*, Friday, July 30, 2004, A01.

89. See Andrew Mollison, "Maestro of the Democrats," *New Leader*, June 27, 1988, 3–4. On the other hand, the leader of a too-united party may need to create excitement, as George Bush apparently intended to do in 1988 by refusing to reveal his choice for vice president until the eve of the convention. James M. Perry and Ellen Hume, "Bush Aiming for Suspense as GOP Starts Convention," *Wall Street Journal*, August 15, 1988, 40. Lyndon Johnson attempted the same stunt in 1964.

90. Evan Thomas, "Center Stage," *Newsweek*, November 17, 2008, 87–99.

91. Adam Nagourney, "Heralding New Course, Democrats Nominate Obama," *New York Times*, August 28, 2008, A1.

92. Institute of Politics, *Campaign for President: The Managers Look at 2016*, 131, 133.

93. Jonathan Allen and Amie Parnes, *Shattered: Inside Hillary Clinton's Doomed Campaign* (New York: Crown, 2017), 279.

94. Michael Barbaro and Michael D. Shear, "Before Eastwood's Talk with a Chair, Clearance from the Top," *New York Times*, August 31, 2012, http://www.nytimes.com/2012/09/01/ us/politics/romney-aides-scratch-their-heads-over-eastwoods-speech.html; Halimah Abdullah, "Eastwood, the Empty Chair and the Speech Everyone's Talking About," CNN, August 31, 2012, http://www.cnn.com/2012/08/31/politics/eastwood-speech/; Amy Argetsinger, "Clint Eastwood Goes Unscripted with Punchy Speech at Republican Convention," *Washington Post*, August 30, 2012, http://www.washingtonpost.com/blogs/reliable-source/post/clint-eastwood-goes-unscripted-with-punchy-speech-at-republican-convention/2012/08/30/3b2a1e02-f317-11e1-892d-bc92fee603a7_blog.html.

95. Institute of Politics, *Campaign for President: The Managers Look at 2016*, 171.

96. See Irving G. Williams, *The American Vice-Presidency: New Look* (New York: Doubleday, 1954); and Joel K. Goldstein, *The Modern American Vice Presidency* (Princeton: Princeton University Press, 1982).

97. Stanley Kelley Jr., "The Presidential Campaign," in *The Presidential Election and Transition, 1960–1961,* ed. Paul T. David (Washington, DC: Brookings Institution, 1961), 70–71.

98. David S. Broder and Bob Woodward, *The Man Who Would Be President: Dan Quayle* (New York: Simon and Schuster, 1992), 13–30; and "Bush Takes Command but Quayle Draws Fire," *Congressional Quarterly Weekly Report*, August 20, 1988, 2307–9.

99. Jamieson, ed., *Electing the President, 2008*, 30.

100. Elisabeth Bumiller, "Palin Disclosures Raise Questions on Vetting," *New York Times*, September 2, 2008, A1.

101. Stuart Rothenberg, "Barney Frank: A Definite No to Nunn," *The Rothenberg Report*, June 20, 2008, http://rothenbergpoliticalreport.blogspot.com/2008/06/barney-frank-definite-no-to- nunn.html.

102. Richard Brookhiser, *The Outside Story* (Garden City, NY: Doubleday, 1986), 155.

103. Jamieson, ed., *Electing the President, 2008*, 27.

104. Gerald M. Pomper, "The Presidential Election: Change Comes to America," in *The Elections of 2008,* ed. Michael Nelson (Washington, DC: CQ Press, 2009), 59.

105. Roy Elis, D. Sunshine Hillygus, and Norman Nie, "The Dynamics of Candidate Evaluations and Vote Choice in 2008: Looking to the Past or Future?" *Electoral Studies* 29 (December 2010): 582–93.

106. Institute of Politics, *Campaign for President: The Managers Look at 2016*, 129.

CHAPTER 5: THE CAMPAIGN

1. See Seymour M. Lipset, Paul F. Lazarsfeld, Allen H. Barton, and Juan Linz, "The Psychology of Voting: An Analysis of Political Behavior," in *Handbook of Social Psychology*, ed. Gardner Lindzey (Reading, MA: Addison-Wesley, 1954), 1124–75; Paul F. Lazarsfeld, Bernard Berelson and Hazel Gaudet, *The People's Choice* (New York: Columbia University Press, 1948), 87–93; Bernard R. Berelson, Paul F. Lazarsfeld, and William N. McPhee, *Voting* (Chicago: University of Chicago Press, 1954), 16–17; and Richard A. Brody, "Change and Stability in Partisan Identification: A Note of Caution," paper delivered at the annual meeting of the American Political Science Association, Chicago, September 1974.

2. David Maraniss, "Aboard the Clinton Campaign, Somewhere Over the Battleground States," *Washington Post*, November 2, 1992, A1.

3. Hillary Rodham Clinton, *What Happened* (New York: Simon and Schuster, 2017), 91, 94.

4. For a theoretically useful elaboration of the distinction between "swing" and "battleground" states, see Darshan J. Goux, "Grading the Battleground: A New Measure of Campaign Activity in the States," paper delivered at the Annual Meeting of the American Political Science Association, Philadelphia, PA, August 2006.

5. David A. Hopkins, *Red Fighting Blue: How Geography and Electoral Rules Polarize American Politics* (New York: Cambridge University Press, 2017).

6. Candidate visit data from Matthew Conlen, "The Last 10 Weeks of 2016 Campaign Stops in One Handy GIF," FiveThirtyEight, December 16, 2016, https://fivethirtyeight.com/features/the-last-10-weeks-of-2016-campaign-stops-in-one-handy-gif. Debates, fund-raisers, media appearances, and addresses to national organizations are not considered public campaign events.

7. Henry J. Gomez, "Hillary Clinton and Donald Trump Kick Off Their Fall Campaigns in Cleveland: 6 Labor Day Takeaways," *Cleveland Plain Dealer*, September 5, 2016, https://www.cleveland.com/open/index.ssf/2016/09/hillary_clinton_and_donald_tru_1.html.

8. Kathleen Hall Jamieson, ed., *Electing the President, 2008: The Insiders' View* (Philadelphia: University of Pennsylvania Press, 2009), 142.

9. Garry Abrams, "See How They Run: Why Do Candidates Dash Madly across the Map? Blame It on a Special Breed Called the Scheduler," *Los Angeles Times*, September 29, 1988, pt. 5, 1.

10. Clinton, *What Happened*, 395.

11. Evan Thomas, "Center Stage," *Newsweek Special Election Edition*, November 17, 2008, 87–99.

12. Elizabeth Bumiller, "McCain Draws Line on Attacks as Crowds Cry 'Fight Back,'" *New York Times*, October 11, 2008, A12.

13. Clinton, *What Happened*, 74.

14. Abby Ohlheiser and Caitlin Dewey, "Hillary Clinton's Alt-Right Speech, Annotated," *Washington Post*, August 25, 2016, https://www.washingtonpost.com/news/the-fix/wp/2016/08/25/hillary-clintons-alt-right-speech-annotated.

15. One study has found at least small effects from campaign visits; see Jeffrey M. Jones, "Does Bringing Out the Candidate Bring Out the Votes?" *American Politics Quarterly* 26 (October 1998): 395–19. Campaigns may allocate a variety of resources, including candidate visits and paid advertising, in a coordinated way, making it impossible for outside researchers or campaign managers to know which affected the voters.

16. Evan Thomas and Peter Goldman, "Victory March: The Inside Story," *Newsweek*, special election issue, November 18, 1996, 124.

17. Heidi M. Przybyla, "Hillary Clinton: I Didn't Think Pneumonia Was Big Deal," *USA Today*, September 12, 2016, https://www.usatoday.com/story/news/politics/onpolitics/2016/09/12/hillary-clinton-didnt-think-pneumonia-big-deal/90287614.

18. Dom Bonafede, "Hey, Look Me Over," *National Journal*, November 21, 1987.

19. Jamieson, ed., *Electing the President, 2008*, 144.

20. Hillary Clinton, *What Happened*, 94.

21. Pew Research Center, "Voter Enthusiasm at Record High in Nationalized Midterm Environment," September 26, 2018, http://www.people-press.org/wp-content/uploads/sites/4/2018/09/Midterm-report-for-release.pdf.

22. Patrick J. Egan, *Partisan Priorities: How Issue Ownership Drives and Distorts American Politics* (New York: Cambridge University Press, 2013).

23. Matt Grossmann and David A. Hopkins, *Asymmetric Politics: Ideological Republicans and Group Interest Democrats* (New York: Oxford University Press, 2016).

24. Henry C. Jackson, "6 Promises Trump Has Made about Health Care," *Politico*, March 13, 2017, https://www.politico.com/story/2017/03/trump-obamacare-promises-236021.

25. Matt Grossmann and David A. Hopkins, "Trump Isn't Changing the Republican Party. The Republican Party Is Changing Trump," *Washington Post*, August 2, 2017, https://www.washingtonpost.com/news/monkey-cage/wp/2017/08/02/trump-isnt-changing-the-republican-party-the-republican-party-is-changing-trump.

26. Erika Franklin Fowler, Travis N. Ridout, and Michael M. Franz, "Political Advertising in 2016: The Presidential Election as Outlier?" *The Forum* 14 (2017): 445–69.

27. Dana Milbank, "True Confessions from the Trail," *Washington Post*, April 24, 2009, A02.

28. John R. Petrocik, "Issue Ownership in Presidential Elections, with a 1980 Case Study," *American Journal of Political Science* 40 (August 1996): 825–50; Byron E. Shafer and William J. M. Claggett, *The Two Majorities: The Issue Context of Modern American Politics* (Baltimore: Johns Hopkins University Press, 1995).

29. James E. Campbell, "Why Bush Won the Presidential Election of 2004: Incumbency, Ideology, Terrorism, and Turnout," *Political Science Quarterly* 120 (Summer 2005): 219–42.

30. CNN, "2016 National Exit Polls," https://www.cnn.com/election/2016/results/exit-polls.

31. See Morris P. Fiorina with Samuel J. Abrams and Jeremy Pope, *Culture War? The Myth of a Polarized America*, 3rd ed. (New York: Longman, 2010); and James Q. Wilson, "How Divided Are We?" *Commentary*, February 2006, 15–21.

32. See Shafer and Claggett, *The Two Majorities*.

33. Donald Trump presidential announcement speech, June 16, 2015, http://www.4president.org/speeches/2016/donaldtrump2016announcement.htm.

34. Brian F. Schaffner, Matthew MacWilliams, and Tatishe Nteta, "Understanding White Polarization in the 2016 Vote for President: The Sobering Role of Racism and Sexism," *Political Science Quarterly* 133 (Spring 2018): 9–34.

35. Michael Tesler, "Views about Race Mattered More in Electing Trump Than in Electing Obama," *Washington Post*, November 22, 2016, https://www.washingtonpost.com/news/monkey-cage/wp/2016/11/22/peoples-views-about-race-mattered-more-in-electing-trump-than-in-electing-obama.

36. Geoffrey C. Layman and Thomas M. Carsey, "Party Polarization and 'Conflict Extension' in the American Electorate," *American Journal of Political Science* 46 (October 2002): 786–802; Geoffrey C. Layman, Thomas M. Carsey, John C. Green, and Richard Herrera, "Activists and Conflict Extension in American Party Politics," *American Political Science Review* 104 (May 2010): 324–46.

37. Harry Enten, "Americans' Distaste for Both Trump and Clinton Is Record-Breaking," FiveThirtyEight, May 5, 2016, https://fivethirtyeight.com/features/americans-distaste-for-both-trump-and-clinton-is-record-breaking/; Lydia Saad, "Trump and Clinton Finish with Historically Poor Images," Gallup Organization, November 8, 2016, https://news.gallup.com/poll/197231/trump-clinton-finish-historically-poor-images.aspx.

38. For more on the Obama campaign's racial strategy, see Marc Ambinder, "Race Over?" *The Atlantic*, January/February 2009, 62–65.

39. Spencer Piston, "How Explicit Racial Prejudice Hurt Obama in the 2008 Election," *Political Behavior* 32 (December 2010): 431–51.

40. Jonathan Knuckey, "'I Just Don't Think She Has a Presidential Look': Sexism and Vote Choice in the 2016 Election," *Social Science Quarterly* 100 (February 2019): 342–58.

41. Lloyd Grove, "When They Ask If Dukakis Has a Heart, They Mean It," *Washington Post Weekly Edition*, October 17–23, 1988, 24–25.

42. Curt Suplee, "Bush's Candidacy Is Being Cooled Off by His Warmth Index," *Washington Post National Weekly Edition*, July 25–31, 1988, 23–24.

43. Peter Goldman, Thomas M. DeFrank, Mark Miller, Andrew Murr, and Tom Mathews, *Quest for the Presidency, 1992* (College Station: Texas A&M University Press, 1994), 657–58.

44. Jamieson, ed., *Electing the President, 2008*, 36.

45. Frank Luntz interview, *Frontline*, November 9, 2004, transcript at https://www.pbs.org/wgbh/pages/frontline/shows/persuaders/interviews/luntz.html.

46. Institute of Politics, Kennedy School of Government, Harvard University, *Campaign for President: The Managers Look at 2016* (Lanham, MD: Rowman & Littlefield, 2017), 163.

47. Kathleen Hall Jamieson, ed., *Electing the President, 2012: The Insiders' View* (Philadelphia: University of Pennsylvania Press, 2013), 34, 60.

48. Michael Kranish, "Mitt Romney Was Hesitant to Reveal Himself," *Boston Globe*, December 23, 2012, http://www.bostonglobe.com/news/nation/2012/12/23/the-story-behind-mitt-romney-loss-presidential-campaign-president-obama/OeZRabbooIw0z7QYAOyFFP/story.html.

49. "Our Cheesy Democracy," *New Republic*, November 3, 1986, 8–9.

50. Larry J. Sabato, *The Rise of Political Consultants: New Ways of Winning Elections* (New York: Basic Books, 1981), 169–70.

51. Ibid., 170–71.

52. Rich Galen, "Nail the Opposition," *Campaigns and Elections*, May/June 1988, 45. See also Rich Galen, "The Best Defense Is a Good Offense," *Campaigns and Elections*, October/ November 1988, 29–34.

53. Sabato, *The Rise of Political Consultants*, 166.

54. Galen, "The Best Defense Is a Good Offense," 30.

55. Diana Owen, "The Campaign and the Media," in *The American Elections of 2008*, eds. Janet Box-Steffensmeier and Steven E. Schier (Lanham, MD: Rowman & Littlefield, 2009), 17.

56. Jill Lawrence, "McCain Seen as 'Bare-Knuckled Fighter' Who Won't Take No for Answer," *USA Today*, October 9, 2008, 4A.

57. Steven E. Schier and Janet Box-Steffensmeier, "The General Election Campaign," in *The American Elections of 2008*, eds. Box-Steffensmeier and Schier, 64–67.

58. Helene Cooper and Michael D. Shear, "Facing Criticism, Obama Defends Ads Attacking Romney's Record at Bain Capital," *New York Times*, May 21, 2012, http://www.nytimes.com/2012/05/22/us/politics/obama-defends-attacks-on-romneys-record-at-bain.html.

59. For a study suggesting that negative advertising reduces voter turnout and lowers individuals' sense of political efficacy, see Stephen Ansolabehere, Shanto Iyengar, Adam Simon, and Nicholas Valentino, "Does Attack Advertising Demobilize the Electorate?" *American Political Science Review* 88 (December 1994): 829–38.

60. John G. Geer, *In Defense of Negativity: Attack Ads in Presidential Campaigns* (Chicago: University of Chicago Press, 2006).

61. See Richard M. Nixon, *Six Crises* (New York: Doubleday, 1962), and especially Theodore H. White, *The Making of the President, 1960* (New York: Atheneum, 1961), for a discussion of two candidates' contrasting attitudes toward their "camp" of reporters. For the 1964 election, see Theodore H. White, *The Making of the President, 1964* (New York: Atheneum, 1965). For 1968, see Theodore H. White, *The Making of the President, 1968* (New York: Atheneum, 1969), 327ff. For 1972, see Timothy Crouse, *The Boys on the Bus* (New York: Random House, 1973). For 1976, see Jules Witcover, *Marathon: The Pursuit of the Presidency, 1972–1976* (New York: Viking Press, 1977). For 1980, see Jack W. Germond and Jules Witcover, *Blue Smoke and Mirrors* (New York: Viking Press, 1981), 213–15, 260–64. On 1984, see Martin Schram, *The Great American Video Game: Presidential Politics in the Television Age* (New York: Morrow, 1987).

62. In 1984, Mondale's backers felt President Reagan was avoiding the issues in a campaign that stuck to broad, patriotic themes. The "great communicator," they argued, was exploiting the media with his carefully staged events. Many in the media agreed and did negative stories about the Reagan campaign's manipulative tactics. Negative coverage of this sort gave the Reagan camp grounds for complaints of their own concerning an anti-Republican "spin" to nightly newscasts. See Michael J. Robinson, "Where's the Beef? Media and Media Elites in 1984," in *The American Elections of 1984*, ed. Austin Ranney (Durham, NC: Duke University Press), 166–202. Allegations of bias in the ABC newsroom tainted the 1992 campaign, fueled in part by the decision of anchor Peter Jennings to invite Clinton to respond to a speech President Bush gave after the Los Angeles riots. See Tom Rosenstiel, *Strange Bedfellows* (New York: Hyperion, 1993), 141.

63. Institute of Politics, *Campaign for President: The Managers Look at 2016*, 43.

64. Jamieson, ed., *Electing the President, 2012*, 59.

65. See the documentary film *Journeys with George* (2002), directed by Alexandra Pelosi and Aaron Lubarsky.

66. Mark Leibovich, "Being Hillary," *New York Times Magazine*, July 19, 2015, 32.

67. Clinton, *What Happened*, 320.

68. Peter Johnson, "Worlds of Politics, Comedy Converge," *USA Today*, January 26, 2004, 1D.

69. Bill Carter, "Candidate Delivers a Ratings Boost," *New York Times*, October 20, 2008, C6.

70. See Matthew A. Baum, "Talking the Vote: Why Presidential Candidates Hit the Talk-Show Circuit," *American Journal of Political Science* 49 (April 2005): 213–34.

71. See Jonathan H. Bernstein, "The Expanded Party in American Politics," PhD dissertation, University of California, Berkeley, 1999.

72. Frank I. Luntz, *Candidates, Campaigns, and Consultants* (Oxford: Basil Blackwell, 1988), 52.

73. Ibid.

74. Mark Petracca, "Political Consultants and Democratic Governance," *PS: Political Science and Politics* 22 (March 1989): 11–14, at 13.

75. Ibid.

76. Luntz, *Candidates, Campaigns, and Consultants*, 57.

77. Dick Kirschten and James A. Barnes, "Itching for Action," *National Journal*, June 4, 1988, 1478.

78. James Moore and Wayne Slater, *Bush's Brain: How Karl Rove Made George W. Bush Presidential* (New York: John Wiley and Sons, 2003); Lou Dubose, Jan Reid, and Carl M. Cannon, *Boy Genius: Karl Rove, the Brains behind the Remarkable Political Triumph of George W. Bush* (New York: Public Affairs, 2003).

79. Sabato, *The Rise of Political Consultants*, 26.

80. Bonnie Siegel, "The Dos and Don'ts of Branding a Candidate," *Campaigns and Elections*, June 13, 2017, https://www.campaignsandelections.com/campaign-insider/the-dos-and-don-ts-of-branding-a-candidate.

81. Luntz, *Candidates, Campaigns, and Consultants*, 72.

82. Occasionally the roles are reversed and consultants find themselves more "dovish" than their employers. In the 1972 general election campaign, George McGovern ditched Charles Guggenheim, his media adviser, because the latter refused (on pragmatic grounds) to produce negative ads. See Sabato, *The Rise of Political Consultants*, 121.

83. See Jonathan Bernstein, "The New Presidential Elite," in *In Pursuit of the White House 2000*, ed. William G. Mayer (Chatham, NJ: Chatham House, 1999); Robin Kolodny and Angela Logan, "Political Consultants and the Extension of Party Goals," *PS: Political Science and Politics* 31 (June 1998): 155–59.

84. Luntz, *Candidates, Campaigns and Consultants*, 50.

85. Adam Sheingate, *Building a Business of Politics: The Rise of Political Consulting and the Transformation of American Democracy* (New York: Oxford University Press, 2016), 179–80.

86. Ryan Lizza, "Kellyanne Conway's Political Machinations," *The New Yorker*, October 17, 2016.

87. Kirk Victor, "The Braintrusters," *National Journal*, February 13, 1988, 394–95.

88. Ibid., 397.

89. Ibid.

90. Ibid., 393.

91. Ibid., 392.

92. Ibid., 393.

93. Sabato, *The Rise of Political Consultants*, 69.

94. Quoted in Scott C. Ratzan, "The Real Agenda Setters: Pollsters in the 1988 Presidential Campaign," *American Behavioral Scientist* 32 (March/April 1989): 451–63, at 451.

95. Quoted in Paul Simon, *Winners and Losers* (New York: Continuum, 1989), 165.

96. Sabato, *The Rise of Political Consultants*, 71.

97. Ibid., 21.

98. Gerald M. Goldhaber, "A Pollster's Sampler," *Public Opinion*, June/July 1984, 50.

99. For one example of this phenomenon, see Carey Goldberg, "Political Battle of the Sexes Is Tougher than Ever," *New York Times*, October 6, 1996, sec. 1, 1.

100. Richard Morin and Dan Balz, "'Security Mom' Bloc Proves Hard to Find," *Washington Post*, October 1, 2004, A05.

101. Ryan Lizza, "How Obama Won," *The New Yorker*, November 17, 2008, 46.

102. Ibid.

103. Ana Marie Cox, "McCain Campaign Autopsy," *Daily Beast*, November 7, 2008, http://www.thedailybeast.com/blogs-and-stories/2008-11-07/mccain-campaign-autopsy.

104. Institute of Politics, Kennedy School of Government, Harvard University, *Campaign for President: The Managers Look at 2012* (Lanham, MD: Rowman & Littlefield, 2013), 160.

105. Jamieson, ed., *Electing the President, 2012*, 29.

106. Ibid., 28.

107. Ibid., 19.

108. Roger Simon, "Obama Pollster: Mitt Wasn't Trusted," *Politico*, November 7, 2012, http://www.politico.com/news/stories/1112/83469.html.

109. Institute of Politics, *Campaign for President: The Managers Look at 2016*, 178.

110. Lyndsey Layton, "Cheney Hopes Aloha Stop Sways Hawaiians," *Washington Post*, November 2, 2004, A08.

111. Andy Barr, "Palin Disagrees with Michigan Move," *Politico*, October 3, 2008, http://www.politico.com/news/stories/1008/14253.html.

112. Katharine Q. Seelye, "McCain Camp Finds Some Hope in Pennsylvania," *New York Times*, November 3, 2008, A20.

113. Rosenstiel, *Strange Bedfellows*, 302.

114. Mark R. Levy, "Polling and the Presidential Election," *Annals of the American Academy of Political and Social Science* 472 (March 1984): 85–96, at 86.

115. Danny N. Bellenger, Kenneth L. Bernhardt, and Jac L. Goldstucker, *Qualitative Research in Marketing* (Chicago: American Marketing Association, 1976), 8.

116. Myril Axelrod, "10 Essentials for Good Qualitative Research," *Marketing News*, March 14, 1975, 10.

117. Elizabeth Kolbert, "Test-Marketing a President," *New York Times Magazine*, August 30, 1992, 21.

118. William D. Wells, "Group Interviewing," in *Focus Group Interviews* (Chicago: American Marketing Association, 1979), 2.

119. Jerry Hagstrom and Robert Guskind, "Calling the Races," *National Journal*, July 30, 1988, 1974.

120. Robert G. Kaiser, "Hearts, Not Minds," *Washington Post*, June 30, 2008, C1.

121. Institute of Politics, *Campaign for President: The Managers Look at 2012*, 118.

122. Institute of Politics, *Campaign for President: The Managers Look at 2016*, 183.

123. Goldman et al., *Quest for the Presidency, 1992*, 257–58.

124. Howard Kurtz, "Why Obama Went Low Key in His Democratic Convention Speech," *The Daily Beast*, September 7, 2012, http://www.thedailybeast.com/articles/2012/09/07/why-obama-went-low-key-in-his-democratic-convention-speech.html.

125. Luntz, *Candidates, Consultants, and Campaigns*, 83–88.

126. Sabato, *The Rise of Political Consultants*, 182.

127. T. W. Farnam, "The Influence Industry: Obama Campaign Took Unorthodox Approach to Ad Buying," *Washington Post*, November 14, 2012, http://www.washingtonpost.com/ politics/the-influence-industry-obama-campaign-took-unorthodox-approach-to-ad-buying/2012/11/14/c3477e8c-2e87-11e2-beb2-4b4cf5087636_story.html.

128. Sarah Perez, "Nielsen: 16M U.S. Homes Now Get TV Over-the-Air, a 48% Increase Over Past 8 Years," *TechCrunch*, January 15, 2019, https://techcrunch.com/2019/01/15/nielsen-16m-u-s-homes-now-get-tv-over-the-air-a-48-increase-over-past-8-years.

129. Brian Stelter, "Enticing Text Messagers in a Get-Out-the-Vote Push," *New York Times*, August 18, 2008, A12. In the event, the news of Biden's selection leaked to the press before the Obama campaign could release the text message to supporters. See Jose Antonio Vargas, "Overload Slows Texts Announcing the No. 2," *Washington Post*, August 24, 2008, A10.

130. Leticia Bode, "Political News in the News Feed: Learning Politics from Social Media," *Mass Communication and Society* 19 (2016): 24–48.

131. Daniel Kreiss, Regina G. Lawrence, and Shannon C. McGregor, "In Their Own Words: Political Practitioner Accounts of Candidates, Audiences, Affordances, Genres, and Timing in Strategic Social Media Use," *Political Communication* 35 (2018): 8–31, at 22.

132. Institute of Politics, *Campaign for President: The Managers Look at 2016*, 232.

133. Ibid., 228.

134. Matt Apuzzo and Sharon LaFraniere, "13 Russians Indicted as Mueller Reveals Effort to Aid Trump Campaign," *New York Times*, February 16, 2018, https://www.nytimes.com/2018/02/16/us/politics/russians-indicted-mueller-election-interference.html.

135. Earl Mazo, *Richard Nixon* (New York: Harper, 1959), 21–22, 362–69.

136. See White, *The Making of the President, 1960*, 282–83; Herbert A. Selz and Richard D. Yoakum, "Production Diary of the Debates," in *The Great Debates: Kennedy versus Nixon, 1960*, ed. Sidney Kraus (Bloomington: Indiana University Press, 1977), 73–126; Elihu Katz and Jacob J. Feldman, "The Debates in the Light of Research: A Survey of Surveys," in *The Great Debates*, ed. Sidney Kraus, 173–223.

137. Gerald M. Pomper, "The Presidential Election," in *The Election of 1984: Reports and Interpretations*, ed. Gerald M. Pomper (Chatham, NJ: Chatham House, 1985), 76.

138. Richard Brookhiser, *The Outside Story* (Garden City, NY: Doubleday, 1986), 272.

139. Marjorie Randon Hershey, "The Campaign and the Media," in *The Election of 2000*, ed. Gerald M. Pomper (New York: Chatham House, 2001), 60–63.

140. Richard L. Berke and Kevin Sack, "In Debate 2, Microscope Focuses on Gore," *New York Times*, October 11, 2000, A1.

141. Robert V. Friedenberg, "The 2000 Presidential Debates," in *The 2000 Presidential Campaign: A Communication Perspective*, ed. Robert E. Denton Jr. (Westport, CT: Praeger, 2002), 135–66.

142. Jodi Wilgoren and Richard W. Stevenson, "Day after Debate, Candidates Assess the Performances," *New York Times*, October 2, 2004, A10; Dan Balz, "Debate Leads to Shifts in Strategy," *Washington Post*, October 3, 2004, A01.

143. Richard Morin, "Singling Out Mary Cheney Was Wrong, Most Say," *Washington Post*, October 17, 2004, A05.

144. Dan Balz and Jim VandeHei, "A Deep Divide on Domestic Front," *Washington Post*, October 14, 2004, A01; Elisabeth Bumiller and David M. Halbfinger, "Bush and Kerry, Feeling Like Winners, Go to Las Vegas," *New York Times*, October 15, 2004, A21.

145. Evan Thomas, "The Great Debates," *Newsweek Special Election Edition*, November 17, 2008, 100–10.

146. Adam Nagourney and Jeff Zeleny, "Rivals Display Stark Contrasts in Clashes on Iraq, Economy," *New York Times*, September 27, 2008, A1.

147. Joe Klein, "Obama's Debate Strategy: Unilateral Disarmament?" *Time*, Swampland blog, October 3, 2012, http://swampland.time.com/2012/10/03/the-debate.

148. Nate Silver, "Romney Erases Obama's Convention Bounce in Forecast," FiveThirtyEight, October 9, 2012, http://fivethirtyeight.blogs.nytimes.com/2012 /10 /09/oct-9-romney-erases-obamas-convention-bounce-in-forecast.

149. Peter Baker, "For the President, Punch, Punch, Another Punch," *New York Times*, October 17, 2012, http://www.nytimes.com/2012/10/17/us/politics/in-second-debate-obama-strikes- back.html.

150. Brian Montopoli, "Conservatives Assail Debate Moderator Candy Crowley," CBS News, October 17, 2012, http://www.cbsnews.com/news/conservatives-assail-debate-moderator-candy-crowley.

151. Jonathan Allen and Amie Parnes, *Shattered: Inside Hillary Clinton's Doomed Campaign* (New York: Crown, 2017), 328.

152. Jamieson, ed., *Electing the President, 2012*, 114.

153. Allen and Parnes, *Shattered*, 327–28.

154. James Fallows, "Slugfest," *Atlantic*, September 2012, http://www.theatlantic.com/ magazine/archive/2012/09/slugfest/309063.

155. Jamieson, ed., *Electing the President, 2012*, 107.

156. Sarah Huisenga and Rebecca Kaplan, "Portman to Play Obama in Romney Debate Prep," *National Journal*, August 27, 2012, http://www.nationaljournal.com/2012-conventions/ portman-to-play-obama-in-romney-debate-prep-20120827.

157. Patrick Healy, Amy Chozick, and Maggie Haberman, "Debate Prep? Hillary Clinton and Donald Trump Differ on That, Too," *New York Times*, September 23, 2016, https://www.nytimes.com/2016/09/24/us/politics/presidential-debate-hillary-clinton-donald-trump.html.

158. Clinton, *What Happened*, 104, 105.

159. See Patrick Healy, "Pact on Debates Will Let McCain and Obama Spar," *New York Times*, September 21, 2008, A23.

160. Kim Severson, "What's for Dinner? The Pollster Wants to Know," *New York Times*, April 16, 2008, F1; Steven Levy, "In Every Voter, a 'Microtarget,'" *Washington Post*, April 23, 2008, D01. See also Douglas B. Sosnick, Matthew J. Dowd, and Ron Fournier, *Applebee's America: How Successful Political, Business, and Religious Leaders Connect with the New American Community* (New York: Simon and Schuster, 2006); Mark J. Penn with E. Kinney Zalesne, *Microtrends: The Small Forces behind Tomorrow's Big Changes* (New York: Twelve Publishers, 2007).

161. Alan S. Gerber and Donald P. Green, "The Effects of Canvassing, Telephone Calls, and Direct Mail on Voter Turnout: A Field Experiment," *American Political Science Review* 94 (September 2000): 653–63; Alan S. Gerber and Donald P. Green, "Do Phone Calls Increase Voter Turnout? A Field Experiment," *Public Opinion Quarterly* 65 (Spring 2001): 75–85; Donald P. Green, Alan S. Gerber, and David W. Nickerson, "Getting Out the Vote in Local Elections: Results from Six Door-to-Door Canvassing Experiments," *Journal of Politics* 65 (November 2003): 1083–96; Donald P. Green and Alan S. Gerber, *Get Out the Vote! How to Increase Voter Turnout*, 3rd ed. (Washington, DC: Brookings Institution, 2015).

162. Alec MacGillis, "Obama Camp Relying Heavily on Ground Effort," *Washington Post*, October 12, 2008, A04.

163. Zack Exley, "The New Organizers: What's Really behind Obama's Ground Game," *Huffington Post*, October 8, 2008, http://www.huffingtonpost.com/zack-exley/the-new-organizers- part-1_b_132782.html.

164. Michael Silberman, "Welcome to the New Media Campaign Tools of 2012," *Mother Jones*, March 13, 2009, http://motherjones.com/politics/2009/03/welcome-new-media-campaign-tools- 2012-0?page=1; David Herbert, "Obama's 'Project Houdini' Revealed," *National Journal*, November 10, 2008, http://www.nationaljournal.com/njonline/no_20081107_4999.php.

165. Alexis C. Madrigal, "When the Nerds Go Marching In," *The Atlantic*, November 16, 2012, http://www.theatlantic.com/technology/archive/2012/11/when-the-nerds-go-marching-in/265325.

166. See Sasha Issenberg, "Obama's White Whale," *Slate*, February 15, 2012, http://www.slate.com/articles/news_and_politics/victory_lab/2012/02/project_narwhal_how_a_top_secret_obama_campaign_program_could_change_the_2012_race_.html.

167. Adam Nagourney, "Campaigns Adjust Their Pace to Meet Short Season," *New York Times*, September 10, 2008, A20.

168. See Jules Abels, *Out of the Jaws of Victory* (New York: Holt, 1959).

169. Robert Alford, "The Role of Social Class in American Voting Behavior," *Western Political Quarterly* 16 (March 1963): 180–94; and Campbell et al., *The American Voter*, chapter 13.

170. For extensive recital of these critiques, see Christine M. Black and Thomas Oliphant, *All by Myself: The Unmaking of a Presidential Campaign* (Chester, CT: Globe Pequot Press, 1989).

171. David Shribman and James M. Perry, "Self-Inflicted Injury: Dukakis's Campaign Was Marred by a Series of Lost Opportunities," *Wall Street Journal*, November 8, 1988, 1.

172. Karen M. Paget, "Afterthoughts on the Dukakis/Bentsen Campaign," *Public Affairs Report*, January 1989, 1, 4.

173. John Jacobs, "Dukakis Admits Campaign 'Mistakes,'" *San Francisco Examiner*, October 14, 1989.

174. Elisabeth Bumiller, "Palin Disclosures Raise Questions on Vetting," *New York Times*, September 2, 2008, A1.

175. Jeanne Cummings, "RNC Shells Out $150K for Palin Fashion," *Politico*, October 22, 2008, http://www.politico.com/news/stories/1008/14805.html.

176. Ben Smith, "Palin Allies Report Rising Camp Tension," *Politico*, October 25, 2008, http://www.politico.com/news/stories/1008/14929.html. This article was the first to use the term "going rogue" to

describe Palin's increasing lack of cooperation with McCain campaign handlers (quoting an anonymous Republican official). Adopting the phrase as a flattering descriptor of her independent spirit, Palin later used it as the title of her first book.

177. Michael Cooper and Dalia Sussman, "Growing Doubts on Palin Take a Toll, Poll Finds," *New York Times*, October 31, 2008, A1.

178. Michael Kranish, "The Story behind Mitt Romney's Loss in the Presidential Campaign to President Obama," *Boston Globe,* December 23, 2012, http://www.boston.com/news/politics/2012/president/2012/12/23/the-story-behind-mitt-romney-loss-the-presidential-campaign-president-obama/2QWkUB-9pJgVIi1mAcIhQjL/story.html; Noam Scheiber, "The Internal Polls That Made Mitt Romney Think He'd Win," *New Republic*, November 30, 2012, http://www.newrepublic.com/blog/plank/110597/exclusive-the-polls-made-mitt-romney-think-hed-win.

179. Adam Nagourney, Ashley Parker, Jim Rutenberg, and Jeff Zeleny, "How a Race in the Balance Went to Obama," *New York Times*, November 7, 2012, http://www.nytimes.com/2012/11/08/ us/politics/obama-campaign-clawed-back-after-a-dismal-debate.html.

180. John Heilemann and Mark Halperin, "The Intervention," *New York*, November 2, 2013, http://nymag.com/news/features/heilemann-halperin-double-down-excerpt-2013-11.

181. Molly Ball, "The Final Humiliation of Reince Priebus," *The Atlantic*, July 30, 2017, https://www.theatlantic.com/politics/archive/2017/07/the-final-humiliation-of-reince-priebus/535368.

182. Fareed Zakaria, "Donald Trump Has Run the Worst Campaign in Modern History," *Washington Post*, October 27, 2016, https://www.washingtonpost.com/opinions/donald-trump-has-won-the-worst-campaign-in-modern-history/2016/10/27/5c870118-9c7e-11e6-b3c9-f662adaa0048_story.html.

183. Abby Phillip, John Wagner, and Anne Gearan, "A Series of Strategic Mistakes Likely Sealed Clinton's Fate," *Washington Post*, November 12, 2016, https://www.washingtonpost.com/politics/a-series-of-strategic-mistakes-likely-sealed-clintons-fate/2016/11/11/82f3fcc0-a840-11e6-ba59-a7d93165c6d4_story.html.

184. There are several sources readers can consult about the technology and tactics of polling. Many years ago, George Gallup published *A Guide to Public Opinion Polls* (Princeton, NJ: Princeton University Press, 1948). See also *Opinion Polls, Interviews* by Donald McDonald with Elmo Roper and George Gallup (Santa Barbara, CA: Center for the Study of Democratic Institutions, 1962); and Charles W. Roll Jr. and Albert H. Cantril, *Polls* (New York: Basic Books, 1972). In 1972, Representative Lucien Nedzi of Michigan held congressional hearings on the possible effects of information about polls on subsequent voting. See *Public Opinion Polls, Hearings before the Subcommittee on Library and Memorial*, Committee on House Administration, House of Representatives, 93rd Cong., 1st sess., H.R. 5503, September 19, 20, 21, and October 5, 1972. A further flap occurred in 1980, as the result of Jimmy Carter's concession of defeat and the television network predictions of a Reagan victory before voting was completed on the West Coast. See Raymond Wolfinger and Peter Linquiti, "Tuning In and Turning Out," *Public Opinion*, February/March 1981, 56–60; John E. Jackson, "Election Night Reporting and Voter Turnout," *American Journal of Political Science* 27 (November 1983): 615–35; *Election Day Practices and Election Projections, Hearings before the Task Force on Elections of the Committee on House Administration and the Subcommittee on Telecommunications, Consumer Protection, and Finance of the Committee on Energy and Commerce*, U.S. House of Representatives, 97th Cong., 1st and 2nd sess., December 15, 1981, and September 21, 1982, and Percy Tannenbaum and Leslie J. Kostrich, *Turned-On TV/Turned-Off Voters: Policy Options for Election Projections* (Beverly Hills, CA: Sage, 1983).

185. Robert Sherwood, *Roosevelt and Hopkins* (New York: Harper, 1948), 86. See also Archibald M. Crossley, "Straw Polls in 1936," *Public Opinion Quarterly* 1 (January 1937): 24–36; and a survey of the literature existing at that time, Hadley Cantril, "Technical Research," *Public Opinion Quarterly* 1 (January 1937): 97–110.

186. Maurice C. Bryson, "The *Literary Digest* Poll: Making of a Statistical Myth," *The American Statistician* 30 (November 1976): 184–85; Peverill Squire, "The 1936 *Literary Digest* Poll," *Public Opinion Quarterly* 52 (Spring 1988): 125–34.

187. Frederick Mosteller et al., *The Pre-Election Polls of 1948*, Bulletin 60 (New York: Social Science Research Council, 1949).

188. Jan Crawford, "Adviser: Romney 'Shell-Shocked' by Loss," CBS News, November 8, 2012, http://www.cbsnews.com/news/adviser-romney-shellshocked-by-loss/; Matt Viser, "New Film Shows Flawed, Human Mitt Romney," *Boston Globe*, January 18, 2014, http://www.bostonglobe.com/news/nation/2014/01/18/mitt-romney-family-side-downplayed-campaign-revealed-documentary/0Jh53bme1OjV9SuM0Q8ytN/story.html.

189. Jamieson, ed., *Electing the President, 2012*, 77.

190. Nate Cohn, "A 2016 Review: Why Key State Polls Were Wrong about Trump," *New York Times*, May 31, 2017, https://www.nytimes.com/2017/05/31/upshot/a-2016-review-why-key-state-polls-were-wrong-about-trump.html.

191. On the import of early projections, see Philip L. Dubois, "Election Night Projection and Turnout in the West," *American Politics Quarterly* 11 (July 1983): 349–64. Dubois argues (against a number of other

studies) that the early projections did have a significant impact on turnout. For a sophisticated analysis of the policy problems involved, see Tannenbaum and Kostrich, *Turned-On TV/Turned-Off Voters*.

192. Michael Cousineau, "Exit Poll Wrong Call in Senate Race Leaves Anger, Hurt, Red Faces," *Union Leader* (Manchester, NH), November 7, 1996, A1.

193. Joan Konner, "The Case for Caution: This System Is Dangerously Flawed," *Public Opinion Quarterly* 67 (Spring 2003): 5–18, at 7. See also Paul Biemer, Ralph Folsom, Richard Kulka, Judith Lessler, Babu Shah, and Michael Weeks, "An Evaluation of Procedures and Operations Used by the Voter News Service for the 2000 Presidential Election," *Public Opinion Quarterly* 67 (Spring 2003): 32–44.

194. Matt Krantz, "Exit Poll Rumors Push Dow into Loss," *USA Today*, November 3, 2004, 4B.

195. The design of the ballot in Palm Beach County probably led a number of voters intending to vote for Democratic nominee Al Gore to cast ballots instead for Reform Party candidate Pat Buchanan. This alone may have cost Gore the presidency. See Henry E. Brady, Michael C. Herron, Walter R. Mebane Jr., Jasjeet Singh Sekhon, Kenneth W. Shotts, and Jonathan Wand, "Law and Data: The Butterfly Ballot Episode," *PS: Political Science and Politics* 34 (March 2001): 59–69.

196. The U.S. Supreme Court first became involved in the Florida recount legal struggle on November 24, 2000 (*Bush v. Palm Beach County Canvassing Board*, 531 U.S. 1004). The court granted a stay sought by Bush halting the recount of ballots ordered by the Florida Supreme Court on December 9 (*Bush v. Gore*, 531 U.S. 1046), foreshadowing its eventual 5–4 decision on the merits in Bush's favor on December 12 (*Bush v. Gore*, 531 U.S. 98). Al Gore formally conceded the election in a nationwide address the following day.

197. See, for example, Howard Gillman, *The Votes That Counted: How the Court Decided the 2000 Election* (Chicago: University of Chicago Press, 2001); Cass R. Sunstein and Richard A. Epstein, eds., *The Vote: Bush, Gore and the Supreme Court* (Chicago: University of Chicago Press, 2001); and Ronald Dworkin, ed., *A Badly Flawed Election: Debating* Bush v. Gore, *The Supreme Court, and American Democracy* (New York: New Press, 2002).

198. See Henry E. Brady, Justin Buchler, Matt Jarvis, and John McNulty, *Counting All the Votes: The Performance of Voting Technology in the United States* (Berkeley, CA: Survey Research Center and Institute of Governmental Studies, 2001), http://ucdata.berkeley.edu/pubs/countingallthevotes.pdf.

199. For example, precincts in Florida using the problematic punch-card ballots were more likely to contain significant minority populations than places with other ballot types. See Josh Barbanel and Ford Fessenden, "Racial Pattern in Demographics of Error-Prone Ballots," *New York Times*, November 29, 2000, A25. See also Michael Tomz and Robert P. Van Houweling, "How Does Voting Equipment Affect the Racial Gap in Voided Ballots?" *American Journal of Political Science* 47 (January 2003): 46–60. Their data are from South Carolina and Louisiana.

200. Ford Fessenden and John M. Broder, "Study of Disputed Florida Ballots Finds Justices Did Not Cast the Deciding Vote," *New York Times*, November 12, 2001, A1.

201. Henry E. Brady, "Detailed Analysis of Punch Card Performance in the Twenty Largest California Counties in 1996, 2000 and 2003," University of California, Berkeley, 2003.

202. Robert Pear, "Bush Signs Legislation Intended to End Voting Disputes," *New York Times*, October 29, 2002, A22.

203. Richard Wolf, "Another Mess at the Polls? The Voting Equipment's New, But Problems Are Likely on Election Day," *USA Today*, October 29, 2008, 1A.

204. Wolf, "Another Mess at the Polls?"; Drew DeSilver, "On Election Day, Most Voters Use Electronic or Optical-Scan Ballots," Pew Research Center, November 8, 2016, http://www.pewresearch.org/fact-tank/2016/11/08/on-election-day-most-voters-use-electronic-or-optical-scan-ballots.

205. John Colapinto, "Enter Laughing," *The New Yorker*, July 20, 2009, 28.

CHAPTER 6: APPRAISALS

1. See William Crotty, *Party Reform* (New York: Longman, 1983); Austin Ranney, "Farewell to Reform—Almost," in *Elections in America*, ed. Kay Schlozman (Boston: Allen and Unwin, 1987); "Democrats Alter Nominating Rules," *Congressional Quarterly Weekly Report*, April 14, 1990, 148.

2. Bloomberg Politics, "Who's Winning the Presidential Delegate Count?" July 25, 2016, https://www.bloomberg.com/politics/graphics/2016-delegate-tracker.

3. Alan Rappeport, "From Bernie Sanders Supporters, Death Threats Over Delegates," *New York Times*, May 16, 2016, https://www.nytimes.com/2016/05/17/us/politics/bernie-sanders-supporters-nevada.html.

4. Astead W. Herndon, "Democrats Take Major Step to Reduce Role of Superdelegates," *New York Times*, July 11, 2018, https://www.nytimes.com/2018/07/11/us/politics/superdelegates-democratic-party.html.

5. Aaron Blake, "RNC Moves to Shrink 2016 Primary Calendar," *Washington Post*, January 24, 2014; Zeke J. Miller, "GOP Takes Control of 2016 Primary Debates," *Time*, August 8, 2014.

6. On polarized Congressional floor voting, several scholarly studies and graphs indicating its record levels are available at "The Polarization of Congressional Parties," http://voteview.com/political_polarization.asp; note particularly the work by Nolan McCarty linked there. On polarization among partisans in the American public, see Pew Research Center, "Political Polarization in the American Public," June 12, 2014, http://www.people-press.org/2014/06/12/political-polarization-in-the-american-public.

7. There are many examples of the party reform school of thought. See, for example, Woodrow Wilson, *Congressional Government* (Boston: Houghton Mifflin, 1889); Henry Jones Ford, *The Rise and Growth of American Politics* (New York: Macmillan, 1898); A. Lawrence Lowell, *Public Opinion and Popular Government* (New York: Longmans, Green, 1913); E. E. Schattschneider, *Party Government* (New York: Farrar and Rinehart, 1940); James M. Burns, *Congress on Trial* (New York: Harper, 1949); Committee on Political Parties, American Political Science Association, *Toward a More Responsible Two-Party System* (New York: APSA, 1950); James MacGregor Burns, *The Deadlock of Democracy: Four-Party Politics in America* (Englewood Cliffs, NJ: Prentice Hall, 1963); Lloyd N. Cutler and C. Douglas Dillon, "Can We Improve on Our Constitutional System?" *Wall Street Journal*, February 15, 1983; and Lloyd N. Cutler, "To Form a Government," *Foreign Affairs* 59 (Fall 1980): 126–43. The work of the Committee on Political Parties, representing the collective judgment of a panel of distinguished political scientists in 1950, is the statement we refer to most often.

8. Committee on Political Parties, *Toward a More Responsible Two-Party System*, 1.

9. Ibid., 66.

10. Ibid., 15.

11. A sample of this literature might include Pendleton Herring, *The Politics of Democracy: American Parties in Action*, rev. ed. (New York: W. W. Norton, 1965); Austin Ranney and Willmoore Kendall, *Democracy and the American Party System* (New York: Harcourt, Brace, 1956); David B. Truman, *The Governmental Process* (New York: Knopf, 1953); John Fischer, "Unwritten Rules of American Politics," *Harper's*, November 1948, 27–36; Peter Drucker, "A Key to American Politics: Calhoun's Pluralism," *Review of Politics* 10 (October 1948): 412–26; Murray Stedman and Herbert Sonthoff, "Party Responsibility: A Critical Inquiry," *Western Political Quarterly* 4 (September 1951): 454–86; Julius Turner, "Responsible Parties: A Dissent from the Floor," *American Political Science Review* 45 (March 1951): 143–52; William Goodman, "How Much Political Party Centralization Do We Want?" *Journal of Politics* 13 (November 1961): 536–61; and Austin Ranney, *The Doctrine of Responsible Party Government* (Urbana: University of Illinois Press, 1954).

12. Herring, *The Politics of Democracy*, 327.

13. Ibid., 420.

14. Committee on Political Parties, *Toward a More Responsible Two-Party System*, 19.

15. Gallup Organization, "Party Images," https://news.gallup.com/poll/24655/party-images.aspx.

16. David A. Hopkins, *Red Fighting Blue: How Geography and Electoral Rules Polarize American Politics* (New York: Cambridge University Press, 2017).

17. Christopher Hare, Keith T. Poole, and Howard Rosenthal, "Polarization in Congress Has Risen Sharply. Where Is It Going Next?" *Washington Post*, February 13, 2014, http://www.washingtonpost.com/blogs/monkey-cage/wp/2014/02/13/polarization-in-congress-has-risen-sharply-where-is-it-going-next.

18. See Frances E. Lee, *Insecure Majorities: Congress and the Perpetual Campaign* (Chicago: University of Chicago Press, 2016).

19. Polsby, *Consequences of Party Reform*; Byron E. Shafer, *Quiet Revolution: The Struggle for the Democratic Party and the Shaping of Post-Reform Politics* (New York: Russell Sage Foundation, 1983).

20. For evidence on this point, see Paul M. Sniderman and Richard A. Brody, "Coping: The Ethic of Self-Reliance," *American Journal of Political Science* 21 (August 1977): 501–21; and Richard A. Brody and Paul M. Sniderman, "From Life Space to Polling Place: The Relevance of Personal Concerns for Voting Behavior," *British Journal of Political Science* 7 (July 1977): 337–60.

21. Evidence indicates that a sizable contingent of voters do make decisions based on this criterion. In general, perceptions of national conditions weigh more heavily than changes in voters' personal fortunes over the previous four years. See Donald R. Kinder and D. Roderick Kiewiet, "Sociotropic Politics: The American Case," *British Journal of Political Science* 11 (April 1981): 129–61; and Gregory Markus, "The Impact of Personal and National Economic Conditions on the Presidential Vote: A Pooled Cross-Sectional Analysis," *American Journal of Political Science* 32 (February 1988): 137–54. Some argue that this type of "retrospective voting" is not rational, since it often applies even to events such as natural disasters which incumbents clearly cannot control; see Christopher H. Achen and Larry M. Bartels, *Democracy for Realists: Why Elections Do Not Produce Responsive Government* (Princeton: Princeton University Press, 2016).

22. See, for example, Jack Citrin, Herbert McClosky, J. Merrill Shanks, and Paul M. Sniderman, "Personal and Political Sources of Alienation," *British Journal of Political Science* 5 (January 1975): 1–31;

and Arthur H. Miller, "Political Issues and Trust in Government: 1964–70," along with the "Comment" by Jack Citrin, both in *American Political Science Review* 68 (September 1974): 951–1001.

23. In systems like the United States, with its extremely frequent elections, this would require a lot of voting. See Anthony King, *Running Scared: Why America's Politicians Campaign Too Much and Govern Too Little* (New York: Martin Kessler, 1997).

24. See Lincoln Dahlberg and Eugenia Siapera, eds., *Radical Democracy and the Internet: Interrogating Theory and Practice* (New York: Palgrave Macmillan, 2007).

25. Eitan D. Hersh, "The Problem with Participatory Democracy Is the Participants," *New York Times*, June 29, 2017, https://www.nytimes.com/2017/06/29/opinion/sunday/the-problem-with-participatory-democracy-is-the-participants.html.

26. Jürgen Habermas, *Legitimation Crisis* (Boston: Beacon Press, 1975).

27. An earlier statement of main themes in this section is Aaron B. Wildavsky's "On the Superiority of National Conventions," *Review of Politics* 24 (July 1962): 307–19.

28. Everett Carll Ladd, "Party Reform and the Public Interest," *Political Science Quarterly* 102 (Autumn 1987): 355–69. See, more generally, Gary R. Orren and Nelson W. Polsby, eds., *Media and Momentum: The New Hampshire Primary and Nomination Politics* (Chatham, NJ: Chatham House, 1987).

29. See Austin Ranney, *The Federalization of Presidential Primaries* (Washington, DC: American Enterprise Institute, 1978), 507; see also Commission on Presidential Nomination and Party Structure (Morley Winograd, chairman), *Openness, Participation and Party Building: Reforms for a Stronger Democratic Party* (Washington, DC: Democratic National Committee, 1979), 32–37.

30. Nelson W. Polsby, "Was Hart's Life Unfairly Probed?" *New York Times*, May 6, 1987.

31. A classic statement is Moisei Ostrogorski, *Democracy and the Party System in the United States* (New York: Macmillan, 1910), 158–60. See also Elmo Roper, "What Price Conventions?" *Saturday Review*, September 3, 1960, 26.

32. See Herbert McClosky, Paul J. Hoffmann, and Rosemary O'Hara, "Issue Conflict and Consensus among Party Leaders and Followers," *American Political Science Review* 54 (June 1960): 406–27; Jeane Kirkpatrick, *The New Presidential Elite: Men and Women in National Politics* (New York: Russell Sage Foundation, 1976); and John S. Jackson III et al., "Political Party Leaders and the Mass Public: 1980–1984," paper presented at the annual meeting of the Midwest Political Science Association, Chicago, April 1987.

33. Gerald M. Pomper, *Elections in America: Control and Influence in Democratic Politics*, rev. ed. (New York: Longman, 1980), 185–87.

34. Alan D. Monroe, "American Party Platforms and Public Opinion," *American Journal of Political Science* 27 (February 1983): 27–42, at 38.

35. Ibid., 27–42.

36. This argument roughly corresponds to one of the main approaches to calculating the strategic advantage of members of a coalition, pioneered by Irwin Mann and Lloyd Shapley. The argument proceeds as follows: "the Shapley value defines the power of actor A as the number of permutations (orderings) in which A occupies the pivotal position (that is, orderings in which A can cast the deciding vote) divided by the total number of possible permutations." See George Rabinowitz and Stuart Elaine MacDonald, "The Power of the States in U.S. Presidential Elections," *American Political Science Review* 80 (March 1986): 65–87, at 66. This approach shows the large states to be the winners. Their influence is more than proportional to their size. This model is often supplemented by an analysis that attempts to determine the influence of the average voter within each state. Along these lines, Lawrence Longley and James Dana Jr. concluded that residents of California (the most advantaged state) have more than twice the "relative voting power" of the inhabitants of Arkansas (the least advantaged state). See Longley and Dana, "New Empirical Estimates of the Biases of the Electoral College for the 1980s," *Western Political Quarterly* 37 (March 1984): 157–75. Yet these calculations assume that all patterns of state voting are equally likely (not a realistic assumption).

37. There are, of course, many other plans for "reform," involving almost all possible combinations of these three alternatives. For example, President Nixon at one point recommended that the 40 percent plurality plank that usually goes with the direct election proposal be applied instead to the present Electoral College setup. See David S. Broder, "Mitchell Recommends Electoral Compromise," *Washington Post*, March 14, 1969. A second example is the complicated "federal system plan" proposed by Senators Bob Dole and Tom Eagleton in 1970 (see *Congressional Record*, March 5, 1970, S3026). These plans had the following characteristics: (1) they were too complex to solve any problems of public confusion or public perception that they are not "democratic," and (2) they had no significant body of congressional support.

38. Alex Vandermaas-Peeler, Daniel Cox, Molly Fisch-Friedman, Rob Griffin and Robert P. Jones, "American Democracy in Crisis: The Challenges of Voter Knowledge, Participation, and Polarization," Public Religion Research Institute, July 17, 2018, https://www.prri.org/research/american-democracy-in-crisis-voters-midterms-trump-election-2018.

39. See Eric R. A. N. Smith and Peverill Squire, "Direct Election of the President and Power of the States," *Western Political Quarterly* 40 (March 1987): 31–44. Smith and Squire argue, following Shapley's

logic, that the importance of states should be calculated according to the ease with which undecided voters can be influenced.

40. George C. Edwards III, *Why the Electoral College Is Bad for America* (New Haven, CT: Yale University Press, 2004); Robert W. Bennett, *Taming the Electoral College* (Stanford, CA: Stanford University Press, 2006). For counterarguments, see Tara Ross, *The Indispensable Electoral College* (Washington, DC: Gateway Editions, 2017).

41. Darshan J. Goux and David A. Hopkins, "The Empirical Implications of Electoral College Reform," *American Politics Research* 36 (November 2008): 857–79.

42. On September 18, 1969, by a vote of 339 to 70, a direct-election plan with a 40 percent plurality runoff provision was passed by the U.S. House of Representatives. See *Congressional Record*, September 18, 1969, H8142–43; for the content of the bill, see *Congressional Record*, September 10, 1969, H7745–46. For more recent discussion of proposed reforms, see Committee on the Judiciary, U.S. Senate, *Hearings on the Electoral College and Direct Election*, 95th Cong. (Washington, DC, 1977), and Bennett, *Taming the Electoral College*.

43. In 1968, the figures were similar when George Wallace ran a strong third-party campaign in the race between Richard Nixon and Hubert Humphrey. As in 1992, a fourth candidate would have needed only 6 or 7 percent of the national total to keep either major-party candidate from having the required 40 percent (Nixon won with only 43 percent, although he received 56.2 percent of the electoral vote).

44. The article that deals most clearly with the Electoral College in terms of its virtues of conciliation and broad coalition building is John Wildenthal, "Consensus after L.B.J.," *Southwest Review* 53 (Spring 1968): 113–30.

45. Roscoe Drummond, "Perils of the Electoral System," *Washington Post*, November 14, 1960. An argument in some ways parallel to our own is contained in Anthony Lewis, "The Case against Electoral Reform," *The Reporter*, December 8, 1960, 31–33. See also Allan Sindler, "Presidential Election Methods and Urban-Ethnic Interests," *Law and Contemporary Problems* 27 (Spring 1962): 213–33.

46. David A. Hopkins and Darshan J. Goux, "Repealing the Unit Rule? Electoral Vote Allocation and Candidate Strategy," paper delivered at the Annual Meeting of the Midwest Political Science Association, Chicago, IL, April 2008.

47. Or, even worse, the Supreme Court, fearing "chaos," might step in and put its thumb on the scale, as in 2000. See Richard A. Posner, *Breaking the Deadlock: The 2000 Election, the Constitution, and the Courts* (Princeton: Princeton University Press, 2001); Richard A. Posner, "*Bush v. Gore* as Pragmatic Adjudication," in *A Badly Flawed Election*, ed. Dworkin, 187–213.

48. Hopkins and Goux, "Repealing the Unit Rule?" 7.

49. See Arthur Schlesinger Jr., "A One-for-All Electoral College," *Wall Street Journal*, August 19, 1988, 16; Arthur Schlesinger Jr., "How to Democratize American Democracy," in *A Badly Flawed Election*, ed. Dworkin, 215–29.

50. Despite popular misconceptions, even the 1964 Republican platform, written by supporters of Barry Goldwater, contained explicit promises to preserve these programs.

51. David R. Mayhew argues in *Divided We Govern: Party Control, Lawmaking and Investigations* (New Haven, CT: Yale University Press, 1991) that sheer legislative productivity is not harmed by divided government, with its constraints on party responsibility.

CHAPTER 7: AMERICAN PARTIES AND DEMOCRACY

1. Steven E. Schier and Todd E. Eberly, *Polarized: The Rise of Ideology in American Politics* (Lanham, MD: Rowman & Littlefield, 2016); Morris P. Fiorina, with Samuel J. Abrams and Jeremy C. Pope, *Culture War? The Myth of a Polarized America*, 3rd ed. (New York: Longman, 2010); Herbert McClosky, Paul S. Hoffmann, and Rosemary O'Hara, "Issue Conflict and Consensus among Party Leaders and Followers," *American Political Science Review* 54 (June 1960): 406–27.

2. This parallels in many respects an argument to be found in Robert A. Dahl, *A Preface to Democratic Theory* (Chicago: University of Chicago Press, 1956).

3. Nate Cohn, "The Wall Is Not Popular. (And Neither Is Trump)," *New York Times*, January 12, 2019, https://www.nytimes.com/2019/01/12/upshot/trump-border-wall-polls.html.

4. Richard A. Brody and Benjamin I. Page, "Policy Voting and the Electoral Process: The Vietnam War Issue," *American Political Science Review* 66 (September 1972): 979–95. See also William Schneider, "The November 4 Vote for President: What Did It Mean?" in *The American Elections of 1980*, ed. Austin Ranney (Washington, DC: American Enterprise Institute, 1981), 212–62; and Nelson W. Polsby, "Party Realignment in the 1980 Election," *Yale Review* 72 (Autumn 1982): 43–54.

5. See Dahl, *A Preface to Democratic Theory*, 124–31. The famous general statement from which this application is derived is Kenneth J. Arrow, *Social Choice and Individual Values*, 2nd ed. (New Haven, CT: Yale University Press, 1963).

6. Christopher Ellis and James A. Stimson, *Ideology in America* (New York: Cambridge University Press, 2012).

7. Jack Citrin, Eric Schickler, and John Sides, "What If Everyone Voted? Simulating the Impact of Increased Turnout in Senate Elections," *American Journal of Political Science* 47 (2003): 75–90; and Sides, Schickler, and Citrin, "If Everyone Had Voted, Would Bubba and Dubya Have Won?" *Presidential Studies Quarterly* 38 (September 2008): 521–39.

8. See Nelson W. Polsby, *Consequences of Party Reform* (New York: Oxford University Press, 1983).

9. Ibid. See also the argument made by Marty Cohen, David Karol, Hans Noel, and John Zaller, *The Party Decides: Presidential Nominations before and after Reform* (Chicago: University of Chicago Press, 2008).

10. See Jack Dennis, "Trends in Public Support for the American Party System," *British Journal of Political Science* 5 (April 1975): 187–230. A recent version of this argument is found in Fiorina, *Culture War?*

11. For the story on split-ticket voting and its effects, see Gary C. Jacobson, *The Electoral Origins of Divided Government* (Boulder, CO: Westview Press, 1990). See also Morris Fiorina, *Divided Government*, 2nd ed. (Boston: Allyn and Bacon, 1996).

12. See Richard J. Ellis, *Democratic Delusions: The Initiative Process in America* (Lawrence: The University Press of Kansas, 2002); David S. Broder, *Democracy Derailed: Initiative Campaigns and the Power of Money* (New York: Harcourt, 2000).

13. See Bruce E. Cain, Sara Ferejohn, Margarita Najar, and Mary Walther, "Constitutional Change: Is It Too Easy to Amend Our State Constitution?" in *Constitutional Reform in California: Making State Government More Effective and Responsive*, eds. Bruce E. Cain and Roger G. Noll (Berkeley, CA: Institute of Governmental Studies Press, 1995), 265–90.

Index